HANS KOHN

Prelude to Nation-States

The French and German Experience, 1789-1815

D. VAN NOSTRAND COMPANY, INC.

Princeton, New Jersey   Toronto   London   Melbourne

Van Nostrand Regional Offices: *New York, Chicago, San Francisco*

D. Van Nostrand Company, Ltd., *London*

D. Van Nostrand Company (Canada), Ltd., *Toronto*

D. Van Nostrand Australia Pty. Ltd., *Melbourne*

PRINTED IN THE UNITED STATES OF AMERICA

To ROBERT WELTSCH
to whom I dedicated
forty-five years ago
my first book
Nationalismus (Vienna, 1922)

Preface

THE quarter of a century between 1789 and 1815 was a crucial time in the history of Continental Europe. It brought the first break with the remnants of feudalism; it gave the people the knowledge that it could and was entitled to change the existing social and political order and it determined the character of nationalism and the rising nation-states in the two leading nations of the Continent. It explains much of their following history, and its influence has not ended yet. Since 1945 the two nations have lost their dominant position in Europe, but their different behavior and "ideas" were to set in the intervening time the model for the aspirations to form nation-states everywhere, outside the English-speaking nation-states which with their religious matrix and their late-seventeenth and mid-eighteenth-century background have remained incomprehensible to most European observers. For that reason Germany underestimated the strength and the intervention of Britain and the United States in both world wars.

Within this late-eighteenth and early-nineteenth-century context, France and Germany set the often conflicting models for the emerging nation-states which evolved in the nineteenth century in Europe and in the twentieth century in other continents. This process is far from finished. Thus this historical study, like probably all historical studies, is of some importance for an understanding of our present-day world. For me personally it has been a work of many years. It establishes the bridge between the *Idea of Nationalism* and the various books which followed and which deal with nineteenth-century European and twentieth-century worldwide nationalism, books like *Prophets and Peoples, The Making of the Modern French Mind, The Mind of Germany, Pan-Slavism, Its History and Ideology,* and *The Age of Nationalism.*

I have always loved teaching because, among other things, it has kept me in contact with young minds, which have now become half-a-century younger than mine. In that way I have remained in touch with living history. For real teaching is always a give and a take, and it is difficult to say who is more enriched by this partnership. Perhaps it has taken time away from my research and writing. I do not regret it. One (*one,* not the only but probably the most important) task of the university is to continue the long chain of learning which started with the ancient Greeks and which assures us of the continuity of our civilization. Naturally, and legitimately, each generation adds its own point of view, changes the tradition, "revolts" against the "burden of the past." When we were young, we did it too. I am glad that the present generation follows this pattern, perhaps sometimes with greater consciousness than we did. Yet with many of them I always found a common language and a common ground, and with many of their complaints I have been in full agreement.

Fellowships at the Institute of Advanced Study in Princeton and at the Center for Advanced Studies at Wesleyan University, Middletown, Connecticut, and a grant from the Rockefeller Foundation gave me generously the opportunity of organizing my material, "uninterrupted" by students, though, as I said above, I in no way resent this kind of interruption. I am equally grateful to the publishing house of D. Van Nostrand in Princeton which accepted the financially perhaps not too rewarding task of publishing this book. Some parts of the book appeared, several years ago, in the *Journal of the History of Ideas, The Review of Politics,* the *Journal of Modern History,* and the *American Historical Review.* But only the frame of a confrontation of the birth of the nation-state in France and the simultaneous attempts to create a German nation-state, under the influence of the French Revolution and yet in opposition to it, gives real meaning to the various and contradictory manifestations of nationalism. Nationalism is as little one and the same in various regions as religion is. It is conditioned by the "character" of the nations, a vague and yet indispensable concept, by their social structure, their predominant political theories. In that sense the book is a contribution to the comparative study of nationalism, the approach which I think the only fertile one. It is the approach which I followed twenty years ago in my *Prophets and Peoples.*

Let me give only two examples from more recent history. There is, of course, no monocausal process in history. Yet the character of nationalism is in modern times certainly one of the causative factors of national history. Jules Michelet, a nationalist French historian, who attracted large audiences to his lectures at the Collège de France, celebrated in his *Le Peuple* (1846) the "shining bayonets" of the French people, but he was consciously a son of the common people and of revolutionary Paris. The circumference of his sympathy was very wide and he praised the equality of all human beings. The great German historian Heinrich von Treitschke who attracted even greater audiences to his lectures at the University of Berlin similarly glorified German arms; but he insisted on a strictly hierarchical order of society and his circumference of sympathy was confined to the Germans.*

France and Germany faced in 1871 and in 1919 very similar situations; defeat on the battlefield, loss of important national territory, the end of an imperial dynasty finding its main support in the army, a civil war (quickly suppressed) which pitched the urban working class against the ruling classes. For years France and Germany hovered between the restoration of a dynasty and a republic. In 1925 the imperial field marshal Paul von Hindenburg became president of the German Republic (what an irony, that the republic retained the title of Reich with all its mystical implications!) and, treated with infinite reverence, ended by calling upon Adolf Hitler. Hindenburg became the grave digger of the Republic. Different was the fate in France. There in 1873 the defeated imperial Maréchal MacMahon became the chef d'état. Six years later he had to go and the (Third) Republic took over and lasted for seventy-one years, longer than any form of government in modern Germany or modern France. Even Charles de Gaulle, a man infinitely superior to the two field marshals and who saved France and her position in the world of the twentieth century by abandoning Algeria and French military bases in Africa and Asia, and this without any loss of prestige for France or himself, soon ran into popular opposition, in elections and in the press.

Neither France nor Germany achieved, as Britain or Switzerland did, a firm consensus in support of civilian democracy. Yet in France, so far, common sense, democracy, and the heritage of the Enlightenment have again and again prevailed. In Germany (but not in German-speaking Switzerland or in the Germanic Netherlands) the rejection or distrust of the Enlightenment put an end to the feeble attempts at democracy and favored the revival of pre-modern forms of societal organization and political ideology, both after 1848-1849 and after 1919. In spite of the very high and in many ways exemplary development of German scholarship in the late-nineteenth century and the general spread of literacy there, one could speak of nineteenth and early-twentieth-century Germany as a politically and socially retarded nation.†

The roots of these contrasting developments in the two leading nations of the European Continent can be traced back to the quarter of a century between 1789 and 1815. The present book is an attempt to deal with some (naturally not all) facets of this situation which was one of the factors dominating European history from 1792 to 1945.

H. K.

Austin, Texas
May 1967

* See Hans Kohn, *Prophets and Peoples, Studies in XIX Century Nationalism* (New York: Macmillan 1946) and Andrew Dorpalen on Treitschke.

† See Hans Kohn, *The Mind of Germany* (New York: Scribner's, 1960) and his *Nationalism and Liberty* (London: Allen and Unwin, 1954).

Contents

x   *Contents*

I

Introduction · Patterns
of Nation-Statehood

THE present international system, which comprises such diverse agencies as the United Nations and the North Atlantic Treaty Organization, the Warsaw Pact and the South East Asia Treaty Organization, the International Labor Organization and the Universal Postal Union, is based upon the recognition of the nation-state as its constituent unit. The existence of nation-states with similar structural aspirations—from public education to industrialization, from modern communications to general suffrage—has made the universal organizations of the present time possible. The nation-state is a very recent development in history. It was not only unknown to Antiquity and to the Middle Ages, but was practically nonexistent in Asia or Africa until the middle of the twentieth century. There were instead city-states and empires (many of them theoretically world empires), feudal and dynastic states, states based on religion as the foremost cementing link, and tribal agglomerations. The modern nation-state emerged in the great Western revolutions of the seventeenth and eighteenth centuries, in Holland, England, and the United States, based upon a new integrating force or group-consciousness—nationalism.

More and more after 1815 the nation-state became the "normal" form of political, cultural, and economic organization in Europe, from Norway to Greece, from Ireland to Estonia. In spite of their "international" ideology, the communist societies too were organized as nation-states and have, in the course of their history, emphasized this national character more and more. In the two decades since the end of World War II, the nation-state, though frequently and understandably beset by great difficulties, has become the "normal" manifestation of the political will of Asian, African, and Latin American societies. Thus by 1966 the peoples of all continents had chosen—in different ways according to their past conditions of life, their social structure, and their political ideas—the nation-state as their basic form of organization. As the last third of the twentieth century opened, nationalism had become the dominant pan-movement on a global basis, the first that made, with the simultaneous development of the means of communication, a universal intercourse possible and necessary.

This development started on the European continent with the French Revolution. The Napoleonic wars and the first half of the nineteenth century witnessed the growth of the ideal of the nation-state and the struggle for its realization in Europe. The rapid spread of this trend from then on was a sign of the progressing westernization of the earth. Supported by the impact of science and technology, of urbanization and secularism, the rise of the nation-state marked the gateway to modernity. How far various peoples proceeded on the road to modernity depended on local circumstances and the vicissitudes of history.

The manifestations of nationalism and the temper of the various nation-states show very great differences. Yet, with all due regard to local variations, nationalism, above all in Europe, has followed three fundamental patterns. One of them shaped the political life and the national consensus of England and Anglo-America, of Holland, Switzerland, and Scandinavia. It has established regimes of great stability which have successfully fused modernity and tradition. The two other patterns were less successful in leading to a similar fusion.

The French nation-state was established in the Revolution of 1789, the fruit of the Age of Enlightenment. It has become the guiding model for many other countries and for liberal trends in search of their identity. Yet in France herself the spirit of 1789 was often opposed by traditional values of the *ancien régime,* and the struggle between *les deux Frances* expressed itself in revolutions and counterrevolutions, in coups d'état and changing constitutions. On the whole, however, the spirit of 1789 has proved its vitality and its durability, and France represented to the rest of continental Europe the modernity of a nation based upon individual liberty, equality, and a cosmopolitan outlook. France was a step ahead of other nations by the fact that the new nationalism originated in the wars of the French Revolution and that nationalism and the modern nation-state emerged at the same time.

A third model was presented by the rise of German nationalism in the period of the Napoleonic wars. This rise preceded by five decades the formation of a German nation-state, a lapse and a sequence repeated in many other cases; yet it shaped the future nation-state decisively. It was a nation-state not only different from the states of the English-speaking peoples but also from France. The Germans themselves were deeply conscious of this difference and often regarded it as a proof of the superiority of the German model. The French and the German models of the nation-state, which were both delineated between 1789 and 1815, deeply influenced the character of rising nation-states everywhere, whereas the model of the English-speaking peoples remained confined to a relatively very small number of nations. The conflict between France and Germany which dominated European history until 1945 was seen by the German patriots from 1812 on and by French patriots at least from 1870 on as the conflict of two different models of basic ideas of political and cultural life.

The establishment of the German nation-state at the end of a victorious war against the "hereditary" enemy on January 18, 1871, was, for German self-awareness, closely connected not only with the medieval empire of the Hohenstaufen but also with the "spirit of 1813," which was interpreted as a repudiation of the un-German "spirit of 1789." The events of 1848-49, in which the Prussian army put an end to the patriotic efforts of German intellectuals, professional men, and artisans to follow the French model, did not become part of the national tradition. The German spirit of 1813 with which the present study deals, engendered in a much restricted and partly falsified form the "spirit" of 1871, of 1914, and even of 1933. German nationalism, with its anti-Western, anti-Enlightenment, and Germanophile attitude, became the model for many similar conservative nationalist trends, from Russia to India, from Spain to Latin America—an overcompensation for political backwardness in the modern world by claims to "spiritual" superiority based upon the legendary glories of pre-modern traditions.

The retardation of the fulfillment of German national aspirations led to a reinterpretation of German thought and the rejection of its cosmopolitan and humanistic components. This attitude made itself felt in full strength for the first time in 1859, though it was clearly represented in the intellectual climate of the "War of Liberation" of 1813. When the centenary of Friedrich Schiller's birth was celebrated, the German dramatist Friedrich Hebbel (1813-1863) noted in his diary on December 3, 1859:

> The Schiller festivities offered an occasion for declaring him the most national poet of the Germans. This, however, he was only in the sense that he denied his nation as this nation itself [in its majority] then did, and that he helped to express its cosmopolitan trend better than anyone else.

During the years from 1789 to 1815 (Schiller died in 1805) many German intellectuals transferred their loyalty from a cosmopolitan humanism which looked upon 1789 as the fulfillment of the Enlightenment to a German-centered nationalism.

Throughout the nineteenth century and the first half of the twentieth, France and Germany, competing for the leadership of continental Europe, followed the separate ways on which they had set out in the French Revolution and the Napoleonic wars. As will be shown, neither of the two concepts of the nation-state was followed by the French or the Germans without ambiguity or equivocation. History never presents clear-cut issues. It is characterized by its complexity and its contradictions. Yet to a certain and sometimes to a high degree, Goethe's words

> Nach dem Gesetz, wonach du angetreten,
> So musst du sein, dir kannst du nicht entfliehen*

are valid not only for the individual but also for the highly fluid and complex group phenomenon of a modern nation. The rise of the nation-state in France and Germany determined, at least for almost a hundred and fifty years, the course of the history of these two nations and established two conflicting models for the rise and character of nation-states not only in Europe but also in other continents.

* You must develop according to the law under which you set out on your way; you cannot escape from yourself.

La Révolution française a opéré par rapport à ce monde de la même manière que les révolutions religieuses agissent en vue de l'autre; . . . ou plutôt elle est devenue elle-même une sorte de religion nouvelle, religion imparfaite, il est vrai, sans Dieu, sans culte et sans autre vie, mais qui néanmoins, comme l'islamisme, a inondé toute la terre de ses soldats, de ses apôtres et de ses martyrs.

—TOCQUEVILLE, *L'Ancien Régime et la Révolution,* Book I, Ch. iii.

ART. 3.—*Les citoyens sont inviolables et sacrés entre eux; ils ne peuvent, dans aucun cas, se contraindre que par la loi.*

ART. 4.—*Les étrangers, la foi du commerce et des traités, l'hospitalité, la paix, la souveraineté des peuples sont choses sacrées. La patrie d'un peuple libre est ouverte à tous les hommes de la terre.*

ART. 5.—*Le pouvoir de l'homme est injuste et tyrannique: le pouvoir légitime est dans les lois.*

—SAINT-JUST, "Essai de Constitution," April 24, 1793.

Part One • France

II

France in 1789

CONTINENTAL Europe at the end of the eighteenth century entered the Age of Nationalism. In its original context nationalism was the response to a deep crisis, a search for regeneration, for better foundations of social life, for new concepts of public and private morality. The crisis was an all-European phenomenon: its origins could be found in the 1680's—in the decade which witnessed the Revocation of the Edict of Nantes in France and the Glorious Revolution in England. The crisis was resolved before the end of the eighteenth century among the English people, both in Great Britain and in North America: this priority in achieving modern nationhood endowed them with their great cohesiveness and their political inventiveness. On the continent of Europe at the end of the eighteenth century the crisis was more pronounced in the West than in the East, where the new spirit penetrated only slowly and against great resistance; what was a broad movement in the West touched only a few isolated minds in the East. Yet everywhere a revolutionary transformation was soon to take place; the French Revolution and its consequences marked a turning point for the whole continent. The first great revolutionary movements in the second half of the eighteenth century remained confined to the outskirts of the civilized world, perhaps in conformity with the then prevailing Rousseauan spirit: to Corsica—where Pasquale Paoli (1725-1807) fought Genoa and France and inspired Rousseau and Bonaparte; to Russia—where a few years later Yemelyan Pugachev led primitive peasants and Cossacks in a desperate attempt to destroy the oppressive upper classes; and to the English colonies in North America—where in the year of Pugachev's execution (1775) George Washington was named chief of the Continental Forces. But now the crisis was to resolve itself in a revolution in the very heart of European life. The revolution occurred in France, as Tocqueville has shown, for the very reason that France was in many ways the most advanced country on the continent, that the old institutions and abuses were weakest there and had a rapidly dwindling hold on the public mind, which felt more strongly than people did anywhere else that it had the right to change them. Thus France set the pace for the continent; 1789 became one of the decisive dates for France and for Europe.[1]

The French in 1789 thought of France, and only indirectly of Europe. For almost two centuries the French monarchy had established the pattern for all the continent: its political leadership was often disputed; its cultural primacy was hardly ever questioned. Now this ascendancy was threatened by the many weaknesses which the once proud structure revealed. The government seemed incapable of coping with the administrative and financial problems with which it found itself burdened. Many Frenchmen began to demand a reform that would render the state more efficient and which would release new energies to regenerate the nation. In the spirit of Voltaire, the French sought a constitution based on reason rather than on outworn precedent; in the spirit of Rousseau, they called for a common patriotic effort and for an aroused national will. The philosophy of the Enlightenment filled them with the certainty that the laws of nature were fighting on their side. This knowledge endowed them with a new audacity, a will to action, an assurance of their ability to realize their new ideal on the ancient soil of France.

France had participated in the War of the American Revolution; aristocrats had served as officers in the republican army. Many of them joined the Order of Cincinnati, which was approved by Louis XVI in December 1783, "to preserve inviolate those exalted rights and liberties of human nature for which they had fought and bled and without which the high rank of a natural being is a curse instead of a blessing." The French members of the order met every Fourth of July at the residence of Charles Hector Comte d'Estaing (1729-1794) to celebrate the anniversary of the Declaration of Independence. Leading French intellectuals like Marie Jean Marquis de Condorcet (1743-1794) and Jacques Pierre Brissot (1754-1793) explained the constitution of the United States to the French public. In 1787 a Gallo-American Society was founded, and in the same year the new "national party" voiced demands for a Declaration of Rights and for acceptance of the principle of free consent to taxation, inspired by the American model.[2] In a tragedy performed in Paris in 1791, General Washington, addressing a British officer, prophesied that the French would be the first to follow in the path of liberty:

> La raison dit: "Sois homme et rentre dans tes droits."
> Peut-être le Français, objet de votre haine,
> Sera-t-il le premier qui brisera sa chaine.[3]

Even before the English colonists in America expressed in their

Declaration of Independence the philosophy of the century, the widely read Abbé Guillaume Raynal (1713-1796), looking to England and her overseas settlements, had asked whether France, with the fertility of her soil, the mildness of her climate, and the refinement of her civilization, could not become an incomparably great nation if Frenchmen lived under the rule of liberty. If the patriotism of a free constitution had infused an overflowing vitality into England despite her bad climate and her scarce resources, what could not be expected from France? [4] Such reflections were not rare. Early in 1787, André de Chénier (1762-1794), in a "Hymne à la Justice" that remained in manuscript for many years after his death, lamented the fate of France, the beautiful and generous land that kind gods had created for happiness. He confronted her with the progress and greatness of the English, "whose courage has submitted only to the laws of a free and wise senate." France seemed to him a vast prison house where the poor suffered from starvation and oppression. Heartbroken, the poet wished to flee to a land where "the strings of his lyre would be moved by a wind carrying the sweet name of virtue and liberty." [5]

The English example inspired aristocratic officers and middle-class jurists, writers, and poets, but its influence did not penetrate deep. The common law and the spirit of experimental inquiry and of commercial enterprise, dominant in England, were alien to most French. The English language was familiar to few. French education was steeped in the knowledge of the ancient world: Livy and Sallust, Tacitus and Plutarch were the masters who influenced the thought and character of young noble and professional men from their earliest years. With the deepening of the crisis, the European mind turned to its source. The German classicists from Winckelmann to Goethe found in the imitation of the ancient Greeks the way to greatness and to personal fulfillment. Their neo-Hellenism had no political implications, nor could it serve the demands of an advancing class. In the stillness of German life it signified to an intellectual aristocracy a pedagogic ideal: the perfection of the individual and finally of the human race by aesthetic education. For these Germans, art and thought, not the ballot box or civic virtue, were the guides to a better life: they were not stirred by the tumultuous democracy of the Athenian marketplace: they breathed the rarefied air of a serene worshiper on the Acropolis.

Though the image of Sparta, thanks largely to the influence of Rousseau, continued to play a role, the small and backward Peloponnesian state could hardly appeal to the citizens of a mighty and civilized empire. In his fanatical subjection to an all-consuming stern ideal, Saint-Just knelt before Sparta's altar, while Camille Desmoulins (1760-1794) found in Athenian liberty the soil that would nourish the flowering of creative art and civilized life. But infinitely more intimate was France's tie with Rome. Though the French sometimes compared their character with that of the Greeks, they regarded their land not only as the oldest daughter of the Roman Church, but as the heir of the Roman genius for law and government.

In their favorite Latin authors the late-eighteenth-century French found an idealized republican past of virtue, simplicity, and justice in sharp contrast to the corruption of the royal court and the iniquities of their age. This picture harmonized with their reading of Rousseau and the glorification of primitive stages of human development. Cicero attracted them because he was a great lawyer and forensic orator, as so many of them wished to be. They saw in him not only an unsurpassed master of his art but also a Horatio Alger hero for their own time, a self-made man of humble birth whose advancement depended on hard work and a blameless record.[6] The young Robespierre was one of many lawyers in whom the study of the classics had nurtured a patriotic spirit and a love for the institutions of republican Rome. Every plea he made before the bar was full of classical allusions.[7] Not without reason did Lamartine, describing the last meal of the Girondins awaiting their death, have Pierre Vergniaud (1753-1793) say: "Living and dying for the liberty of the world, we mistook the period; we thought ourselves in Rome, and we were in Paris."[8]

Thus the new France saw herself as Rome renascent—republican Rome first, imperial Rome later. The Roman fashion pervaded all manifestations of public and private life. Many of the symbols of the Republican and Imperial regimes were derived from ancient models. When the revolutionary armies established new states and republics, they gave to these creations of the moment names from the Roman past; the Constitution of 1795 officially prescribed that the legislators in session were to wear uniform costumes closely patterned after Roman dress. Even the Parisian masses imitated antiquity: François Noël Babeuf (1760-1797) adopted the name "Gracchus" and in his paper *Le Tribun du peuple* compared the French Revolution to the war between patricians and plebeians in ancient Rome.

Neo-Hellenism in Germany emphasized personal perfection and universal harmony; the new Rome in France stressed the political virtues of the stern patriot and his combative spirit. This ancient mold, which ill suited the critical attitude of eighteenth-century individualism, was transmitted in schools maintained by the Roman Church and imbued with the traditions of authoritarianism.[9] The models of Sparta and Rome, of Lycurgus and the republican patriots, were not conducive to an understanding of liberty and tolerance, to a civilized respect for one's fellowmen, or to the intricacies of free discussion and patient inquiry.

The nationalism that grew up in France under the impulse of the Revolution was not the fruit of a tradition of individual liberty as in the English-speaking countries. It was filled with a spirit of fierce pride and admiration for the hard splendor of power and authority. These revolutionary democrats did not understand liberty in the way that it was understood by the Englishmen who agreed to limit their own rights in order to limit those of others. They understood it, as Sorel so well said, in the way of the king of France, who recognized no other right but his own:

> This attitude was called Roman liberty, and this conception, renewed by Rousseau and his whole school, adapted itself marvelously to the classical formulas, for a long time approved in France by the monarchy. It belonged to the French way of life and tradition. For some, this Roman pride went hand in hand with force of character and the most valiant steadfastness of the soul: they fought for their principles, succumbed with a stoic faith, or retired with dignity after the defeat of their party. For the others, the great majority, it was above all a pride of State, jealous and suspicious of competitors, implacable to the defeated, arrogant towards foreigners, but perfectly pliant to force and extremely capable of reconciling itself to submission to a master, whoever he might be, a crowd, a faction, a dictator, a general, be his name the People or the Committee, Robespierre or Bonaparte.[10]

This new nationalism set the pattern for most of the continent, with its spirit of exaltation and exclusiveness that contrasted with the individualism and cosmopolitan benevolence of the eighteenth century. This nationalism admired in its glorification of the past not the periods of quiet and patient progress, but the spectacular deeds of ambition; not reason, but will; not reflection, but enthusiasm; not readiness to compromise, but a desire for decisive action.[11] The older nationalism that developed among the English-speaking peoples in the century between the Glorious Revolution and the outbreak of the French Revolution respected the privacy of the individual: the nation-state was regarded as the protective shell for the free interplay of individual forces. The nationalism of the French Revolution revived the ancient ideal of the polis, where the duty and dignity of the citizen lay in political activity and his fulfillment in complete union with the nation-state.

Soon the French came to feel that they even surpassed the ancients. Had they not accomplished greater deeds than the ancients themselves? Had they not lighted a brighter beacon than had ever shone before on the path of mankind? In the most civilized century of history, they had outgrown the old masters and had set an example that would endure. On January 8, 1791, the rector, professors, and fellows of the University of Paris presented to the session of the National Assembly an address in which they declared their loyal adherence to all its decrees and expressed the new feeling that France had become worthy of the ancient models:

> Turning for an answer to the shades of all the great men who have immortalized the republics of Greece and Italy, we rediscover in the monuments of Athens and Rome those generous sentiments of liberty and patriotism with which their ashes are still aglow. . . . We used to speak of fatherland and liberty, and looking around us we found neither liberty nor fatherland. . . . But times have changed, thanks to the vigils of our legislators, thanks to the virtues of a citizen king. . . . We shall no longer see in the ancients men of a higher race and, as Montesquieu calls them, colossi and giants. Already, gentlemen, our own history offers us objects of comparison worthy of these great models; already the French have felt that they have a fatherland and have proved that it is sweet to die for it.

III

Influences on the Rise
of French Nationalism

THE model of Antiquity and to a lesser degree the influence of Anglo-American nationalism were only two of several important strands woven into the pattern of the French Revolution. Another was the eighteenth-century belief that all men and nations obey the same rational laws and that right legislation was to make this imprescriptible law evident to every man. Even Rousseau—the first great writer to succumb to the religious passion of intense patriotism, the fulfillment of human personality in a boundless love of the fatherland—viewed the nation in this light and hence as a community unmoved by the desire for glory and deaf to clarion calls to battle. This faith in reason and the laws of nature, governing man here on earth no less than the stars in their movements, was not confined to France. It united the educated classes all over Europe—princes and nobility, writers and their readers. Division of mankind into classes and castes, variety of religious faith and national tradition, separation of peoples by military and trade policies—all seemed to belong to a past when the light of reason had not yet penetrated the superstitions and prejudices belonging to that darker age. When Condorcet greeted the future Emperor of Russia, Paul I, at the session of the Académie des Sciences on June 6, 1782, he expressed what was then the common feeling:

> The princes hasten to destroy the barriers that alleged national interests—phantoms created by cupidity and ignorance—erected between the peoples and at the same time those that all kinds of prejudices set up among subjects of the same realm. At last we realize that all men form but one family and have but one interest. The word "mankind"—that feeling which embraces men of all countries and of all ages—is on the lips of the mon-

archs as well as on those of the philosophers: it seems to unite, in one and the same attitude, those whose ambition it is to enlighten men, and those whose duty it is to watch over their happiness and to defend their rights.[1]

Thus, when the French set out to reform the monarchy, many of them conceived their aim and actions to be applicable to all nations. Did not men everywhere partake of the universal morality that seemed to underlie the efforts of the patriots? What the French were doing seemed to be only a part of a general movement and to anticipate developments that were soon to follow everywhere. Educated men of all nations interpreted the beginnings of the French Revolution as they had the American Revolution, in the light of man's "natural" striving for liberty. For a long time the educated classes had followed everything written in France with close attention and deep respect. Now they witnessed the French appearing to shake off the chains of superstition and past tradition and to live according to the light of reason. What had been philosophical faith now seemed to assume reality. Paris was the new Zion, the new Mecca, where the generous dream of the eighteenth century, the heavenly city of the brotherhood of man built here on earth, was coming true.

Count Honoré Riqueti de Mirabeau (1749-1791), who represented the Third Estate as deputy for Aix and Marseilles, struck a chord that echoed all over Europe when he exclaimed on August 14, 1789:

> All constitutional progress in the laws and government of great states promotes the growth of reason and of human perfectibility. You will usher in the fortunate era when everything will assume the place, the form and relationship assigned to it by the immutable nature of things, and when common liberty will banish from the whole earth the absurd oppressions that weigh men down, the prejudices of ignorance and cupidity that divide them, the senseless jealousies that torment the nations, and will bring about the rebirth of a worldwide brotherhood without which all public and individual advantages are so doubtful and precarious. You labor for our sake, for the sake of succeeding generations, for the sake of the whole world, and you will march on with a firm but measured step towards this great achievement.[2]

The French Revolution was greeted as a new revelation, not by the oppressed masses of the earth, who hardly heard of it, but by the intellectuals, by the enthusiasts among them. Even old Hegel, looking back many years later on the dream of his youth, spoke of the religious fervor that hushed mankind at the sight of the divine spectacle.[3] Rising above all national and religious differences, a new common spiritual fatherland seemed ready to receive the faithful from all corners of the earth. French patriots displayed together on many occasions the flags of France, the United States, Britain, and Poland. Many foreigners flocked to Paris, among them Jean Baptiste du Val-de-Grâce, Baron de Cloots (1755-1794), who later took the name of Anacharsis Cloots, a Prussian of Dutch descent. He had at an early age come under the influence of French rationalism and played an active part in the Revolution. On June 19, 1790, he led an "embassy of the human race," a group of thirty-six foreign enthusiasts in their national costumes, to the National Assembly, which he addressed in the capacity of "l'orateur du genre humain." Many French and foreign intellectuals felt that the cause of the Revolution was universal. With a grandiloquence similar to Cloots's, the last article of the draft of the French constitution that Saint-Just submitted to the Convention on April 24, 1793, announced: "Le peuple français vote la liberté du monde." [4]

This cosmopolitanism found its most extreme expression in a letter from Anacharsis Cloots to Madame de Beauharnais:

> Why, indeed, has nature placed Paris at an equal distance from the pole and the equator, but for it to be a cradle and the metropolis for the general confederation of mankind? Here, the States-General of the world will assemble, and I predict that the time is not so remote as people believe. Let but the Tower of London fall to pieces like [the Bastille] of Paris, and there will be no more tyrants. The French flag cannot wave over London and Paris, without soon being hoisted all round the globe. . . . Then provinces, armies, conquerors, or conquered nations will no longer exist. . . . People will travel from Paris to Peking as they do from Bordeaux to Strasbourg; the ocean, by a bridge of ships, will join its shores; and East and West will embrace in the field of confederation. Rome was the metropolis of the world through war; Paris will be so through peace. The more I reflect, the more I conceive the possibility of one single nation, and the facility with which the Universal Assembly, sitting at Paris, will conduct the government of the whole human race. . . . Men will be what they ought to be, when each will be able to say: The world is my country, the world is my own native land. Then, there will be no more emigrants. There is but one nature, and one society.

In a much more restrained way the French minister of foreign affairs Pierre Lebrun wrote on November 11, 1792, to his London representative François-Joseph Noël:

> It is pretty certain that our principles will spread everywhere by themselves, a little sooner or a little later, precisely because

they are principles of pure reason—"de la saine raison"—for which the major part of Europe is now ripe.

The French were confirmed in this opinion by foreign delegations like that of several English patriotic societies who on November 7, 1792, submitted an address to the Convention which read:

> Frenchmen, you are already free; the Britons prepare themselves to become free. The triple alliance, not of crowned heads, but of the peoples of America, France, and Great Britain, will bring liberty to Europe and peace to the world. After the example set by France, revolutions will be easy. We should not be surprised if very soon an English National Convention will receive similar congratulations.

This address was printed and sent to all departments of France.

In August 1792, during the critical hours when the Prussian offensive against the French Revolution had started, the Legislative Assembly accorded the right of French citizenship to the leading humanitarians of the age—to Bentham and Wilberforce, to Washington and Madison, to Schiller and Klopstock, to Pestalozzi and Kosciuszko, and others who

> have served by their writings and by their courage the cause of liberty and have prepared for the enfranchisement of the peoples, and therefore cannot be regarded as aliens by a nation which its enlightenment and its courage have set free. . . . [If] one is not allowed to hope that men will some day form, before law as before nature, a single family, a single community, the friends of liberty and of universal brotherhood should not therefore be less dear to a nation that has proclaimed its renunciation of all conquest and its desire to fraternize with all peoples.

The eighteenth-century belief that barriers between nations would crumble before an upsurge of universal benevolence faintly lingered on, but it had become a dream for the distant future. What emerged in its place was the new reality of the nation, setting itself apart from mankind and often against it, soon to override its own pious desire for the renunciation of conquest. For with the French Revolution, which emerged from, and in many ways consummated, the eighteenth century, the century came to a close and the Age of Nationalism began.

Though poets and writers abroad might look upon the new France as the common fatherland of mankind, nowhere outside France did the people, regardless of the fact that they carried much heavier burdens than the French, respond spontaneously to the call of the Revolution. Peasants and artisans, shopkeepers and professional men clung to their traditional ways of life. Only where the French armies penetrated were the new ways of life accepted, often under protest, always incompletely, and in most cases but for a brief while. When the peoples were finally stirred into action—and the impulse rarely reached the mass of the population—they were not moved by generous universal visions and faith in the rights of man, but by the new gospel of nationalism that the French armies, not always willingly or wittingly, had carried with them across Europe.

IV

The Revolution as National Regeneration

DESPITE its European implications, the French Revolution began as an effort at national regeneration, a reformation of the French state, head and members. It drew its strength from its national character; what remained a dream of intellectuals outside France became there a social reality.[1] Only in France did the Revolution produce, for a short time at least, a unity of spirit and purpose in the national ranks. The French monarchy, the symbol around which the nation had grown up and the link that united the disparate elements of the realm—provincial and feudal rights, castes and legal traditions—had, like the absolute monarchs everywhere, tried to achieve this unity. The monarchy was historically too closely tied up with the privileges of clergy and nobility to be able to adjust the machinery of the state to the pressing demands for reform.

The absolute monarchy had created the French state, the legal framework for the life of the nation. By the end of the century, the structure was not only cumbersome and creaking under the burden it had to carry, but top-heavy, without a broad enough base to support its growing weight. In spite of its time-honored relics, the eighteenth-century state tended to be a rational construction. It has been compared to a mechanism: it was devoid of the warmth of pulsating life, of the impulse and vigor imparted by emotional loyalties and by active self-identification. What was in it, was not of it. While the monarch claimed to represent the state and to determine the national will, both state and will seemed distant to the nation, not theirs. A very great monarch in whom the love and loyalty of the people centered might have temporarily filled the void. But the weakness at the top grew at the very time when the immensity of the needed reforms demanded an authority of unprecedented strength, supported by an active and enlightened public opinion. Nobody thought of abolishing the monarchy in 1789; its prestige was still intact. If Louis XVI had been a stronger man, if Marie Antoinette had shown a greater sense of responsibility, the monarchy could have carried through the necessary reforms. Just as in Russia in 1914-1917, an important factor in the outbreak and course of the Revolution was the character of the rulers.[2] The French people in 1789 looked to the King for guidance. Robespierre believed that France was fortunate in having a prince worthy of cherishing and protecting liberty, who would inaugurate a new era in France by giving men happiness through legislation founded upon virtue.[3]

French participation in the American War of Independence had a deeper effect on the finances of the government than on the minds of the people. The heavy military expenditure for that venture created a threat of bankruptcy to the state. Tax reforms met with resistance from the privileged classes. Royal administration was diffused and encountered everywhere a multitude of difficulties caused by outdated local laws, privileges, and vested abuses. The precarious position of royal authority aroused hopes in the French aristocracy of the sword and robe that they might recapture the power they had lost to the absolute monarchs. The spirit of the Fronde revived, but it was a spirit of the past that could contribute nothing to the problems of the present beyond nostalgic reminiscences about the "liberties" enjoyed by the free Frankish men in the good old days. The revolt of the nobility, the first act of the French Revolution, was no more than an ineffectual prelude—or rather, a belated epilogue. It appealed to feudal forces that were in full decay; it opened the way unwittingly to new social forces that had gathered strength throughout the century and were supported by the intellectual culture of the time.

When the King decided to call the Estates General, which had met for the last time in 1614, its convocation was a victory for the nobility; it promised the end of the absolutist period, the revival of the ancient liberties. But that dream soon evaporated; the historical continuity had been broken for too long. The nation was no longer the king and the estates, among whom the two privileged orders played the decisive role, sanctified by tradition, fortified by economic power, invigorated by learning. The tradition had lost its magic spell; the economic power and the learning had shifted to the Third Estate, and the Third Estate felt its growing might. It was no longer willing to abide by the rules of 1614. Much of its rise it owed to the monarchy, which had used it in the struggle against the aristocracy. Thus it was ready to cooperate with the King. Assembled at Versailles, the delegates of the Third Estate assured him: "Your faithful commons will never forget what they owe their kings; never will they forget that natural alliance of throne and people against the aristocracies, the power of which can only be established on the ruins of royal authority and public happiness.

The convocation of the Estates General raised hopes high. The country suddenly seethed with political activity. Electoral assemblies met; the wishes and grievances of the privileged classes and of the people were discussed and formulated all over the realm; hundreds of pamphlets appeared. The demands for reform of administration, taxation, and the judicial system, confined until then to small articulate groups, became widespread and uniform. A rational constitution, guaranteeing the natural rights of man, was to insure the happiness of the kingdom and its citizens through patriotism and virtue. In these demands the urban bourgeoisie took a leading role. They called for an efficient state and broader freedoms not only for moral and legal reasons but in the interests of economic security and increased production as well. Over the last century they had built up their fortunes by hard work and careful accounting; they wished similar methods applied to the affairs of the state. No longer did they regard these affairs as the exclusive concern of the king, with which they did not feel themselves entitled to interfere. Their own affairs and those of the state had become too interdependent; the finances of the realm were now a national concern, the concern of those classes which by their own not unjustified estimate were the producers of wealth and the experts in finance.

But in whatever direction the bourgeoisie moved, they found themselves hindered by obsolete privileges, glaring abuses, and the inertia of vested interests. They had acted not only as the lever in the economic progress of the country: most of the great writers of the century, whose thoughts the aristocracy had eagerly accepted had come from lower classes, and members of the bourgeoisie had filled with distinction important positions in the administration, the very positions that demanded initiative and hard work, while the highest ranks in state and church alike were reserved to often less competent members of the aristocracy. The Third Estate felt its strength, and yet it was "enchained." Remove its chains and it would be able to carry the burden of the state to a future of prosperity and happiness, of law and progress for all.

The bourgeois were not thinking of their own class alone. They assumed the leadership because they constituted the only class socially and educationally advanced enough to represent the people at large. Among them, the lawyers were best able to speak in public, to present a case and maintain a wide acquaintance with public affairs. They were elected by the peasants not because they imposed themselves, but because they seemed best fitted to represent their constituents and the constituents' interests. The bourgeoisie was convinced that it worked for the regeneration of France to the benefit of all Frenchmen. In a country where government was good and efficient, where rational laws prevailed and where the liberties and rights of every citizen were protected by the constitution, the foundation for human happiness would be firmly laid.

This confidence of the middle classes was not the work of agitators, nor did any plan for the seizure of power inspire it. It was a spontaneous manifestation of the actual social and intellectual situation. It found a classic formulation in the pamphlet that the Abbé Emmanuel Joseph Sieyès (1748-1836) published in January 1789, in which he asked, *Qu'est-ce que le Tiers Etat?* The answer he gave expressed the prevailing thought. The Third Estate was the nation.

> Who will dare to say that the Third Estate does not contain everything that is needed to form a complete nation? It is a strong and robust man, one of whose arms is still in chains. The elimination of the privileged orders would not diminish the nation, but enhance it. What is the Third Estate? Everything, but an everything shackled and oppressed. What would it be without the privileged orders? Everything, but an everything free and flourishing. Nothing can be accomplished without it, everything could be accomplished infinitely better without the others.

The state had been the king; the nation had been represented by the three estates. Now all that was changed.

> The Third Estate includes everything that belongs to the nation; and everything that is not of the Third Estate cannot consider itself as being of the nation. What is the Third Estate? Everything.

The new nation envisioned by Sieyès was not an emotional body of passionate beliefs. It was an orderly association of individuals, living under a common law, established by a legislature in which they were represented.

> Qu'est-ce qu'une nation? un corps d'associés vivant sous une loi commune et représentés par la même législature.[4]

The agitation caused by the convocation of the Estates General strengthened the Third Estate and the feeling of national unity. For the first time in more than a hundred and fifty years—and in a time of great crisis, when decisive measures were needed—the representatives of the kingdom as a whole were to work together to regenerate by their common efforts "the immense French empire." They no longer had to think

in provincial or traditional terms, but for the first time as an interdependent whole, a nation, one nation. Not yet manifest at the time of
the elections when the *Cahiers de doléances* were discussed and accepted, the nation became a reality when the men sent to the capital
from all parts of the kingdom met together.[5]

V

Traditional Loyalties
and National Unity

NASCENT patriotism was expressed in many of the *cahiers* and in the debates preceding the meeting of the Estates General, but this patriotism was still tempered by attachment to traditional local rights, and the demand for unity was confined on the whole to legal reforms. Though Mirabeau overstated the case by calling France in 1789 "une agrégation inconstituée de peuples désunis," the various parts of the future nation were far from forming a "royaume un et indivisible," the famous phrase with which the second title of the Constitution of 1791 began. What Voltaire had predicted as a possibility—"our grandchildren will perhaps be astonished one day to learn that France was composed of provinces which, by the very laws, had become hostile each to the other"—now became true.[1] The disparate elements were first drawn together by the traditional loyalty to the crown and the newly emergent demand for rational reform.

The strongest resistance to French national unity came from those provinces that had joined the kingdom only recently by treaties that guaranteed their rights. In their own eyes, such provinces constituted sovereign states, nations in themselves. This was the case with Navarre and Béarn. The kingdom of Navarre did not participate in the elections to the Estates General, and sent deputies only at the last minute; they took no part in the deliberations and protested against the abolition of provincial privileges. The parliament of Béarn, a province, united with the crown of France in 1620, declared on June 20, 1788:

> As citizens and magistrates of a country alien to France, though subject to the same king, we must put before Your Majesty the peculiar rights of the two nations that the precipitate action of your administrators has confused. . . . Béarn has

been since time immemorial an independent sovereignty and has continued to be so.

When the National Assembly decided on August 4 to abolish all provincial privileges, the indignant Bishop of Lescar declared, "Let us quit France and remain Béarn," and a meeting at Pau, the capital of Béarn, on August 31, 1789, demanded the convocation of the Estates of Béarn to examine the question. The Estates did not wish to renounce their ancient constitution, "which derives from the most respectable social pact of which a nation could avail itself, except to adopt a better one, depending on the result of the work of the National Assembly.[2]

The Dauphiné in southeastern France, which came under the crown in the fourteenth century but retained its privileges and its own parliament in Grenoble, felt differently. In July 1788 the three orders of the province met at Vizille and resolved that they would never separate their cause from that of the other French provinces, and while they wished to maintain their peculiar rights, they would never abandon those of the nation. The nobility agreed to the demands of the Third Estate for better representation and greater influence. This attitude set an example and electrified French opinion to such an extent that the Estates of Béarn turned for advice in October 1789 to those of the Dauphiné. The reply came:

> Let us no longer think of what we have been, but of what we wish to be today, free Frenchmen under one king. To enjoy our national rights we should retain only those of our particular privileges which cannot harm the happiness of our fellow citizens, and we should envisage the whole of France as our fatherland. People of Béarn, of Brittany, of Dauphiné, let us glory in being French and let us fly to the help of the fatherland.[3]

Most Frenchmen in 1788-1789 found themselves somewhere between the two extremes presented by Béarn and Navarre on one hand and the Dauphiné on the other. They faced the same dilemma as did the mayor of Morlaas in Béarn on May 16: "Up to what point is it fitting for us to cease to be Béarnais in order to become more or less French?" Sieyès dismissed this sort of dilemma with hopeful assurance: "You will always be a Breton, always a Provençal, but you will soon bear with us the name of Frenchman, and we shall be able to pride ourselves on this in places other than the theater when that name designates a free man." [4]

The national spirit showed itself in 1789 stronger in the large cities than in the countryside.[5] Many of the complaints voiced were of a local nature, but as the grievances were similar everywhere, the demands assumed a national uniformity. The quest for a better constitution was well-nigh universal; it was national in scope but philosophical in origin:

it looked not to the nation for its sanction, but to the laws of nature. "France cannot be regenerated and reborn to a new life," the Third Estate of the Sénéchaussée of Nîmes declared, "but by reconstituting her on those principles which are as ancient as the world, which are engraved on all hearts, the nature of which is to exist eternally though often forgotten." [6] The words most frequently repeated were eighteenth-century words—liberty and happiness, goals to be reached through a spirit of true patriotism. But the emphasis shifted from the patriot king of the eighteenth century to the patriot citizen of the French Revolution; the traditional term for treason, *lèse-majesté*, changed to *lèse-nation* or *lèse-patrie*, even sometimes with a more universal outlook to *lèse-liberté* or *lèse-humanité*. The hope for an enlightened nation was eloquently expressed by the nobles of Caen in Normandy, who saw

> the three orders unite in spirit and sentiment, and transform by all the resources of genius and virtue this disturbed nation into a gentle society of brothers, . . . a state, issuing from a crisis that presaged ruin, raising itself to the pinnacle of fame and prosperity, triumphing over itself in submitting all passions to the salvation of the fatherland. [7]

The electoral meetings and discussions, the compilation of the *cahiers*, the publication of many hundreds of pamphlets—all created a sudden intellectual effervescence in a nation in which various censorships had stifled free expression of public opinion. Many of the writers were unknown, many of the pamphlets were published anonymously. Some of them addressed themselves to women as well as men; others offered easy panaceas for the great crises of the time, with frequent assurances of the efficacy of virtue and moral effort. [8] Public impatience grew with the worsening of the crisis, when the basic financial disorder was aggravated by bad harvests and consequent rising prices and unemployment. These in turn swelled the floating population of the large cities, especially of Paris. Thus at a time when happiness and prosperity were promised as the imminent result of national effort and will, circumstances made the prospect of attaining them ever more remote.

Against this background of gathering storm clouds, events quickly belied the serene confidence of the *cahiers* and pamphlets of the beginning of the year. The King, enthusiastically addressed as the restorer of French liberty, instead of assuming leadership and cooperating with the Third Estate, sought the support of the aristocracy to maintain the old order. Even as late as September 9, the public in the Théâtre Français acclaimed and demanded the repetition of the verse in *Marie de Brabant*, a play by Barthélemy Imbert (1747-1790):

> Puisse un roi, quelque jour l'idole de la France,

De l'hydre féodale abattre la puissance,
Et voir l'heureux Français, sous une seule loi,
Au lieu de vingt tyrans ne servir qu'un bon roi! [9]

The convocation of the Estates General was originally sought by the aristocracy to limit the absolute power of the monarchy, but under pressure of the middle classes and of the philosophy of the century, this intention gave way to an irresistible demand for a total regeneration of the state. This change frightened the nobility; many discerned the implications more clearly than most members of the Third Estate itself. Faced by the unforeseen alliance of throne and nobility, the Third Estate turned to the Parisian masses for support. It was their pressure that determined the rapid course of events.

Orderly and peaceful realization of the new order was impeded not only by aristocratic opposition but also by passions aroused among the people. The sufferings and uncertainties of the economic crisis made them demand rapid social changes, or even, in many cases, a return to the security of ancient regulations. The deliberations of the National Assembly, the enthusiastic harangues of street-corner orators, the outbreaks of violence in the villages and in the cities—all these factors contributed to a disintegration of authority. The traditional signposts of organized society disappeared in the storm of ideas and passions, conservative fears and social unrest. In these critical hours, nationalism was ultimately to provide a new basis for authority, a direction for the ship of state, a unifying bond for the integration of the social order. But it was no longer the rational and serene nationalism of the eighteenth century; it was a passionate faith, transcending the bounds of reason and becoming a law unto itself.

VI

Sieyès and the Third Estate

THE birth of one France was the work of the Third Estate, of the middle classes, who were its articulate exponents, and of the people—of all those who did not belong to the two privileged orders. Sieyès in his famous pamphlet took up the aristocratic plea advanced early in the eighteenth century that the nobles were the descendants of the Frankish conquerors, while the people were Celtic Gauls:[1]

> Why should one not send back into the Frankish forests all the families who maintain the foolish pretension of descending from the race of the conquerors and of inheriting their rights? Should there be any distinction between birth and birth, then the descendants of the Gauls and the Romans would at least be equal to those of primitive and barbaric Germanic tribes. But, in reality, the races cannot be distinguished in France. Their blood has so intermingled that the ancestors of the Third Estate are the fathers of the whole nation.[2]

While the higher clergy belonged to the aristocracy, the lesser clergy shared the life of the people from whom it sprang. The first step towards the fusion of the three estates was taken on June 13, 1789, by three priests of Poitou who, in going over to the Third Estate, declared:

> We come, preceded by the torch of reason, led by love of the commonweal, to place ourselves at the side of our fellow citizens, of our brothers. We hasten to you at the call of the fatherland, which urges us to establish among the orders the concord and harmony on which depend the success of the Estates General and the salvation of the state.[3]

On June 17, 1789, the Third Estate declared themselves to be the National Assembly. Two days before, Sieyès had demanded the abolition of the obsolete Estates General: the Third Estate, which represented the majority of the nation, should constitute itself "the assembly of the known and verified representatives of the French nation" and invite the members of the other orders to join it. After some discussion about a shorter name, the Assembly accepted the suggestion and proclaimed itself to be the representative of the general will of the nation:

> The title of National Assembly is the only one that fits the assembly in the present state of affairs, either because the members who compose it are the only legitimate and publicly known and verified representatives, or because they were sent directly by almost the entire nation, or because the representation is one and indivisible, and thus no deputy, no matter from which order or class he was elected, has the right to exercise his function apart from the present assembly.

The Assembly, which invited the two privileged orders to join "in the name of the God of Peace and of the national interest," to deliberate in the spirit of "concord so necessary in this moment, for the salvation of the public good," proceeded immediately to the great task set forth in the *cahiers*, the making of a constitution. On the night of July 9, the name of National Constituent Assembly was adopted.

The resistance to this assumption of full powers by the Third Estate was broken by popular uprisings. They reached threatening proportions in the *jacqueries* of the countryside, with the burning of manor houses and the spread of anarchy and fear. More famous and more conspicuous, however, became the popular uprising in Paris that led to the fall of the Bastille on July 14, 1789, an event unimpressive in its immediate result —the liberation of seven insignificant prisoners—but of great symbolic value. The apparently impregnable fortress of the old regime and of royal authority, ineptly defended, fell before the resolute attack of an unorganized and poorly armed mob, a handful of free men, as Elisée Loustallot (1762-1790) called it in the first number of his newspaper, *Révolutions de Paris, dédiés à la nation*, published on July 15. "O sainte liberté," he exclaimed, "quelle est donc ta puissance!" [4]

The month of August 1789, starting with the famous night of the fourth and culminating in the Declaration of Rights on the twenty-sixth, destroyed the historic framework and the ideological foundation of old France. In the speed with which interests, privileges, and prejudices, rooted in the traditions of many centuries, were abandoned, the philosophy of the eighteenth century celebrated its supreme victory. Liberal members of the high nobility took the lead. The Vicomte de Noailles called for the establishment of a government that would be admired and followed by the whole of Europe. The Duc d'Aiguillon set the tone:

> In this century of light, when sane philosophy has assumed command, in this fortunate epoch when we are united for the

public good and, free of all personal interests, are going to work
for the regeneration of the state, it seems to me, gentlemen,
necessary, before establishing this highly desirable constitution
which the nation awaits, to prove to all citizens that we intend
and wish to anticipate their desires, and to establish as promptly
as possible that equality of rights which must exist between all
men and which alone can assure their liberty

Thus upon the initiative of the nobility the old division of the French
into classes and castes was swept away. The delegates of provinces
followed. Going far beyond—or rather, contrary to—their mandates,
they renounced all their historical rights and privileges. The session of
August 4 has rightly been called "the heroic suicide of particularism."
Traditions of centuries, which the communities had regarded with pride
and defended with vigor for such a long time that they almost seemed
to belong to the nature of things, disappeared in one night, never to return. This sudden change, though prepared by the criticism of the century, could not have taken place but for the impact of the new and
overwhelming emotion of national unity. Provinces, principalities, and
cities renounced privileges and historical rights of an infinite variety.
Article X of the Decree of August 11 established the unity of the nation:

"Une constitution nationale et la liberté publique étant plus
avantageuses aux provinces que les privilèges dont quelque-
unes jouissaient et dont le sacrifice est necessaire à l'union intime
de toutes les parties de l'Empire, il est déclaré que tous les
privilèges particuliers des provinces, principautés, pays, cantons,
villes et communautés et habitants, soit pécuniaires, soit de toute
autre nature, sont abolis sans retour et demeureront confondus
dans le droit commun de tous les Français.

The first half of the month of August established national unity; the
second established liberty through the Declaration of the Rights of
Man and the Citizen, the fruit of the constitutional development of the
English-speaking countries and of the rational individualism of the
eighteenth century. The Declaration established the base and framework
of the new order, a nation of free individuals protected by law. The people were sovereign, but they derived their power from the law, and the
law derived its power from reason. The Declaration limited the om-
nipotence of the nation-state in Article II: "The aim of all political association is to preserve the natural and imprescriptible rights of man. These
rights are liberty, property, security, and resistance to oppression"; and
in Article XVI: "Any society in which the guarantee of rights is not
assured or the separation of powers not determined has no constitution."
The Declaration proclaimed and protected the rights of the individual

as the center and fountainhead of society and of the nation. The objection has been voiced that this conception does not correspond to the facts of nature and history: the individual nowhere exists except in society and finds himself everywhere indissolubly a part of the collectivity. But the Declaration opposed to the practice of the ages the hope of the new age; in making the autonomous individual the starting point and the justifying end of all society, the Declaration stands out in the history of the emancipation of man. Though conditioned in its wording and in the underlying thought by the century of which it was the climax, it transcends that, and any, century. Men will always recur to it when they seek to protect the dignity, privacy, and happiness of the human being against growing pressure from the group. Throughout the nineteenth century, continuing and expanding faith in the Declaration succeeded in preventing the new god of nationalism from degenerating into Moloch.[5]

In July 1789 Sieyès exposed the underlying principles of the Declaration and enlarged upon some of its implications. According to him, the individual should find his liberty limited only where it begins to encroach upon the liberty of another. This point is determined by law. Everyone has a right to protection of his person, property, and liberty, but not everyone, as Sieyès saw it, can participate actively in the affairs of the state. The rights of man and the citizen do not necessarily involve political rights: even in democratic societies women had then no political rights, though they enjoyed the full protection of human and civil rights. Political rights demand not only intellectual maturity but also an active interest in public affairs. Sieyès, who rejected privileges of birth and of wealth, believed that only the better educated and more responsible part of the population should become legislators, but he hoped that with the growth of education all people above a certain age would come to share equal political rights.

Like the authors of the Declaration, Sieyès included among the fundamental rights freedom of thought and expression in all its forms. But he wished to guarantee not only the positive right of action but also the negative right of abstention. Man has the right to speak out or to attend an assembly or demonstration; he has equally the right to remain silent or to stay at home. The privacy of the individual was to be protected against all regimentation. In one respect, Sieyès went beyond the original Declaration. He demanded the right to public assistance for every citizen unable to provide for his needs or to find work. Because the liberty of the individual presupposed for Sieyès the framework of national solidarity, he added fraternity to liberty and to equality before the law.[6]

The liberty on which the Declaration insisted was personal liberty, not national independence; the equality was legal equality before the law and equal admissibility to all public offices and employments, not equality of wealth or income. Neither national self-determination nor socialism could be directly derived from the Declaration.[7] It was not an expression of the rights of the French nation, but of universal rights. Pierre Samuel Dupont de Nemours (1739-1817) voiced on August 8, 1791, the general conviction: "It is not a question of a declaration of rights which would last for one day. It is a question of the fundamental law of the laws of our nation and of that of other nations, which will endure throughout the centuries."

The lawmakers of 1789, however, put equal emphasis on the enduring value of the individual and the temporary necessity of national unity. Revolutionary France swung away sharply from the historic confusion of internal divisions: its desire for rational order and its passion for national unity pushed it further towards excessive centralization than the monarchy had gone, a process culminating in Napoleon's regime. France did not follow the example of English self-government or of American federalism. Though there was a trend to constitute the nation as a federation of autonomous democratic provinces or communities with the national government deriving its power from them, the unitarian conception prevailed. The nation became rigidly one and indivisible, with all its life emanating from the center and flowing from there to the periphery.[8] The idea of a sovereign nation applied to such a centralized nation can render its power more dangerous than that of a sovereign monarch. *In Deo vivimus, movemur et sumus* became *In natione vivimus, movemur et sumus*. Formerly, at least in Western civilization, God and the earthly sovereign were different, and man could appeal from the sovereign to God. In the Age of Nationalism, outside the English-speaking countries, the omnipotent nation sometimes absorbed God as it did the free individual, and became the *summus arbiter* and *summum bonum*, the all-in-all.

This danger was present even in the French Revolution. Hardly was the Declaration proclaimed before it was infringed. The National Constituent Assembly regarded itself as a sovereign body without any division or separation of powers. It embodied the national will, which did not tolerate checks or balances. Though the monarchy still commanded the loyalty of the overwhelming majority of the people, who could scarcely imagine a France without a king, and though a compromise was found on October 10, 1789, calling Louis XVI "by the grace of God and the constitutional law of the state, King of the French," [9] all rights resided in and emanated from the nation, of which the monarchy became an organ without much function. But in that troubled time, when all authority was open to question, the sovereignty of the Assembly was more theoretical than real. The legal dictatorship of the Assembly soon faced the actual dictatorship of the Parisian masses, of the active and articulate members of the Parisian commune. Their relationship was complex. At the beginning the Assembly sought the support and protection of the masses against king and nobility; soon, however, the Parisian mob opposed the elected representatives of France and tried to force them far beyond the mandates they had received. In fact, neither the Assembly nor the Parisians inquired into the will of the people as a whole. By the end of 1789 France found herself more divided than at the beginning of the year.[10]

The Age of Nationalism generated passions that threatened to burst the dikes set up by eighteenth-century reason. It coincided with the transition from rural to urban economy, with the growing social dynamism and mobilization of capitalism, with the quicker pace of life spurred on by mechanized industrialization and popular education. The traditionally organized and integrated communities of villages and guilds gave way to the unorganized masses of the cities, increased by migration from the country. Masses and mass psychology created new problems. Lacking the stability and security of a traditional society, the masses were more easily swayed by utopian hopes and stirred by unreasonable fears, many of which manifested themselves as national or social messianism and irrational hostilities born of prejudice. With the new mobility of the age, elites, on the other hand, formed in a more rapid succession: for them as well as for the masses, nationalism became the medium for organization and self-expression. In the course of this development the elites grew more and more skillful in manipulating the hopes and fears of the masses.

From the time of the French Revolution on, social and economic questions played an increasingly important part. In preceding centuries, and in precapitalistic societies in general, immobility of status, willing acceptance of the social hierarchy, and resignation to the station into which one was born gave little scope to a desire for social change or economic advance. Wherever enlightenment penetrated, rational criticism gave rise to new ambitions; wherever the influence of capitalism spread, traditional ties were loosened or broken to allow the rise of new men and new classes. This process was far less advanced in France in 1789 than in Britain. Nevertheless, serfs were almost unknown in France by then; peasants were no longer attached to the soil and had been free for generations to move about and own property. Many of them were being absorbed into the bourgeoisie. But the rapid growth of the population and the division of land through inheritance created an agrarian crisis which was aggravated by the fact that the burden of taxation fell most heavily upon the peasants, who were least able to carry it. Their serious economic grievances drove them to revolt, though they had hardly any social revolutionary consciousness. Nor was there any clear class consciousness among the workers in the cities. The leaders of the revolutions in Paris were not wage earners, but the lower middle class, owners of small workshops and shopkeepers. They alone fulfilled the necessary conditions: they were able to read, they provided the active members of the clubs, and they were filled with a spirit of initiative.[11]

For all its lack of class consciousness in the modern sense, the French Revolution brought into sharp relief the psychology of masses on the move under the impulsion of great collective emotions. This was as true of the crowds in Paris as of the bands of peasants who spread the Great Fear through the countryside in 1789. In such aggregations of people, often brought together by a trivial incident or uncontrollable rumor about the designs of a few of the leaders, the individual, losing himself in the "herd," sheds control and restraint. His fears and hopes are magnified out of proportion to reality. Many peasants had concrete grievances against individual aristocrats: they constructed them into an abstract image of the whole aristocracy, endowing it with the worst features observed. Thus an adversary-type was built up in their minds that obscured and replaced reality, but impressed itself more strongly upon the imagination because it appeared more consistent and less complex. It responded to the need for simplification and understanding; it seemed to explain the otherwise inexplicable economic crisis and the difficulties of life by which the people found themselves suddenly harassed.

While this new adversary-type could be charged with full responsibility, the national or social group believed itself, in contrast, the virtuous sufferer, the innocent victim of dark forces. It felt frustrated, through no fault of its own, and was convinced that once the adversary was removed, everything would be set right and happiness would follow. To the black picture of the adversary was opposed the shining white of the idealized self. National and social mass struggles started to assume an apocalyptic fervor; one had to win a decisive battle against the arch-enemy and the millennium would arrive. These hopes and fears generally aggravated the crisis that had produced them; with the growth of passions and suspicions, unrest spread and endangered more and more the functioning of government. This rapid worsening of the situation created an uncritical state of mind in which the conviction became general that hostile plots were the root and cause of the growing misfortunes. The suspicion of a conspiracy of the aristocracy—and soon afterwards of foreign monarchs—became even more convincing to the aroused masses because they attributed to their opponents the same passionate faith, the same absorption in the cause, the same drive to unite and act, as that by which they themselves were animated, or with which their own leaders tried hard to imbue them.[12]

Rational doubts and aversion to precipitate action found scant support in the new mental climate. For with the French Revolution, ever stronger stress was laid upon will and action as against reason and reflection. Men began to shake off religious acquiescence; their growing feeling of collective strength gave them confidence that a strongly determined human will could and must find ways to accomplish its ends. Scientific discoveries seemed to prove the power of human ingenuity and inventiveness. With emerging individualism, men willed themselves; with rising nationalism, nations willed their national selves. A new audacity began to characterize the period. Above all, a new impatience, born of insecurity, anxieties, and high-flown aspirations—all of them the result of changing conditions in a world where mobility was replacing status—drove man to throw himself forward into the unknown future. "Il fuit en avant." This spirit of aggressiveness began also to influence the conduct of war in the Age of Nationalism. Its spirit became offensive, aiming at the annihilation of the enemy by quick blows. George Jacques Danton (1759-1794) summed it up on September 2, 1792, in his famous words, "Le tocsin qu'on sonne n'est pas un signal d'alarme, c'est la charge sur les ennemis de la patrie. Pour les vaincre, il nous faut de l'audace, encore de l'audace, et la France est sauvée." The first year of the Age of Nationalism witnessed at one and the same time the supreme recognition of the dignity of human personality in the Declaration of Rights and the rise of collective passions and mass forces deeply hostile to the rights of the individual. Januslike, the new age faced two ways.

VII

Self-Determination and Equality

AT THE beginning, the emphasis was on unity and equality. On November 30, 1789, Corsica, an island alien to France in history, traditions, and language, was accepted as an integral part of France, a decision welcomed by the Corsicans.[1] In the same month, after negotiations with the Pope, Charles François Bouché (d. 1794) submitted a bill proposing the annexation of two ancient papal enclaves in French territory, the Comtat Venaissin and the city and state of Avignon, and their irrevocable union with the county of Provence and thus with France. In opposition to this proposal, however, the parishes of the Comtat invoked a new principle, the principle of self-determination, of the free expression of popular will, as it had been proclaimed by the French Revolution at its inception and implied in the Declaration of Rights. The people of the Comtat protested "before the universe" against all treaties made without their knowledge and their direct participation:

> Considering that any claim or assumption of sovereignty can be lawfully founded only on the free consent of the people, and that the expression of its will must precede any change of government; considering, moreover, that the people handed over by proceedings in which it has had no part would consider itself abandoned, for men cannot be bought and sold like mere lands and chattels.

Though the small territory in question was on all sides surrounded by and economically dependent upon France, and though its people were French-speaking and their geographical position on the road to Italy was of the highest strategic importance, the French Assembly bowed to the will of the people of the Comtat. Only when repeated plebiscites made certain beyond all doubt that the majority of the inhabitants of Avignon and the Comtat freely desired union with France did the National Assembly, on September 14, 1791, accept them.[2]

The Declaration implicitly recognized the right of self-determination; explicitly it established the legal equality of all people in France. On December 21, 1789, the Comte de Clermont-Tonnerre demanded that no one be excluded from the right to vote "on account of the profession which he exercises, or of the religion he professes." Three days later, Protestants, comedians, and the hangman received full legal equality. Speaking to an actor in 1790, the president of the Jacobin club in Rouen stressed the fact that prejudice had ceased to exist. "All men are equal by nature," he said, "they are now equal also by law. Today the applause of society proves to you that talents, honesty, and above all patriotism are the only titles of consideration for free men." With similar insistence it was asked: "Is it not true that all Frenchmen are born and are citizens before being Christians, before being Protestants, before being Jews?" [3] Under these conditions, the integration of Jews into the new national body became possible and necessary. The Jews living in the south of France, especially in Bordeaux, were largely of Spanish descent and had for a long time shared French cultural life. They were admitted to full equality on July 28, 1790. Other considerations arose in the case of the Jews in eastern France, particularly in Alsace, who in language and custom differed from the French. They were accepted into the French Union on September 27, 1791, but under the condition that they would cease to remain a nation within a nation and that they would fully adopt the ways of life of the body politic, with which, despite differences of descent and traditional background, their interests, inclinations, and loyalties were henceforth to fuse completely.[4]

The concern for human equality brought the questions of the colored peoples and of slavery in the French Empire to the fore. Eighteenth-century humanitarianism drew the attention of French intellectuals to the situation in the colonies. Montesquieu, following Locke, pointed out the evil of slavery:

> It is useful neither to the master nor to the slave. Not to the slave, because he can do nothing through the motive of virtue; nor to the master, because by having an unlimited authority over his slaves he insensibly accustoms himself to the want of all moral virtues, and thence becomes fierce, hasty, severe, choleric, voluptuous, and cruel.[5]

Camille Desmoulins dreamed of becoming "an Alexander in philanthropy . . . to embrace in his love all mankind." [6] Bernardin de Saint-Pierre (1737-1814) had presented in his *Voyage à l'Île-de-France* a moving picture of life among the slaves. A royal ordinance of 1784 tried to improve their lot. Condorcet expressed his opposition to slavery in the *Journal de Paris* in 1777, and four years later published in Neuchâtel under the pseudonym of "Schwartz" a pamphlet called *Réflexions sur l'esclavage des nègres,* which was reprinted in Paris in 1786, one year before the famous Société des Amis des Noirs united Condorcet, Brissot, Lafayette, Sieyès, and Mirabeau in the cause of emancipation.

The Declaration of Rights aroused much fear among the French settlers in St. Domingue, where the free mulattoes demanded equality with the whites. On May 15, 1791, it was granted to them by the National Assembly, but the imperial government was unable to enforce the edict in the colonies. There mulattoes continued to be excluded from the right to vote in the colonial assemblies. Jeremy Bentham, who became an honorary French citizen on August 26, 1792, sent to the Convention in 1793 a pamphlet called *Emancipate Your Colonies!* The Convention did not go that far, but on February 4, 1794, when three delegates from St. Domingue—a white, a mulatto, and a black man—presented themselves before the Convention, a motion to abolish Negro slavery in all the colonies was approved by a rising vote. It was decreed that "all men, without distinction of color, domiciled in the colonies, are French citizens and enjoy all the rights assured under the Constitution." This decision was reversed, however, and slavery was re-established in the French colonies in July 1802.[7]

More powerful than these legal attempts to achieve the union of Frenchmen was the spontaneous movement of fraternization that swept the country in 1790 and culminated in the famous Fête de la Fédération celebrated on the first anniversary of the capture of the Bastille. It originated in the late fall of 1789 in the provinces, where various National Guards formed local federations with neighboring departments and promised to support each other in the common defense of the National Assembly and its laws.[8] Responding to this movement, the Parisians proposed on June 5, 1790, the organization of a great national federation:

> Hardly ten months have passed since the memorable moment when, from the walls of the conquered Bastille, a sudden cry arose: Frenchmen are free! On the same day, let a more moving cry ring forth: Frenchmen, we are brothers! Yes, we are brothers, we are free, we have a fatherland. . . . How beautiful will be the day when all Frenchmen are allied! A nation of brothers, regenerators of the empire, a citizen-king, rallied for a common oath at the altar of the fatherland, what a new and imposing spectacle for the nations! . . . On July 14 we achieved liberty; on July 14 we shall swear to preserve it. On one and the same day, at one and the same hour, let a general cry, a unanimous cry, reverberate throughout all parts of France: Long live the nation, the law and the king!

Such a union of the friends of the fatherland would strengthen it so that it would no longer have any enemies; it would make all those who still hesitated vie for the honor of seeing their names inscribed "dans ce pacte de famille, monument de notre gloire et garant éternel de la félicité de cet empire."

On July 14, 1790, the national festival was celebrated in Paris on the Champ de Mars and all over France. Its immediate purpose was to create a united National Guard throughout the country, "animated by an identical spirit to defend the public liberty and to uphold the laws of the empire and the legitimate authority of the monarch." As commander of the National Guard of Paris, the Marquis de Lafayette (1757-1834), in the presence of the King, the legislative body, and an immense crowd estimated at 300,000, swore an oath at the altar of the fatherland. The oath promised to unite the French among themselves and with their king for the defense of liberty, constitution, and law, for the protection of the security of persons and property, the unhindered circulation of grain and other foodstuffs throughout the kingdom, and the payment of taxes. With the disintegration of the governmental apparatus and the growing economic crisis, a supreme moral effort seemed needed to induce the people to sacrifice their individual and local preoccupations to the fatherland, "the reality of which was to appear that day to all." [9]

On June 26, 1793, a decree ordered the erection "in all communities of the empire of an altar of the fatherland on which will be engraved the Declaration of Rights, with the inscription: The citizen is born, lives, and dies for the fatherland"—an inscription running counter to the very spirit of the Declaration.[10] Though the festivals became ever more spectacular and though all the arts were mobilized in their behalf, the spirit of July 14, 1790, never returned. Finally, on July 14, 1805, no public mention was made of the significance of the day. But for those who had been present, and for later generations, it remained the bright hour of the birth of a nation. Chénier commemorated the event and its mood:

> Dieu du peuple et des rois . . .
> Ici sont rassemblés, sous ton régard immense,
> De l'Empire français les fils et les soutiens,
> Célébrant devant toi leur bonheur qui commence,
>   Egaux à leur yeux comme aux tiens.
>
> D'un mortel isolé connaissant la faiblesse,
> D'un mortel citoyen sentant la dignité,
> Forts de leur union, sans maître, sans noblesse,
>   Agrandis par l'égalité.

Nous jurons d'obéir, de donner notre vie
Au peuple souverain dont émane la loi;
Nous jurons d'obéir à cette loi chérie,
   Nous jurons d'obéir au roi.

Plus d'ordres différens, plus même de province;
La France désormais, en son immensité,
Ne voit qu'un seul empire, un seul peuple, un seul prince,
   Unis dans la même cité.[11]

Another song of the period, celebrating the spectacle of a duke and a stevedore, a charcoal *vendeuse* and a marquise, abbés and soldiers, monks and young women, working together to make the festival a success, wished to see the blessings of union extended beyond national limits:

> Patrie, élevons ton autel
> Sur les pierres de la Bastille,
> Comme un monument éternel,
> Où le bonheur des Français brille.
> Venez, de tous les lieux divers
> Que renferme ce grand empire,
> Donner aux yeux de l'univers
> L'exemple à tout ce qui respire!
> Que par la paix et l'union
> Tout étranger soit notre frère,
> Et que la Fédération
> S'étende par toute la terre.[12]

All classes and ranks participated; rich and poor were united; the traditional divisions not only of provinces but of religions disappeared.[13]

> Such was that Festival of the Federation, an image anticipating a new world, a veritable prophecy in action, perhaps the most astounding and loftiest vision of the future a great people had ever seen. Without doubt, that oath—bound to hopes, alas! too soon disappointed—was not upheld; but nevertheless France had written there, and in a manner impossible to destroy, the first page of a book destined to be taken up again and continued.[14]

VIII

Divisions and Unity
in the New Nation

HARDLY had the enthusiasm of the oath of union manifested French brotherhood for one memorable day when this unity was broken. The deep rifts that became apparent then, still exist. Rich and poor had fought together to overthrow the absolute monarchy. The nation was no longer the king and the estates; it was the people as a whole. All of them were "children of the fatherland," they were the "sovereign"; but the question now arose how many among them could and should actively determine the fate of the nation. Universal suffrage for adult males was not known at that time, not in Britain and not even in the United States; the idea of suffrage for women scarcely occurred to anyone.[1] The Constitution of 1791 divided French male citizens into several categories according to their wealth, which qualified them for the right to vote or for that of being elected. While property owners alone were thus recognized as active citizens, the new order made it possible for anyone to become a property owner; there were no longer any classes fixed by law. This division into active and passive citizens was widely accepted at first, but opposition soon spread, with a demand for equal voting rights for all men above the age of twenty-five. Condorcet pointed out the discrepancy between the electoral law and the Declaration of Rights. Jean Paul Marat (1743-1793) in his *Ami du peuple* protested against the formation of a new privileged class. These democratic demands did not emanate from the people itself. The peasants were indifferent to the vote; the workers in the cities, patriotic and anti-aristocratic, willingly accepted the decisions of the Constituent Assembly. The agitation for universal suffrage was carried on by a minority from the wealthy and educated classes.[2]

It was only in 1791 that the people in Paris began to take up the issue. Their protests were directed less against the requirement of a minimum income—which was very low—than against the necessity of paying a "marc of silver" to become a candidate for election. Two of the Parisian sections declared that though the law was the expression of the general will, those who on July 14 had saved the fatherland at the risk of their lives were excluded from making its laws:

> The art of government consists in governing all by all. Abolish those decrees that violate your sublime Declaration of the Rights of Man and the Citizen; restore to us our brothers to enjoy with us the benefits of the Constitution which they await impatiently and which they have upheld with courage. Let the totality of citizens sanction your decrees, else there is neither Constitution nor liberty.

But even by the middle of 1792 the majority of Frenchmen, including the workers of Paris, were neither democrats nor republicans. Events, however, proved stronger than opinions. The growing economic crisis, the religious conflict, and above all, the passions of war mobilized the masses and widened the social rift in France.

Hardly had national union reconciled Catholics and Protestants and healed the wounds left by the wars of religion when a new religious conflict, as bitter as that of the seventeenth century, divided the nation. The Civil Constitution of the Clergy nationalized the Catholic Church in France on July 12, 1790. Many Europeans welcomed a measure that subordinated the church to the state and removed the danger of an independent body within the body politic. Therein the revolutionaries only followed the lead given to them by the absolute monarchs—above all, by Joseph II of Austria. The many cases of corruption visible in at least the higher ranks of the church had produced a widespread demand for reform. Many German intellectuals compared the measures of the Constituent Assembly to Luther's struggle for a reformed and at the same time more national church. The nascent nationalism, in its unitarian tendencies, was deeply suspicious of all dependence upon foreign powers, especially upon the Papacy, which was regarded as hostile to the very principles on which the French Revolution wished to build the nation.

But soon their intentions led the patriots further than any extreme Gallicanism ever went. Was it not necessary, they asked, in the new age of reason and progress, to subordinate the traditional church to the new "religion" of the national state? Did not the new nationalism provide a stronger tie of brotherhood, a better promise of happiness on earth, a more trustworthy source of virtue than the church? The Civil Constitution not only ended the spiritual and financial dependency of the clergy upon Rome, but undermined the dogmatic and administrative structure of the church. The regenerated French state was to have its own regenerated church, a church of the French nation and of the French people, Christian perhaps—in that vague sense in which the enlightened humanitarianism understood religion; certainly not Roman. The Constitution ordered the election of clergy and bishops by the people. Members of other religions and freethinkers, not only Catholics, had the right to vote. Was there any guarantee that men would be elected for their devotion to the Catholic faith? The solemn oath they had to swear on assuming office spoke only of loyalty to France. They promised to be "faithful to the nation, the law and the king, and to maintain with all their might the Constitution decreed by the National Assembly and accepted by the king." [3]

Faced by this dilemma, forced to choose between faith and patriotism, many bishops and priests refused to take the oath and to sever their spiritual ties with Rome. The church in France was split wide open. But the struggle was not simply one between two ecclesiastical doctrines; it was a conflict in the conscience and mind of many Frenchmen, who were now torn between loyalty to the nation, which they wished to see reformed and regenerated, and allegiance to their inherited faith and the sacraments on which their eternal salvation depended. The religious conflict, perhaps more than any other question, divided France on matters that touched on the most intimate resources of man's life.

Hitherto, the fundamental acts of human life—birth and baptism, marriage and death—had been the province of the church and received from it their meaning. The law of September 20, 1792, not only allowed divorce but introduced the registration of all acts of personal and family status by state authorities. The church registers were closed; in the town halls new registers were opened. The center of life shifted visibly: the intimate events of man's career here on earth—hitherto so indissolubly linked with heaven—belonged henceforth to the nation and received from it their meaning and legitimacy. Formerly, at least within Western civilization, state and church had divided control over man's body and soul and had often fought over them; and in this divided authority lay a guarantee of liberty. Now, body and soul were in danger of being subjected to the state alone. This danger hardly existed in England and the United States, where the religious matrix survived into the Age of Nationalism and the traditions of individual liberty and local self-government were deeply rooted. [4]

The opposition of classes and the controversy over religion were both involved in a third issue dividing the nation. Though this conflict separated only a small minority from the main body, it went to the root of the question concerning what made up the nation. King, nobility, and church had constituted for many centuries the glories of France. Was not the fatherland, the true *patrie*, embodied in the monarch, especially in an enlightened monarch, a king-patriot? The men of the eighteenth century were agreed that fatherland was not a geographic term, nor necessarily a point of emotional attachment created by community of descent, language, or tradition. The term fatherland implied political order with just laws and institutions and a promise of happiness for its citizens. The men of the Revolution accepted this concept, but they interpreted it in their own way. The Abbé Volfius, the future Constitutional Bishop of the Côte d'Or, defined fatherland at the festival of federation at Dijon on May 18, 1790:

> It is not at all this soil on which we live, these walls which have seen our birth. The true fatherland is that political community where all citizens, protected by the same laws, united by the same interests, enjoy the natural rights of man and participate in the common cause.

The party of the king understood fatherland in a similar legal and nonterritorial sense, but they appealed to a different concept of law, involving not the natural rights of man, which seemed to them to destroy the lasting foundations of society and to lead to strife and chaos, but the habits and customs which, slowly changing through the centuries, had assured the peace and progress of that society. One of the aristocratic émigrés defined fatherland in 1796:

> Fatherland is a word without meaning if it does not signify the whole body of laws under which one has lived; that is what forms the fatherland. A fatherland that limits itself to territory says nothing to the heart of man; to love a fatherland when it has lost its laws, its customs, its habits—that is an absurd idolatry. France without its king is for me only a corpse, and of the dead, one loves only the memory.[5]

Patriotism at the end of the eighteenth century implied loyalty to ideas and institutions rather than to the gods of the soil or the blood. In both its forms it had universal connotations: the men of the Declaration of Rights broadened their vision of the fatherland to include all peoples progressing towards liberty, equality, and fraternity; the nobility, also citizens of the eighteenth century, fought side by side with nobles of other lands for common ideals and concepts.

The emigration of the nobility as a protest against legal changes in France was at first compared to the emigration of the Huguenots, who had agitated from abroad and even fought against the Catholic monarchy of France. They felt themselves allied with men of their faith of all nations, and such sentiments sometimes dominated the émigrés from the French Revolution as well. "I shall march," declared one of their more extreme leaders, Louis Joseph Prince de Condé (1736-1818):

In spite of the horror which the idea of dipping one's sword in French blood must naturally inspire in a descendant of Saint Louis, I shall march at the head of the nobility of all nations, and, followed by all men loyal to their king who gather together under my flag, I shall attempt to deliver an unfortunate monarch.

But times were changing: the concept of the fatherland was undergoing a transformation in both camps, expressed in a more fervent attachment to the native soil.

Many of the émigrés were seized by a nostalgic love for the land they had left and the idea of which they carried with them. Charles de Villers (1765-1815) wrote in 1798:

Republican today, monarchical tomorrow, in the diversity of human affairs it is always France that remains; it is the land which has nourished our early years and given us its habits and its language; we have derived from there that national character, that firmness in misfortune, that gaiety which support and comfort us; there live our parents, our friends, everything that is dear to us.

This attachment was even stronger in the hearts of the revolutionary patriots whom the vicissitudes of the Revolution forced into death or exile. When Danton was urged to flee to safety to escape the guillotine, he declined—"parce qu'on n'emporte pas la patrie à la semelle de ses souliers." And the Prince Victor de Broglie (1757-1794), mounting the scaffold, admonished his infant son, the future minister under Louis Philippe, to forget the death of his father and to remain faithful to the ideas of the Revolution. When Lazare Carnot (1753-1823) escaped from Paris in 1797, he concluded his written justification of his point of view:

O France! My fatherland! O great people, truly great people! It is on your soil that I had the happiness to be born; I cannot cease to belong to you except by ceasing to exist. You embrace all the objects of my affection, the work that my hands have helped to build. Receive this my vow to serve your immortal glory and your constant prosperity, which I renew each day and which I address at this moment to all that you contain of virtuous and honest souls, to all those who preserve within themselves the sacred spark of liberty.[7]

Napoleon's coup d'état of 18 Brumaire, 1799, opened up not only for Carnot but for many aristocratic émigrés the possibility of a return to France.

The conflict between the traditionalist and the revolutionary camps of the French nation was aggravated by the religious schism. The philosophers of traditionalism—the Vicomte Louis Gabriel de Bonald

(1754-1840) and the Comte Joseph de Maistre (1753-1821)—rejected the individualist and, as they regarded it, abstract conception of man underlying the philosophy of the Enlightenment and the Declaration of Rights. For them, society was ordered by preordained laws: the true religion was the foundation of the true state, and the true state was the protector of the true religion. Rationalist and individualist criticism of religion could only lead to the destruction of state and society. In 1796 Bonald published his *Théorie du pouvoir politique et religieux* and Maistre his *Considérations sur la France*. Each might be considered a reply to Condorcet's *Esquisse d'un tableau historique des progrès de l'esprit humain*, which was published posthumously in 1796 after the author's suicide in prison during the Terror. In the most tragic period of the Revolution, when he himself faced persecution and death, Condorcet voiced the supreme confidence of enlightened men in the power of reason. This optimistic position Bonald and Maistre rejected. To them, man's claim to autonomy appeared an act of revolt against eternal law, an act of hubris that must of necessity lead to moral and political anarchy. Only the restoration of religion—they meant the Roman Catholic Church—and of the hereditary monarchy by the grace of God could save France. Maistre warned:

> Let us not indulge in the dreams of Condorcet, of that philosophy so dear to the revolution that used its life to prepare the misfortune of the living generation, benignly bequeathing perfection to our posterity. . . . We are corrupted by the modern philosophy which said that everything is good.[8]

Maistre felt that on the contrary, man was not good, that he had been vitiated by original sin—"But I see another law in my members, warring against the law of my mind, and bringing me into captivity to the law of sin which is in my members" (Romans 7:23)—and he pointed to events of the Revolution to prove how quickly a civilized nation could return to primitive savagery, once it abandoned the principles of true religion. Only under the guidance of unshakable authority could man lead a civilized life. In contrast to Rousseau, Bonald stated: "We are evil by nature, good by society." [9] According to Bonald, the men of the Enlightenment misunderstood the nature of man and of society; the Revolution was less a failure of the heart than of reason.

Rarely have the two opposing principles been stated with as much incisiveness as in the years of the French Revolution. In their extreme forms, both contentions were utopian: the ideal state of true religion had no more existed than could the ideal state of the perfect man and of pure reason ever come into existence. Yet to both parties, the desirability and feasibility of idealized and abstract conditions seemed so evident that they could only explain doubt or resistance as motivated by personal interest or profit, by secret plots and dark conspiracies. Opponents were seen either as tyrants and enemies of the people or as foes of all divine and human order; complex events were explained either as conspiracies of aristocrats, Jesuits, rich profiteers, or as machinations of freemasons, atheist intellectuals, alien agitators. The critical intelligence and the sense of moderation of the French people have generally though not always restrained these dangerous oversimplifications. Among the English people they played no great role after the Glorious Revolution, thanks to inherent common sense—or as some might call it, a lack of metaphysical imagination—and a tradition of compromise. On the other hand, they have dominated significant trends of modern German and Russian thinking.

Though the two opposing interpretations of nationalism were first stated with sharp logical clarity in France, they were by no means confined to that country. The various forms of nationalism are not only determined by the traditions and character of each people; they are also shaped by the answers man gives to the ultimate questions on the meaning of life and history. Representatives of both—a liberal and optimistic concept of man and a concept that is pessimistic and authoritarian—can be found in the Age of Nationalism in practically every nation, but from case to case their strength and influence vary. In France, traditionalist nationalism, born in opposition to the French Revolution, was strongly represented; but though it attracted the masses in the form of authoritarian democracy, it has so far never prevailed for any length of time. The faith in the liberty of the individual, underlying the Declaration of Rights, has so far reasserted itself again and again.

The division of the French nation into two camps, the Revolutionary patriots and the émigrés, seemed to render the demand for national unity even more imperative. At first there was much opposition to legal action against the émigrés, as such action seemed contrary to the principles of the Declaration; but a decree of November 9, 1791, threatened the émigrés who fought against the French Revolution with death. In the debate, Condorcet declared that though every man had the right to change his fatherland, there nevertheless existed moral obligations by which one was bound even to an unjust fatherland.[10] The unwise behavior of many émigrés brought few friends into their camp abroad. The Habsburg Emperor Leopold II, an enlightened and moderate man who ruled from 1790 to 1792, showed little inclination to listen to their demands, but some minor German princes in western Germany, especially the Saxon Prince Clemens Wenzeslaus, Elector and Archbishop of Trier, who resided at Coblenz, supported them in their call for intervention in France to restore the monarchy. On the whole, the émigrés evoked little animosity towards the Revolution; public opinion abroad was more aroused by the excesses of the revolutionaries than by the vituperations of the exiles. When the war they sought actually broke out in 1792, it was the aggressive spirit of the Revolution, not the determination of the monarchs, that brought it about.

The French Revolution, which at first carried a message of universal peace, drove France and Europe into a war more prolonged and more devastating than any since the wars of religion. In this war France, threatened by disintegration as a result of the fall of the uniting symbol of monarchy, found a new authority and a new stability in the nation-state, first in the Republic and then in the plebiscitarian democracy of the Empire. Both received their impulse from the desire for indivisible national unity and for national glory. When the monarchy was abolished by the Convention on September 21, 1792, France was not yet republican. A republic seemed—to judge by both the teachings of Rousseau and the example of the United States—suitable either for a small, peaceful community or a loose federation, and hardly fitted for the rigors of war.[11] The French Revolution, like the monarchy, desired a unitarian strong state. Danton, on September 25, 1792, demanded:

> France must be an indivisible whole: she must have unity of representation. The citizens of Marseilles wish to clasp hands with the citizens of Dunkerque. I therefore ask the death penalty against whomsoever wishes to destroy the unity of France, and I propose that the National Convention decree unity of representation and execution as the foundation of the government to be established. Not without trembling will the Austrians learn of this holy harmony; then, I swear to you, our enemies will perish.

The new Republic was accepted by the French without enthusiasm and without any solemn adherence. It was only among the armies fighting on the northeastern frontiers that the Republic was acclaimed. There the new nationalism received its sanction. When on September 29 Pierre Louis Prieur (1756-1827), the Commissar of the Convention, proclaimed the Republic to the army of the Ardennes, one of the officers, hearing of the end of the monarchy, asked: "For whom shall we fight from now on?" Prieur answered: "You will fight for your homes, for your wives and children, for the nation, for the Republic. If you have neither the wish nor the courage to defend this noble cause, withdraw." The French historian François Aulard (1849-1928) pointed out that French republican nationalism was born in war and remained for a long time in the French mind indissolubly linked with glory and the battlefield. The Republic appeared at the very moment when the defeated enemy was in retreat. For the soldiers, as for the whole of France, she personified victorious patriotism. Not the monarchy but the nation triumphed over the foreigner. Victory on the battlefield converted France from loyal monarchism to republican nationalism.[12]

IX

Missionary Nationalism and the Problem of Liberation

On May 22, 1790, the National Assembly voted enthusiastically that the French nation should renounce the undertaking of any war for the purpose of conquest. This declaration corresponded to the enlightened spirit of the eighteenth century—though not to the practice of its kings —and to the universalism of the Declaration of Rights. At the same time, it corresponded to obvious facts: France seemed dangerously weakened, threatened by a financial and administrative chaos that all the decrees of the Assembly could not halt, and by the disorganization of the army, with increasing disputes between officers and soldiers. But despite her good intentions, an aggressive spirit was not lacking in France. The tenuous character of the borderline between aggression and defense in periods of revolutionary change was overlooked in the enthusiasm of righteousness. The feudal rights of German princes and bishops in Alsace, firmly anchored in international law, guaranteed by the Treaty of Westphalia and by the solemn promises of Louis XIV, were abolished by unilateral French action. On October 31, 1790, Philippe Antoine Merlin de Douai (1764-1838) maintained on behalf of the Committee on Feudal Rights of the Convention that Alsace had become French by the will of the people and that the will of the people took precedence over legal treaty rights. Nevertheless, there is no doubt that the National Assembly was deeply in earnest in renouncing war. Its determination never to use force against the liberty of any people was incorporated in the Constitution.[1]

Respect for the liberty of other peoples similar to that shown in the case of Avignon and the Comtat Venaissin was also shown in the annexation of Savoy and Nice after the outbreak of war in 1792. One of the foreign enthusiasts for the French Revolution, a friend of Thomas

Paine and an honorary citizen of France, the American poet Joel Barlow, was deeply impressed:

> Here we see a sovereign people, uninfluenced by any fears, hopes or connections from abroad, deliberating in the most solemn manner, whether they will extend their territorial boundaries by the admission of seven new provinces, having about four hundred thousand free men who had sent their deputies to solicit a union.

When the French Army of the South entered Savoy on September 19, 1792, the municipality of Chambéry greeted them with the words: "We are a people not conquered, but liberated." The following month, the deputies elected in Savoy constituted themselves the National Assembly of the Allobroges and voted union with France.[3]

This liberalism changed after the first French victories in the field. Liberty was no longer understood to imply respect for the rights and wishes of others when they differed from one's own conceptions; liberty claimed as a right and even as a duty the imposition of its benefits. On November 19, 1792, the Convention declared that "France will extend help and fraternity to all peoples wishing to recover their liberty." This implied possible interference with the affairs and laws of other states. The question arose, What would happen if some people, probably at the instigation of vested interests or enemies of progress, refused to wish to "recover their liberty"? Was France not bound to bring liberty to these peoples even against their wish? From the beginning of the Revolution, strong voices demanded that France free not only herself but mankind.

In the hopeful atmosphere of the constitutional monarchy, this desire was expressed with moderation and peaceful intent. Such was the expectation of Mirabeau on August 25, 1790:

> The influence, sooner or later irresistible, of a strong nation of twenty-four million men, speaking the same language and reverting in their social life to the simple notions of liberty and equality, will find in all the countries of the world missionaries and disciples and will undoubtedly conquer all Europe in the name of truth, moderation, and justice, but not all at one time and not in a single day.[4]

But as the divisions in France grew and the economic situation deteriorated—events which were believed by many to be a result of dark machinations and hidden enemies—the country's passions and fears increased to such a degree that violence directed abroad seemed to offer an outlet for the unrest within.

It was then widely believed that kings and their cabinets desired and plotted war, while free peoples demanded only peace. Was it not necessary, for the peace of France and for the salvation of mankind, to overthrow all monarchies and liberate the peoples everywhere in order to banish the scourge of war? Maximin Isnard (1755-1825) exhorted the Assembly on November 29, 1791:

> Let us proclaim to Europe that if the cabinets engage the kings in a war against the peoples, we shall engage the peoples in a war against the kings.

Isnard expected that in a war between free peoples and despots, those who were misled by the tyrants would fraternize with the free men.

> Les peuples s'embrasseront à la face des tyrans détronés, de la terre consolée et du ciel satisfait. . . . Let us at last tell Europe that ten million Frenchmen, kindled by the fire of liberty, armed with the sword, the pen, with reason and eloquence, could by themselves alone, if they became angered, change the face of the world and make all the tyrants tremble on their thrones of clay.

The agitations of the émigrés naturally angered the French, but the danger they presented was far overestimated. In the Declaration of Pillnitz on August 27, 1791, the Habsburg Emperor Leopold and the King of Prussia lent some verbal support to the demands of the émigrés, but they did so more as a matter of form than from any intent of action. The Emperor was anxious for peace; no foreign power was eager to intervene in France. Britain observed strict neutrality, and Russia's attention was concentrated upon Poland. The French revolutionists ascribed to the kings the same wholehearted purposefulness they themselves possessed. In reality, there was neither unity nor will to action among the monarchs. By their assumption that the dangers were real, the French created the very dangers they feared. Warlike sentiments were expressed by many Frenchmen. On December 16, 1791, Brissot told the Jacobins: "A people who regained liberty after ten centuries of slavery needs war to consolidate liberty." Gouverneur Morris, United States minister in Paris, wrote to George Washington at this time: "It happens, therefore, that the whole nation, though with different views, are desirous of war; for it is proper, in such general statements, to take in the spirit of the country, which has ever been warlike." [5]

There were voices raised against the war fever. Robespierre opposed it because he wished first to fight the domestic enemy and thought war might aggravate the economic crisis. The moderates, the Feuillants, feared that the war turning into an ideological conflict would deal a final blow to the monarchy in France and upset the whole of Europe. [6] But on April 20, 1792, the Assembly by all but seven votes declared war on Emperor Leopold to protect France's independence against "the King's unjust aggression." *L'amour sacré de la patrie* swept France. In Strasbourg the officer Claude Joseph Rouget de Lisle (1760-1836) sang the "Chant de guerre pour l'armée du Rhin," later called the Marseillaise. The war spirit was fanned by foreign enthusiasts such as Anacharsis Cloots. A number of them from Germany had assembled in 1791 in Strasbourg. They were a small but varied group: Catholic priests like the former monk Eulogius Schneider (1756-1794) and Anton Josef Dorsch (1758-1819), who became a professor at the Catholic Academy; Eduard von Clauer, a Prussian nobleman; and Christian Friedrich Cotta (1758-1838), the famous publisher's brother, who, after editing a Stutt-gart monthly called *Teutsche Staatsliteratur,* published after July 1791 the *Strassburger Politisches Journal für Freiheit und Aufklärung.*[7]

These circles conducted a lively propaganda among the Germans across the border. The pamphlet, *Letzter Ruf der freigewordenen Franken an die unterdrückten Deutschen* [Last appeal of the French who have become free to the Germans who are oppressed] in August 1791 combined the benevolence of universal liberation with the fierce nationalism of wars remembered and envisaged. "Feel your slavery, noble Germans," was its message:

> Understand at last that your princes wish to use you as un-fortunate tools for slaughter against us Frenchmen, who offer you friendship. . . . Tear off the fetters of slavery . . . ; we offer you our help, we are ready to fight and die with and for you, we protect your freedom, your property and your home— you are free with us and you are our brothers. But if you wish to remain slaves . . . then you are not worthy of being spared by us, and we shall make you beggars, as our tyrant did a cen-tury ago. We shall not spare your blood and property, we shall win or die for our liberty, for we are French.[8]

The feeling of an international mission and of nationalist pride were mingled inextricably in the initial stages of the war. Anacharsis Cloots himself harped on the theme of French greatness and destiny. To the Jacobins he declared on January 1, 1792, that he demanded war for the very reason that he wished peace: war would establish domestic unity.

> Frenchmen, Jacobins, Feuillants, these terms will fuse har-moniously when it is necessary to defeat the nobles and the princes. . . . Let us cross the Rhine. The fate of the universe depends on the speed and the greatness of our measures.

In the same speech, besides voicing his concern for the universe Cloots promised that as the result of the war France would be established within her natural boundaries on the Rhine and on the peaks of the Alps.

This general ebullience reached a climax with the outbreak of the war for which the French patriots had agitated. They used in their propaganda the specter of an invasion of France by a coalition of all European monarchs and the émigrés. Many Frenchmen saw tyrants everywhere, and liberty only in France. They believed that the monarchs, as clairvoyant about the "inevitable" course of history as themselves, must take all possible measures to prevent their own downfall.[9] The French ambassadors abroad reported correctly that no threat of foreign aggression existed. "Peace is still in our hands, our ambassadors abroad concluded," writes a modern French historian.[10]

> That is the same conclusion at which history, more enlightened than our fathers were, has arrived, on the strength of authentic documents. Believing themselves menaced by the kings of Europe and designing to arouse the people against them, the French out of fear, tradition, and fanatical propaganda wished war and abandoned themselves to the parties which had been preparing it since 1791.

The Prussian offensive began on August 19, 1792. The encounter at Valmy, a village in the Department of the Marne, on September 20, insignificant in itself, marked a turning point. The young untrained French volunteers were believed to have no chance against the well-drilled heirs of the Frederician tradition, but the sansculottes stood firm under a violent cannonade, shouting "Vive la nation!"—the first baptism by fire of the new patriotism. In November the victory at Jemappes in southwestern Belgium opened for the French Army of the North the route to the heart of the Austrian Netherlands. Animated by contradictory principles and sentiments, the French found themselves faced with the dilemma of their practical application in conquered territory.[11] Soon an old-fashioned economic consideration outweighed the new motives and slogans. France was in a dire economic position; she could not meet her domestic needs, let alone the expenses of a foreign war. Under these circumstances—accompanied by high-sounding declarations—the invaded countries were made to pay for the expenses of the war and a heavy burden was put on the very people whose liberation and happiness had been promised as one of the aims of that war. Not only did the invading armies live off the land, but the new territories were included in the French monetary system in the hope of strengthening its crumbling foundations; heavy fines and contributions were imposed upon the wealthier inhabitants of the invaded countries. All this was done officially for the benefit of the liberated peoples.

The cosmopolitan spirit of liberty that the French Revolution of 1789 evoked lingered on in 1793 as a pale ghost to which desultory compliments were paid from time to time. But the liberty of man was no longer the concern of every member of the human fraternity. It was now the mission of the French to establish a new order that might ultimately secure liberty and equality on earth. The road lay through the terrors of war, and the French had to accept the burden—in the interests of mankind, but not without profit and glory for France. "Allons!" Robespierre exhorted the Jacobins on July 29, 1792. "Il faut que le peuple français soutienne le poids du monde. Il faut qu'il soit parmi les peuples ce qu'Hercule fut parmi les héros." Officially the war was not regarded as a war among nations, but as a war of principles. On April 20, 1792, Antoine Merlin de Thionville (1762-1833) explained the intentions of the French as war against kings, peace for nations. "The French nation does not support a war of nation against nation, but defends a free people against the unjust aggression of a king." On November 19, 1792, the Convention ordered the French generals to help and defend those peoples who found themselves persecuted for the cause of liberty.

To give to the national war a greater appeal and to find support for it abroad, it was regarded as an international civil war, as a reenactment of the French Revolution on a broader stage. The enemy was not the alien nation, but its domestic oppressors; but woe to the nation that did not feel itself oppressed. In this spirit Robespierre demanded a brotherhood of nations in his address to the National Convention on April 24, 1793:

> The Committee has completely forgotten to consecrate the duties of fraternity that unite men with all the nations, and their right to mutual assistance. It seems to have ignored the bases of a universal alliance of the peoples against the tyrants. One would think that your declaration has been drawn up for a herd of human beings confined to one corner of the globe, and not for the immense family to which nature has given the earth to live and sojourn there.

To rectify this situation Robespierre proposed four articles that would secure for the French the esteem of all peoples. "It is true that they might have the disadvantage of embroiling you irrevocably with the kings," he said. "I confess that this disadvantage does not frighten me; it will certainly not frighten those who do not wish a reconciliation with them." Then followed his four articles:

> (1) The men of all countries are brothers, and the different peoples must do their utmost to aid each other, like citizens of the same state
> (2) Whoever oppresses a nation thereby declares himself the enemy of all nations.
> (3) Those who fight a people to arrest the progress of liberty and to destroy the rights of man must be persecuted by all

nations, not as ordinary enemies but as rebellious brigands.

(4) The kings, the aristocrats, the tyrants, whoever they may be, are slaves in revolt against the sovereign of the earth, the human race, and against the liberator of the universe, nature.

Though no vote was taken on this proposal, it reflected the spirit, doubly terrifying in its confused sincerity, which underlay much of the aggressiveness of the armies of the National Convention.[12]

Under the impact of these ideas, the French revolutionary war degenerated into a war of conquest. The very day that the Legislative Assembly declared war, Condorcet insisted that "each nation alone has the right to make its own laws, the inalienable right to change them; to wish to deprive a foreign people of it by force is to betray one's own fatherland, to become the enemy of the human race." On October 24, 1792, the diplomatic committee of the Convention ordered the French generals in enemy territory never to disown the eternal sacred principles of the sovereignty of the peoples, and never to invite them to adopt French laws nor propose to them any form of government.

> On entering enemy territory, the general shall proclaim in the name of the French nation that the country is liberated from the dominion of its former sovereign, and free to give itself, under the protection of the armies of the Republic, such form of government as it shall be pleased to adopt.

And even on February 13, 1793, Carnot emphasized the principle that each people, however small a territory it inhabits, is an absolute master within it and equal in right to the greatest. No people may subject another to common laws without the latter's free consent.

> Nous Français ne connaissons de souverains que les peuples humains; notre système n'est point la domination, c'est la fraternité.[13]

At the beginning the application of these principles did not create great difficulties. The Belgians at first welcomed the French. They wished to become independent of the Austrians, but they certainly did not wish to exchange dependence upon the Austrian "tyrant" for a dependence upon French "liberty." They were deeply attached to their own traditional institutions and most reluctant to accept the more "progressive" French order. They resented French armies living off the land. They began to suspect that they were exchanging a distant and rather mild "oppressor" for one much nearer home and more impetuous. Under these circumstances, Cambon reinterpreted the practical application of the principles so recently proclaimed. It was discovered that the war was directed not only against the kings but also against all those who supported the king or the traditional institutions of their country, and that meant all those who did not enthusiastically adopt French institutions. Clearly, they were enemies of the liberty of their own people and even of the human race.

For all its "pure and honest intentions," the French Republic insisted that the enemies of liberty had to be punished and the people had to be taught how to be free. Property belonging to the "accomplices of tyranny" was confiscated and used to defray the cost of the war for liberty. All local taxes were abolished as obsolete survivals of tyranny. As a result, local administrations lost their revenues and became entirely dependent upon France. Under these conditions it was clearly France's "duty" to offer her resources to the freed peoples. Unfortunately, these resources were the assignats, paper money of fast-dwindling value, that was now imposed on the reluctant beneficiaries:

> In entering into a contract with a people who wish to be free, in suppressing its taxes and offering to it a part of our resources to aid it in reconquering its liberty, we are offering it our revolutionary money [Cambon declared]. Then we shall not need to buy at great expense of cash, clothing and food in the country itself; common interest will unite the two peoples to fight tyranny.

No attempt was made to deny the right of self-determination, but "true" friends of liberty knew that the vote could only be given to men who "really" wished to be free and adhered to the French principles. Logically, only such persons could hold public office.

Decrees of the Convention in December 1792 put these proposals into effect. The French generals, upon entering enemy territory, were immediately to suppress all established authority, abolish all taxes, and proclaim the sovereignty of the people. New governments were to be chosen in elections in which only those could vote or be nominated who had taken the oath of liberty and equality. Thus the freed peoples became "conquered for liberty." A small minority in Belgium welcomed this change, especially among the revolutionary clubs in large cities, clubs which were partly composed of Frenchmen. Most Belgians, however, wished to maintain liberty and equality according to *their* laws and traditional concepts, and to preserve the Catholic religion. They desired an independent and sovereign Brabant in accordance with the Constitution of January 1790. In their meeting of December 24, 1792, the representatives of Brussels informed the National Convention:

> The Belgians are not ungrateful, but they are jealous of the right of sovereignty, the exercise of which the French Republic has restored to them, and they will never be so despicable as to accept a master voluntarily.

"Our customs," the representatives of Louvain wrote at the beginning of 1793,

> Our customs, our habits, our usages, our inclinations, our national character and even our soil—in a word, everything— present differences between these provinces and the various departments of France too marked for any single, identical legislation to be able to lead us to happiness through absorption into the immense French Republic.

Only Liége, with its distinct history, inclined towards union with France.[14]

In a proclamation to the Belgians in February 1793, the commissioners of the National Convention defended France against the accusation of atheism. On the contrary, they declared, true Christianity was being realized in France, where "all things recall the first centuries of Catholicism." Citizens were beginning to enjoy the virtuous pleasure of fraternity. The poor, those cherished children of the hero of the Gospels, were no longer objects of disdain. "The hero of the Gospels" may have sounded like a strange description of the Son of God in the ears of Belgian Catholics; they may have been similarly bewildered when they heard:

> France wants you all to be free, all equal in rights; all its decrees that are so boldly calumniated by those perverse men who seek to usurp your sovereignty, while failing to defend it, lead to this great end.

Some of the commissioners expressed themselves, however, with greater frankness. If the Belgians adhered obstinately to their clericalism and their *constitution nationicide,* their opinions could not be taken into account. "The wish of an infantile or imbecile people would count as nothing, because it militated against itself." And even more drastically another commissioner affirmed that "the right of conquest, which for the first time has become useful to the world and just, must form the political education of the Belgian people."

Under pressure from the French army and the revolutionary clubs, the Belgians voted for union with France, and the National Convention, having abandoned the principles guiding its predecessor in the case of Avignon, declared itself satisfied that it had received an expression of the free will of the Belgian people. But the true picture was presented in a report on March 12, 1793, by Charles François Dumouriez (1739-1823), the commanding general of the Army of the North, in which he warned the National Convention that it had been deceived, that the Belgians felt despoiled of their wealth and intimidated in the expression of their will, and finally, that the uprisings against the French were not engineered by the aristocrats, but were a spontaneous reaction of the peasants, for whom resistance became a holy war.

The spring of 1793 also saw the union of parts of the Rhineland with the French Republic. There, too, especially in Mainz, where revolutionary sentiment was strong among the educated middle class, the French had originally been welcomed. But the enforced circulation of the *assignats* and requisitions without payment created deep resentment. On March 19 a "National convention of Free Germans," elected by the "right" kind of people, met and on March 20 its representatives presented the demand for union with France to the National Convention in Paris:

> It is little to have caused the edifice of the former tyranny to crumble; it was necessary in order to rebuild that of public happiness. The representatives of the people know the unanimous wish of their constituents; in asking the union of their country with the French Republic they voice only the sentiment that is in all hearts.

This wish of the "Rheno-Germanic peoples" coincided with the laws of nature, and even with strategic geography. "Nature herself has desired that the Rhine should be the frontier of France," the representatives went on; and they did not hesitate to invoke ancient times. "It was so in the first centuries of the French empire." What the great expansionist kings of France had striven for without success, the national effort of a free people had achieved in a short time. "This union, so much desired, which the intrigues of kings have never been able to effect, has cost but a slight effort on the part of the victorious armies of liberty." [15]

In spite of the preservation of appearances, the National Convention realized that the peoples would not rise spontaneously against the "common enemy," the monarchs, and thus make the Republic safe against monarchist plots. In a letter to Joseph Servan (1757-1807) on November 26, 1792, Brissot insisted that French liberty would never be safe as long as a Bourbon sat on a throne; therefore he proposed an expedition against Spain. Only when the French frontiers were on the Rhine and the Pyrenees divided free peoples could France feel secure, in a continent formed of republics living according to Jacobin ideas. This new tendency towards aggrandizement aroused England as Burke's philippics had not done. The impression grew that the National Convention was following in the footsteps of Louis XIV, merely replacing his universal monarchy with a universal republic, more dangerous because it evoked a stronger response abroad and a more active enthusiasm at home.

On February 1, 1793, the National Convention declared war on Britain and ordered the occupation of the Netherlands. But military reversals were close at hand. Austro-Prussian victories, internal insurrections, and quarreling factions created by April 1793 a situation in which the French Republic felt threatened with extinction. A resurgent army determined to fight out the war, and a merciless liquidation of domestic opposition saved the Republic. But this dictatorship did not strengthen the respect for individual liberty or the spirit of tolerance and settlement by agreement in the nascent French nationalism.

X

Revolutionary Terror and National Virtue

THE war tempted the French to abandon liberty as conceived in 1789 in their relations with other peoples; it now offered an opportunity to the extremists at home to reinterpret liberty for the French themselves. Domestic and foreign policy are generally carried on in the same spirit: ruthlessness at home does not permit a liberal policy towards external enemies. Through an exalted sense of mission, France was led to disregard the traditional laws of nations. Were they not embalmed in treaties, old parchments gathering dust, which the new life-force of dynamic revolution could and must tear up? Nor was the constitutional order at home secure. After the manifesto of the Duke of Brunswick on July 25, 1792, all officials and local and provincial bodies were asked to be permanently at their posts. All citizens able to bear arms were ordered to place themselves in a state of permanent mobilization; everyone had to wear the *tricolore cocarde;* it was strictly forbidden, under heavy penalty, to wear any other insignia.[1] On August 10 the revolutionary masses of Paris overthrew the Constitution and the monarchy. The Declaration of Rights was no longer respected. Opposition papers were suppressed and suspected persons arrested. "Lorsque le peuple se met en insurrection, il retire tous les pouvoirs pour les reprendre." [When the people rise up, they destroy all existing authority in order to regain it themselves.] But who was the people? It was a minority of the French nation, a part of the population of Paris.[2] This minority, Maximilien Robespierre (1758-1794) and Antoine Saint-Just (1767-1794) believed, was the true French people, the sincere patriots, while the others, the majority, had not yet freed themselves from the mold of the past and were spiritually still slaves.[3] For the sake of France and the Revolution, they had to be forced into freedom and patriotic virtue.

Liberty was no longer the right of the individual, nor that of the Frenchman; it was reserved for the virtuous patriot, for the soldiers of liberty who formed a tribunal of public conscience and devoted themselves unreservedly to fighting tyrants and conspirators in France and abroad. Only on virtue could a true republic be founded. Yet how rare was this virtue! "Virtue!" Robespierre exclaimed on July 26, 1794,

> Virtue! It is a natural passion without doubt, but how could these venal souls, who were accessible only to dastardly and savage passions, know it? But it exists, I swear it, O sensitive and pure souls, it exists, this tender, imperious, irresistible passion, torment and delight of magnanimous hearts, this profound horror of tyranny, this compassionate zeal for the oppressed, this sacred love of mankind, without which a great revolution is but a startling crime, destroying an earlier crime. It exists, that generous ambition to found on earth the first republic of the world.[4]

Revolutionary patriotism became in 1793 a religion that had little in common with the spirit of 1789.[5] Its zealous missionaries wished to impose it, even if that meant disregarding for the moment—and it might be a very long moment—the rights of the individual and the majesty of the law. The abolished constitutional monarchy was not followed by a constitutional republic accepting the fundamental principles of 1789; in its own eyes, the Revolution inaugurated an entirely new era in the history of mankind. History seemed divided into three ages. The first started with the Creation and terminated with the birth of Christ; the second began with His coming and with the Gospels, and found its consummation in the French Revolution; the third era dawned in 1792. To order man's life, a new calendar was needed to mark the character of the new era, its conformity to the eternal laws of reason and nature, and thereby its permanence and finality.[6] A new religion was required to replace Christianity, which was the heritage of a past era and no longer befitted the new man. The new age was not atheistic; it was far removed from the skepticism and agnosticism of the eighteenth century; it believed fervently in the new gospel of man and reason, which had become flesh in the French nation and in the revolutionary masses of Paris, imbued with the fullness of faith.[7]

The new gospel easily incited the masses to warlike actions. Among the men of 1789 Mirabeau alone foresaw the dangers arising from the fact that the people were sometimes more susceptible to passionate militancy than were cabinets or diplomats. In a speech of May 20, 1790, he warned against the fanaticism born of utopian hopes and against noble self-delusions. At a time when few French patriots thought a popular regime could lead to interminable wars of conquest, Mirabeau pointed out that throughout history the democratic peoples, the representative assemblies of free nations, were easily induced to desire war in order, as they believed, to undo "injustices" and to right all wrongs. "You will not be deceived by cabinet ministers; but will you never be deceived by yourselves?" he asked. Would public opinion, which exercised so much pressure on free governments, be able to restrain itself? "Look at the free peoples: they have always distinguished themselves by more ambitious and more barbarous wars." Liberty demands the restraint of reason and the respect of law. In times of overpowering passions, liberty can easily become the first victim.

But at the moment when France and the Revolution seemed lost, passion appeared more essential than liberty. The invading armies appeared bent upon defeating France and depriving her of that position of leadership in Europe which the reforms of 1789 had sought to restore. There was widespread apprehension that the émigrés, arriving in the wake of the enemy, would abolish the gains of the Revolution and revive the *ancien régime* with its privileges and abuses. National survival, national unity, and the social advances of the Revolution faced one and the same danger. National interest had to merge with revolutionary enthusiasm around a new symbol that would replace the monarchy. The time was extremely short in which a united nation could be forged. Threatened by the despotism of the kings, Marat declared, France had to organize the despotism of liberty.[8] Parliamentary democracy reflected the spirit of diversity, the meeting ground of opposed and conflicting interests and their harmonization by slow debate. It allowed pressure groups and egoistic motives to influence the formation of the general will and to corrupt it. Only a dictatorship of virtuous men, devoted exclusively to the interests of the whole nation and reflecting the true general will, could meet the crisis. Any opposition to their leadership would be treason to the nation. The severity of the laws of the Terror was accentuated by the wide and vague interpretation given to words like "treason." Robespierre justified their harshness by explaining that these laws would be applied only to enemies of the people.

The oppressive nature of the Terror was felt less in actual executions than in the general fear and insecurity which it created. It was assumed that private acts or thoughts were closely watched. Spying and denunciation were officially encouraged. Devoted citizens formed committees of surveillance. Every citizen had to carry his *certificat de civisme*, which he received only after examination of his beliefs and character. No one was supposed to relax or to lead a private life. Everyone had to be an enthusiastic citizen at all times. The revolutionary leaders were convinced that a government that represented the revolutionary will of the people and was free from the dividing pressures and passions of special interests would not be "the iron hand of despotism, but the reign of justice and reason." In a free nation morality would rule instead of egotism, principle instead of habit, and the love of glory would furnish a better incentive than love of money. The revolutionary leaders spoke and acted as though this perfect people and this perfect French nation, the consummation of the rational development of mankind, actually existed. All those who did not live up to this expectation or did not conform were outside the people, the true people.

"The people is sublime," Robespierre said on June 14, 1793, "but individuals are weak." And Saint-Just made his meaning clear when he declared on October 10:

> You have to punish not only the traitors, but even those who are indifferent; you have to punish whoever is passive in the Republic and does nothing for her. For, since the French people has manifested its will, everything opposed to it is outside the sovereign; whatever is outside the sovereign is an enemy.[9]

In this struggle all other considerations gave way to the cause. The Jacobins, as Louis Maribon-Montaut (1754-1842) said, "sacrificed everything to their fatherland. Quand il s'agit de la patrie, il n'est ni frères, ni soeurs, ni père, ni mère." [10] The nation-state took control of the people's soul.[11]

Of all the revolutionary leaders, none represented the spirit of fervent patriotism, of virtuous exaltation, and of inflexible will better than Saint-Just. He was the embodiment of the new dynamic voluntarism. No obstacle was allowed to deflect him or to cause him to hesitate. As a very young man, on May 15, 1790, when some counterrevolutionary pamphlets were burned, he put his hand into the flames, following the Roman example, and swore to die for the fatherland. As Barère wrote in his memoirs, Saint-Just was the first to say that the secret of the Revolution lay in the word "dare"; and he dared. A worthy disciple of Sparta, he despised the bourgeois desire for a comfortable and secure life in the shadow of peace, and even more the drive for profit and wealth:

> The pure love of the fatherland is the only foundation of liberty. There cannot be any liberty in a nation where consideration for the glamour of wealth plays any part in the service of the state. . . . One builds a republic only by frugality and virtue. What can glory and wealth have in common? [12]

Saint-Just's extreme youth did not permit him to be elected to the first two assemblies. Only in September 1792, at the age of twenty-five, did he take his place in the National Convention, where his maiden speech on November 13 was a passionate plea for the death penalty for Louis

XVI. "One cannot be king innocently. This man must either be king or perish." Sharing only two years later the fate of so many revolutionaries on the guillotine, Saint-Just left to posterity no theoretical work, only speeches and letters and a number of fragments in which during hectic and feverish months he sketched his ideal republic:

> A republican government has virtue for its guiding principle; without it, terror. What do they wish who wish neither virtue nor terror? . . . A vigorous government is said to be oppressive. That is an error. The question is wrongly stated. What is needed in government is justice. A government which exercises justice is for that very reason neither vigorous nor oppressive, because it oppresses only that which is evil.

A revolution, he felt, could only be rescued from its enemies by dictators or by censors, the former saving it by force, the latter by virtue.[13]

Saint-Just proposed a strictly patriotic and military education as the foundation of his republic:

> The fatherland is by no means the soil; it is the community of affections, so that, each one fighting for the safety or the liberty of what is dear to him, the fatherland finds itself defended. If every man comes out of his door with a gun in his hand, the fatherland is quickly saved. Each one fights for what he loves; . . . the result is that each fights for all.

To achieve this, children should be brought up in common by the state, the boys to be trained as future soldiers and subjected to rigid discipline and Spartan austerity, while the girls were to be left to learn the virtues of domesticity.[14] Such a nation in arms must develop its own technique of warfare. It would fight with an energy and combative spirit hitherto unknown. As representative of the Committee of Safety along with Le Bas, Saint-Just was sent to the eastern front, where he proclaimed that the French would march from all sides like thunderbolts, without stopping, without allowing the enemy time to breathe.[15] He demanded of the people's representatives delegated to the armies that they be the fathers and friends of the soldiers, sleeping in their tents, taking part in their military exercises, ready day and night to listen to them, having as little as possible to do with the generals so that the ordinary soldiers would have confidence in their justice and impartiality; in short, they must set an example of unflagging energy and of permanent vigilance. "Ceux qui font des révolutions dans le monde, ceux qui veulent faire le bien, ne doivent dormir que dans le tombeau"[16] [Those who start revolutions in this world, those who wish to do good, must not sleep except in the grave].

In his demand for a new art of warfare, Saint-Just spoke both as a proud patriot and a fervent revolutionary:

> We have lacked until today institutions and military laws conforming to the republican system which is in the process of being founded. In a time of innovation, all that is not new is pernicious. The military art of the monarchy suits us no longer; those were other men and other enemies. . . . Our nation has already a character of its own; its military system must differ from that of its enemies. Since the French nation is driven in this war by all the strong and generous passions, love of liberty, hatred of tyrants and of oppression, and since, on the contrary, her enemies are mercenary slaves, automatons without passions, the system of war of the French army must have the spirit of shock troops.[17]

Frenchmen were no longer fighting as subjects of a king, but as a nation. Their war had to be nationalized in all its aspects. Formerly armies fought, but individual civilians, commercial exchange and intellectual intercourse remained unaffected. Now the National Convention proposed measures against the liberty of individual Englishmen sojourning on the soil of France and against British commerce. In their justification Saint-Just declared the war to be a national war only on the part of the French; on England's side supposedly the court and the ruling classes were waging the war, not the people. Therefore a measure taken against English commerce was not directed against the English people, but only against their rulers. Weakening the rulers would enable the English people, if they were worthy of liberty, to break their chains. "The court of London is our Carthage, not England." The English merchant class, Saint-Just maintained, did not constitute the English nation, and all laws against English commerce should be gratefully received by the English people, oppressed by that very merchant class. On the other hand, he justified the detention of English subjects in France by declaring that patriotism was engraved in every heart. "Whatever reason has banished a man from the earth on which he was born, his heart clings to it as a tree clings to the soil, else he is depraved. The love of his cradle is the last virtue to depart from the heart of even an ungrateful man." [18]

The nationalization of the war changed the character of French nationalism. The missionary zeal of the Revolution and its own fears and insecurities had ultimately roused hesitant Europe into action; the danger of an invasion of France in its turn determined the French to resist with all their strength a return of the *ancien régime*.[19] The safety of the new nation-state, which had not yet had time to take firm root, overshadowed all other considerations. "When the fatherland is in danger," Danton proclaimed on September 2, 1792, "no one can refuse his service without being declared infamous and a traitor to the fatherland. Pronounce the death penalty for every citizen who refuses to march . . . or who directly or indirectly opposes the measures taken in the interest of public safety." [20] As the war became more pronouncedly nationalist, the former emphasis on international peace and on universal philanthropy waned rapidly, as did the concern for individual liberty. To the passion for national strength and unity, the interests of humanity and of individuals alike were sacrificed.

On August 14, 1793, the National Convention announced the *levée en masse:* "The French people proclaims through its representatives that it rises en masse for the defense of its independence, of its liberty, of its constitution, and in order to deliver its territory from the presence of despots and their satellites." In the eighteenth century, wars had been fought with limited contingents and limited efforts. This time every inhabitant of France was drawn into the war, and felt it to be his cause—at least, according to the theory which governed the war effort. For the first time the government requisitioned everybody and everything—again, at least in theory. The distinction between civilian and soldier disappeared. "Tous les Français sont en réquisition permanente pour le service des armées." This is the central sentence of the famous decree of the Convention of August 23, 1793, which inaugurated a new epoch in warfare:

> All citizens must discharge their debt to liberty. Some will give their labor, others their wealth, some their counsel, others their strength; all will give the blood that flows in their veins. Thus all Frenchmen, all sexes, all ages are called . . . to defend liberty. From this moment until . . . the enemy is driven from the territory of the Republic, all citizens of France are in permanent requisition for the service of the armies. The young men will go forth to battle; the married men will make arms and transport food; the women will make tents, uniforms, and will serve in the hospitals; the children will prepare lint from old linen; the old men will gather in the public places to rouse the courage of the warriors, to excite hatred of kings and to preach the unity of the Republic. National buildings will be converted into barracks, public squares into factories of arms, and the earth of cellars will be examined to extract the saltpeter from it. Saddle horses will be requisitioned to complete the corps of cavalry; draught horses, other than those employed in agriculture, will be used for artillery and transport. The Committee of Public Safety is . . . authorized to set up all the buildings, factories, and workshops which shall be considered necessary for the execution of this work and to requisition for that object, in the whole extent of the Republic, the craftsmen and workers who can contribute to success.[21]

A few days later, on September 5, Danton urged the transformation of the nation into an armed camp:

> I demand that you vote at least one hundred millions to make weapons of all sorts, so that their manufacture does not stop for one minute, so that the forges thunder day and night, for if we had had enough weapons, we should all have marched. Que la France toute entière soit un immense camp, hérissé de fer, couvert de bouches en feu. Never will the fatherland in danger lack citizens.

The national response did not come up to expectations. Where the appeal to virtue failed, law had to enforce it. But even here the French revolutionary government never went to the lengths of twentieth-century governments or of total war. For the intellectual climate at the beginning of the "bourgeois" century such a complete militarization of life would have been unbearable. The laws introducing general military service were extremely mild. All citizens between eighteen and forty, unmarried or widowers without children, were declared available for military service on February 24, 1793, but they were only to be drafted when not enough volunteers came forward. This system of conscription was made permanent on September 5, 1798, and all young men from twenty-one to twenty-five had to serve. The decision was by no means popular. There were many cases of evasion and desertion.

Clearly, it was not enough to mobilize men and industry. Scholars and artists, writers and orators were put to the service of the nation to kindle the people's enthusiasm. Attempts were made to form new revolutionary elites. In Brittany Pierre-Louis Prieur of the Marne organized a republican youth movement. The boys were drilled in the use of arms by citizen-soldiers, given a flag inscribed "Hope of the Fatherland" and swore to emulate their fathers in its service.[22] In the spring of 1794, four thousand young men between the ages of sixteen and eighteen, sons of trusted Jacobins, were brought together in a military camp where they were reared in a Spartan spirit to form the cadre of the republican armies.

All these efforts bore fruit. On June 26, 1794, the victory of Fleurus in southwestern Belgium turned the tide. The invading armies were repelled. France was saved. But it had been saved by the army, and even after the hour of danger had passed, the army remained preeminent in national life. The occupation of foreign countries brought much needed economic support to the hard-pressed government. The veterans who as a result of domestic conditions could not be absorbed into economic life at home were accustomed to the different standards and conditions of the army and intoxicated with glory. The armies came to be identified with the Republic; they were its creation, the living symbol of republican nationalism; their first victories were its first triumphant manifestation. Their success provided a justification for the new government and proved that it could represent France at least as gloriously as the great monarchs had done. Thus with the national emergency past, when the French put an end to the Terror, the deaths of Robespierre and Saint-Just did not mean a return to the monarchy, but the consolidation of the Revolution. The leaders who put an end to the Terror did not press for peace. Though the people, after the rigors of the Terror, longed for a new ease of life, they could be swayed without difficulty to pursue the road to glory. Robespierre prepared the way for Napoleon, the ideologue for the soldier, the virtue of the revolutionary zealot for the cold Machiavellianism of power.[23]

XI

War and the Spirit of Nationalism

LOYALTY to the nation-state had stood a severe test. Popular songs and public festivals celebrated the new religion of the fatherland, of liberty and of national glory:

> Le vieillard veut marcher, le jeune homme s'élance,
> Et l'étendard sacré, si cher aux nations,
> Aux peuples asservis signal de délivrance,
> Brille devant nos légions . . .[1]

Frenchmen had shown themselves worthy of entering, and dominating, the new age. As Marie-Joseph Chénier (1764-1811) told the Convention on November 5, 1793:

> Free of prejudices and worthy of representing the French nation, you will found on the ruins of dethroned superstitions, the only universal religion which brings peace and not the sword, which makes citizens, not kings or subjects, brothers and not enemies, which has neither sects nor mysteries, which has equality as its only dogma, laws as oracles, magistrates as priests, who burn the incense of the great family only before the altar of the fatherland, the common mother and divinity.

In innumerable odes and prayers the new god of the fatherland was invoked.

> Ce Dieu n'est point le Dieu des prêtres,
> Injuste, cruel, orgueilleux;
> Le créateur de tous les êtres
> Nous fit naître pour être heureux.
> Qu'en nos mains l'encensoir se brise:
> Rejetons un culte imposteur;
> Abjurons l'esprit de l'église,
> Mais respectons le Créateur.
>
> Vérité, raison et lumière,

Tels sont ses dignes attributs;
Son temple est la nature entière,
Et son encens sont nos vertus.
Entendons sa voix qui nous crie:
On doit chérir l'humanité;
Ne vivre que pour la patrie,
Et mourir pour la liberté.[2]

Though the number of those who wished to live for the fatherland and were ready to die for liberty was great, many continued hostile or lukewarm. Though the days of the calendar, cities and streets, and new-born children received names not of Christian derivation, but expressing the virtues of the new civic religion or the kindness of Mother Nature, the old faith lived on.[3] The Terror, which wished to impose salvation by force, did not achieve its ends. Its leaders attributed the resistance of the people not to human nature but to counterrevolutionary monsters, against whom extreme measures were necessary. When Lyons surrendered after a two months' siege in October 1793, it was threatened with total destruction:

> All that was inhabited by the rich will be demolished; nothing will remain but the houses of the poor, the homes of patriots who were massacred or proscribed, the buildings especially employed for industry, and the monuments dedicated to humanity and public education. The name of Lyons will be effaced from the list of cities of the Republic; the group of remaining houses will henceforth carry the name "Liberated City."

A similar vengeance was to be wreaked on Toulon, when the city was captured on December 19, 1793. Those who had fought the Convention were condemned by a tribunal composed of followers of the Convention who had been imprisoned, but not executed, during the siege. The Convention ordered the demolition of the city, which was to lose its name and to be called "Port la Montagne." The words that Mme Roland is said to have uttered on the scaffold: "O Liberté! Que des crimes on commet en ton nom!" were not without justification.[4]

The Jacobin Terror of 1793-1794 was the prelude to the totalitarian revolutions of the twentieth century, but it was only a pale and short prelude. Robespierre and his friends were imbued with, and restrained by, eighteenth-century humanitarianism. There was no monolithic party dominating the country and the parliamentary assembly. The Committee of Public Safety never dominated the whole of France or even the Convention. There was no infallible leader of undisputed authority. Even Robespierre did not control the party or the Committee. The revolutionaries were not a close-knit disciplined group; discussion remained possible and factionalism could not be suppressed. The Convention and the French people soon grew tired of exaltation and disgusted with bloodshed and exceptional laws. The Revolution of 1789 wished to bring France liberty under law; a prolonged state of terror was compatible with neither liberty nor law. Even Robespierre turned against the *enragés,* the maximalists, who wished to perpetuate the Revolution. When Robespierre was overthrown, French patriotism lost its religious, mystic fervor. After Thermidor, the National Convention used moderation following its triumph over royalist reaction and extremist insurrection and worked towards the secure establishment of the revolutionary gains and a general reconciliation. The Place de la Révolution where the guillotine had functioned was renamed Place de la Concorde. It is significant that no statue has been erected in France to Robespierre, no street or square has been named in his honor.

Yet the Terror left its evil heritage in the history of French nationalism, and of continental nationalism in general. In England the Glorious Revolution put an end to reaction and also to exaltation and civil war. It secured the gains of the Puritan Revolution in an evolutionary spirit of agreement and compromise. The French Revolution followed a different course: it began with a "glorious revolution" in 1789, but it was quickly followed by civil war, by the proclamation of a struggle *jusqu'au bout*— to the bitter end—against domestic opposition and of war *jusqu'au bout* against external enemies. No true conciliation settled the issues. The spirit of *jusqu'au-boutisme* has reappeared in France again and again. The use of bitter and excessive language to describe the activities and motives of adversaries became frequent. Politeness and chivalry, regard for form and respect for the fellowman in one's opponent gave way to heated overstatements. Carnot objected to the terms of the surrender of Ypres because they showed "a certain esteem and condescension for enemies toward whom we must proclaim hatred and contempt, unless we wish the French soldier to turn soft and to take pity on the fate of hypocritical and bloodthirsty enemies of our liberty." A theoretical love of peace was always proclaimed, but it was to be a peace that put an end to tyranny and injustice—these terms covering everything which appeared contrary to the alleged national interests of the moment.

The new attitude showed itself in the treatment meted out to countries which the French armies invaded after 1793. The victory of Fleurus at the end of June 1794 delivered Belgium once more into French hands. In the following months Germany west of the Rhine and the Low Countries fell under French control. There was no longer any question of plebiscites nor of the liberation of peoples. The humanitarianism of 1789 was gone. The invaded lands were to pay for the costs of victory; most of them were to be annexed to France, and their institutions accommodated to the higher and more progressive principles of the victor nation, until the conquered subjects were finally ready to be received as French citizens. The pleas of Belgian patriots for respect of their autonomy and tradition were rejected. It seemed superfluous to consult the Belgian people. "The people always will the good, but they don't always see it clearly." The National Convention had no doubt that for the Belgians the true good was best served by their inclusion in France. Accordingly, it was so decreed on October 1, 1795.

The Belgians felt this as an imposition of foreign domination. Before then, they had lived under a Habsburg prince whom they had shared first with the Spaniards and later with the Austrians. That did not mean their subjection to Spain or to Austria.

> The ancient provincial constitution had remained in force, administration was carried on in the national languages [French and Flemish], the Estates had maintained their right to vote taxes. The Spanish kings or the German emperors had never regarded the country as an integral part of Spain or Austria.

They preserved Belgium's national individuality and the Belgian people regarded them as "their" princes, the heirs of the Dukes of Burgundy. Neither the Spaniards nor the Austrians infringed on the national civilization; there was no attempt at Hispanization or Germanization. Belgium had not been ruled by indigenous sovereigns since Charles V, yet it had never had to submit to foreign domination. This autonomy was now abolished at one stroke; even the old names disappeared. The Austrian Low Countries and the Bishopric of Liége became nine French departments "newly reunited." One still spoke of Belgium as one spoke of Champagne or Burgundy; but "the name lost its national significance and became no more than a geographical expression." [5]

The period of the Convention and of the Directory laid the foundation for the expansionist policies of the Napoleonic empire. The same period established the image of Britain as the archenemy of the Revolution. When the victories of the revolutionary armies revealed the weakness of the continental enemy their hatred was directed against the mighty island power apparently so secure in her traditions of liberty. The French Republic carried on the struggle of the French monarchy against the "hereditary" enemy. The liberal France of the eighteenth century had looked up to England as an example. Now Britain became in French eyes the leader of world reaction. The virtues and heroism of the new France were pitted against British plutocracy and Albion's perfidy. To Robespierre, Pitt became "an agent of a past century," attempting to turn the wheel of history back to the age of barbarism and despotism. His agents and spies were suspected of fomenting trouble everywhere, of supporting all the factions with which Robespierre had to struggle, and of corrupting the civic spirit of France.[6] In this struggle, which continued that of Louis XIV and anticipated Napoleon's, the Committee of Public Safety anticipated the Emperor's later economic measures against Britain. Rejecting the economic theories of the physiocrats and of Adam Smith, it revived mercantilism under the more modern form of economic nationalism. Like the older mercantilism, this new economic policy did not result from the pressure of business interests, but from considerations of warfare and national power.

But the old conflict received a new justification. It was no longer a contest of power between royal houses and cabinets. The Revolution resumed the struggle of the monarchy against Britain in a moralistic and nationalist spirit. It wished to break the maritime and commercial ascendancy "usurped by England" in the interests of freedom of the seas and the liberty of all peoples. In proposing a French Navigation Act, Bertrand Barère stressed the fact that it was fundamentally different from the English one. The latter was the work of tyrants; the former, "decreed in the midst of a democratic revolution," was a step towards liberty, towards achieving equality for all nations who were weary of being tributaries to foreign industry.[7] The Directory tried not only to exclude British imports but to establish a continental monopoly for French industry. In the exaltation of victory which the French poets celebrated in 1794, their wrath and their scorn were directed above all against England. The "Hymne à la victoire" which Charles François Lebrun (1739-1824) wrote after the battle of Fleurus thanked God "who fought on our behalf" for "this vast coffin of Fleurus,"

> Où des rois expire l'orgueil,
> Où périt l'insulaire avare;
> C'est là qu'au fer de nos soldats,
> L'Anglais fourbe, lâche et barbare
> A payé ses assassinats.

And Chénier, glorifying the recapture of Toulon, had no doubt that "the insolent rival of a magnanimous people will everywhere be beaten down," for

> Le Français au combat marche avec la vertu,
> Et l'Anglais marche avec le crime.

The French were going to save mankind from English brigandage:

> L'Univers se soulève; il remet en nos mains
> Le soin de récouvrer le public héritage,
> Et les bras des nouveaux Romains
> Renverseront l'autre Carthage.

In 1797 Rouget de Lisle sang a "Chant des vengeances," a *Hassgesang* against the England which had the audacity not to succumb to France:

> L'affreux brigand de la Tamise
> N'a point succombé sous nos coups! . . .
> Vengeance! Nous ferons justice
> A Londres, à nous, à l'univers.
> Artisan des malheurs du monde,
> Trop fier dominateur de l'onde,
> En vain crois-tu nous échapper:
> Sur tes rochers inaccessibles,
> Le géant, de ses bras terribles,
> Va te saisir et te frapper.[8]

In less than a decade the French Revolution had traveled the long road from universal philanthropy to military glory. "O terre des guerriers: o France! o ma patrie!" a poet addressed the fatherland in 1797; even the desire for peace was expressed with a bellicose flourish:

> Tu fus long-tems l'effroi, sois l'amour de la terre,
> O république des Français.
> Que le chant des plaisirs succède aux cris de guerre:
> La Victoire a conquis la Paix.[9]

The French nation was turning away from mankind to concentrate on itself. "Let us leave to the philosophers," François Robert (1763-1826) told the National Convention on April 26, 1793,

> Let us leave to them the problem of examining humanity in all its relationships: we are not the representatives of the human race. I wish therefore that the legislator of France would forget the universe for a moment to concern himself with his country alone. I desire that kind of national egoism without which we shall be false to our duties, without which we shall legislate here for those who have not mandated us, and not in favor of those for whose profit we can legislate all matters. I love all men; I particularly love all free men; but I love the free men of France better than all other men in the universe. I will not seek, therefore, to know what is the nature of man in general, but what is the character of the French people.[10]

During a discussion in the Conseil des Anciens about the right of the Republic to confiscate the property of the émigrés, François Martin Poultier (1753-1826) argued that the needs of the nation take precedence over the rights of an individual:

> If the nation suffers, the danger becomes general; the privations of an individual only bring private inconveniences. We cannot, therefore, compare a nation and a few individuals.

The nation can exercise its right in a different way, and the general interest can authorize it to take extraordinary measures that the law cannot allow an individual. The rights of the citizen, passing into the hands of the people, take on an entirely different importance, and they can be regulated differently, as the common good requires.[11]

But even in October 1794 Jean Baptiste Clauzel objected in the National Convention to a proposed resolution which, invoking the authority of Rousseau, declared that at this moment humanity was incompatible with patriotism and that freedom of the press could only lead to serious inconvenience. Clauzel maintained that the principles which the Convention professed were contrary to those on which the resolution was based. If it was true that the philosopher of Geneva, that friend of humanity, had really written the passage which the resolution quoted, then it was an error on his part—no man is exempt from committing errors. Anton Claire Thibaudeau (1765-1854) objected even more strongly:

They dare to assert that patriotism is incompatible with humanity, when patriotism is nothing else but love of one's fellowmen, but enlightened humanity. It is high time that the Convention declare itself, and that it put an end to these fluctuations with which they wish to impress public opinion.[12]

But these fluctuations were part of the complex and often contradictory picture presented by the nationalism of the French Revolution. It oscillated between the promise of a happier era for individual and mankind alike and the actuality of emphasis on national interest and pride. By an elaborate system of education, it tried to implant both firmly in men's minds and hearts.

XII

Education in the
Age of Nationalism

THE French Revolution inherited from the age of Enlightenment faith in the importance of education. The seventeenth century discovered the rationality of nature; its laws became comprehensible to man, who thereby gained the power of mastering it. Knowledge was power. The eighteenth century placed *les sciences morales et politiques* beside the natural sciences; an understanding of the rationality of man and society would provide power to educate the human race and to improve society. On the occasion of his reception into the French Academy on February 21, 1782, Condorcet praised the advance of education in his age:

> As enlightenment spreads, methods of instruction grow more perfect. The human mind seems to expand and its frontiers recede. A young man who leaves our schools has acquired more real knowledge than the greatest geniuses, I do not say of antiquity, but of the seventeenth century itself, could acquire by long study. These new fields of knowledge which date almost from our own day—the object of which is man himself and the goal of which is the happiness of man—will make no less certain progress than did the physical sciences. This entrancing idea, that our descendants will surpass us in wisdom and enlightenment, is no longer an illusion.[1]

The need for secularization and modernization of education was recognized in the last decades of the monarchy, but very little was accomplished.[2] As in so many other fields, it was left to the energy of the French Revolution and Napoleon to carry through the reform. The need for universal education in the formation of a nation was evident to all; the French Revolution established the first comprehensive system of national education and set the pattern for the future. The Reformation emphasized everyone's duty to be able to read the Bible; the enlightened monarchs desired the spread of education to improve administration; the new nation-state, based upon the active participation of its citizens, recognized that education was the duty of society towards its members. In a variety of goals and methods, the quarter of a century from 1789 to 1814 shaped the pattern for the wide fluctuations in all modern education, from a broad and critical humanism to a narrow authoritarian nationalism.

In his First Memorandum on Public Instruction, Condorcet demanded in 1790 an education that would sharpen critical faculties. "Public authority does not have the right in any matter to teach opinions as truth," he warned:

> It is not entitled to impose any belief. . . . If one arouses a blind enthusiasm for an exclusive doctrine, one makes the citizens incapable of judgment; if one tells them what they must worship and believe, then one wishes to create a kind of political religion, a fetter for the mind. One violates liberty in its most sacred rights under the very pretext of teaching that it is to be cherished.[3]

Condorcet confessed in a moving passage that "for a long time, he regarded these views as dreams which could only be realized in the distant future and for a world in which he would no longer exist." But, he discovered, "a happy event has suddenly opened up an immense prospect for the hope of the human race, a single moment has put the span of a century between the men of today and the men of tomorrow."[4] The school system which Napoleon put on a firm basis a decade later did not correspond to Condorcet's hopes: it sought to produce loyal servants of the state and to indoctrinate men with the political religion that Condorcet had feared and condemned.

This shift in emphasis from liberty to authority was not the only change of original intentions regarding education. Condorcet denied that different countries need different laws and institutions. Were not reason, justice, the rights of man, the interest of property, liberty, and security the same everywhere, and did they not form identical foundations for laws and institutions?[5] But Chénier, in his speech to the National Convention on the importance of public instruction, considered that the purpose of education was "to make republicans."

> It is, moreover, to make Frenchmen, to give to the nation a physiognomy of its own, peculiar to it; finally, it is to dwell upon the importance, the extent, the geographic situation of France, upon her influence on Europe and the world, upon the powerful interest that commands her to perfect the public reason and to accelerate the progress of the human mind.[6]

But whatever the various interpretations, all the legislative bodies of the French Revolution were agreed upon the necessity of an inclusive system of general education that would raise new generations of virtuous and patriotic citizens. Several projects were submitted, among others by Talleyrand and Condorcet. The most radical project was the one by Louis Michel Lepeletier de Saint-Fargeau (1760-1793), whose educational theories were taken up, after he was assassinated by royalists, by his friend Robespierre. The project called for a Spartan system of education to regenerate the national spirit which had been degraded by the vices of the old regime. Lepeletier proposed to educate all boys from five to twelve and all girls from five to eleven at public expense in national establishments removed from family life. Patriotic songs and the most striking deeds in the history of free peoples and of the French Revolution were to be taught, together with the fundamentals of the constitution. Manual training, gymnastic exercises, and work on the soil formed an important part of the curriculum.

All the new programs stressed technical education and training in science and manual skills. Condorcet hailed such emphasis as the beginning of "a great revolution in the application of physics and chemistry to the needs and happiness of man." His enthusiastic predictions promised that with a few more obstacles overcome, an immense horizon will open before our eyes. Everything heralds one of these fortunate eras in which the human mind passes suddenly from the obscurity of painful research into the brilliant daylight of great results, and thus enjoys in one day the labor of several generations.[7] In another departure from tradition, most of the projects stressed the importance of educating both sexes and of extending instruction beyond the formal school age. Condorcet suggested that citizens of all ages gather every Sunday to be taught the Constitution, and through it, the principles of public morality and the rights of man.

Yet even in the official proposal which he submitted to the Legislative Assembly on behalf of the Committee of Public Instruction on April 20, 1792, Condorcet asked that love of the fatherland must not be taught in an emotional way.

> Let us not employ, to inspire love of the fatherland, the means by which religious or political charlatans know how to bind the people to institutions that flatter their ambitions or their pride. Let us help to develop the human faculty during the weakness of childhood, but let us not abuse this weakness by molding it according to our beliefs, our interests, or our pride.

By developing their sense of truth and justice, Condorcet believed, citizens of the fatherland could be educated without becoming charlatans of patriotism.[8] This dispassionate approach was not shared by the Jacobin

Society of Paris, which asked the societies in the provinces in a circular of February 27, 1792, to emulate the spread of Christianity through apostles and missionaries by sending out apostles of liberty and equality into the villages every Sunday to distribute the Declaration and the Constitution, newspapers and pamphlets, and to explain them to the villagers. "These missionaries sent by you will establish the most august and formidable alliance that has ever existed, the alliance of the whole French people. They will be the forerunners of the teachers whom, one day, the National Assembly will send out for the new public education." [9]

This education was not only to enlighten the mind but to instill a new morality, a civic religion which would be detached from the religion of the past and would create national unity and pervade all aspects of life. Some of the suggestions made at the time went to great lengths, such as one by a Parisian priest who wished to extend the new unity and uniformity even beyond the grave. At the beginning of 1792 Charles Alexandre de Moy (1750-1834) published a pamphlet entitled *Accord de la religion et des cultes chez une nation libre*, in which he claimed for the nation the right of supervision over all religious details. "A single law—the national law—must command everyone, and no special law can or may exempt any citizen from the legitimate control of the national law." He suggested that priests and ministers should no longer distinguish themselves by wearing clerical clothes, nor should church bells be rung except on occasions of public interest. With special vehemence he protested against cemeteries reserved for various creeds: the man who was to be buried was above all a citizen before he was a Catholic, Protestant or Jew. With separate cemeteries, he complained, the national society would only include all the living; it would loose its hold at the moment of death. "In dying, the citizen would isolate himself and split off from the great society." [10]

Naturally, a society in which uniformity could be demanded even of the dead was eager to mold the rising generation. The Republic had a difficult task to accomplish: teachers had to be trained, textbooks written, new principles laid down, new methods worked out:

> Republican catechisms were widely distributed to inspire the youth with patriotic sentiments by comparing the old regime with the achievements of the Revolution, by contrasting examples of civic virtue and aristocratic corruption. The conviction was fostered that the Republic, even in its excesses, was superior to all other forms of government and that the "free man" was the model for all mankind.

A good example of this civic morality is provided—though in rather questionable poetry—by the "Commandments of the Republican":

La république tu serviras,
Une, indivisible seulement.
Aux fédéralistes tu feras
La guerre éternellement.
En bon soldat tu te rendras
A ton service exactement.
Pour tous les cultes tu seras,
Comme le veut la loi, tolérant.
Les beaux arts tu cultiveras;
D'un état ils sont l'ornement.
A ta section tu viendras
Convoquée légalement.
Ta boutique tu fermeras
Chaque décadi strictement.
La constitution tu suivras
Ainsi que tu en as fait serment.
A ton poste tu périras
Si tu ne peux vivre librement.[11]

Though the schools steeped the students in patriotism, their nationalism did not abandon the eighteenth-century traditions of reason and liberty. When Joseph Lakanal (1762-1845) submitted his report on the establishment of normal schools to the Convention, he stressed the hope that

in the Pyrenees and in the Alps the art of teaching will be the same as in Paris, and this art will be that of nature and genius. Human reason, cultivated everywhere with an equally enlightened assiduity, will produce everywhere the same results. These results will be the re-creation of human understanding in a people who will become an example and model for the world.

And Bertrand Barère, who in 1794 in his *Rapport sur l'éducation révolutionnaire, républicaine et militaire* had pleaded for the religion of the fatherland, published in 1797 a pamphlet *De la pensée du gouvernement révolutionnaire* in which he stated that he wished to protect that same religion from too much propaganda, lest freedom be impeded.[12] The new schools established by the Convention continued the eighteenth-century trend towards rational enlightenment and secularization. Study of the Christian religion was replaced by that of the Declaration and the Constitution. The Commission of Public Instruction issued a circular letter on November 19, 1794, pointing out that France had broken with "the opinions which had misled all the centuries and all the peoples." Therefore, only those were wanted as teachers who were brought up in the philosophy of the present day and for whom reason was the sole authority.

The national education that the French Revolution inaugurated went far beyond the school itself. There were numerous academies, scattered all over the country, which pursued their researches independently, without any central encouragement. Most of them were insignificant in achievement. In 1795 the National Convention established in Paris a new Institut National des Sciences et des Arts which was to belong to the whole Republic. Its staff was to perfect the sciences and the arts by uninterrupted research, by publications, and by correspondence with foreign societies, and to carry through literary and scientific enterprises that would be of public utility and enhance the glory of France. This Institute, like the great central schools founded by the Convention— the Conservatoire National des Arts et Métiers, the Ecole des Travaux Publics, and the Ecole Normale—served not only to emphasize the unity of France, but also to strengthen the Republic. Scientific research was organized in the service of national defense. Experiments were undertaken with new weapons, with balloons to be used for military observation, and with telegraphic signals. In the spirit of rational unity the metric system was introduced and soon helped to establish in many other lands a new uniformity of measures and weights.[13]

XIII

Arts and Letters in the
Age of Nationalism

Out of the new patriotic pride the first steps were taken to make Paris the artistic center of the world. In 1793 the Convention opened in the Palace of the Louvre the Musée de la République, the first national museum in Europe. It was governed by the principle that artistic treasures belong to all, and that the national state, the new patron of the arts, must make them accessible to the people. At the same time, the state expected the cooperation of artists. During the war, Robespierre remarked: "To defeat the tyrants, we should count on our presses as well as on our artillery. Why have we neglected this force, the power of the press?" [1] Newspapers and pamphlets were sent for distribution to the armies; writings critical of Robespierre were suppressed. But not only the pen was used for the defense of the fatherland; all the arts were mobilized by the Committee of Public Safety to glorify the Republic, to create a new Republican style, and to mold the new national spirit. To represent and inspire it, public buildings were adorned with murals and statues. On May 16, 1794, the Committee called upon poets

> to celebrate the principal events of the French Revolution, to compose hymns and patriotic poems and republican plays, to write about the historical actions of the soldiers of liberty, the traits of courage and devotion of republicans, and the victories won by the French armies.

It also called upon citizens, men of letters,

> to transmit to posterity the most noteworthy facts and the great epochs in the regeneration of the French, and to give to history that severe and firm character appropriate to the annals of a great people conquering its liberty, attacked by all the tyrants of Europe.

It exhorted them "to infuse a republican morality into works destined for public instruction" and it promised competitive contests and national awards for these labors.[2]

For obvious reasons, music played a greater role than the visual arts as a persuasive force. Through the centuries, the church had employed music to strengthen a congregation's feeling of community and to deepen religious emotions. The army used music to fuse individuals into marching columns through rhythm and to arouse flagging and hesitant minds to endurance and action. Early in the new century, Schopenhauer was to set music above all other arts because it best represented the emotional urge and the elemental will underlying all manifestations of life. The French Revolution found in music its perfect instrument. The great celebrations and festivals of the period were held under the open sky, and tens of thousands participated. To create among them a solemn feeling of communion, to lift their hearts in an emotional response, the memory of which would remain with them, a musical art was called for, something stimulating and dynamic. In his opera *La Reprise de Toulon,* François Joseph Gossec (1734-1829) arranged the Marseillaise for choir and brass instruments, and it was this orchestration of the Marseillaise that intoxicated the masses. Upon the suggestion of Lafayette, Bernard Sarrette, a captain on the General Staff, organized the *Musique de la garde nationale,* an orchestra of seventy military musicians for whom he provided new percussion instruments and brasses to create an effect of greater power and pomp. The modern military orchestra was born in the French Revolution, and the new instrumentation soon influenced the orchestras of opera and concerts as well. When the Conservatoire National de Musique et d'Art Dramatique was founded in 1795, Sarrette became its first director.

Robespierre entrusted Gossec with creating the musical arrangements for the Festival of the Supreme Being. At this festival an immense crowd sang the Marseillaise to the accompaniment of an orchestra that included two hundred drummers alone. The last verse of the Marseillaise was accompanied by artillery salvos. The mighty music and the community singing roused the passion of the attendant crowds. In this respect, music was no longer a matter of private enjoyment, intended for those who had an ear for it, but a political factor, a "democratic" force for swaying the people to action.[13] The theatrical impact and heroic character of the new enlarged orchestra and the big chorus could not fail to influence opera—from *La Vestale* of Gasparo Spontini (1774-1851), celebrating the glory of Napoleon, to the music-drama of Richard Wagner, which helped to create the myth of the German hero. With the French Revolution a new heroic age dawned, in which the people itself, the nation, began to play its role on the world stage.

The law of October 25, 1795, which organized national education, also established several national festivals—those of the Republic, Youth, Husbands and Wives, Old Age, Gratitude, Agriculture, and Liberty, in addition to the great anniversaries of January 21, July 14, and August 10.[4] But the institution of national festivals goes back to the beginning of the revolutionary period: the Fête de la Fédération was its first and perhaps its greatest manifestation. Sieyès suggested these festivals—in which he hoped France would surpass ancient Greece—as the most fitting institution "à moraliser les hommes, à les policer de plus dans leurs relations sociales et à leur inspirer, soit en particulier, soit en commun, une bonne émulation d'estime et de gloire."[5] In a similar vein Talleyrand demanded in 1791 national festivals and theaters inspired by the example of the Greeks and Romans to arouse a "love of the fatherland, that almost unique morality of the free peoples of antiquity."

While the Revolution found hardly a single great musician to express popular mass sentiments, it was fortunate in having in Jacques Louis David (1748-1825) a painter whose heroic classical canvases fitted the temper of the time, and to whom was consigned the direction of the festivals. He supported the Revolution from the beginning, and when in September 1792 he was elected a member of the Convention, he devotedly followed Robespierre's policies. Cato and Brutus were his inspirations, and the somber style of his great pictures—"Licteurs rapportant à Brutus les corps de ses fils" (1789), "Derniers moments de Michel Lepeletier de Saint-Fargeau," and "Marat assassiné dans sa baignoir" (1793)—exemplified the republican virtues. A member of the Committees of Public Instruction and of General Safety, and later president of the Convention, David was, under Robespierre, dictator of the arts in France. Later he supported Napoleon with the same enthusiasm; he was named Napoleon's "first" painter and commissioned to paint four *tableaux* which were to decorate the throne room.

The festivals fulfilled their national task: they helped to make patriotism the common "religion" of all Frenchmen. Marie-Joseph Chénier (1764-1811) declared in his speech to the Convention on November 5, 1793:

> Liberty will be the soul of our public festivals; they will exist only for it and through it. We must sow great memories throughout the year and make all our civic festivals an annual and commemorative history of the French Revolution. . . . Il faudra consacrer dans l'avenir les époques immortelles où les différentes tyrannies se sont écroulées devant le souffle national et ces grands pas de la Raison, qui franchissent l'Europe et vont frapper les bornes du monde.

Three weeks later, Danton took up the suggestion, and recalling the Greek Olympic games, asked that "the cradle of liberty be the center of the national festivals." He demanded that "the Convention consecrate the Champ de Mars to national games, that it order a temple to be erected there where the French people can gather in great numbers." Such gatherings would nourish the "sacred love of liberty and augment the resources of national energy"; through such institutions France would conquer the world.

Jacques Nicolas Billaud-Varenne (1756-1819) delivered before the National Convention on April 20, 1794, a report on

> the theory of democratic government and its power to restrain ambition and to temper the fervor of the military spirit; on the political goal of the current war; and on the need for inspiring the love of civic virtue by public festivals and moral institutions. [La théorie du gouvernement démocratique, et sa vigueur utile pour contenir l'ambition, et pour tempérer l'essor de l'esprit militaire; sur le but politique de la guerre actuelle; et sur la nécessité d'inspirer l'amour des vertus civiles par des fêtes publiques et des institutions morales.]

In this report he explained the all-inclusive task of this education in patriotism:

> Take hold of man from his birth, lead him to virtue by the admiration of great things and by the enthusiasm which they inspire. Let every heroic deed have its trophy, let every generous sentiment be celebrated in frequent public festivals. These lively and touching spectacles leave profound impressions which uplift the soul, which enhance genius, and which electrify both civic sense and sensibility: civic sense, which is the sublime principle of self-abnegation; sensibility, which is the inexhaustible source of all affectionate and sociable instincts. These repeated gatherings are gradually conducive to creating a need in men of seeking each other's company and mingling together; they accustom them to finding their highest pleasure in meeting together, and their joy in a general participation in the same ecstasies and the same enjoyments. Let the fatherland, the common mother, clasp all her children in her arms without distinction. . . . Let her care extend up to the last moments of existence; and consider how useful it would be to have the mother country herself preside at the funerals of all her citizens. Death is a reminder of equality, which a free people must consecrate by a public act which will ever recall to them that necessary warning. Funeral pomp is a comforting homage that effaces even the hideous imprint of death; it is the last farewell of nature. It is only the perverse man whom public reprobation will

hurl down into the grave with the scorn and indignation which must pursue crime even beyond annihilation.[6]

The festivals, though arranged by the authorities for the people, were intended to be truly popular in nature—spectacles in which the people themselves participated and played the leading role. The most elaborate of them was the one dedicated to the worship of the Supreme Being, instituted by Robespierre himself. In his address on the relations between religious and moral ideas and the republican principles and on national festivals, delivered before the Convention on May 7, 1794, Robespierre introduced his proposals in memorable words spoken at the moment when French republican arms were triumphing on all fronts:

> It is little to destroy the kings; it is necessary to make all peoples respect the character of the French people. In vain shall we carry the renown of our arms to the ends of the world if old passions rage unchecked in the bosom of the fatherland. Let us beware of becoming intoxicated with success. Let us be terrible in defeat and modest in triumph, and let us establish peace and happiness in our midst through wisdom and morality. That is the true aim of our efforts; that is the most heroic and difficult task.

To that end, Robespierre advocated that the French people recognize the existence of the Supreme Being and the immortality of the soul, that it detest bad faith and tyranny, that it succor the unfortunate, the weak, and the oppressed, that it do all the good it could for others and be unjust to none.

> To recall men to the thought of divinity and to the divinity of his own being, festivals will be instituted which will receive their names from the glorious events of our revolution, from the virtues which are the dearest and most useful to men, and from the greatest benefactions of nature.[7]

The fall of Robespierre and the decline of revolutionary enthusiasm somewhat dampened the ardor of these celebrations, but the Thermidor republicans tried hard to preserve them and to put them on a more permanent and organized basis. Characteristic was the Directory decree of July 31, 1796, which regulated the celebration of the Festival of August 10. It declared that since all free peoples celebrated fervently (*avec ivresse*) the memorable epochs of their history, and above all the days of their liberation—just as the Romans regarded the expulsion of the Tarquins one of the events most worthy of remembrance—the tenth of August, the last day of royal despotism in France, would be no less dear to the French. It was decreed that in every commune in France the public officials should march in a procession led by a detachment of the National Guard to the public square. There the history and significance of the day were to be explained to the assembled people and an inscription hung on the Tree of Liberty that read: "Honor to those courageous men who overthrew the throne. The French no longer recognize any other masters than the laws." This ceremony was to be accompanied by martial music. Schoolteachers were to take a public oath that they would inspire their pupils with republican sentiments and with respect for the virtues, talents, and courage of the founders of the Republic. Patriotic songs were to follow this oath. The fathers and mothers of the defenders of the fatherland were to be accorded a distinguished place among the spectators of the public games following the ceremony, this place to be marked by an inscription surrounded by laurels.

With Napoleon the national festivals came to an end, not because he neglected the direction of public opinion, but because in these celebrations active participation by the people was too pronounced. The unity of the nation which Napoleon's festivals were intended to advance was no longer a matter of spontaneous emotion; it reposed in Napoleon himself. The institution of the national festivals was originally meant to form a commemorative cycle of the great events of popular liberty rather than of military glory, of the defeat of domestic tyranny rather than of external enemies. Under Napoleon, the emphasis shifted from the former to the latter. The first years of the Revolution, though they certainly produced no masterpieces, had greatly stimulated popular artistic expression in poems and songs and plays; the national festivals were carried on this wave. Napoleon distrusted all such spontaneous manifestations.

What was true of the festivals, also applied to the theater, which the Revolution had regarded less as a place of amusement than as an institution for the patriotic and moral education of the citizens. The Revolution opened the theater to the masses, but it was to be a different theater. "A theater of little women and slaves is no longer fit for men and citizens," Marie-Joseph Chénier pointed out in the dedication of his play *Charles IX, ou L'Ecole des Rois* in 1789. In his "Treizième étude de la Nature," Jacques Henri Bernardin de Saint-Pierre (1737-1814) called for a French national Shakespeare who would present to the people the drama of Saint Joan.

> I wished that this subject, treated by a man of genius in the manner of Shakespeare, would produce a patriotic play, and that this famous shepherdess would become among us the patron saint of war as Saint Geneviève is that of peace; that this play would be reserved for occasions of peril to the state; that it

then be performed before the people in the same way that the standard of Mohammed is shown to the people of Constantinople in similar circumstances; and I do not doubt that at the sight of her innocence, of her services, of her misfortunes, of the cruelty of her enemies, and of the horror of her suffering, our people, transported, would exclaim: "War! War against the English!"

On August 2, 1793, the Convention decreed that from August 4 to September 1—that is, during the period when many people from the provinces would assemble in Paris to celebrate the Festival of August Tenth—the theaters were to present "republican tragedies, like *Brutus, William Tell, Caius Gracchus.*" When, on August 6, the Théâtre de la République performed *Brutus*, the notice boards hailed the play as "De, par et pour le peuple."[8] On March 10, 1794, the Committee of Public Safety called for the immediate reopening of the former Théâtre Français, which after the Revolution was renamed "Théâtre de la Nation" and closed by the Convention in 1793 for performing *Pamela, ou La Vertu récompensée* by François du Neufchateau (1750-1828), a play regarded as too moderate in tone. The theater was now to be used exclusively for performances given at various times "of, by, and for the people." The building was to be called Théâtre du Peuple and decorated within "with all the attributes of Liberty." Artists from other theaters were to be requisitioned to perform there before citizens selected by their municipalities for distinctive patriotism. Similar free spectacles were to be given in the provinces. The plays performed on the Parisian stage during the Revolution presented the common people as heroic defenders of the fatherland and models of domestic and conjugal virtue. Royal censorship of theaters was abolished on January 13, 1791, but the National Convention reintroduced a strict control which was strengthened by the vigilance of the Jacobin clubs, to make sure that "the stage be redeemed, that Reason come there to speak the language of liberty, to throw flowers on the tombs of its martyrs, to sing of heroism and of virtue, and to teach a love of law and of the fatherland."[9] Thus, festivals and theaters cooperated to form the backbone of patriotic education and to cement the unity of the nation.

XIV

Nationalism and Linguistic Unity

THE UNITY of the nation was the ceaseless concern of the patriots. "The Republic will never be one, indivisible and prosperous," Carnot reported to the Convention of January 29, 1793, "until all come to the aid of each." Better communications, he believed, would assure a greater uniformity of language and customs and would help to overcome indifference to the general affairs of the nation. In anticipation of the brain trusts and planned economies of the twentieth century, Carnot suggested that every year a group of scholars and artists visit the whole of France to examine conditions and then to present an annual report on the general state of the country, as a basis for a plan to promote national prosperity and rationalize the administration.[1] Such a program and, even more, the efforts towards uniform education seemed to demand the acceptance of French as the one national language taught in all schools throughout the country.

French in the eighteenth century had been voluntarily accepted without any political pressure as the language of the educated classes throughout Europe. In the nineteenth century, its use extended as far as Latin America and the Near East. But the French rarely indulged in linguistic nationalism. While the Germans and the Italians, under the impact of nationalism, wished to unite all the populations speaking German and Italian into a nation-state, the French, except for a brief while during the Revolution, made no attempt to impose political sovereignty on the basis of a common language, nor to impose language as an element of political community. However, the passionate demand for uniformity and the sharp rejection of federalism during the Revolution gave rise to a nationalist effort to institute French as the mother tongue in all corners of the French Republic. The French felt that as a result of their revolutionary efforts and sacrifices, their political civilization was, after 1789, far ahead of that of other peoples. Free and French seemed synonymous; people enjoying the freedom of the French Republic should be proud to speak the language in which the Declaration of Rights was conceived and written. For a short while, nationalism made the French forget that the Declaration was the expression of universal reason, valid in all languages.

On January 27, 1794, Bertrand Barère submitted on behalf of the Committee of Public Safety, a report "Sur les idiomes étrangers et l'enseignement de la langue française," in which he spoke of French as the most beautiful language of Europe, "the first to proclaim frankly the rights of man and the citizen, the one language which was destined to give the world the most sublime thoughts of liberty and the greatest speculations in politics." He proposed that an instructor of French be sent to each canton where non-French languages were spoken to teach French and the Declaration of Rights. The Jacobin club of Strasbourg was of the opinion that "as long as diversity of tongues is not proscribed in the Republic, as long as the language of free men is not the sole one used in France, we shall have among us men who are not French." This linguistic nationalism was strongest in Alsace. Saint-Just and Philippe Le Bas (1764-1794), as representatives of the people, invited the women citizens of Strasbourg "to abandon the German fashions, because their hearts are French." [2]

The main non-French languages spoken in France at the end of the eighteenth century were Basque, Catalan, Breton, Flemish, German, and Italian. Provençal was also still widely used throughout southeastern France. These conditions disappeared only in the nineteenth century with the spread of general education, military service, and improved communications, which brought many travelers to these outlying parts of the country. The secluded valleys of the Pyrenees and the lonely fishing villages of Brittany were drawn into the main stream of national life, but Basque, Breton, and German survived even in the nineteenth century, and some of these languages received a new lease on life under the impulse of regional nationalism. In Alsace in the eighteenth century French was spoken mainly by Protestants, while the Catholic population adhered to German, which was favored by the royal administration. Leading periodicals like the *Bürgerfreund* and the *Elsaessischer Patriot* appeared in German, and when Goethe came to Strasbourg in 1772, he found the intellectual life of the city and the university more German than French.[3]

Political union with France in no way implied the imposition of the French language. Breton had not developed fully as a language until Brittany became an integral part of France. Before the union of the two countries in 1532, independent Brittany under her native dukes had used French as the official language and as the language of the court. No Breton literature was then produced; only in the sixteenth and seventeenth centuries, under the influence of the church was the vernacular language cultivated. Mystery plays, translated from French or Latin, were performed by peasants in Breton, and Breton devotional books were published. The Jesuit Father Julien Maunoir (1606-1683), though himself born in Upper Brittany where Breton was not spoken, developed a religious mysticism linking the Breton language and the true faith. Addressing himself to St. Corentin, the first bishop of Quimper—who founded the see in the fifth century at the time when the Celts immigrated to Brittany from Britain—he exclaimed:

> It has been the grace of the Armorican language, O great saint, that you planted the faith in Cornwall with very special blessings from heaven which bestow a venerable character on the idiom which you use. For thirteen centuries no kind of infidelity has stained the language which served you as a medium for preaching the gospel of Jesus Christ, and the man has yet to be born who will see a Breton, speaking Breton, preach any other religion but the Catholic one. The Bishops who have held firm to the idiom that you honored with your blessed lips have advantages and favors to which no other nation can pretend.[4]

A long line of priests followed Father Maunoir in establishing the tie between the Catholic tradition and the Breton language throughout the countryside. But cities like Rennes were French in the eighteenth century; the strongly developed feeling of provincial unity was not based upon language, nor was there any sign of a Breton nationalism except for the strength of religious fervor, which played its part in the civil wars of the French Revolution. It was only after the Revolution that a Breton national movement and, with it, a Breton literature of any importance developed. "We look in vain for any manifestation of originality in Breton literature until we reach the nineteenth century. The consciousness of nationality then awakened and found expression in verse." [5] The unifying tendencies of the French Revolution never seriously threatened the survival of the Breton language or of other vernaculars.

But during the Revolution and the Napoleonic wars[6] there were strong elements working in favor of linguistic unification. The state intervened in the administrative, cultural, and economic life of all parts of the territory to an unprecedented degree, and all functions were centralized in the capital. Men from all parts of the country served together in regiments which became schools of the French language and of French sentiment; marching over the roads of almost all Europe, the soldiers began to look upon French as the language of military glory. For the French revolutionary patriot, unity of language meant primarily a union of souls. To speak French seemed both a proof of patriotic loyalty and of rational enlightenment. "Multiplicity of idioms may have been useful in the ninth century and under the overlong reign of feudalism," a contemporary wrote. "Today, when we all have the same law as our master, when we all are French, we should have but one language, just as we have one heart."

The spread of French was also advanced by the festivals and the schools. At the former, delegates from neighboring departments and often from the capital participated. For their sake, the common language was used, and the solemn texts which were recited were in French. There had not yet developed among the Basques or Alsatians, the Bretons or Flemish, any national sentiment which would have demanded the translation of these texts into the vernacular. Sacred texts had been received habitually in a foreign language. The place of Latin in the church was taken in the new faith by French. In the enthusiasm of the Revolution the outlying provinces joined the center voluntarily; Alsace, for instance, became French in sentiment, and partly in language, through the Revolution. Higher education in France before the Revolution stressed Latin more than French, classical authors more than French writers. All that was now changed. In spite of the facile comparison with Roman republicans, the French patriots, feeling themselves heralds of a new epoch, wished to reduce the role of "dead languages" in the curriculum and to give first place to French, to the history of the fatherland, and to science. J. B. E. Legendre wrote in his *Coup d'oeil sur l'éducation publique* in 1792:

> The three or four years which follow the beginning of schooling should not be devoted to the study of a language which is of practically no use during the course of life, but to the study of French, which by its beauty, vitality, and tenderness has almost become the universal language.

In these years, when the fatherland was in danger, and only then, voices were raised against tolerance of the "idioms" which were believed to be vehicles of foreign and especially of clerical propaganda. It seemed difficult to explain the new principles and laws to those who did not speak French; on the other hand, the counterrevolution had easy access to them through priests who used Basque or Breton, Flemish or German. Barère, in the name of the Committee of Public Safety, denounced the idioms on January 27, 1794:

> Federalism and superstition speak Breton; emigration and hatred of the Republic speak German; the counterrevolution speaks Italian, and fanaticism speaks Basque. Let us break these dangerous instruments of error. It cannot be our task to uphold these barbarous jargons and these vulgar idioms, which

can only serve the fanatics and the counterrevolution. . . . The
monarchy had good reason to resemble the Tower of Babel;
but in a democracy, to leave the citizens ignorant of the national
language and incapable of controlling the government means to
betray the fatherland. It means to fail to recognize the blessings
of the printing press, for every printer is a teacher of the language and the legislation. . . . In a free people language must
be one and the same for all.

Abbé Henri Grégoire (1750-1831), Bishop of Blois, a Jansenist and a
Liberal, who fought for racial equality in the colonies, a spokesman for
international cooperation and later an opponent of Napoleon's policies,
affirmed in his report of June 6, 1794, "Sur la necessité et les moyens
d'anéantir les patois, et d'universaliser l'usage de la langue française,"
that because the political state of the world banished the hope of having
all peoples speak a common language,

one can render the language of one great nation uniform, so
that all its citizens can exchange their thoughts without hindrance. This enterprise, which no people has as yet fully carried
out, is worthy of the French people, who are centralizing all
branches of social organization and who ought to be eager to
establish as soon as possible in a republic which is one and
indivisible, the single and invariable use of the language of
liberty. All members of the sovereign body are admissible to all
offices. It is desirable that all be able to fill them successively
and then return to their agricultural or mechanical professions.
Under these conditions we are faced with the following alternative: if these offices are occupied by men incapable of expressing themselves and writing in the national language, will
the rights of the citizen be safely guaranteed in legal and administrative matters transacted in imprecise terms? If, on the
other hand, ignorance of French excludes anyone from office,
then we might soon see a rebirth of that aristocracy which
formerly employed the patois to patronize those whom they
insolently called *les petites gens*. Society would then soon be
again divided into two separate classes, and ignorance of the
language would compromise social happiness and destroy
equality.

After Thermidor, this linguistic nationalism soon disappeared. Even
at its height it had been motivated more by concern for the gains of
the Revolution than by any romantic glorification of language. It
quickly gave way to a spirit of tolerance towards the use of non-French
languages within the national territory. During the Terror a decree of
July 20, 1794, had forbidden the use of any language but French for
public transactions or even for those under private seal. On September

2 of the same year, this law was suspended indefinitely. The schools were not forced to teach French, but nevertheless the private schools, which were granted a new lease on life, were eager to do so. By the end of the revolutionary period, the number of people who were able to speak French had increased enormously.[7] Under Napoleon the prefects cared above all for efficiency and smoothness of administration and for that reason favored the spread of the French language. But their efforts in that direction were not inspired by nationalism. They obeyed the same motives as did the enlightened monarchs of the eighteenth century. Napoleon himself, though he utilized and satisfied the national desire for glory, was no French nationalist, nor did he try to promote French nationalism.

XV

Napoleon and Nationalism

A SINCERE patriotism, a deep attachment to the soil and people of France, inspired Robespierre. It provided a moving lyrical undertone to the tragic sternness of his reports:

> Yes, this delightful land which we inhabit and which nature caresses with love is made to be the domain of liberty and happiness; this sensitive and proud people are truly born for glory and for virtue. O my fatherland! if fate had caused me to be born in a foreign and distant country, I would have addressed heaven continuously with wishes for thy prosperity. I would have been moved to tears by the recital of thy combats and thy virtues. My attentive soul would have followed with a restless ardor all the movements of thy glorious revolution: I would have envied the fate of thy citizens; I would have envied that of thy representatives. I am French, I am one of thy representatives. . . . O sublime people! Accept the sacrifice of my whole being. Happy is the man who is born in thy midst; happier is he who can die for thy happiness.[1]

This feeling for France was unknown to Napoleon. At no time in his life had he the desire to die for the happiness of the French people. The patriotic sentiment he knew in his youth was the rhetorical patriotism of a late-eighteenth-century adolescence which had been instructed by the classics and Rousseau. But even so his was a patriotism directed against France. Napoleon the Corsican shared his fellow countrymen's hatred of their French conquerors and their admiration for Pasquale Paoli (1725-1807), the leader of the Corsican fight for independence in which the young Napoleon longed to join. What attracted him most to Rousseau in his early youth was Rousseau's idolization of primitive agrarian Corsica.[2] "My relatives, my country, and my veneration for Paoli and Rousseau were my only passion," Napoleon wrote later of this period of his life. When, at the age of ten, he entered the military school at Brienne-le-Château in the department of the Aube in northeastern France, Napoleon knew little French.

> As I still spoke French badly and found it hard to accustom myself to a completely different mode of living, I generally kept away from my companions at first and preferred to occupy myself with my books. Extraordinarily sensitive as I was, I suffered infinitely from the ridicule of my schoolmates, who used to jeer at me as a foreigner. My pride and sense of honor would tolerate no insult to my country [Corsica!] or to the beloved national hero Paoli.

At the beginning of 1786 Buonaparte received his commission as a sublieutenant in the French garrison town of Valence in southeastern France. There his thoughts returned incessantly to his native land. The words which he wrote in May 1786 were characteristic of his feeling throughout the period:

> What tragedy awaits me in my country! My fellow countrymen are loaded with chains! and have to bear, trembling, the weight of the oppressor's hand! [The oppressor was the King of France, whose uniform Napoleon wore.] You Frenchmen! It is not enough that you have robbed us of what we love the most, you have even destroyed our manners and customs! What attitude shall I adopt, how shall I speak when I arrive in my country? When his country no longer exists, a good citizen should die. If one man could save my countrymen by sacrificing his life, I would at once rise and thrust the avenging sword into the breast of the tyrant in order to revenge my country and its injured rights.[3]

For the French people the Revolution meant a full awakening to nationalism; Napoleon abandoned his Corsican patriotism to embrace the revolutionary cause. Was he swayed by the promise of liberty which it held out to Frenchmen and Corsicans alike? Political liberty soon came to have as little meaning for him as nationalism, but he sensed the dynamic possibilities in this enthusiastic upsurge of a great people. Edmund Burke wrongly believed that the Revolution had dealt a mortal blow to French strength, leaving the country a great void. In a memorandum which he sent in September 1792 to Emperor Leopold II, Mirabeau remarked that Burke "has said something very stupid, for this void is a volcano, whose subterranean agitations and approaching eruptions no one can neglect for a moment without imprudence." Even more clearly than Mirabeau, Napoleon understood the dynamism of the French Revolution, this immense release of energy, this gateway to ceaseless activity and boundless ambition. His personality was admirably

suited to his time. In a period which exalted the individual and his op-
portunities, Napoleon—as Nietzsche so clearly sensed—was an extreme
individualist for whom France and Europe, nation and mankind, were
but instruments for achieving his individual destiny.

The same quest for an efficient government that brought about the
Revolution in 1789 helped Napoleon to power ten years later. The
French longed for a strong man who would safeguard the main achievements of the Revolution in orderly security and stabilize the new frontiers and glorious conquests in peace. Of all the institutions of the young
republic, the army alone possessed the necessary prestige and power.
Of its young generals, Buonaparte appeared the most promising. He
did not disappoint the country's expectations. A man of rare vitality and
capacity for work, of penetrating intelligence and prodigious memory,
he proved a great administrator and organizer, continuing the line of
enlightened absolutist monarchs of the eighteenth century and surpass-
ing them by far, becoming the last and the greatest of them. Like them,
he did not understand and had no use for nationalism and the new
popular forces. Like them, he believed in the state, in direction from
above, in efficiency and rational order. But unlike some of them, he
considered himself less the first servant of the state than its master. His
primary end was not the welfare of his subjects nor the *raison d'état* of
France; not even, except for brief moments, the perpetuation and glory
of his dynasty. All these limited goals he accepted, and from time to
time promoted each one or all of them, but they did not satisfy or
contain him. His ambitions knew no definite limits, his activities had no
fixed and stable direction. He felt that his will was strong enough to
triumph over the nature of man and the nature of things alike. To him,
the impossible was only "a phantom of the timid soul and the refuge
of the coward." Despite his youthful Rousseauan nationalism, he was an
eighteenth-century cosmopolitan for whom civilization was one and
the world the stage. He started the cult of force that found so many
adherents a hundred years after his death. "There is only one secret for
world leadership—namely, to be strong, because in strength there is
neither error nor illusion; this is the naked truth." "Succeed! I judge men
only by the results of their acts." He was a dynamic force, for whom the
world was but "an occasion to act dangerously." [4]

Unlike the men of the eighteenth century, Napoleon knew no moderation nor could his temperament accommodate itself to peace. He did
not believe in harmony, but in mastery, not in compromise but in struggle and decision. In 1802, after the peace treaty with the British signed
at Amiens, France had everything she could desire; but Napoleon was
unwilling for her to become a great state among other states and for
himself to be a king equal to other kings. He had to be the first of all,

the emperor of the Occident, the successor to Charlemagne and to Caesar; soon his ambitions went beyond the legacy of Rome, to Byzantium and to Asia. His triumphs he owed to the disunity of his adversaries, to their hesitation and half-measures. But his hubris drove him on until he succeeded in arousing the peoples, in overcoming the jealousies and pettiness of the rulers, in uniting Europe—not under his leadership, but against him. He was repeatedly offered favorable peace terms that would have left France in possession of many of her conquests; he rejected them. He could not resign himself to the French nation-state of the nineteenth century. He did not belong to the Age of Nationalism.

The constitutional liberties for which 1789 and the nineteenth century strove meant little to Napoleon. He did not deny them: he denatured them. He paid lip service to universal suffrage and deprived the people of any effective vote. With supreme contempt, he drew up many meaningless constitutions and had them confirmed by plebiscite. The people had no share in the government of their affairs; their public spirit was not encouraged. Yet in his declarations, he always took care to emphasize his wish to "rattacher les grandes autorités de l'état à la masse de la nation, d'où dérive nécessairement toute autorité nationale." He admitted no doubt that as "l'élu du peuple" he alone represented the majority of the nation. He praised democracy if it was democracy on his terms—"true" democracy. Napoleon's effective coups d'état with their subsequent plebiscitarian endorsements did not strengthen French respect for constitutional legality. The order which he undoubtedly brought to France was not the animated coherent working of creative national forces; they were cowed or dormant, deprived of all spontaneity. What remained of movement was directed from above by an administrative system that insured quick obedience but did not allow for discussion or free cooperation. All public and intellectual life was closely supervised and the formation of parties or associations was prohibited. Though Napoleon was personally not cruel and his regime was devoid of brutality and mass executions, it created an atmosphere of enforced silence, of distrust and denunciation, of arbitrary arrests and insecurity.

Napoleon's dictatorship differed from twentieth-century totalitarianism in another respect. In his contempt for public opinion, for ideologues and writers, he failed to know how to make use of them. He made little attempt to mold public opinion. He did not flood the country with newspapers and pamphlets, he did not spread popular reports of his great campaigns and victories, nor did he try to explain the virtues of his legislation. He distrusted even a controlled use of the printed word. The revolutionary period had abounded in pamphlets and newspapers. Napoleon allowed in Paris only nine newspapers to be published, which in the spring of 1803 had a combined circulation of less than 20,000 copies, and one semiofficial newspaper in each department. As there was to be only one party in France and only one opinion, there seemed to be no need for diversified newspapers. The few that did appear had to be protected against "the spread of false news." They were threatened with suppression if they published "articles contrary to the respect due to the social pact, to the sovereignty of the people, and to the glory of [French] arms." Even pamphlets praising the Emperor and populariz- ing his soldiers were extremely rare. The number of printers was limited, too; they and the booksellers had to be licensed and were required to take an oath that they would not print or sell any publication which might conflict with "their duty to the Emperor and the interests of the state." No less close was the supervision over the theater and literature. Both became "official"; as a result, they were conventional in style and content, with the sources of creative inventiveness drying up.[5] While the armies of Napoleon carried French power to the furthermost limits of Europe, the French spirit was in danger of losing the leadership it had exercised for so long.

Similarly, Napoleon did not concern himself with the promotion of elementary education or the education of women. His reforms confined themselves mainly to higher schools for the training of capable and loyal civil servants. "Public instruction," declared Pierre Louis, Comte Roederer, who in 1802 was put in charge of all affairs concerning it, "can and must be a very powerful machine in our political system. Through it the legislator will be able to recreate a national spirit and then to make use of it himself." The concern of the Enlightenment for education evaporated; what remained was paternal care of good and useful subjects. Napoleon centralized education, as he centralized the state. The decree of March 17, 1808, organized the "University," the general corporation charged with the direction of the political and moral formation of French youth. Its bases were the teachings of the Catholic religion. Superimposed on them was loyalty to the Emperor and the imperial monarchy—the depository of the happiness of the people— and to the Napoleonic dynasty—the preserver of the unity of France and of all the liberal ideas proclaimed by the constitutions—and obedience to teachers and parents. Napoleon more and more acknowledged only the official world, the armor of the state; for the nation and its intellectual life he had little use. He underestimated their importance, both in France and abroad.

In a speech to the Senate, Napoleon said on July 9, 1810, "A new order of things now guides the universe." But this order, though rational in its outline and efficient in its application, broke upon the one obstacle which it did not take into account: the human element, the popular reluctance to accept the imposed form. Napoleon's society was planned by a great strategist in the camp of a victorious army. Distrusting spontaneous manifestations of liberty, he regarded the order of the army and the discipline and élan of war as an antidote to social anarchy. He did not see that long wars threatened to produce anarchy and to destroy much of the substance on which every living order must be based. He tried to compensate the French for the political immobility that he imposed with economic activity.

Napoleon appealed to the ambitious self-love of the French that the success of the revolutionary armies had fanned, to their feeling of superiority. He wished his rule to be "a dictatorship of persuasion based upon popularity." To some, he promised to continue the gains and heroism of the Revolution; to others, he appeared as a conservative force.

> So artfully was the system of Buonaparte contrived that each of the numerous classes of Frenchmen found something in it congenial to his habits, his feeling, or his circumstances, providing only he was willing to sacrifice to it the essential part of his political principles. . . . To all these parties, Buonaparte held out the same hopes under the same conditions.—"All these things will I give you, if you will kneel down and worship me." Shortly afterwards, he was enabled to place before them to whom the choice was submitted, the original temptation in its full extent—a display of the kingdoms of the earth, over which he offered to extend the empire of France, providing always he was himself acknowledged as the object of general obedience, and almost adoration.[6]

The dynamism of Napoleon's temperament did not allow him to formulate and follow a consistent foreign policy, conforming to the interests of the French state, as Richelieu had done. His aspirations led him in too many directions. Everywhere he found England in his way, whether he tried to expand throughout Europe or to recreate the Mediterranean empire of the Romans that he, himself a Mediterranean, regarded as his legacy. From his earliest years, his glance had embraced distant lands and his plans mapped out roads for future adventure. When he started for Egypt in April 1798 as general-in-chief of the Army of the Orient, he carried with him a directive to "drive out the English from all their possessions in the Orient," to cut the Isthmus of Suez, and to take all necessary measures to assure the French Republic free and exclusive possession of the Red Sea. The daring march to the Pyramids and across the Sinai Desert was motivated not by the arbitrariness of a freebooter, but by the logic of a great vision: to make Egypt, as it had been for Alexander and Caesar, the starting point for the conquest of Asia, for an advance toward India, for a decisive battle in the heart of the new British Empire. If he had been successful, Napoleon would have attained the triumph of vast land masses over sea power, the re-opening and control of the ancient land routes to the East, the revival of the decayed civilizations and glories of the Levant and the Orient. This "mirage" of a renaissance of the lands long relegated to obscurity by the rise of oceanic sea power beckoned him on all his life. It was inextricably linked with his hostility to Britain, the mistress of the sea, and his jealousy of Russia, the empire of the East. Napoleon him-self vacillated between recreating the empire of the West—and pro-tecting it and its Mediterranean civilization against the threats from the north and the east—and the limitless horizons of the earth. In the twenty years of his career he had to confine himself to uniting Europe; he was stopped at the Channel and on the snowfields of Russia from going beyond.

XVI

The Empire of the West

WHEN Napoleon had himself crowned Emperor of the French on December 2, 1804, many regarded this step as a betrayal of the Revolution. The revolutionary hero seemed dead, buried under glittering uniforms and high-sounding titles, church incense and court ceremonial. Beethoven tore up the dedication of his Third Symphony to General Buonaparte and replaced his name by the lament, "To the memory of a great man." Stendhal, watching the coronation ceremonies in Paris, looked with disgust at the Emperor as a new Caesar and called his accommodation with the Pope "an alliance of all the charlatans." He "rinsed out the bad taste" in his mouth by reading Alfieri, the tragic dramatist and early nationalist of eighteenth-century Italy.[1] In reality, Napoleon never ceased to incarnate two early aspects of the French Revolution: its universalism and its quest for efficient government. To other aspects such as nationalism and liberalism he often paid lip service, but found little actual use for them. His own nature drove him to disregard or misinterpret the forces of liberty long before he became an emperor. (That he became one, while the "great leaders" of the twentieth century, men like Hitler and Stalin, did not, was due to the different circumstances of the two periods: in Napoleon's time nationalism had not yet sufficiently consolidated nations, nor was it possible to elaborate a doctrine of the masses or to forge a mass party, so that a hereditary dynasty seemed the only guaranty of continuity.) Napoleon did not revive the title of King of France, because it seemed to imply an abdication of popular sovereignty, while the title of Emperor flattered the nation and its desire for glory without alarming it unduly. The imperial title preserved the feeling that national sovereignty was unimpaired—"My policy consists in ruling men according to the will of the great majority. In this way I believe one recognizes the sovereignty of the people"[2]—and did not recall the struggle with the royal government for liberty.

The new title did not strike the French as strange nor as incompatible with republican achievements. The same law that proclaimed Napoleon Emperor charged him with the government of the French Republic. The term "empire" had been widely used in eighteenth-century France and by French republicans to connote a vast and prosperous land with a great future—as it had been used by American patriots for the thirteen colonies and later for the young and growing United States. It was in no way contrary to liberty and it was full of the promise of human happiness. Napoleon, however, thought less of this modern meaning of the word than of its ancient and hallowed significance, the memory of the Roman Empire as the guarantor of peace and justice in a universal world order. When he married Marie Louise (1791-1847), the daughter of the last Holy Roman Emperor, her imperial descent and the fact that the mother of his son was the niece of the last Queen of France, Marie Antoinette (1755-1793), probably meant as much to him as the practical advantages of an alliance with Austria. In his renovation of the empire of the West, he naturally recalled Charlemagne, who like him had rebuilt the Roman Empire in the West and as ruler of the Franks had united France, Italy, and Germany. Soon after Charlemagne the Frankish Western empire disintegrated into the warring camps of French and Germans. Napoleon hoped to revive and to preserve its greatness and force and to bring to a close the long struggle between French and Germans for its heritage. Like Charlemagne, he wished to found his empire in collaboration with the Roman church, but without allowing papal claims to weaken his power. No longer should the church have the power to war with the emperor for supremacy. The secular ruler should hold undisputed sway.

An eighteenth-century agnostic, Napoleon was willing to use the church to support order and morality among his subjects and to solidify his reign. He regarded the church as an institution of his empire and the Pope as an imperial official. "Paris was to be the metropolis of Christendom, the center and guide of the religious as well as of the political world." [3] To the Ecclesiastical Committee he declared on March 16, 1811:

> The present epoch carries us back to the time of Charlemagne. All the kingdoms, principalities and duchies which formed themselves out of the debris of the empire have been rejuvenated under our laws. The church of my empire is the church of the Occident and of almost the whole of Christendom.

He announced the convocation of a Council of the Occident in order that "the church of my empire be one in its discipline, as it is in its faith." When he annexed the Papal State on May 17, 1809, he did so on the strength of the theory that the secular domain of the Pope had been a fief of Charlemagne, "Empereur des Français et notre auguste prédécesseur," and that the true sovereignty remained with the donor and his heirs, who could revoke or modify the gift. The expenses of the papal office were charged to the imperial budget, and the autonomy of the Gallican church of 1682 was extended to the church in the whole empire.

In 1811 this empire, with its frontiers on the Elbe, the Ebro and the Adriatic Sea, was practically coextensive with that of Charlemagne. French prefects administered its affairs in Rome and Florence, Genoa and Turin, Antwerp and the Hague, Hamburg and Mainz, Trier and Cologne, Barcelona and Saragossa. In addition, it included the Illyrian provinces on the Adriatic coast and the Kingdom of Italy with Milan as its capital. Around this mighty nucleus, there was an outer circle of closely controlled vassal states—Spain and Naples in the south, the Confederation of the Rhine, the Helvetic Confederation, and the Duchy of Warsaw in the east. By its hold on the Vistula and the Ionian islands, Napoleon's empire went far beyond that of Charlemagne, stretching out in the direction of the Orient, towards the reunion of Byzantium with Rome.

This empire of the West had two capitals, Paris and Rome; on February 17, 1810, the latter was proclaimed "the second city of the empire." The emperors, after their coronation in Notre Dame in Paris, were to be crowned once more before the tenth year of their reign in Saint Peter's. The Pope was invited to reside where he pleased, but preferably in Paris or Rome. In 1810 the yet unborn heir to the throne received the title King of Rome, which all future heirs were to bear—an appellation recalling that of the uncrowned Holy Roman Emperors. It carried an infinitely greater majesty and promise than the title Prince of Wales borne by the heirs to the disputed realm of the sea. Napoleon set out to monumentalize his two capitals as centers of triumphant empire. An imperial palace was planned for the Capitol in Rome, and excavations were begun to lay bare the forums of antiquity.

Napoleonic rule imposed upon the provinces and satellites of his empire new concepts and new life, of which much quickly vanished after his fall; yet some invigorating efficiency remained and ended many outworn traditions and institutions. Wherever Napoleon went, he brought with him rational reforms and administrative progress. When he started for Egypt, the decree of the Directory of April 12, 1798, charged him "to improve by all means at his disposal the fate of the natives." He took with him a great number of carefully chosen scholars and scientists in all fields and with their help he founded on August 22, 1798, the Institut d'Egypte, of which Gaspard Monge (1746-1818), a mathematician and one of the founders of the Ecole Polytechnique, became the first president. Scientific research into the antiquity, the geography, the fauna and flora, and the present state of Egypt was eagerly promoted, to go hand in hand with the spread of enlightenment among its people. On October 2, 1798, the first issue of a literary and philosophical journal *Décades égyptiennes* appeared. The French hoped that through modernization Egypt would become the cradle of the regeneration of Islam and that civilization, science, and industry would return to the country that had once been their center. As this renascence developed under French inspiration, a close tie between France and the Middle East was to result; the spread of enlightenment would entail a growth of French influence.

Though Napoleon's rule in Egypt was short-lived, his hopes were not all disappointed. It is true that his progressive reforms did not reach the people and did not influence their life, but modern Egyptology owes its origin to the work of his scholars and found its initial expression in the famous *Description de l'Egypte,* which in its nine volumes of text and twelve volumes of plates presented the first survey of the antiquities, the natural resources, and the modern society of the land of the Nile. French civilization and language remained predominant in Egypt with the tiny educated upper class for well over a century. When a few years after Napoleon's expedition the vigorous and ruthless Albanian soldier Mohammed Ali laid the foundations of the first semimodern Islamic state in Egypt, he did it partly under the inspiration of the legacy Napoleon's administration left in the ancient land.[4]

More immediately far-reaching were the effects of Napoleon's administration in the Belgian departments that the Convention had incorporated into France. Under the Directory they had merely felt bewildered and oppressed; under Napoleon, they were infused with fresh energy and benefited from the new social order created by the Revolution. The ties with the traditional past of estates and provinces, castes and guilds, privileges and rights, still so potent in 1792, were broken. When Napoleon's domination ended, a return to 1792 was no longer possible. His rule had not aroused a Belgian nationalism, for whatever national feeling had existed had been closely connected with the old regime and provincial autonomy, which were now no more than a distant memory. But Napoleon succeeded in preparing the soil for a future growth of a new Belgian nationalism. Meanwhile,

> If one did not feel oneself French, one did not feel oneself Belgian either. One was satisfied to live by making the best of one's opportunities without considering them as good in themselves. Instead of a true national sentiment, there were only vague aspirations towards a better future which no one could define.[5]

The Belgians recognized the good qualities of the new administration
—its useful innovations and the security it afforded to the rising spirit
of enterprise and individual advancement—but they suffered from a
lack of civil liberties and they felt the French administrators to be
aliens. Napoleon carried out the program of enlightened absolutism
that the Holy Roman Emperor Joseph II had tried to implant in Belgium,
and the reforms rejected twenty years before were now accepted. But
measures toward frenchifying instruction and administration and the
conflict with the Catholic church alienated many Belgians. Religious
publications such as the *Jerusalems herstelling* (1811) by the priest
Stichelbaut kept love of the mother tongue and devotion to the church
alive. When the French occupation ended with the Allied victories in
the spring of 1814, the Belgians did not aid the French, nor did they, like
the Dutch, rise against them. A return to the old regime was unacceptable
to the younger generation that had grown up during the last twenty
years; most of the people did not wish to abandon the achievements of
the Napoleonic era. But the Belgians had no national program of their
own: Napoleon's regime nowhere directly encouraged the growth of
spontaneous group activity and national sentiment, though indirectly
it helped to generate them.

Napoleon was ready to use national aspirations as far as they seemed
compatible with his system, but without having any sincere desire to
satisfy them. He never thought seriously of an independent Poland or
an independent Italy, though from time to time he gave vague encouragement to those who believed in them. For him, nations had no reality.
He created and dissolved new states incessantly, and shifted frontiers and
rulers restlessly. Nor did he encounter opposition from nationalism in
the beginning. The people dissatisfied with his rule were less moved by
national sentiments than by dislike of alien troops who stayed on and
lived off the land and in many cases behaved without tact or restraint.
The people were motivated much more by loyalty to religion or to traditional ways of life than by nationalism. Only towards the end of his
reign did Napoleon succeed, against his intention, in arousing nationalism in some of the peoples subject to or threatened by his rule. Thus
indirectly and unwittingly, Napoleon became a midwife to the birth
of the Age of Nationalism on the continent of Europe.

At the end of 1811, Marshal Louis Nicolas Davout (1770-1823), the
commanding officer in Hamburg, warned Napoleon of the mounting national sentiment in Germany and of the dangers to French rule that this
growth of German nationalism involved. Napoleon rejected the warning;
he did not believe in the possibility of nationalism and in his rebuke he
pointed to the peaceful character of the German people. Germany
seemed to him quiescent and obedient. "If there were a movement in

Germany, it would ultimately be for us and against the small princes." [6] Whatever understanding of nationalism there was in Napoleon's mind applied to Italy. He was the first to create an Italian republic and later a kingdom of Italy, and thus to give a powerful impetus to the slowly awakening demands for Italian unity and nationhood. Later on, he was to say that he had planned eventually "to create a single state out of this great peninsula." But while he had the power, he repeatedly divided Italy up arbitrarily according to what he believed were the momentary interests of his empire and dynasty. On behalf of these interests, had his empire survived, he might have crowned a second son King of Italy and united the country around his throne. [7]

Only when all hopes for empire and dynasty had vanished and Napoleon himself was a captive on St. Helena did he begin to build up a consistent legend about his intentions and plans to promote the liberty of nations and the happiness of Europe. This legend deeply influenced the thought of following generations and prepared the way for a brief rebirth of empire and dynasty. In a famous passage, Napoleon espoused simultaneously the cause of national unity for the four great continental peoples—the French, the Spanish, the Italians and the Germans—and the cause of a united Europe where the same views and interests, laws, and principles, would prevail throughout the continent. Even then, his words betrayed the vagueness of his thinking on these issues. His decisions had been dictated by changing strategic needs of his war plans against England and Russia. Napoleon wished at times to consolidate France, Spain, and Italy into a compact Latin bloc that would be an impregnable barrier against "all the nations of the north." He asked himself why no German prince had used the German demand for unity to his profit:

> Certainly, if heaven had willed that I be born a German prince, I would infallibly have governed thirty million united Germans; and from what I think I know of them, I believe that, once they had elected and proclaimed me, they would never have abandoned me, and I would not be here now.

Napoleon believed he might have led a willing and obedient German nation to dominion over Europe. Little in these words betrays any attachment to France or to the happiness of peoples. But at the same time he sounded a different note.

> Le premier souverain qui, au milieu de la première grande mêlée, embrassera de bonne foi la cause des peuples, se trouvera à la tête de toute l'Europe et pourra tenter tout ce qu'il voudra.

But, even provided that the interests of the various nations and of the whole of Europe did not conflict, the leader of the peoples of the whole continent might discover that it was difficult to "try anything he wished." [8] The cult of force and of limitless empire dominated Napoleon's mind to the last; his dream did not change on St. Helena. With great sincerity he told Benjamin Constant (1767-1830) a few months before he had to leave France: "I wished for the empire of the world; and to insure it, unlimited power was necessary to me. To govern France alone, a constitution may be better." [9] The Age of Nationalism in the nineteenth century rejected the emperor of the world and demanded constitutions.

Napoleon's European union—his continental system—was a weapon in his struggle with England. "Let us be masters of the Channel for only six hours, and we shall be masters of the world." In this struggle, he claimed to represent the interests of mankind and to defend the liberties of all peoples. But the peoples did not agree: they feared Napoleon and the French much more than the English. The English employed the advantages of commerce and inspired jealousy; Napoleon used the means of war and imposed tyranny. In his *De l'esprit de conquête et de l'usurpation dans leurs rapports avec la civilisation européenne* (1813) Benjamin Constant regarded war as the instrument of the past, commerce as that of enlightened civilization:

> War and commerce are only two different means of arriving at the same goal—the possession of what one desires. Commerce is an attempt to receive by agreement what one no longer hopes to conquer by force. A man who would always be the strongest would never think of commerce. It is experience which, in demonstrating to him that war—that is to say, the employment of his force against that of another—is exposed to various resistances and checks, leads him to have recourse to commerce—that is to say, to a more pleasant and certain way of compelling the interests of others to consent to what accommodates his own interest. . . . Carthage, fighting with Rome in ancient times, had to succumb: she had the force of circumstances against her. But if the fight between Rome and Carthage were taking place today, Carthage would have the universe on her side. Elle aurait pour alliés les moeurs actuelles et le génie du monde. [10]

Napoleon rejected the possibility of the application of English liberty in France:

> In the case of a nation like the English where everything is influenced by public opinion, even the actions of the Cabinet and the resolutions of Parliament, it will be easily understood that the press enjoys unlimited freedom. Our constitutions, on the other hand, do not require the interference of the people in state affairs. If the people were not satisfied with this, the exist-

ing organization would have to be completely altered; but it has been proved that such a force of public opinion produces nothing but confusion and excitement, so that a strict surveillance of the press would have to be set up.[11]

On St. Helena, Napoleon spoke more enthusiastically about liberty and the English model. Aware of the contradiction between his words and his acts, he pointed out:

> There is no comparison between my situation and that of the English government. England is able to work on a soil which extends to the very bowels of the earth while I labor only on a sandy surface. England reigns over an established order of things while I had to take upon myself the great charge, the immense difficulty, of conciliating and establishing. I purified the Revolution, in spite of hostile factions. I combined together all the scattered benefits that could be preserved; but I was obliged to protect them with a nervous arm against the attacks of all parties; and in this situation it may truly be said that the public interest, the state, was myself.[12]

While Napoleon rejected liberty, he offered equality:

> I have always been of the opinion that sovereignty lay in the people. The imperial government was a kind of republic. Called to the head of it by the voice of the nation, my maxim was the career open to talents without distinction of birth or fortune.[13]

He had no racial prejudice. Repeatedly he suggested the encouragement of intermarriage between whites and blacks as the best way of establishing peace and civilization in the colonies. To that end he proposed to authorize polygamy, provided that every man took wives of different races and that their children, brought up under the same roof and upon the same footing, would from their infancy learn to consider themselves as equal and in the ties of relationship forget differences of color.[14] On St. Helena he regretted the expedition to St. Domingue. "I ought to have treated with the black chieftains: I ought to have appointed Negroes as officers in their regiments, and made [Pierre Dominique] Toussaint L'Ouverture (c. 1746-1803) viceroy." [15] He not only gave equality to the Jews, but he welcomed their influx into France. In his opinion they supplied very good soldiers for the French army, and in addition, they brought great wealth to France. He was convinced that if his empire had lasted, many more Jews would have immigrated to France, for all the Jews would gradually have come to settle in a country where equality of laws was assured them, and where all honors stood open to them.[16] What Napoleon demanded was loyal and obedient subjects, useful to the state; as long as they were that, he did not inquire into their religion, race, or nationality.

In his feeling for equality Napoleon favored universal military service. "An emperor puts his confidence in national soldiers, not in mercenaries." In a talk with an Englishman who objected to conscription, Napoleon maintained that its burden fell equally upon all ranks. "Oh, how shocking that a gentleman's son should be obliged to defend his country, just as if he were one of the *canaille!* That he should be expected to expose his body, or put himself on a level with the vile plebeian! Yet God made all men alike." [17] Even under Napoleon, conscription was far from all-inclusive. As in the days of the Convention and the Directory, only young unmarried men served, and the wealthy were allowed to buy substitutes. The heaviest manpower burden fell, not upon France, but upon the newly acquired provinces and vassal states. At the same time conscription was very unpopular. In 1811 the number of evaders was estimated at 160,000 for France, and bribery, self-mutilation, and marriages between young men and old women to evade service were not rare. When the Grand Army crossed the borders of Russia in 1812, Frenchmen formed less than half its numbers. The wars of Napoleon had ceased to be national wars: only in the defense of French territory in 1814 and 1815 something like the original national enthusiasm reappeared.[18]

XVII

Nationalism and Liberty

NATIONALISM was at a low ebb in France when Napoleon returned from Russia. The nation was tired of wars and tired of glory. Even Napoleon's retreat to the Rhine at the end of 1813 and his appeal to the memories of 1793 did not rekindle the burnt-out flame. The people had been deprived of initiative and activity for too long. Glory depended on success; when fortune deserted Napoleon, it was quickly forgotten, in the bitter disappointment of the moment, that he had carried the French banners to Madrid and Rome, Berlin and Vienna. He was now held responsible for misfortune and defeat:

> Eh bien! dans tous ces jours d'abaissement, de peine,
> Pour tous ces outrages sans nom,
> Je n'ai jamais chargé qu'un être de ma haine. . . .
> Sois maudit, o Napoléon!
> O Corse à cheveux plats! . . .[1]

The provisional government that Talleyrand formed on April 1, 1814, reminded the French people three days later:

> To end civil discord, you chose as your head a man who appeared on the world stage with the marks of greatness on him. You put all your hopes in him; those hopes have been betrayed; on the ruins of anarchy, he founded nothing but despotism. He should at least, out of gratitude, have become a Frenchman with you. That he has never been. . . . He knew not how to rule, either in the national interest, or in the interest of his despotism. He destroyed whatever he wished to create, and re-created whatever he wished to destroy. He believed only in force. Today he is overthrown by force, a just retribution for his insensate ambition.

Napoleon wished to create an empire out of all proportion; it was time, many Frenchmen felt, that the nation recognized its limits and regained its proper measure. Only on such foundations could true grandeur for France be founded.[2]

A young Frenchwoman who had lived through the Revolution and the Empire observed in 1813:

> All the people have found a patriotic energy to repel us; why did we lack it? What is the fatherland, if not love of long-standing habits, of family, of country, and of quiet happiness? Alas! France at present is nothing more than a garrison where discipline and boredom rule. We will defend this garrison out of obedience, but the inhabitants will not identify themselves with the quarrel, and the conquest of France is but a military affair, threatening only the honor of the army.[3]

Pierre Jean de Béranger (1780-1857), who felt the pulse of the city on March 31, 1814—the day when the victorious allies entered Paris—was convinced that

> If the emperor had been able to read all their hearts, he would doubtless have recognized one of his greatest mistakes, one which the nature of his genius caused him to make. He had gagged the people, he had taken from them all free intervention in their own affairs, and thus obliterated those principles that our revolution had inculcated in us. From this resulted a deep torpor of the sentiments which are most natural to us. For a long time his success took the place of patriotism for us; but, as he had absorbed the whole nation within him, the whole nation fell with him. And in our fall, we did not know, in the face of our enemies, how to be anything more than he had made us.[4]

There still survived republican patriots who had fallen into disfavor with Napoleon because of their outspoken criticism. One of them was Henri Grégoire, who throughout all the vicissitudes of his life remained faithful to the spirit of 1789. A devout Catholic priest, he was the model of a tolerant philanthropist.

> He carried tolerance to an almost unimaginable degree; he seemed to love Jews, Protestants, Anabaptists for their very errors, as a philanthropist most loves those whom he finds the most unhappy. All the pariahs of society found in him a constant defender: at the beginning of his career he worked hard for the improvement of the lot of the Jews, the Irish Catholics, the Negroes, and domestic servants; the same thoughts preoccupied him in his last moments. He had seen in the French Revolution the application of the teachings of the Gospels to political society; Bourdon de l'Oise characterized him perfectly when he reproached him in the Jacobins' club with wishing to christianize the revolution.[5]

The spirit of Grégoire was summed up in a codicil to his will in which he bequeathed six prizes for the best essays on the problems dearest to his heart: how to prove from the Bible and tradition that ecclesiastical or political despotism is contrary to the dogma and morals of the Catholic church; how best to reinvigorate the liberties of the Gallican church; how to imbue scholars, men of letters, and artists with civil courage and dignity so that they do not succumb to a worship of power; how best to extirpate the unjust and barbaric prejudice of the whites against the colored peoples; how to prevent war and to increase the respect of the military for the obligations of a citizen; how to find the causes and remedy for the disparity between technical advance and moral progress.[6] In some ways Grégoire anticipated the reforms planned by Pope John XXIII more than 150 years later.

While Grégoire embodied the humanitarianism of 1789, Lazare Carnot (1753-1823) was the most faithful representative of its nationalism. He voted against the establishment of a hereditary monarchy by Napoleon. In his speech on this occasion he emphasized the fact that he could not consent to regard liberty, a good so superior to all others and without which the others were nothing, as an illusion. "My heart tells me that liberty is possible, that a free regime is easy to maintain and that it is more stable than any arbitrary government." In spite of his refusal to sanction the destruction of liberty, he repeated that he was always ready to sacrifice his dearest affections to the interests of the fatherland.[7] The disaster of 1813 called him from retirement to the defense of his country. He offered Napoleon his services, was appointed commander of the garrison of Antwerp, and proved there "a faithful and incorruptible soldier." When Louis XVIII became King of France, Carnot addressed a memorandum to him in July 1814, in which he emphasized the need of nationalism to unite the French people:

> Only a noble and strong passion can do it, and this passion can only be love of the fatherland. One must therefore insure its birth, one must create a national spirit; that is what we lack, and what we lack to such a degree that we can hardly conceive of it, so that scarcely any of us understands how one can sacrifice one's personal interest to the general interest and forget oneself for the salvation and glory of one's country.

The French, Carnot went on to say, would hardly believe in the possibility of patriotism if they had not seen its development in England, where all private fortunes were tied up with the common good, and where, therefore, everyone was greatly interested in the general welfare. France must develop, he believed, a similar patriotism, though its focus would be different:

England makes it a point of honor to regard herself as the center of great maritime enterprises which unite all nations; France must make it hers to profit from the gifts with which nature has prodigiously endowed her.

He demanded a loving attachment to French soil and its cultivation without any wish for rivalry with the British in foreign trade, supremacy in which was assured to the latter for a very long time by geographic position and the balance of power in Europe. Such a love of the fatherland, Carnot believed, would unite the various national forces in a common sentiment and task and preserve them from adventures and conquest.[8]

At the same time, two of the most influential thinkers of the coming generation, Claude Henri Comte de Saint-Simon (1760-1825), the visionary of early socialism, and Augustin Thierry (1795-1856), his disciple, the future historian, published in October 1814 *De la Réorganisation de la société européenne,* in which they regarded an Anglo-French alliance as desirable but impossible. Half a year later, in their *Opinion sur les mesures à prendre contre la coalition de 1815,* they proposed to found a new Europe on an alliance between the two nations. Such cooperation, they thought, was demanded by interest and necessity alike. Though the authors foresaw that the French would at present reject it, they were convinced that the time would come when such a union would put an end to French turmoil and ills. The two nations were in one respect complementary: Britain had at her disposal accumulated trade capital; France, a fertile soil. More important, however, was their community of political ideas. There was one important difference: Britain had behind her the experience of a hundred and thirty years of the parliamentary form of government upon which the French were only now embarking. Thus the constitutional party in France would find in the British nation much needed support against its two strong domestic enemies—the defenders of despotism and the advocates of an extravagant liberty. The authors regarded France as the only real nation on the continent of Europe at that time; all the other states were merely governments. Therefore, in the relationship between France and Britain, nation could speak to nation and influence the governments to act according to the national will. The Anglo-French alliance, however, would not long remain confined to the two nations. It would form the nucleus around which the other European peoples could organize into free nations.

In line with their reasoning, the two authors demanded that the assembly of the French nation, which Napoleon after his return from Elba had convoked on the Champ de Mai for June 1, 1815, to swear fidelity to the new constitution, should adopt a solemn declaration:

That the English people, by the conformity of our institutions with its own, by that affinity of principles and that community of social interest which are the strongest ties between men, is henceforward our natural ally; that the will of the French nation, that the interest of England and France, the interest of the whole of Europe, demand that this union be rendered more intimate, stronger, and more regular by an accord between the governments; and that, therefore, the assembly order the government that it was to create, to conclude an alliance with the British government.

Saint-Simon and Thierry insisted that the new constitution for France should be postponed until the war crisis of 1815 was averted, so that the nation could deliberate in full freedom.[9]

Their hopes were not realized. The Assembly adopted the Acte Additionnel with which Napoleon hoped to meet the demands for liberal reforms. It was accepted without enthusiasm and without confidence. Napoleon did not like concessions so contrary to his personality and temperament, and the people found them insufficient to safeguard liberty against the return of despotism. But whatever their feeling toward Napoleon, most Frenchmen were willing to fight. They resented the returning Bourbons and émigrés even more than they did Napoleon; they were eager to preserve the social gains of the Revolution, and they felt bitter about the humiliation of France by the invading armies. For the first time, genuine national feeling rallied again around Napoleon.

The defeat at Waterloo brought the Bourbons back. Though the peace terms preserved the French territorial frontiers of 1791, the fall from towering heights of glory and power was too steep not to leave its mark upon French national pride. Strangely, French national resentment turned primarily against England. Waterloo was regarded as an English victory and the outcome of the long wars of the Revolution and of Napoleon was interpreted as a British triumph. That was strange because Britain and Russia protected France in 1815 against the vast territorial demands of Prussia. German politicians, journalists, and writers demanded the annexation of Alsace, of the whole of Lorraine and of the Burgundian Franche-Comté. Even Field Marshal Gneisenau pleaded in an impassionate letter to Prince Hardenberg for establishing "in perpetuity" the security of Belgium, Prussia, and Germany. Most Prussian-German demands of 1871, 1914, and 1940 were anticipated in 1815. Gneisenau also demanded the extradition of Napoleon to Prussia and his execution. "This is a demand of eternal justice—so will es die ewige Gerechtigkeit." Britain saved France in 1815 from a Prussian peace.[10] Nevertheless, French nationalism remained emotionally directed against England for many years. Despite their common concepts of liberty, the two nations did not, as Saint-Simon and Thierry had hoped, unite in the face of a Europe in which nationalism had either not yet awakened the peoples or had turned them away from the concept of a free society based upon rational law to a romantic longing for uniqueness and close communal ties based upon the call of the blood and the lure of the past.[11]

The resentment against the peace treaty of 1815 helped to promote a legendary interpretation of Napoleon which kept his cult alive in France.[12] Yet, in spite of repeated retrogressions to authoritarian rule and the cult of *gloire*, the liberalism of 1789 has proved a lasting heritage in France and in French nationalism. Outside France, the aggressive and absolutist traits of the Napoleonic regime were revived in the twentieth century without the restraints which the survival of the eighteenth-century Enlightenment imposed in France. From his experiences under Napoleon, Benjamin Constant has given a valid characterization of the twentieth-century extremists as men who

> regarded compromise and weakness as ignoble, constitutions and laws as superfluous subtleties, and who despised parliamentary forms for their allegedly unbearable slowness. They preferred rapid and trenchant decisions as in war, and thought unanimity of opinion essential as in an army. Opposition they regarded as disorder; critical reasoning, as revolt; the courts, as military tribunals; the judges, as soldiers who must execute the orders of authority; those who were suspect or accused, as if they were enemies and convicted criminals; and the judgments of the courts as battles in the state of war into which they had transformed government.[13]

The nineteenth century was on the whole a period of the slow but apparently secure growth of constitutional liberties and peaceful commercial intercourse. It was the century which for the first time witnessed in western Europe and North America the activities of organized peace societies. Towards the end of the century, however, Nietzsche predicted the coming of a new and more "virile" age:

> We owe it to Napoleon that several warlike centuries, which have not had their like in past history, may now follow one another—in short, that we have entered upon the classical age of war, war at the same time scientific and popular.

Nietzsche may have been wrong with regard to the warlike "centuries"; it may be that only the decades of 1914 to 1945 were truly "warlike," dominated by the short-lived phenomenon of fascism which glorified war. Perhaps Nietzsche forecast more correctly the coming of the new global era:

> Inescapably, hesitatingly, terrible like fate, the great task and

question approaches: how should the earth as a whole be administered? And to what end should men as a whole—no longer
a people or a race—be raised and bred?

To that end, Nietzsche remarked, "Napoleon wanted *one* Europe, which
was to be the mistress of the world." [14]

Many fundamental traits in Napoleon's nature belong to the second
half of the eighteenth century; others anticipated the first half of the
twentieth century. His global aspirations appeared a "violent anachro-
nism" in the nineteenth-century Age of Nationalism. At its beginning,
for the protection of their tranquillity and diversity, the other peoples
united against him and his universal empire. Their resistance sealed his
fate. In the first war of nationalities he perished:

> Il fit du glaive un sceptre, et du trône une tente,
> Tout son règne fut un combat. . . .
> Il passa par la gloire, il passa par le crime,
> Il n'est arrivé qu'au malheur.[15]

In 1829, long after Napoleon's fall and death, Goethe read the
Mémoires sur Napoléon by Louis Antoine Fauvelet de Bourrienne (1769-
1834), which appeared in that year. Bourrienne was Napoleon's fellow-
student in the military school in Brienne and later his personal secretary.
Still later he turned against Napoleon and ended as an ultraroyalist.
The *Mémoires* did not depress Goethe nor diminish his admiration for
the Emperor. "The power of truth is great," he told Eckermann.

> The halo, the aura of illusions, with which the journalists,
> historians, and poets have invested Napoleon, disappears be-
> fore the terrible reality of this book, but the hero does not lose
> an inch in the process; instead he grows in stature as he grows
> in truth.[16]

In his devotion to the Emperor, Goethe underestimated the titanic and
destructive elements in Napoleon, to whom "the impossible, on the lips
of power, is only a declaration of impotence." A man alone against the
world, Napoleon in his arrogance rose above the common law in the
certainty of his individual mission. What would happen if more than a
century later nations followed his example and rose—without the safe-
guards of the Enlightenment's respect for reasonableness and for the
essential equality of all men and peoples—above the common law, willing
to stand alone to impose themselves upon the world, and bear this burden
in the certainty of a historical or biological mission?

Après la France, l'Allemagne est la nation que la révolution française a le plus remuée

> —Eugène Lerminier, *Au delà du Rhin* (Paris 1835) II, 229

Überdies will jede Nation das ihr eigentümliche Gute so weit verbreiten als sie irgend kann und soviel an ihr liegt, das ganze Menschengeschlecht sich einverleiben, zufolge eines von Gott den Menschen eingepflanzten Triebes, auf welchem die Gemeinschaft der Völker, ihre gegenseitige Reibung aneinander und ihre Fortbildung beruhet.

> —Johann Gottlieb Fichte, 1807

Eine uns eigene grosse deutsche Aufgabe haben wir zu lösen: den echt deutschen Staat haben wir auszubilden, wie er dem Genius der Nation entspricht.

> —Leopold von Ranke, *Zur Geschichte Deutschlands und Frankreichs im 19. Jahrhundert. Sämtliche Werke,* 49/50 (Leipzig 1887), p. 71

Part Two • Germany

XVIII

The French Revolution
and Central Europe

ON THE European continent political life in the modern sense of the
word began with the French Revolution. The eyes of Europe were turned
toward France; contact with the ideas of the French Revolution slowly
awakened the dormant political life and thought in other European
countries, especially in Germany and Italy. Using propaganda and the
force of arms, the French Revolution wished to spread its universal
message of liberty and dignity to all individuals and to all peoples;
it did it as a French message establishing the superiority of French
civilization as the most rational, enlightened, and human type of civilization. French nationalism set the example for the unification of a nation;
in Italy and Germany, French armies swept away most of the feudal
encumbrances which impeded the process of national unification. But the
combination of cosmopolitan individualism with French nationalism,
which appeared natural to the French, was not easily accepted by the
non-French peoples who came under the influence of the French
Revolution. The idea that a tyrant might be expelled, the cult of liberty,
the aspiration toward nationhood one and indivisible, the longing for a
new national cohesion and a new national spirit, the idea of a state
rooted in popular consent and enthusiasm—all these concepts of the
French Revolution spread to Italy and Germany, were eagerly learned
from France. But the emphasis shifted: the tyrants to be expelled were
French influence and French armies of occupation; the liberty worshiped
was not so much individual freedom from authoritarian government as
national freedom from foreign governments. The great Italian nationalist
of this period, Vincenzo Cuoco (1770-1823), summed up this shift in
attitude in his *Saggio Storico* of the Neapolitan revolution of 1799.
"Strange character of all the peoples of this earth!" he exclaimed. "The

desire to give them an exaggerated liberty awakens in them a longing for freedom from the liberators themselves."

Thus the new feeling of nationalism and of national pride which began spreading throughout Europe was soon in sharp opposition to the French nationalism from which it had received its great impulse. It looked for its justification to its own national heritage and strove for the glorification of that heritage. Yet in the first part of the nineteenth century this nationalism hardly influenced the people; it was largely the concern of intellectuals and writers who, fighting against the preponderant influence of French civilization, extolled the beauty of their own language and literature in contrast to that of the French. Out of the myths of the past and out of dreams of the future, German and Italian authors created an ideal fatherland long before an actual fatherland, often very different from the dream, became a reality. The process of building a nation was reversed. In France, as in Great Britain and the United States, the struggle for a new political and social reality, the work of statesmen, jurists, and legislators, had preceded the cultural manifestations of national life; in Germany and Italy the cultural rejuvenation, the work of intellectuals, writers, and teachers, preceded and was separated from the political and social transformation. The nationalism of the French Revolution was in its origin linked with the philosophy of individual liberty and rational cosmopolitanism. Nationalism in Germany and Italy, born under the influence of France and in the struggle against her, necessarily tended, for its own self-preservation, to emphasize elements contrary to the essence of French nationalism. Other nationalisms thus not only became anti-French but could easily lead to a revolt against the spirit of the Enlightenment and its rationalist and cosmopolitan tendencies. The contact between national cultures in the Age of Nationalism not only frequently generated and deepened antagonism between nations but also produced a cultural conflict, an opposition of ideas, which invested the struggle between nations with the halo of a quasi-religious crusade.

Among the European countries deeply affected by the events in France, Germany offers the most fertile field for the study of the development of the idea of nationalism. No other country presents a similar wealth of remarkable personalities and startling theories in the Napoleonic period. The Germans have been for a very long time a people more enamored of the pursuit of pure ideas than the Western nations, and they have throughout shown a greater liking for systematic thoroughness. They have called themselves, and not without justification, a people of thinkers and poets. Inferior in political and social life to their western neighbors, they quickly became their equals in philosophy, poetry, and music in the late eighteenth century. On the other hand, they were in every respect more advanced than their neighbors in the east and southeast. Germany lay in the center of Europe; as the result of history it had ill-defined and shifting boundaries, in this respect resembling rather the lands of eastern than of western Europe, where thanks to geography and history the nations had gained much earlier a distinct geographic and political definiteness. Germany became in many ways a mediator; it received its ideas and civilization from the West; it transformed them and handed them on to the East in their transformed form: this holds especially true of nationalism. It was not Western nationalism but its German form that aroused central and eastern European nationalism. Within Germany itself the emphasis in the Age of Nationalism shifted from the west to the east: from the old German cultural soil which had been fertilized from early times by Roman and Western influences to eastern Germany, an originally Slavic land which had been conquered and colonized by the Germans in the later Middle Ages. Napoleon's Rhenish Confederation represented an attempt to plant the center of Germany firmly in the West and to turn German eyes westward. It was a passing effort which ended in failure. In the Age of Nationalism the Germans looked less and less to their free cities, so numerous in western and southern Germany, and more and more to the court of Berlin for leadership.

Germany not only occupied a central position with regard to cultural influences and ideas but also with regard to social structure and economic development. Nationalism in Britain, in the United States, in France, and in the Low Countries was a middle-class movement. In Germany the middle classes were much weaker than in the West, though much stronger than in the East. In Germany as in Italy they lacked the strength of economic independence based upon freedom of opportunity and a sense of initiative and the experience in self-government and in executive administrative positions. In Russia and in Poland, in Hungary and in the Balkans, the situation was even worse. There, at the end of the eighteenth century, an educated native middle class hardly existed. Whatever middle class there was, was largely of German descent or under German cultural influence. Nowhere in central and eastern Europe was there even the beginning of an industrial working class, and the peasants lived, at least outside western Germany, in the utmost poverty and illiteracy, oppressed by the burden of serfdom, by military service, and by the weight of the system of taxation. In Austria the enlightened reforms of Joseph II had improved the status of the peasants; in Germany east of the Elbe, in southern Europe, in Poland, Russia, and the Balkans the peasants continued to vegetate in misery and degradation. Thus the idea of nationalism began to penetrate at the beginning of the nineteenth century from the West into lands with a different structure, to a soil unprepared for modern industrial societies, so that the nationalism growing up there became different in many of its implications. In seventeenth-century England and under English influence in eighteenth-century France, a surprisingly large number of people were interested in experimental science and in practical political problems and social reforms. In Germany, in southern and eastern Europe, this class was very rare. There nationalism developed under the influence of speculative thinkers; many of them were impassioned dreamers rather than men with a responsible contact with reality.

Western nationalism lived predominantly in the present, German and Eastern nationalism in the past and in the future. The study and interpretation of the past, undertaken largely to provide an inspiration for future action and to find "historical rights" to support and justify exorbitant claims, frequently became a source and prime mover of the new national movements. The motivating forces in the life of modern nations can hardly be discovered in what really happened in the past, but rather in the way in which each people interprets or misinterprets its history. The peoples who wake up to national consciousness gain awareness of themselves and a clearly defined identity through their interpretation of history. There they find or think to find a valid justification for their passionate desires and convincing examples of their own virtues. The road to the future is mapped out as an obligating legacy from the past, as a manifest destiny leading them on. From the material of history they create their national myths.

It is a fascinating task to study these myths—myths of the peoples about themselves and myths about other, especially "hostile" peoples— for these myths open the way to an understanding of the "national soul" in its hopes and its hidden fears which underlie the great collective emotions. It is important to take these myths very seriously. They contain a factual kernel of historical truth which lends them their power of conviction, but which is often uncritically magnified in a flood of popularizing articles and speeches. This myth tends to assume a dogmatic character in elementary education, so much so that it becomes an almost instinctive and self-evident conviction. In Germany and later in the eastern lands, "Westernizers" have fought valiantly in the name of historical criticism and of rational common sense against these more extreme myths. Their efforts had some influence with the educated classes and often promoted a more cautious approach to national claims; but among the masses the myths, with their emotional appeal and their incitement to action, prevailed, and in the Age of Nationalism—different in this from the Enlightenment or the Age of Reason—the masses grew steadily in importance as the determining factor of political life.[1] National myths have been neither consistent nor constant. A nation's consciousness of itself, of its character and its past, has frequently changed in the course of history and under its impact. The German mind and the German self-image were different in the second half of the nineteenth century from what they had been a hundred years before. The new German self-image was prepared by the impact which the Napoleonic wars made on Germany; it was broadened by the defeat of 1848 and by Bismarck's triumph, and then carried to a new height by the spirit of 1914 and the unexpected outcome of the war.

As the land of the center, Germany had a twofold choice. It could stay wide open to the influences from west and east, from south and north, becoming truly the heart of Europe, generous and full of sympathy, a guardian of peace and equilibrium, constitutionally unable and psychologically unwilling to centralize its forces for aggressive and expanding purposes. That was in various forms the idea which inspired the German political scientists of the eighteenth century and motivated their praise of the weakness of the Empire. This idea underlay Goethe's concept of world literature; it bestowed upon the melting pot of the imperial city of Vienna, with its mixture of races and civilizations, the mellow charm of a capital which remained international and European even in the Age of Nationalism. But there was a second choice possible for Germany, and the tendencies of the Age of Nationalism rather invited it. Germany could try to isolate itself from Europe, regarding itself not as a center but as a summit rising from the periphery and at the same time separated from it. Under these conditions the center, thrown back upon itself, could easily feel itself encircled by the periphery, forced to gather its strength for the defense of its lofty and exposed position and to organize it to control the periphery through aggressive expansion which alone seemed to promise security. These alternatives presented themselves not only to Germany but in varying degrees to all non-Western peoples. In this respect, too, thanks to its geographic and historical situation, Germany set the pace and worked out some exemplary solutions. The alternatives were ever present in German nationalism, but as the Age of Nationalism developed, the second alternative—isolation and domination—grew in preponderance.

Thus for the history of nationalism few epochs were as decisive as its development in Germany between 1789 and 1815. Under the impact of the French example, the larger of the German states had begun to adopt rational administrative forms which elsewhere became the mold of the modern nation states. On the other hand, in the venerable and ineffectual constitution of the Holy Roman Empire, medieval universal ideas, long discarded in the West, continued to exercise their influence. Since the end of the Middle Ages no political reality had corresponded to the concept of a German nation, but German writers of the Renaissance emphasized past German greatness and future German mission more extravagantly than humanists had ever dared in other lands, where thoughts were more restrained by reality. The Reformation which originated in Germany and which found in Luther a "national" spokesman gave a strong impetus to the feeling of separateness from and opposition to the universal church and community. Traditions of social subordination and passive obedience to authority combined with daring thought and inventive imagination in the realm of the mind to keep the tension great between a reality and an ideal which seemed to belong to two different worlds without any visible contact. At the same time new forces were slowly taking shape. In the second half of the eighteenth century Germany overcame the consequences of the devastations of the Thirty Years War. The nation, hardly yet conscious of any political existence, nevertheless felt its strength and numbers growing. Its intellectual classes, without any political and social responsibilities, were bursting with ideas which they thought themselves entitled to indulge in freely. Yet ideas influence reality; if conceived and enunciated without a sense of responsibility for social reality, they may easily produce a deformed reality and a psychological attitude which oscillates between overestimation and underestimation, without a frame of reference tested by experience. The idealism of Fichte and Hegel, the dreams of Novalis, the brilliant formulations of Schlegel and Adam Müller opened no doors to a responsible mastery of reality. They were, at their best, lofty excursions in the realm of thought, "verstiegen im Reiche der Gedanken," but dangerous by reason of their claims to explain or change reality through their surrealistic concepts. Yet they exercised a disturbing and profound influence on politics and history in Germany and other lands where the cautious and sober empiricism of a Locke or a Hume, the skeptical and rational clarity of a Descartes or a Voltaire, the critical analysis of a Kant, never took deep root.

XIX

Madame de Staël and Cultural Nationalism

THE Age of Nationalism transformed not only political relations but also cultural contacts. No longer was civilization based on common ideas and traditions exchanged among individuals of various lands within one republic of letters; it was replaced by contacts between national literatures—the term Nationalliteratur now became common in Germany—each written in a different language and above all in a different spirit. The conviction grew that literature and philosophy were not merely the work of individual genius, but were shaped and determined by the conditions of society and the traditions of nationality. Several leading eighteenth-century thinkers raised the point. Germaine Necker, Baronne de Staël-Holstein (1766-1817) was the first to establish it clearly at the turn of the century in her long essay *De la littérature considérée dans ses rapports avec les institutions sociales* (1800). This daughter of a Genevan Calvinist, who as minister of the expiring French monarchy had been the hope of the middle classes, started her literary career with a treatise on Rousseau's writings and character (1788).

Married to a Swedish diplomat, finding in the France of 1789 her spiritual home and the center of her affections, Germaine de Staël became one of the most important figures in the unfolding of early modern nationalism and the first mediator among the national literatures of the period. Burning with ambition to become a leader of public opinion, she was one of the outstanding representatives of the liberal nationalism of the beginning French Revolution which drew its inspiration from the Anglo-American example and which believed with equal firmness in the liberty of the individual, in the national foundation of modern politics, and in the desirability of a universal open society. Widely traveled in many European lands, learned and full of curiosity, she established through her personal contacts and her widely read works an international exchange of national civilizations. Her love of liberty and her great and never satisfied political ambitions brought her into conflict with Napoleon. The ensuing years of exile were put to good use; they made of the French author a European figure.

In her novel *Corinne ou Italie* (1807) and in her treatise on German literature and the German national character *De l'Allemagne* (1810) Mme de Staël set herself a twofold task: on the one hand, to convey the message of French liberal nationalism to Italy and to Germany, to arouse them to political life, to the desire for individual liberty and national unity, and on the other hand, to acquaint the French public with the little known Italian and German literary life of the period. The new intellectual developments in Germany, the philosophy of Kant and Fichte, the poetry of Goethe and Schiller, the intensity of German literary life amongst the romanticists, had passed almost unnoticed in France. Mme de Staël, always deeply impressed by foreign life and full of sympathy for it, introduced to the French a glowing image of Germany which was no longer fully true even when she wrote it and which was soon to give way to new forces shaping a different Germany. But her heart-warming picture of a highly gifted, earnest, and dedicated people of poets and thinkers who led a peaceful, modest, and virtuous existence in small picturesque towns without practical interests or political ambitions deeply influenced the idea which French intellectuals made themselves of Germany. With them it became the foundation of love and admiration for Germany, above all for the German mind, which dominated France until the war of 1870. Mme de Staël contrasted the coldness of Napoleon's classicist imperial style with the inspiration of German poetical enthusiasm. Her Germany was a country of romantic ruins and peaceful sleepy towns, of wise patriarchs and contented burghers, of social tranquillity and profound religious feeling. Above this graceful stillness, unruffled by greed for power or social conflicts, rose the realm of the German mind, detached from all earthly considerations, given to ecstasy and dreams, in quest of the good and the beautiful and always in search of the infinite. The land seemed full of historical monuments and memories. In the beginning of the book she heard the Rhine "telling the great deeds of times long past, and the shade of Arminius seems still to wander along its steep slopes." But the ancient glories appeared dead to her; she was shocked by the political immobility, the idyllic quietness which contrasted with the glorious heroic past.

One could say that the people of the north, the conquerors of the world, left in Germany when they departed from her, under various forms, traces of their past, and that the whole country now seems a place which recalls the sojourn of a great people who have long abandoned it. This immobilized picture of actions which were alive a long time ago leaves a distressing impression.[1]

In the midst of many virtues and charms, the visitor from the West missed the force of public opinion, a national character and a national will, a center of unity for all the wealth of diversity. She found the Germans "by nature inclined to literature and philosophy":

> However, the separation of classes, which is more pronounced in Germany than anywhere else, harms in certain regards the mind itself. The aristocracy has there too few ideas, and the educated classes have too little contact with the practical world. Imagination rather than clarity of thought characterizes the Germans. A center and limits are needed for their prominent talents of thought, which easily rises and loses itself in vagueness, which penetrates and disappears in the depths and confounds itself through too much analysis.[2]

Mme de Staël wished to acquaint the French with German thought and thinkers. Prussia and northern Protestant Germany appeared to her "la patrie de la pensée." But she wished to do more: to arouse in the Germans the desire for national sentiment and united action, an action which by necessity must turn against France and against Napoleon, whose ambitions and aggressions Mme de Staël consistently condemned. Though the political problems of Germany were hardly touched upon in her book, her intentions were unmistakably clear; it was therefore not surprising that Napoleon's censor did not allow the book to appear in 1810. In an extremely polite letter the Minister of Police pointed out to madame that she apparently did not find the air of France to her taste and that on the other hand the French were not yet reduced to a state in which they would have to search for models amongst the peoples whom she admired. "Votre dernier ouvrage n'est point français," the Minister wrote.

When the book appeared three years later, Mme de Staël published the letter in the preface, dated October 1, 1813, a few days before the Battle of Leipzig, and in an important comment she defended her theory of nationalism. "Difference of language, natural frontiers, memories of common history, all these factors contribute to create among men these great individualities which are called nations." They constitute the chief actors of history, they create destiny. "The submission of one nation to another is against nature. Who believes today in the possibility of breaking up Spain, Russia, England, France? Why should it be different in the case of Germany?" When Mme de Staël wrote *De l'Allemagne,* she stated regretfully and apprehensively that the Germans were not a nation. Now, four years later she pointed to the beginnings of German nationalism and its struggle against the French. "Does one not see some German lands [those of the Rhenish Confederation] in fighting against their fellow Germans expose themselves to the contempt of their own French allies?" Against France, which had succumbed to the despotism of Napoleon and to the lure of glory, she upheld the cause of the Germans, who she believed were fighting for liberty and for a true patriotism, and of the English, whom she admired because they had fought during ten years to preserve Europe from anarchy and during ten more years to preserve her from despotism. "The fortunate English constitution was the goal of the hopes and efforts of the French at the beginning of the Revolution; my loyalty has remained where theirs was then." Mme de Staël was faithful to the liberal nationalism of 1789 and its faith in the collaboration of free peoples in the cause of constitutional liberty.[3]

Mme de Staël believed in cultural and political independence and at the same time in cultural and political collaboration. She was afraid of the uniformity which Napoleon's rule might impose upon the whole of Europe. When she visited Russia in 1812 she expressed her preference for Russians dressed in their native oriental costumes instead of in European fashion; in the latter case

> they would enter too easily into that great uniformity of Napoleon's despotism which brings to all the nations, first military conscription, then war taxes, and finally the Code Napoléon, in order to rule entirely different nations in the same manner.

Mme de Staël warned the European peoples against a desire to imitate the French.

> In Vienna they believe too much that good taste requires speaking only French; whereas the glory and even the pleasure of each country consists always in the national character and spirit. . . . The superiority of French manners has perhaps prepared the foreigners to think the French invincible. There is only one way to resist this superiority; it consists in very determined national habits and manners.[4]

Energetic actions, she believed, could not develop except in free countries where the patriotic sentiments flow as irresistibly through the soul as blood flows through the arteries. But free countries must be peaceful countries; otherwise they may lose their liberty. Freedom makes strong, but only freedom with justice. In the early years of the Revolution the French resisted Europe in a war of independence. Then the French were stronger than the whole of Europe because they were united by the force of free public opinion. But with the French revolutionary armies marching from victory to victory, Mme de Staël called for moderation:

> You Frenchmen, you who have repelled the whole of Europe, you who triumph, is it not you who should calm the furious desire for revenge? Give peace to Europe, ask for it if it is necessary. You need it more than your enemies; for that liberty which alone can plead for you effectively before the judgment of history, depends on peace.

If the French did not achieve peace and liberty, nothing could excuse their terrible wars of defense.

> Your victories would be confounded with your carnages and they would leave in your history nothing but annals of death. You may conquer everything but the independent esteem of just minds and courageous souls; yet these are the only approbations which by their impartiality are worthy of consideration.[5]

While exhorting France to peace and cautioning her against the intoxications of triumph and conquest, Mme de Staël approved and praised wars of defense and of national liberation. In a famous passage at the end of her *De l'Allemagne,* deeply influenced by the German romanticists and by her own poetic sentimentality, she saw enthusiasm as one of the great moving, beautiful forces of life and history. It elevates us above ourselves, she wrote, above our immediate interests, and unites us with the divine and with the universal harmony. She called her readers to the greatness of self-sacrifice for the triumph of noble causes and she exalted wars of national liberation.[6] Before the eyes of the defeated of the day, the Germans and the Italians, she held up the vision of a possible victory tomorrow, if ever a true patriotism would be aroused among them. "Men, all men, march to the help of their country when the circumstances demand," she wrote in 1809, at a time when few Germans felt any patriotism and when many of them were aligned on the French side,

> but if they are inspired by enthusiasm for their fatherland, what a beautiful movement does then take hold of them. The soil which saw them born, the earth of their ancestors, the sea which laves the rocks, long memories, far-reaching hopes, all that rises around them like a call to battle; each heartbeat is a thought of love and pride. God has given the fatherland to men who can defend it, to women who for its sake consent to the dangers of their brothers, husbands, and sons. When dangers begin to threaten it, a fever without shivers and without frenzy hastens the flow of blood in the veins; every effort in such a struggle springs from the deepest innermost recesses of the soul.

Let the bugle sound, let the national flag unfurl in the air, and you will see eyes normally so gentle, so ready to become gentle again at the sight of misfortune, suddenly animated by a sacred and terrible will. Neither wounds nor blood will cause any shudders; there is no longer any question of pain or death, but only of a self-offering to the god of the armies; no regret or incertitude interferes any longer with the most desperate resolution; and if the whole heart is in it, one enjoys existence admirably.[7]

But independence of the fatherland was to Mme de Staël only important if it was a fatherland of free individuals, protected against domestic tyranny and its attempts to stifle personal independence and to impose uniformity. In her *Considerations sur les principaux événements de la Révolution Française* which she wrote in 1815 and which was published only after her death, she left a passionate defense of the principles of 1789. The English constitution appeared to her to be the model of liberty and reason, but she rejected the idea advanced by many after the experiences of the Terror of Robespierre and the despotism of Napoleon that the French were unfit for liberty. She pointed out that England had to pass through long periods of bloody turmoil before making liberty secure in a wise equilibrium. To England, she wrote, belonged the glory of having first established representative government, but the vivacity and vanity with which one reproaches the French would attach the French even more strongly to liberty once they made up their minds about the need. "No people of Europe can be compared to the English since 1688; between them and the continent there are one hundred twenty years of social improvements." But the French are following suit.

They are the third nation, if one counts the Americans, that has tried its hand at representative government; and the example of those who preceded them in the attempt finally begins to guide them.[8]

The author who had introduced Italy and Germany to the French now introduced to them English political life and ideals. She understood the dependence of English prosperity on English liberty, and she was confident that in spite of some temporary deviations at the end of the Napoleonic wars the cause of liberty would progress in Britain. Faithful to the convictions of liberal nationalism, she regarded individual liberty as the true bulwark of national strength.

All men are more or less attached to their country. The memories of childhood and the habits of youth form that inexpressible love of the fatherland which one must recognize as a virtue, for it has its source in all genuine sentiments. But in a great state, liberty and the happiness that this liberty gives can also inspire a true patriotism; for that matter nothing is comparable to the power of public feeling in England.[9]

Mme de Staël's devotion to freedom never blinded her to the peculiarities of nationality. In a country as devoid of personal liberty, as remote from England or America, as Russia was when she visited there in 1812, she admired the energy and the will to sacrifice which the whole nation showed in the cause of national defense. The religious and the military spirit predominated so much that they made possible actions which in more civilized countries could be attributed only to liberty. "It is remarkable how pronounced public feeling is in Russia," she wrote.

> The reputation of invincibility which repeated successes have given the nation, the natural pride of the leaders, the devotion of the people, the deep influence of religion, the hatred of foreigners which Peter I had tried to destroy in order to enlighten and civilize his land but which has remained in the Russian blood and which reawakens as occasion arises—all these reasons together make this nation a highly energetic one. . . . Even civil servants have in Russia a rank corresponding to a rank in the army. The spirit of the nation is wholly turned towards war.

Mme de Staël found in Russia, in spite of the progress of civilization since Peter I, a surviving barbarism; "I understand by this word a certain primitive energy which with some nations can take the place of the concentrated strength of liberty." [10]

For all her love of the liberty which Britain and America had and which she hoped would grow in France, the exiled authoress had no desire to see other nations shaped after their model. "Strange craze of the French Revolutionaries who wish to oblige all countries to adopt the same political organization as France!" she wrote.[11] In Russia she deplored the fact that the Russian writers, like so many others on the European continent, imitated French literature, which on account of its very beauties fitted only the French. She recommended to them to turn rather to ancient Greece as a model; but, she insisted, Russian writers must above all derive their poetry from the most intimate depth of their own soul. Years before, in her novel on Italy, contemplating Greeks in their oriental costumes working in Ancona, she had remarked:

> L'art de la civilization tend sans cesse à rendre tous les hommes semblables en apparence, et presque en réalité; mais l'esprit et l'imagination se plaisent dans les différences qui carac-

térisent les nations: les hommes ne se ressemblent entre eux que par l'affectation ou le calcul; mais tout ce qui est naturel est varié. C'est donc un petit plaisir, au moins pour les yeux, que la diversité des costumes; elle semble promettre une manière nouvelle de sentir et de juger.[12]

National differences seemed to her to express themselves above all in letters and philosophy. They alone could transform a territory into a fatherland by endowing the nation with similar tastes and sentiments. Through them and not through force or military strength, a nation could be established on firm foundations. In the military spirit there was too little spontaneity, too much uniformity, to allow that strength in liberty, variety, and self-expression which alone rendered a nation fully alive. The military spirit was the same in all centuries and in all countries; it could not form the true character of a nation.[13] Only intensity of thought and the art of its expression furnished the necessary basis for liberty. Such intensity of thought she found in Italy and above all in Germany, and she expected that these thoughts would transform themselves into generous actions.[14] In 1813, witnessing the German War of Liberation, she believed these hopes realized. "What the philosophers have put into a system, becomes now reality, and the independence of the soul will establish that of the states." [15] But her generosity led her to misread the significance and the strength of the events. The philosophy of the generation of 1813 in Germany had little to do with the ideas of 1789 which Mme de Staël believed would bring to Germany individual liberty and to Europe peace among free nations. Germany in her first great national effort helped to break the domination of Napoleon, whom Mme de Staël so passionately hated, and established national independence from France, but there was neither strength nor enthusiasm enough to establish among the Germans themselves the secure reign of individual liberty. Many of the thinkers and poets so dear to Mme de Staël had promoted a way of thought highly critical of and even opposed to her cherished ideas of 1789. The French Revolution found no enduring response in Germany.

XX

The French Revolution and
Eighteenth-Century Germany

THE first news of the French Revolution evoked a warm and even enthusiastic response in the hearts of many German intellectuals. Few, however, understood its political and social implications; the great majority were hardly interested in them. The elaboration of a constitution, the new political power of the Third Estate, the lifting of all the traditional restrictions upon trade and industry, the emancipation of the peasantry—none of these changes of the foundations of national life made much impression on most of the sympathetic onlookers east of the Rhine. What they approved and greeted was not the changing reality, but the ideas which in so many discourses and pamphlets were proclaimed as the moving force behind it, ideas familiar to educated Germans because they formed the common intellectual climate of enlightened eighteenth-century Europe: the growth of the individual to greater stature through freedom, the realization of the natural laws of reason, the revival of the ancient traditions of liberty and patriotism, and the purifying return to the natural goodness of which Rousseau had been the prophet. Old men like Klopstock and Kant, young men like Friedrich von Gentz (1764-1832) and Georg Wilhelm Friedrich Hegel (1770-1831) welcomed the Revolution as a blessing for mankind, as a revelation of man's moral character. Gentz, who was so soon to become highly critical of the events in France, wrote on December 5, 1790, to Christian Garve (1742-1798), a popular philosophical writer of his day:

> I would regard the failure of the Revolution as one of the greatest misfortunes that have ever befallen the human race. The Revolution is the first practical triumph of philosophy, the first example of a form of government founded upon principles and upon an integrated consistent system of thought. It is the

hope and the solace for so many ancient evils under which
mankind groans. Should this Revolution recede, then all these
evils would become ten times more incurable. I can imagine
vividly how everywhere the silence of despair would admit,
contrary to reason, that men can be happy only as slaves, and
how both great and small tyrants would use this terrible admission to take revenge for the terror which the awakening of
the French nation struck into their hearts.[1]

A few German intellectuals persisted in their enthusiasm even after
the idyllic honeymoon of the Revolution had passed and civil war and
armed conflict with the neighboring states revealed some of the serious
implications of the regeneration of mankind. National feeling and consciousness were so widely unknown in Germany then that political considerations hardly entered into the judgment. Neither the friends nor
the enemies of the Revolution asked themselves whether a France greatly
strengthened by the newly gained national integration would present a
danger to German national interests. The Germans who condemned the
French Revolution did so because it threatened to destroy the traditional
foundations of law and order. The others were convinced that providence
had chosen the French, the most advanced civilized people of the period,
to start the great work of the reformation of the world, to be joined
soon by all other nations. Even the invasion of Germany by the French
armies hardly aroused any patriotic resistance. Nobody thought of Germany, of German honor or of German power. The statesmen tried to
keep their countries as far as possible out of the danger of war and to
profit as much as possible from the changes brought about by the war,
without any regard for the interests of the German Reich or of a German nation which few recognized as a reality and even fewer as a
desideratum. The German poets did not call for patriotic resistance
and did not voice the wrath of an outraged nation; they moaned over
the devastation of the peaceful countryside and the suffering of peasants
and burghers, and they expressed their longing for peace and reconciliation, for the abolishment of arms and armaments, and for the undisturbed
flow of tranquil and unheroic days.[2]

Representative among the leading enthusiasts for the Revolution was
Georg Forster (1754-1794), a widely traveled man and fertile writer
who in 1788 was appointed librarian to the ecclesiastical Elector of
Mainz. The Society of the Friends of Liberty and Equality which was
founded in that city on October 25, 1792, after the example of the
Jacobin clubs of Paris, became the center of French propaganda in the
Rhineland. Addressing it on November 15, Forster exclaimed:

What were we only three weeks ago? What could transform
us so miraculously and so fast from oppressed, maltreated,

silent serfs of a priest into upright, vocal, free citizens, into daring friends of liberty and equality, determined to live as free men or to die? Fellow-citizens! Brothers! The force which could transform us in such a way can also fuse the people of France and the people of Mainz into one nation. Our languages are different—but must therefore our concepts be different? Are liberté and égalité no longer the same jewels of mankind when we call them Freiheit und Gleichheit? [3]

Forster regarded the Rhine as the "natural frontier of the great republic which does not desire to make any conquests but only to receive those nations which join it voluntarily." With these convictions he went to Paris as one of the Rhenish deputies to ask for the incorporation of districts west of the Rhine into France. His cosmopolitan enthusiasm for human freedom misunderstood both the nature of the French Revolution and the mentality of his fellow Germans. The French did not live up to his expectations of a regenerated mankind; the Germans—with the exception of a few writers indulging in lofty theories—had no use for liberty and equality. The citizens of the quiet German free cities were prouder of their peaceful order than desirous of getting out on the dangerous path of the new liberty.

The short-lived "liberty" of Mainz was a rather isolated case in Germany, without any roots in actual conditions. When a young enthusiast of Mainz sent an appeal to freedom, "Aufruf zur Freiheit," to other free cities, a citizen of Frankfurt-am-Main answered with an appeal to tranquillity, "Aufruf zur Ruhe." In mediocre but undoubtedly sincere poetry he pointed out that the subjects of Frankfurt had enjoyed peace without a liberty tree and expressed gratitude for the fact that the French army had not yet liberated them. Such a liberator, the author considered, was much too expensive for a city, because he brought with him hard times for the citizens. Even more outspoken was a "Freiheitslied für Hamburger" which was distributed as a leaflet in 1792. It compared the true liberty of the people of Hamburg with the oppressive and boastful freedom of Mainz and of the French.[4] Yet all these leaflets directed against the Revolution and the invading army showed no hostility to the French. The Hamburg poet was proud and enamored of Hamburg; he expressed no sympathy or concern for Germany. In spite of numerous writings, the French Revolution made hardly any impression upon wider German circles. It aroused neither social unrest nor national consciousness.[5] The political message of the Revolution remained unheeded in a Germany which was unprepared for it. Only the Napoleonic empire and its impact on Germany slowly, in the course of a decade, aroused the Germans, more to national consciousness than to a demand for social and political reforms. In the last decade of the eighteenth century even men who later became fervent patriots felt no concern for Germany's future. Friedrich Perthes, then a young man of twenty in Hamburg, greeted the French victories in 1792 over the German armies: "As man and citizen of the world I rejoice over the progress of the French armies; as a German I wish to cry; for it will be an eternal shame for the Germans to have yielded to the good cause only by force." [6]

Exaggerated fears of the effects of the French Revolution led in some tiny German states to petty police measures combatting imaginary dangers.[7] More serious, because deeply resented by the German educated class, was the suppression of the freedom of discussion in theological and philosophical matters in Prussia under Frederick Wilhelm II, which forced the leading Berlin periodicals to leave Berlin. These measures, however, indicated rather the reaction and inefficiency of many German courts, great and small alike, than the desire on the part of the people to limit or overthrow the arbitrary rule of most of their princes. Hardly any of the German intellectuals who wrote enthusiastic verses or pamphlets about the Revolution ever drew the conclusion that what was right and reasonable in France might be desirable in Germany too. The masses were bound by traditional obedience; the educated classes confined themselves to dreams in the free realm of the mind; both desired above all peace. Many turned against the French Revolution when it began to carry its message by the force of arms into other lands. Klopstock, who had celebrated in Hamburg the Bastille Day of 1790 by wearing the revolutionary tricolor, published in 1795 a poem in which he reminded the French of their sacred promise never again to wage a war of conquest. Not as a German but as a lover of peace and mankind, he bitterly lamented the new desire of the French for glory, their passionate ascent to dizzy heights of success from which, as he warned them, the fall might be disastrous:

> Kein Eroberungskrieg! So scholl das heilige Wort einst,
> Das ihr uns gabt, verehret, als nie verehrt ein Volk ward,
> Und, so deucht es uns, Stimmen Unsterblicher wiederholen:
> Künftig nicht mehr Eroberungskrieg.
>
> Und jetzt führt ihr ihn, den allverderbenden, seid gar
> Grosse Krieger, ersteigt mit schlagendem Herzen, mit heissem
> Durste nach Ruhm, im Orkan der Leidenschaft, des Kampfspiels
> Schimmernde Höh! die . . . Abgrund ist.[8]

The few poets and writers who began to sound a patriotic note made no impression. The fate of Poland, where for lack of patriotism a once glorious and powerful kingdom disappeared from the map of Europe and was carved out among its neighbors, hardly attracted attention or served

as a lesson. In the midst of great political upheavals and military expeditions, Germany slumbered on. In 1798, five years before his death,
Herder tried to wake her up:

> Germany, are you slumbering on? Look what happens around
> you, what happened to yourself. Feel it, wake up! . . . See
> your neighbor Poland, formerly so powerful and proud, kneel-
> ing dishonored and untidy before three victors. Look at the giant
> in the East; you yourself taught him to brandish his sword and
> his club. Look westward: there relying on might and luck an-
> other fighter faces you, full of agility and enthusiasm. And you,
> you still tarry to stand up like a man and wisely to unite? . . .
> Should your name be gone with the wind? Will you, too, kneel
> before strangers, partitioned by them? Do none of your an-
> cestors, does not your own heart, does not your language mean
> anything to you? . . . Courts will not protect you nor princely
> priests. . . . Who does not protect himself, does he deserve
> liberty? [9]

Another solitary voice came from a little known poet of the younger
generation, Johann Christoph Friedrich Hölderlin (1770-1843). Together
with his fellow Swabians, Hegel and Friedrich Wilhelm Josef Schelling
(1775-1854), he studied philosophy and theology at the University of
Tübingen. A few years later, in 1798, Schelling became professor of
philosophy in Jena as Fichte's successor and joined there the circle of
leading romanticists. Schelling was to end his long life as a philosopher
of mystical romanticism, but at Tübingen the three young men, like
most of the academic youth of the day, enthusiastically welcomed the
French Revolution and planted a tree of liberty. Yet Hölderlin, one of
the greatest among poets, whose sensitive soul could not endure the
strain of life and whose creative career was cut short by early madness,
was more influenced by the neoclassical humanism of Schiller than by
the France of 1789. Like the classicists, he sought a state which would
give full scope to the liberty of the harmoniously developed beautiful
human personality. Such a society Hölderlin found in ancient Greece, and
this Greece of his imagination and longings became his spiritual home.
After its image he wished to transform his homeland and the Germans
into "a new kingdom where beauty is queen." [10] In some of the great
odes which he wrote in 1789 and in the following years, he prophesied in
solemn and inspired words the birth of a new Greece, the ripe and
autumnal fulfillment of the Greek spring on German soil. He envisioned
Germany as a priestess, dealing out unarmed advice to kings and nations
assembled around her.[11] But this Germany existed only in his generous
poetic dreams; the actual Germany was far from resembling the Greece
of his imagination.

In his philosophical novel *Hyperion* Hölderlin took the reader to the Greece of 1770, where his hero, full of the glories and beauties of ancient Greece, longed to become the educator and liberator of his nation, but was defeated in his efforts by the meanness of the people around him, to whom he had wished to dedicate his life, and who drove him back into solitude and resignation. In his wanderings Hyperion also visited Germany. The people he found there were in no way better than the modern Greeks: fragmentary human beings, incomplete as personalities, and incomplete as Germans. Nobody seemed farther away from the Greek and Hölderlinian ideal of the fully developed harmonious personality, beautiful and good. Hyperion wrote to his friend,

> I did not expect much and I was prepared to find even less. Humbly I came, like the homeless blind Oedipus to the gate of Athens, where the sacred grove received him and beautiful souls met him—but how different was my fate! Barbarians from of old, and grown more barbarous by their industry and their science and even their religion; utterly incapable of any godly feeling, corrupt to the very marrow, insulting every decent soul by the degree of their exaggeration and meanness, dull and disharmonious like the pieces of a bowl thrown away—

so it was that the Germans appeared to him.

> It is a hard word, and yet I say it because it is the truth: I cannot imagine any people more unharmonious and unfulfilled than the Germans. You see among them artisans, but no human beings; thinkers, but no human beings; priests, but no human beings; masters and serfs, youth and maturity, but no human beings. It is like a battlefield where hands and arms and limbs lie scattered in pieces while the life which has been shed trickles away in the sand.

Hölderlin found among the Germans no spirit and no daring, no seriousness and no liberty; they seemed like calculating barbarians, doing well what they were trained to do in a limited field and yet full of conceit and without any true modesty.

> The Germans are forever complaining that everything on earth is imperfect. If only someone would tell these God-forsaken people that things are so imperfect with them because they corrupt everything pure and defile everything sacred with their coarse hands; that nothing flourishes among them because they do not heed divine nature; that the life with them is empty and replete with care and overfull of cold damp discord, because they scorn genius which infuses vigor and nobility into human activity and serenity into suffering and love and brotherhood into cities and houses.[12]

But though Hölderlin went out to the Germans, like Hyperion to his Greeks, longing to lead them to a higher and fuller life and was repelled by what he found—anticipating Nietzsche here as in other traits of his solitary genius—he was no nationalist. Like Nietzsche, he started from Greece to seek the new man. When he parted from Hegel, his watchword was "The Kingdom of God." In the few years of maturity which fate allowed him, he never ceased to seek a new manifestation of divine beauty in which nature and spirit would fuse as he believed they had fused in ancient Greece. When Hyperion met his friend Alabanda, they lamented together over their people of dead souls, a corpse without will, greatness, or spirit. "It must not stand where it does, the dry and rotten tree. It steals the light and air from the young life which is growing up to make a new world." In spite of the ugly reality, they did not despair; their faith in man was too great for that. They hoped for an awakening, but they did not look to political means to achieve it. They did not expect any help from the state; they only wished it should not hamper or hinder man's growth. For Hyperion knew well that though the state can protect from evil, it cannot produce anything good. "Gracious God!" he exclaimed. "Whoever wishes to make the state a moral educator does not know how much he sins. If man wished to make the state his heaven, he has always made it into hell." When Alabanda asked when the longed-for awakening would come, Hyperion answered:

> Then when the beloved daughter of time, its youngest and loveliest child, the new church, will go forth from these obsolete and defiled forms, when the awakened feeling for the Divine brings back to man his divinity and to his heart beautiful youth. I cannot announce this coming for I have but a dim foreboding, but it will certainly come, certainly.[13]

Hölderlin longed for a new religion and a nobler man; considerations of politics or concern for the state were alien to him.

While the Swabian poets and thinkers went out in quest of the ideal, an entirely different atmosphere prevailed in Halberstadt, where the old Prussian poet Johann Wilhelm Ludwig Gleim (1719-1803) lived. He wrote to Seume on November 1, 1798: "It is an honor to be a German man. Thank God that I am a German!" At the end of 1789 he helped to edit a monthly *Deutsche Monatsschrift* in Halberstadt. Its program announced:

> We are Germans, we are Brandenburgers; and with all our hearts we are lovers of our fatherland. Whatever concerns it, concerns us also most intimately and will not only influence the choice of patriotic themes on our pages but also our attitude to all other subjects.[14]

Gleim and his friends thought above all of Prussia. They were the last guardians of the legacy of Frederick the Great. They were not alone in lamenting Germany's surrender before the French armies. A few helpless patriots spoke up for the Reich among the citizens of the many small states and free cities of southwestern and western Germany. These insignificant principalities, counties, and communities could not feel secure without the protection of the Reich.[15] While the larger German territories like Prussia, Bavaria, and Saxony developed their own political consciousness and were eager for severing all ties of dependence upon the Empire, the very classes which seemed obsolete and doomed before the march of administrative centralization and uniform territorial organization, the ecclesiastical princes, the imperial knights, and the small and sleepy free cities—all of them concentrated in the Swabian, Frankish, and Rhenish circles of the Reich—not only felt loyalty towards the Emperor but many of them sought ways and means to strengthen the Reich. This German patriotism was confined to a small section of the educated class, jurists and publicists. The lower classes were absorbed in local interests, and their horizon was limited by daily work and traditional pleasures; none thought of participation in political life, none claimed the right to give advice or even to think about affairs of state. But most intellectuals were also alien to any national concern, they either served devotedly and obediently a prince and local state or were cosmopolitan and nonpolitical in their culture and outlook.

Among the few patriots a newly awakened romantic interest in the Middle Ages and in antiquarian research turned minds towards the imperial tradition which had seen its days of greatness in the Middle Ages. But they rarely thought of strengthening the Reich. Its very looseness seemed more advantageous to liberty than the straitjacket of the modern centralized state. The weak Empire had much to recommend itself to most German intellectuals of the period, lovers of freedom and peace. The Empire was unable to threaten the tranquillity of Europe by active aggression or to control the liberty of thought and expression by concerted action, yet it provided a tie of sentimental unity and kept the consciousness of historical continuity alive. Among the intellectuals of the small German states this loyalty to the old Reich survived even after its dissolution. When the future historian of medieval Germany, Johann Friedrich Böhmer (1795-1863) wished to volunteer for the War of Liberation in 1813, his father, a typical burgher of Frankfurt-am-Main, wrote him that unfortunately he saw no Germans take to the field but only Bavarians, Württembergians, Hessians, Saxons, and the like. Such a war, he wrote, could accomplish something for Germany's princes, but little for the people who could find happiness only if Germany would form again "under our beloved Emperors" a

Reich as it did before the Treaty of Westphalia.[16]

In 1791 the Academy of the University of Erfurt, a city then forming part of the lands of the Elector of Mainz, the leading ecclesiastical prince of the Reich, sponsored a contest for the best answer to the question, "What means are there to make the German citizen understand the value and the advantage of the German imperial constitution and to arouse his loyalty to it?" None of the replies mentioned the possibility or the desirability of German unity. Ten years later Johann Gottfried von Pahl (1768-1839), a burgher of the tiny free city of Aalen in Swabia, who had been among the early admirers of the French Revolution, became concerned with the disintegration of the Reich. But he was hardly more distrustful of France than he was of Prussia's and Austria's intentions for territorial aggrandizement at the expense of the other German princes and cities. In the small free city of Schwäbisch-Gmünd he began to publish in 1801 his *Nationalchronik der Teutschen* (which he continued until 1809) and in the same year he addressed a patriotic appeal to the Imperial Diet in Regensburg. There he proposed not only a strengthening of the military forces of the Reich but also the formation of a separate federation within the Reich of the smaller German princes without Austria and Prussia. He wished to place this federation under the protection of Russia, which would have to guarantee the weaker members of the Reich against its two great powers. Thus one of the most devoted German patriots at the beginning of the nineteenth century could not envision a future for the Reich except by the creation of a kind of Rhenish Confederation, not under the protection of France, it is true, but still under that of a foreign power.[17] A few poets dreamt of the desirability of German unity,[18] but many years had yet to pass before this dream was shared by a growing number of the educated classes. In June 1809 Seume described the situation in Germany in characteristic lines:

> Hass und Spaltung herrscht in unsern Stämmen,
> Einheit nur kann das Verderben hemmen,
> Und die Einheit fliehn wir wie die Pest.
> Eh' man öffentlich, was recht ist, ehret,
> Jauchzt man, wenn Gau den Gau verheeret,
> Und die Volksschmach wird ein Freudenfest.[19]

Perhaps no German state proved more impregnable to German nationalism at the turn of the century than Prussia. Since the time of Frederick II a Prussian nationalism had begun to grow up, a feeling of pride in the military successes and the personal renown of the great king whose policy weakened the German Reich and who felt no sympathy for German cultural life. He and his father built Prussia in the ideal of a purely military state, held together by the personality of the leader-king and the army. When after his death two weak monarchs succeeded the old warrior—Frederick William II (1786-1797) and Frederick William III (1797-1840)—the Prussian state lost much of its strength and vitality. Within its loosened meshes the public opinion of the educated classes and of the townspeople whom Frederick II had hardly noticed made itself felt for the first time, and this public opinion was there, as in most parts of Germany, adverse to war and patriotic glory and desirous of the benefits of a peaceful and undisturbed life. The war against France in 1793 was thoroughly unpopular. As far as there was in Prussia any feeling of hostility toward a foreign country, it was directed against Austria. The idea of a community of interests with Austria and other German states against France was then as alien to Prussian statesmen as it was to the people under their rule.[20] Prussia's separate peace with France concluded at Basel in 1795, which abandoned the left bank of the Rhine to France and declared Prussia's disinterestedness and neutrality in the wars between France and the Reich, was enthusiastically welcomed by the people and the educated classes alike.

For ten years the Prussians lived in peace and prosperity, unconcerned with Napoleon's victorious expeditions in southern Germany and with the fate of a German nation of which they did not feel a part and of the existence of which they hardly knew. Of the Prussians of that period, Barthold Georg Niebuhr (1776-1831), the famous historian of ancient Rome and one of the first supporters of Prussia's claim to German leadership, wrote:

> They had no feeling whatsoever against the French oppression [in Germany] and no sympathy with the distress of the Reich, mortally wounded in its honor and fortune, as long as they flattered themselves that Prussia would get her share and that they were the chosen people of the new god. They became alarmed only when they noticed that their own existence was threatened, when they recognized that they had been deceived.[21]

In bitter irony Gentz wrote to Mallet du Pan on January 19, 1799:

> Why should the fall of the kings of Sardinia and of Naples, who are at a distance of three or four hundred miles from us, affect us in Prussia? What is to us the destruction of the house of Austria, which is our natural enemy? What does the misery of the whole of Europe mean to us, provided that the French Directory and the Prussian government survive? [22]

In those years of peace "without honor or glory" Prussia's wealth grew and letters and art began to flourish there. Few demands for reform were voiced, and these only mildly. With the same self-satisfaction as characterized the middle class, the Prussian minister Struensee declared in August 1799 to the French chargé d'affaires:

> The salutary revolution which you made from below upward, will happen in Prussia slowly from above downward. The King is a democrat in his own way; he works incessantly for the limitation of the privileged classes in Prussia.[23]

Nothing of that kind happened. There was neither sufficient energy nor strong incentive. Only in East Prussia, Baron Friedrich Leopold Schröter (1743-1815), who was provincial administrator there, began after 1795 with the emancipation of the serfs and the improvement of the economic conditions in the cities, anticipating later reforms and making East Prussia one of the most advanced German regions.

XXI

The Cosmopolitanism
of German Intellectuals

THE birth of the modern nation-state in neighboring France hardly made any impression on Germany. Only twenty years later Germany entered the Age of Nationalism, and then merely with tentative steps, more in cultural aspirations and in the enthusiasm of battle than through the transformation of the political and social structure of the nascent nation. In spite of all the changes and the moving of frontiers and princes over the checkerboard of the old Reich, German life went on unruffled under the surface. The short-lived enthusiasm for the French Revolution died quickly, not only because internal conditions in France disappointed many German sympathizers but also because there could be no application of the French lesson to the German scene. France was a nation, Germany was not. Wieland saw it clearly: "In all convulsions and confusions France is held together by the firm will of the great majority to remain one nation; under similar circumstances Germany would split up and become the prey of foreign countries." A German pamphlet in 1791 stated:

> We have as many nations, as manifold and different national interests, as many conflicting complaints as we have princes. The German townspeople and peasants have no Paris, no common center of their power, their complaints and wishes, no common tie nor goal. The Swabian and the Saxon do not know each other, they have nothing in common but their language.[1]

Intellectual curiosity about the French Revolution was naturally great, for German intellectuals like those of other European countries had been for a century in the habit of closely following events in France. Johann Wilhelm von Archenholz (1743-1812), a Prussian who had fought in the Seven Years War, who had traveled far and had wide interests, wrote in 1793 in *Minerva, ein Journal historischen und politischen Inhalts,* a quarterly which he published in Berlin from 1792 till 1812:

> The French Revolution has pushed everything else aside by its tremendous interest; the best poems remain unread; one snatches only newspapers and such writings as still the ravenous political appetite.

Amongst the German writers who informed the public on the events of France were not only enthusiasts like Georg Forster and the Silesian Konrad Engelbert Oelsner (1764-1808), who acted in 1796 as a French agent to create allied and federated border states under a French protectorate, but also highly esteemed and sober-minded citizens like Gerhard Anton von Halem (1752-1819), a high civil servant of Oldenburg, and Joachim Heinrich Campe (1746-1818), educator, author, and publisher of Braunschweig, where the enlightened ruler, Duke Karl Wilhelm Ferdinand, called upon him to help in the reform of the school system.[2] In 1789 Halem went to Paris accompanied by the young Wilhelm von Humboldt, his former pupil. His letters clearly mirrored the enthusiastic cosmopolitanism of the generation. After crossing the French border—he wrote—

> I cannot describe the sentiments which overwhelmed me when we saw here suddenly the symbol of the happily conquered liberty, the French cockade on the hats and caps of all those whom we encountered—burghers and farmers, old men and boys, priests and beggars—and the happy faces proud of their new superiority over other nations. I could have embraced the first men whom we met. They did not seem to me any longer Frenchmen. My traveling companions and I, too, had ceased, in our sentiments at that time and in the relation to them, to be Brandenburgers and Braunschweigers. All national differences and prejudices disappeared. They on their side had again come into possession of the long missed human rights; we on our side likewise felt that we were human beings.

After his arrival in Paris Halem asked himself whether it was true that the new Hellenes and Romans whom he thought to see around him had really a few weeks before been Frenchmen. Was it not necessary, he asked, to revise German judgment about the French character?[3]

A German poem published in 1796 compared the two "sisters," Gaul and Germany, of whom one had awakened from her sleep and had found happiness, while the other still slumbered but was near the awakening to human rights. This latter hope was premature. Many Germans began to doubt whether France had found her happiness; Germany herself continued for a long time to slumber on, and many

Germans felt happy. They were satisfied when they compared their safe and quiet life with the chaos and the upheavals in the neighboring country. Few understood that the French example might offer a lesson from which Germany could learn.[4] F. Chr. Laukhard, who had served in the Prussian army and later in the French, saw clearly the difference between the two armies and the superiority of the French. Though the Prussian professional soldiers were without doubt better drilled, the French republicans had a patriotic loyalty which Laukhard found wanting among mercenary soldiers. He explained the French victories by the fact that the French soldiers knew why and for what cause they were fighting and drew from this knowledge a vital energy and inspiration.[5]

More clearly than others Gentz recognized at an early stage the importance of the disturbances in France. The influence of Burke, whose *Reflections* he translated into German, had helped to extinguish his former sympathy with the French Revolution. But he was clear-sighted enough to wish to adopt some of its reforms in order to strengthen the resistance to the Revolution:

> One must transplant as much of the means and instruments of the enemy to one's own army and to one's own soil as is compatible with the continuation of an orderly constitution. This can best be done by opposing to the enthusiasm of the Revolution a well-calculated influence on the minds and hearts of the citizens. This should not be neglected even for one moment. It must be the incessant concern of the princes, to educate and guide public opinion.

By all appropriate means—by solemn declarations and sermons, by elementary education and pamphlets, by support and encouragement of literary talent—the princes must shape the ideas of the period and must do it immediately if they wished to survive. Gentz was among the few who had at that time a clear grasp of the importance of public opinion and the active cooperation of the people in the new age. He became Germany's first modern political publicist. Not before the end of the first decade of the nineteenth century, and then only for a very short period, did some German governments begin to understand the lesson which the West offered, that an awakened and free public opinion strengthened national vitality and did not undermine the authority of the state.

Even German thinkers whose sympathy with the French Revolution could have taught them an understanding of the impact of popular forces put the emphasis in the process of national regeneration not on the people but on an authoritarian leader. In the same year when Pahl, moved by the unfortunate peace of Lunéville, proposed a strengthening of the German military establishment, his fellow Swabian Hegel meditated on plans for the reform of the German imperial constitution. There he formulated for the first time his insight that the state is power; without power no state could exist, and therefore, as Hegel proclaimed in the first sentence, Germany was no longer a state. Very different from the German political scientists of that period, he put a discussion of the armed forces of the Reich at the beginning of his treatise and regarded it as the core of the problem. The state to him had its origin and sanction not in the general will of its citizens but in itself and its might. Hegel had little understanding of the importance of cohesion within the state in peacetime, of the vitality infused by popular activity. The test of war was to him the true criterion of the strength of national life. He demanded a powerful Germany, not a national Germany. The reform of the Reich was not to come from awakened popular forces, but through forceful leadership from above. Like Fichte a few years later, Hegel pleaded for a "Zwingherr," a hero who would impose unity and greatness upon the Germans. He did not at that time expect leadership from Prussia. As between her and Austria, all his sympathies were on the side of the latter. Prussia appeared to him a soulless despotism, lacking in scientific and artistic genius, and he warned against an overestimation of Prussia, which only the genius of Frederick II had forced into ephemeral energy. Nor did Hegel, the philosopher and intellectual, expect German regeneration to be brought about by intellectual or moral forces. He did not trust the ability of reason and insight to accomplish it. He was convinced that they must be justified by force: then only does man accept them. Machiavelli had a deep influence on Hegel, as he had on Fichte, in making them abandon eighteenth-century concepts. Hegel's prince was no longer the first servant of the state, recognized by the social contract which the citizens concluded of their conscious and free will, but the great man whom the others obeyed against their will, not only on account of his overpowering personality but because he represented their unconscious will, the will which they will share later, largely thanks to the leader's exertions. Hegel never named the hero whom he expected to bring about German regeneration and whose coming he announced. Some commentators saw the Austrian Archduke Karl, others saw Bonaparte, as the man in whom Hegel set his hopes. Hegel's concept of the state, as he developed it then, showed hardly any influence of the ideas of 1789 and of the liberal nationalism which the French Revolution originally aroused: it mirrored Napoleon and his message, which the march of history seemed to confirm.[6]

Hegel was not alone amongst the Germans of his time to admire the French general and to expect from him the salvation of Germany and of Europe. Karl Theodor von Dalberg (1744-1817), the last imperial Elector

of Mainz and the first statesman of the Rhenish Confederation, one of the
most enlightened and progressive administrators whom Germany knew
at that time, a highly cultivated Maecenas of German letters and himself a scholarly writer of merit, voiced the opinion of many educated
Germans when he wrote of Napoleon in 1802:

> The extraordinary man, whose worth as restorer is even
> greater than his worth as victor, who has made possible what
> seemed impossible, who has established order on the ruins and
> horrors of anarchy in France, who brought peace to his con-
> temporaries, this extraordinary man has the necessary greatness
> of soul to rise above the class of benefactors of single nations,
> to become the benefactor of mankind and to support far around
> constitutions, tranquillity, peace, and concord.[7]

At the beginning of the century most German statesmen and writers
hailed Napoleon either as the prince of peace or as the regenerator of
Germany; the masses welcomed the progressive reforms where French
administration introduced them, or remained indifferent. The disenchant-
ment with Napoleon among the educated classes began to spread only
after 1808. Even then many remained loyal, either to his political leadership or to the inspiration of greatness which he seemed to embody.
When in 1806 the millenary German empire, the Holy Roman Empire
of the German nation, came to an end, only the romanticists looked
longingly back to this ancient abode of medieval traditions and customs;
many more looked to the Rhenish Confederation, the Rheinbund,
to take the place of the old Empire and to unite the Germans on a
new and better basis. In the summer of 1806 Gerhard Anton von Halem
greeted the Rhenish Confederation as a new German Bund, a sapling
which would grow and take the place of the old oak tree which the
tempest of the times had uprooted. He saw in Dalberg a guarantee that
the German intellectual life would prosper in the new confederation,
from which he expected the salvation not only of his generation but
even of their distant descendants:

> Am Rhein, am Rhein, da wächst mit unsern Reben
> Hervor ein neuer Bund,
> Ein Deutscher Bund, und neues, deutsches Leben
> Keimt aus erregtem Grund.
>
> Die Knospe schwillt, indes im Sturm der Zeiten
> Die alte Eiche fiel.
> Die Knospe schwillt; den Schössling treu zu leiten,
> Sei edler Deutschen Ziel!
>
> Es gilt das Heil von uns und späten Erben,
> Der Bundestag ist nah.

Was kümmern wir? Kann deutscher Geist ersterben?
Ist nicht ein Dalberg da?

The medieval empire seemed dead; where could the Germans hope to find a new unity except in the Rhenish Confederation? In comparison with the old Reich, the new Bund seemed turned toward the future, founded on the progressive ideas of the present time, inspired by the greatest personality of the age, the restorer of the unity of Western civilization on a new rational basis, of the empire of Charlemagne, which would end almost a thousand years of hostility and rivalry among French and Germans and Italians and bring a securely founded peace. Did not Napoleon himself, in assuming the protection of the Rhenish Confederation, declare it to be his goal to obviate every kind of dissension and disorder? As his chargé d'affaires stated:

> Having thus provided for the dearest interests of his people and his neighbors, and having assured, as far as it lay in his power, the future peace of Europe and that of Germany in particular, heretofore constantly the theater of war, . . . he hoped that the nations of Europe will at last close their ears to the insinuation of those who would maintain an eternal war on the continent of Europe. He trusts that the French armies which have crossed the Rhine have done it for the last time, and that the German people will no longer witness, except in the annals of the past, the terrible pictures of chaos, devastation and carnage which war invariably brings with it.

Though Austria and Prussia remained outside the Rhenish Confederation, the other German princes were easily won over by the favors which Napoleon bestowed upon them. The ecclesiastical principalities, the many small territories ruled by counts and barons, the tiny free cities were incorporated into the larger states, which thus became rounded-off territories and could reform and modernize their administrations. The larger of these territories, like Bavaria, Württemberg, and Baden, took Napoleon's enlightened despotism as a model, but even the chief reformers, among them Count Maximilian Joseph Montgelas (1759-1838) in Bavaria and Duke (later King) Frederick I of Württemberg from 1797 to 1816 did not follow the progressive social measures of the French Revolution. They neither completely abolished feudalism nor did they liberate the peasants. Only in the territories which came under direct French administration were the legal and social gains of the French Revolution fully introduced. On the other hand these lands suffered under the censorship and the suppression of free public opinion which was characteristic of Napoleon's regime everywhere. The execution on August 26, 1806, of the bookseller Johann Philipp Palm, who was accused of having distributed the pamphlet *Deutschland in seiner tiefen Erniedrigung* [Germany in her deep humiliation] in Braunau, caused great resentment in Germany, but this execution was an isolated case. On the whole, the persecution of free opinion in Napoleonic Germany was not worse than it was in France itself, and certainly not more oppressive than it was "normally" in Austria and Prussia even during the years of the "War of Liberation." [8]

It is probable that Napoleon had the intention of developing the Rhenish Confederation into a unified German structure. His restless ambitions did not give him time or opportunity for any constructive long-range activity of that kind. He shifted princes and frontiers too frequently to allow the growth of stability. But an even greater hindrance was the fact that the newly consolidated German middle states were too jealous of their newly gained sovereignty and not willing to subordinate it to the unity and interests of a German nation, the existence or desirability of which they did not acknowledge. Only the educated German classes supported the idea of integrating the various member states of the confederation into a national structure. The armies of Bavaria and Württemberg were proud to fight as independent armies on the side of the greatest military genius of the times and to earn laurels under his leadership. Young Germans rejoiced that they were Napoleon's contemporaries. The masses in the Rhineland greeted Napoleon enthusiastically in 1804, and the people of Cologne unyoked the horses of his carriage and dragged it forward in triumph. When the French troops drove the Prussians out of Hanover, the population welcomed the French as liberators and immediately removed everywhere the Prussian eagles. Bavarian writers propagated the theory that the Bavarians were really not Germans, but descendants of the Celtic Boii and therefore closely related to the Gauls.

One of the most widely read authors on constitutional law and politics of the period, Christoph Freiherr von Aretin (1773-1824), a member of one of the leading Bavarian families, published in 1809 *Die Pläne Napoleons und seiner Gegner in Deutschland*. In it he praised Napoleon as the true representative of Deutschheit, of the German character, which so many Germans of the period identified with cosmopolitanism—and Napoleon appeared as the embodiment of rational cosmopolitan aspirations—while he castigated Napoleon's enemies as a Protestant conspiracy of Prussia and Britain against the good of mankind. A similar point of view was voiced in Baden by the local statesman and popular novelist, Count Karl Christian Ernst Benzel-Sternau (1767-1849). This admiration of Napoleon was in no way confined to southern and western Germany. A Protestant Prussian parson, Bodenburg, glorified in an ode in 1804 both Napoleon and King Frederick William III. He called

Napoleon a mythical hero, "Du aus der Vorwelt Wundertagen erstandener Heros." The Prussian king was glorified because he had kept peace with the French, had renounced achieving greatness through arms, through the thunder of battle and tears and blood, and had instead sought the happiness of his people through the benefits of peace. On May 9, 1805, the *Berlinische Nachrichten* published an editorial maintaining that no period in history seemed more destined to realize the blessings of eternal peace than the age of Napoleon.

Austria's war against Napoleon in 1805 and Prussia's war against him in 1806 hardly evoked any sympathy in other German lands. Napoleon's victories seemed only to confirm the general conviction that he represented an irresistible force, the "wave of the future" which was destined to overwhelm Europe. The unbroken success of his arms, the progressiveness of his administration, the never before encountered power of personality created a legend to which the greatest minds of Germany succumbed, the more willingly because national sentiment was unknown to them. The day before the Battle of Jena (in which on October 14, 1806, the Prussian army ignominiously collapsed) Hegel wrote from Jena, which the French had occupied: "As I did before, now everybody wishes success to the French army" [wie ich schon früher tat, wünschen nun alle der französischen Armee Glück]. Three months later he saw in the victories of the French armies the proof that "education and intelligence defeat crude efficiency" [Bildung über Roheit und der Geist über geistlosen Verstand und Klügelei den Sieg davonträgt]. For the following years Hegel lived and worked in Bavaria, the leading state of the Rhenish Confederation, and his loyalty to Napoleon remained unshaken until the Emperor's final defeat in 1814. Even during 1813 he regarded the movement of "liberation" with bitter irony and the "liberators" with contempt. On April 29, 1814, when Napoleon's fate seemed sealed, he lamented his doom as an immense tragedy, as the defeat of the one great man by the mass of mediocrity.

Hegel's unwavering loyalty to Napoleon was shared by Goethe. In July 1812 when Napoleon's armies had crossed the Russian border, Germany's most representative poet welcomed Maria Louise, the Empress of France, in a poem which glorified her husband. The historical events of the time seemed to him a grandiose struggle between land and sea, between the continent and Britain, a struggle in which he foresaw Napoleon's victory:

> So tritt durch weisen Schluss, durch Machtgefechte
> Das feste Land in alle seine Rechte.

Goethe rejoiced that the hero to whom history had given more than to anyone else had now found fulfillment of his fondest wishes in the birth of his son and thereby in the secure foundation of the dynasty. He was convinced that father and son together would close with mild hands the temple of Janus and establish the reign of peace.[9]

Goethe was minister of state in one of the Thuringian duchies, that of Saxe-Weimar, the territory of which included Jena, the scene of the famous battle and the site of the university where Schiller and Fichte taught and where the romanticists formed their first famous circle. That the minister Goethe remained alien to the spirit of German nationalism was hardly any exception in that period. But while many German writers and intellectuals discovered nationalism after 1810 or were converted to it by the force of events, Goethe remained untouched by the prejudices of national interests or the lure of the national past. Whatever tribute he paid to nationalism he had offered in the Storm and Stress of his early youth, under the influence of Herder,[10] who was one of the first to regard in his *Von Deutscher Art und Kunst* the terms "German" and "creative" or "original" as almost synonymous, while "French" represented the opposite.[11] In the years of his maturity, Goethe never indulged in the glorification of German "depth" or of German character. Though for him classical antiquity remained the absolute model and ideal, he rejected every identification of the Germans with the Greeks and warned against basing modern patriotism upon the example of the ancients.

In the spring of 1807, Franz Passow (1786-1833) came as a young man to teach at the gymnasium in Weimar where Goethe's son August went to school. Passow himself was a classical philologist, who later became professor of Greek at the University of Breslau and was the author of a widely used *Handwörterbuch der Griechischen Sprache*. He wrote on December 27, 1807, to Friedrich Heinrich in Munich:

> My whole soul is tied to the beautiful thought of restoring at least in individuals what the Germans as a whole have lost ignominiously—an enthusiasm for fatherland and freedom—by revealing to them Greek antiquity and the development of the Greek mind.

But Goethe warned against all political applications of the Hellenic past to modern times. "Der Freiheitssinn und die Vaterlandsliebe, die man aus den Alten zu schöpfen meint, wird in den meisten Leuten zur Fratze," was his severe judgment. The demand for liberty and the love of the fatherland which so many of his contemporaries thought to recreate after the ancient model, seemed to Goethe to degenerate all too easily into a grimace or travesty. He rejected the narrow patriotism of the ancients and demanded an ever-growing cultural intercourse among the nations, a free trade in ideas and thought. The review *Kunst und Altertum* which he edited served largely the purpose of propagating his idea of Weltliteratur—world literature, above and beyond all national literatures.[12] The older Goethe grew, the more he turned to humanism for guidance, the farther and more radically he separated himself from nationalism both as a statesman and a writer.

The young Goethe's most popular dramas, *Goetz von Berlichingen* and *Faust*, had helped to restore the interest in the German past and in the Middle Ages. But nobody rejected the romantic glorification of the Gothic past more sharply than Goethe did in 1827. He declared:

> The Greek mythology, the most highly conceived embodiment of the best and purest humanity, merits praise more than the ugly devilry and witchery which could develop only in somber periods full of anxiety out of a confused imagination and which could find nourishment only in the dregs of human nature.[13]

He found the illustrations of the great French romantic painter Eugène Delacroix, which with rare sympathetic genius captured the mood of the early Faust, much too "wild." What he enjoyed most in the French translations was the fact that the serene clarity and orderliness of the French language of necessity attenuated the enthusiasm and turbulent originality of his youthful style.[14]

Politically and culturally, the mature Goethe never felt any hostility towards the French. After the Battle of Jena, Heinrich Voss, the son of the famous translator of Homer, then a teacher at the Gymnasium at Weimar, wrote to Schiller's widow: "With the situation as it is, I wish, from the bottom of my heart, further victory to the French and an early peace." [15] To Goethe himself "the awakening of German political nationalism remained forever alien; the universal power of the enlightened world emperor was infinitely nearer to his heart and mind." Toward Germany Goethe remained cool and detached, not only "in den Jahren der Not," but also in "den Jahren der Erhebung." The depth of the national "misery" did not move him, the height of the nation's "rise" did not arouse him. When in October 1813, after the allied victory at Leipzig, the Prussians and Austrians entered Weimar, the Austrian Field Marshal Count Wenzel Joseph Colloredo was quartered in Goethe's house. The host received him wearing the decoration of the French Legion of Honor, in spite of Colloredo's protest. A few days later, Goethe explained to Wilhelm von Humboldt that he could not very well take off a distinction which the French Emperor had bestowed upon him because this Emperor had lost a battle.

Humboldt was surprised that neither Goethe's son nor Schiller's was eager to volunteer. Goethe opposed the formation of volunteer corps composed of students and other sons of the educated classes. If one has to make war, he insisted, it should be done by professional soldiers, not by young intellectuals who offered their services out of enthusiasm. Even after Saxe-Weimar joined the Allies, there was little enthusiasm for the war in the territory which only a few weeks before had loyally stood by the Rhenish Confederation. Few hastened to offer their services to the common German cause. Goethe's son hesitated for a long time; when he joined, he did so against the express will of his father, who used all his influence to keep him away from active service.[16] After the defeat of the French, Goethe never equated German victory in arms with cultural or moral superiority. He never compared French superficiality and Parisian immorality to German depth and spiritual culture. In the last years of his life, he emphasized again and again how much he owed to the French in the development of his mind and art, and he readily acknowledged the moral and intellectual leadership of the French.

On November 16, 1829, Goethe wrote that in his opinion the French were the culturally most alive nation and that they would therefore greatly influence the moral world.[17] His famous praise of Paris was recorded by his secretary Eckermann on May 3, 1827:

> But now conceive a city like Paris, . . . where the best works, both of nature and art, from the whole earth are open to daily inspection; conceive this metropolis of the world, where every walk over a bridge or across a square recalls some mighty past, and where some historical event is connected with every street corner. In addition to all this, conceive not the Paris of a dull, unintellectual time, but the Paris of the nineteenth century in which, during three generations, men like Molière, Voltaire, Diderot, and others have kept up such a current of intellectual life as cannot be found anywhere else in a single spot on the whole earth. . . . We Germans are of yesterday. We have indeed made considerable progress this century; but a few centuries more may have to elapse before so much culture will spread among our people that they will appreciate beauty like the Greeks . . . and that it will be said of them, it is long since they were barbarians.[18]

Barbarians the Germans appeared to him as they did to Hölderlin's Hyperion, but in Goethe's statement none of the bitterness of the younger man reverberated, none of the enthusiasm for raising the Germans to the heights of the Greeks; with Olympian objectivity the old sage surveyed the world of nations and civilizations and his preference went not only to the ancient Greeks but to the modern French.

Of lesser importance than Goethe and Hegel, yet deservedly famous in their days, were the novelist Jean Paul Friedrich Richter (1763-1825) and the Swiss historian Johannes von Müller (1752-1809). Richter under the name Jean Paul, was at the beginning of the nineteenth century one of the most widely read authors. He admired Napoleon and saw in him one of the great geniuses of mankind, a creative force among the general mediocrities of the period. When Jean Paul later turned away from Napoleon, he was not motivated by German nationalism but by pacifism and liberalism. He had welcomed Napoleon and had desired his victory over England, because he expected that after this success Napoleon and a confederation of German princes under his protectorate would guarantee a long-lasting peace. "Do we not gladly share," he wrote, "since the last wars again the common name of Franks and do we not remember from history, that the majority in France are not Gauls but transplanted Germans?" [19] But Napoleon soon disappointed him. In 1812 he began to see the Emperor as a man of force whose rule was shaken by his hubris. "I would like to pray," he had already written a few years before, "Almighty, Thou has sent from Corsica a force which changes everything; recall to him the existence of human weakness which he unfortunately finds only in others." [20]

When in 1809 the publisher Perthes asked Jean Paul to contribute to his new periodical *Vaterländisches Museum,* he objected in his reply of December 23, 1809, to the use of the word "unterjocht" [subjected] for the German people; he found it an untruthful description of the real situation. In his contribution to the first issue of the periodical he wrote against the self-pity of the Germans.

> Let us remember that with the French incursion into Germany we did not exchange republican liberty—which was not here—for despotical serfdom—which cannot come from a country where it does not exist—but only more or less moderate monarchs against more or less moderate monarchs.[21]

Jean Paul's vision was high and wide; it was inspired throughout by his faith in liberty and peace. "Our period," he wrote in December, 1812,

> Our period is great and without precedent because not countries but three continents are laboring to transform themselves to greater similarity, and the olive tree of peace can no longer strike its roots in one garden, but only in the whole globe. The compass needle and the pen, ships and printing presses have abolished the isolation of the nations and they all now stand together on one scaling ladder, one Jacob's Ladder. If we find anywhere in world history footsteps of the progress of mankind, then they are on the roads to liberty and light; at present liberty is spreading through laws to colonies, Negroes, Jews, and serfs; the antagonism between the various classes gives way to common patriotic attraction, since all classes oppose one breast to the enemy on the battlefield. Liberty more often creates intelligence than intelligence produces liberty.[22]

Johannes von Müller, who lived in 1806 in Berlin as Prussian court historiographer, opposed Napoleon's universal monarchy for many years. The events of that year changed his mind. After the dissolution of the German Empire he wrote to Perthes:

> World events have grown beyond all political calculations. Wrath and fear have left my heart. The scene becomes too solemn. The Ancient of the Days sits in judgment, the books are open, and the nations and their princes are being weighed. A new order is in preparation, something entirely different from the expectations of those who are only its blind tools.

From Berlin he wrote on October 21, 1806, to his brother:

> From all signs of history, as far as I can understand them, it has become finally manifest to me that all the parts of the world where one can live in mildness of civilization are being given to this One; it is no longer of any use to write, speak, or fight against it; why should I go to Russia and squander myself in such Don Quixotism?

Thus he stayed on in Berlin and met Napoleon on November 20, 1806. Napoleon's personality impressed him as it did Goethe.[23] On January 29, 1807, Müller delivered an oration on Frederick the Great in French before the Berlin Academy and ended it by asking the soul of the Prussian King in heaven to recognize that victory, greatness, and power always come to those who resembled Frederick the most. Thus Müller paid his compliments to Frederick and to Napoleon; respect for Frederick, he said, united the French, whom he always dearly loved, and the Prussians, whose glory he was.[24] In the same year Müller entered the services of the newly created Kingdom of Westphalia and its King Jerome, Napoleon's brother, first as secretary of state, then as minister of education. An early death saved him from the need or the temptation to change his opinion about Napoleon.

Another popular writer and orator of the period, Ludwig Gotthard Kosegarten (1756-1828), was not spared this change. Appointed professor of history of the University of Greifswald while the city was occupied by the French, Kosegarten had to deliver the oration on Napoleon's birthday in August 1809. There he expressed the hope that the Confederation, which so far had called itself modestly only the Rhenish Confederation, would in the future include all lands where German was spoken. Only thus could the various parts of Germany which had become alienated from each other by different governments, constitutions, and religions, become united. Supported by the most powerful man, as long as this support was needed, Germany's hundred tribes could finally grow into an ordered and live organic body. Then for the first time the north

German and the south German, the Protestant and the Catholic, would meet as brothers. No longer then would there be talk of Saxons, Bavarians, Swabians, and Franks; every German would be honored by the name of German. Thus Kosegarten glorified Napoleon as the father and promoter of German unity.[25] He was one of many German scholars and writers, princes and statesmen, who visualized for Germany a future of close cooperation with Napoleon and the French. There was then even less national feeling of opposition against the French among the common German people than among the educated classes.

XXII

A E I O U: Austria's
Historical Consciousness

I N THIS general atmosphere of acquiescence or indifference, Austria
astonishingly enough formed in 1809 the only exception. There for a
brief time German national feeling came alive not only in isolated poems
or essays but in the aroused consciousness of a people and in a patriotic
literature supported and encouraged by the government. For a few
months the eyes of the isolated German patriots scattered throughout the
German lands turned to Vienna, the seat of the former imperial dynasty.
Conditions in Austria, however, were so peculiar that that land could
hardly set an example for the rest of Germany. Like Prussia, but for a
longer time and to a higher degree, Austria had formed a state sui generis,
and its development had singled it out among the German lands. This
differentiation began consciously in the fourteenth century under the
Habsburg Duke Rudolph IV. The Austrians called him The Founder
(Der Stifter); he built St. Stephen's Cathedral, founded Vienna University, invented the title Archduke, and forged the Privilegium Maius which
gave a legal foundation to Austria's claims for a special position. Thus
Austria, "although it still kept one foot within the German orbit, stepped
out of it. It learned to regard itself as a sovereign political entity, like
the neighboring states of the Přemyslids, Arpads, and Piasts, which had
all taken the step out of the Reich long before." [1]

Austria was no longer a German borderland, but began to see itself as
the center for an organization of the various peoples of the Danubian
area. Such a policy could be achieved at that period through dynastic
marriages. Already the Babenbergs, who preceded the Habsburgs as
rulers of the Ostmark (the "Eastern March"), had intermarried, mostly
with the Bohemian and Hungarian royal houses. The Habsburgs continued to strengthen such ties even more markedly, a policy well indi-

cated in the noted line, *Bella gerant alii, tu, felix Austria, nube.* The famous double wedding between the children of Rudolph von Habsburg and Přemysl Otokar II of Bohemia at the end of the thirteenth century was paralleled in the middle of the fourteenth century in the marriages of the two daughters of Charles IV of Bohemia with Rudolph IV of Habsburg and his brother, and the policy culminated in the notorious Viennese "Double Marriage" of the grandchildren of Maximilian of Austria. The ensuing union of Austria, Bohemia, and Hungary under the Habsburgs in 1526 only reaped the harvest of the policy of many centuries.

Maximilian's father, the Habsburg Archduke Frederick the Younger, who died in 1493 as the Roman Emperor Frederick III, though neither a successful ruler nor a remarkable personality, broadened the Habsburgs' hold far beyond their Danubian lands. Through the marriage of his son with the heiress of Burgundy he laid the foundations of the world empire of his great-grandson Charles, who ruled in Spain and the Americas, in Burgundy and in Germany, the last embodiment of the Roman and Christian dreams of world order. For more than three centuries after the death of Frederick III the imperial dignity remained almost uninterruptedly connected with his house, so that Empire and Habsburg became almost synonymous. This mediocre prince expressed a strong premonition of the coming greatness of his house in the mysterious combination of the five vowels A E I O U which he used to inscribe as a family emblem on his buildings and belongings. In his own interpretation they meant "Alles Erdreich ist Oesterreich untertan" [All the earth is subject to Austria] or "Austriae est imperare orbi universo" [Austria must rule the whole world]. This naive confidence was, in the stress and storm of later periods, reinterpreted into the still confident but rather obscure and apocalyptic "Austria erit in orbe ultima" [Austria will be the last on earth]. As far back as the fifteenth century the Habsburgs were conscious of a special dynastic mission.

Austria, as it grew through family reunions and the imperial dignity in the sixteenth and seventeenth centuries, was a unique state. It was a territorial state and at the same time a universal empire, fusing into the service the two great universal ideas of Western Christianity, the succession of the Roman Empire and the guardianship of the Catholic Church. It was a product of German expansion and colonization and it was at the same time multilingual and multiracial; it was the head of the ill-defined and amorphous Holy Roman Empire of the German Nation and the organizational and strategic center of the Danubian basin, the Donauraum, where it stood on guard for Europe against the Turks. It was wide open to the cultural influences that came from France, Italy, and Spain. It radiated them in all directions and adapted them into a new and distinct civilization by assimilating influences from the eastern plains and the Levant. In the eighteenth century when the Hohenzollern transformed their different inherited and conquered lands into a rationalized state structure, the Habsburg princes—Maria Theresa and her two sons—created a dynastic Austrian state. But the impetus which they gave to their lands was lost after 1792. For more than half a century, during the most critical period, the government was in the hands of rulers neither willing nor able to arouse popular forces in support of the monarchy.

With the French Revolution the ideas of liberty and nationality began to spread to Austria, though they did not penetrate deeply and did not touch the masses. A purely dynastic state seemed doomed in the Age of Nationalism; yet the survival of a supranational state in the heart of Europe, where Germanic, Slavic, and Romance peoples and civilizations had been intermingling for centuries, could have supplied a much-needed corrective to the nationalist excesses of the age. Such a state could have counteracted the urge for national independence to which the interests of individual liberty and international good will were too often and too willingly sacrificed. But no such state could be founded in the nineteenth century upon the sole pillars of bureaucracy and army, of church and nobility. It could not exist if it did not call upon the spontaneous collaboration of peoples and classes whom it should have united to mutual aid. Austria became in the Age of Nationalism a state of officials and not of citizens; its goal was tranquillity and order, not movement and growth. The greatest and most needed experiment for which favorable conditions existed in Austria remained untried. The Habsburgs in the nineteenth century did not understand how to mobilize the forces of liberty and federated nationality. The great Habsburgs of the eighteenth century had protected the peasants and townspeople against the privileges of the nobility and favored education and enlightenment against the encroachment of the church. The French Revolution frightened their successors to seek the support of aristocracy and clergy; they never fully recovered from the shock which they experienced again in 1848. In spite of this, the Austrian monarchy lasted throughout the Age of Nationalism, and though it was not bold with wisdom, it was in the later decades of the century civilized with moderation and restraint. It never tried to impose uniformity. Though it hardly ever attempted to create a favorable public opinion, it did not hinder popular forces from organizing, growing, and expressing themselves[2] and thus it retained, almost to the last, the passive loyalty of the masses.[3] But it did not activize them for its own invigoration.

XXIII

Austria's Brief National Awakening

AT THE time of the French Revolution none of the nationalities living under Habsburg rule had developed a modern national consciousness. The official language in Hungary was Latin, the court aristocracy was largely educated in French, the educated and commercial classes in all the provinces spoke and wrote in German, and only the peasants used the vernacular. In Hungary the feudal estates were opposed to the enlightened reforms of Joseph II not out of nationalism but, as in Belgium, out of conservative attachment to traditional privileges. When the Emperor wished to replace Latin by German as the official language in Hungary, this reform, which would have modernized public administration and replaced the Magyar nobility by German-speaking imperial bureaucrats, aroused the opposition of the Hungarian estates, who countered by demanding the use of Magyar. "The vindication of the use of the Magyar language could not be a sincere one," wrote a leading Hungarian historian. "The same counties which [arguing in 1784 against the decree of the Emperor] emphasized the possibility of an administration in the Magyar tongue, declared it in 1811—that is, twenty-seven years later—an impossibility." [1] To maintain its fiscal privileges the Hungarian nobility insisted on retaining the customs barrier separating Hungary from the other Habsburg lands. As long as the nobility refused to accept equality of taxation, the only way of making it contribute to the Empire's finances was to levy custom duties on Hungarian corn and cattle exported into Austria.

As far as the people was politically conscious, it was attached to ancient, hallowed symbols and to vested historical privileges. Joseph II, despairing of the realization of his enlightened reforms, decided, in the last years of his life, to return the crown of St. Stephen to Hungary. A delirium of enthusiasm swept over the land when this mystic embodiment of "Hungarian freedom" was brought home. [2] The new spirit of 1789, to which the masses were impermeable, hardly touched even the educated classes. Joseph's younger brother, the Grand Duke Leopold of Tuscany, a wise and enlightened ruler who was soon to succeed as Emperor, recognized this clearly. He wrote on June 4, 1789, to the Archduchess Christine: "It is difficult to help the people against their convictions because it is difficult for a government or even the most enlightened minister to know better what is suitable and useful for the nation than the people themselves, their individuals and their representatives." But some of the Hungarian counties began to voice their feudal objections to reform in modern words. For their vested privileges they appealed to the new theories of state. "Pacto sociali, quo regna coalescunt, evictum est, maiestatem ab origine apud populos esse". With these words the representatives of the county of Pesth insisted that according to the social contract in which states are formed, the sovereignty rests with the people. Similarly the representatives of the county of Bihać in Croatia insisted: "Omnis nacio propter se ipse coivit in societatem, et consequenter nacio quae sui tantum commodi causa societatem inivit ipsamet summum ius in se ipsam habet" [Every nation has entered into social life for its own sake, and therefore the nation which formed the society is itself the depository of the fullness of rights]. Thus the nobility invoked the sovereignty of the "people" against reforms proposed by the monarch.

Soon, however, the revolutionary events in France frightened the ruling classes into an alliance with the monarchy. Leopold II, who intended to continue the enlightened work of his brother Joseph II in a spirit of wise moderation, died after less than two years on the imperial throne. His successor Francis II, whose spirit continued to dominate until 1848 while his actual reign encompassed the critical years from 1792 to 1835, was the embodiment of mechanized bureaucracy, distrustful of the people and of spontaneous forces and protecting himself against them by oppressive policy and restrictive censorship. He never had the slightest understanding of modern patriotism. When someone was recommended to him for being an ardent patriot, the Emperor gave the characteristic reply: "He may be a patriot for Austria, but the question is whether he is a patriot for me." All opposition of the new course was regarded as "Jacobin"; everywhere a conspiracy of Freemasons and other "dangerous" elements was suspected. There were a few isolated cases of men who wrote or spoke in the style of the French Revolution, among them the Hungarian Josef Ignaz Martinovicz, who founded a Society of Equality and Liberty, and a few citizens involved in the famous "Jacobin Conspiracy" in Vienna in 1794. The trial against them produced no more dangerous indication of a plot than dancing around a small tree of liberty and some enthusiastic and scurrilous outpourings in verse and prose. But the government wished to set an example; several of the accused were executed, others sentenced to long terms of imprisonment. The purpose was achieved. Political life and active participation ceased entirely in the monarchy.[3] Even the famous Austrian anthem, the "Gott erhalte," composed by Joseph Haydn and written by Lorenz Leopold Haschka, one of the leading scribes in the service of governmental reaction, hardly expressed the feeling of the people; it was a manifestation of the court, not of the nation.[4]

The inefficiency of the administration was fully revealed in the wars which Austria fought against the French Revolution. The Emperor's younger brothers, Archdukes Karl (1771-1847) and Johann (1782-1859), both more popular than he, repeatedly demanded reforms and tried to activize the administration and the people. Their efforts were in vain. Before the energy of the new French nationalism, the ancient German Reich was doomed. Though Francis—until 1806 the head of the German nation as constituted in the Holy Roman Empire—was in no way animated by any German patriotism in his wars against France, Austria nevertheless showed more concern for German interests than did Prussia or other German states. Revolutionary France regarded Austria as its archenemy and wished to base its foreign policy upon a close alliance with Prussia. This friendly feeling was then heartily reciprocated by the Prussian government and Prussian public opinion. In a sequence of swift blows the Reich crumbled. Prussia's separate peace with France at Basel in 1795, Austria's peace treaty of Campoformio in 1797, and the Congress of Rastatt in 1799 prepared the dissolution of the Empire. The left bank of the Rhine was ceded to France, the secularization of the ecclesiastical principalities destroyed the last pillar of imperial influence, and the smaller German states began to compete for the favors of France. True, a Viennese poet had expressed in 1796, after the first victories of Archduke Charles over the French armies of Jourdan and Moreau, the hope that German unity under the protection of the widespread wings of the imperial eagle of the Habsburgs would save Germany from French domination; but this hope was not fulfilled.[5] Neither German unity nor any patriotic desire for it were forthcoming. Ten years later, the formation of the Confederation of the Rhine on August 1, 1806, sounded the death knell of the Reich. On August 6, Francis II laid down the imperial crown. Two years before, he had assumed the title of Francis I, Emperor of Austria. The world-imperial dream of the Habsburgs—the legacy of Rome transferred to the Germans—was ended. Austria became a territorial state. Its population and its geographic position could have secured to the Habsburgs the leadership in Germany, Italy, and the Balkans. But their realm was never strong and united enough to fulfill this function. No common patriotism animated the peoples and called them to participate in an Austrian idea and mission. The government did not encourage it; it distrusted "enthusiasm"; it preferred tranquillity and order.

Only in the year 1809, when Austria alone among the states of the former German Empire took up arms against Napoleon, the government made a short-lived effort to arouse a national consciousness among the people.[6] Vienna became for a brief while the center of German nationalism; a patriotic literature flowered; Austrian poets like Josef Freiherr von Hormayr, Heinrich von Colin, Ignaz Castelli, and Karoline Pichler gained popularity with their songs and plays.[7] Hormayr also inspired the *Vaterländische Blätter für den Oesterreichischen Kaiserstaat*, which Johann Michael Armbruster founded in 1808 "to bring the inhabitants of the hereditary lands of the Emperor and King together to make them mutually better acquainted and to promote love of the fatherland through knowledge of it" [die Bewohner der k.k. Erbstaaten mit sich selbst näher bekannt zu machen und Vaterlandsliebe durch Vaterlandskunde zu befördern].

German romanticists like the brothers Schlegel, Friedrich von Gentz, and Adam Müller flocked to Vienna, where the memories of the Reich survived; for through its fascination with the past, romanticism rekindled interest in the medieval imperial tradition. Even Arndt, who later turned his hopes to Prussia, wrote a popular song, "Oesterreich an Ehren und an Siegen reich," and he called upon the Austrians: "Up then, friends, speed to the Rhine, and Mainz and Wesel and Landau quickly attacked and captured," and with the Austrians envisioned back on the Rhine, Arndt appealed to the Germans: "Then let us shout: Freedom and Austria! and: Franz is our Emperor, not Bonaparte. . . . Austria is the rallying point, the House of Habsburg shall rule; for we want a German master." In his army order of April 6, Archduke Karl proclaimed: "Europe's liberty has taken refuge under our banners; your victories will untie her fetters, and your German brothers, now as yet in the ranks of the enemy, await their redemption." Turning to the German nation, he informed them: "We fight to save the independence of the Austrian monarchy and to return to Germany the independence and national honor which are its due. Our resistance is its last support for salvation, our cause is Germany's cause."

But the war was lost; in their appeal to German nationalism the Austrian patriots had no success. The Germans did not heed the appeal. Some remained neutral; none took up the war against Bonaparte. No German state fought on Austria's side for the cause of Germany. The armies of Bavaria and Württemberg fought with the French, and their peoples greeted the French army rapturously as it marched through their lands. The German masses had no feeling for German nationalism or unity; they cared only for peace. The German princes owed too much to

Napoleon to desert him and trusted his destiny. Nor did the patriotic upsurge last in Austria. The people in Vienna very quickly forgot their short-lived national enthusiasm. The peace treaty which inflicted such heavy losses upon the monarchy was welcomed by the Austrian population; the delights of peace seemed far preferable to the exertions of war. Little hostility was manifested toward Napoleon, who in 1805 and in 1809 could show himself freely and without elaborate protection to the inhabitants of the enemy capital.[8] Together with the short-lived patriotism, civic liberty in Austria was buried under a pompous tombstone erected by a paternalistic bureaucracy. Count Philipp Stadion (1763-1824) intended to carry through reforms similar to those introduced at that time by Stein in Prussia. He failed; his place was taken by another Rhenish aristocrat, Count Clemens Lothar Metternich (1773-1859), an eighteenth-century nobleman, deeply hostile to the spirit of 1789 and to the idea of nationalism. The patriotic upsurge of 1809 was stillborn.

Characteristically, the only truly patriotic struggle on Austrian soil in 1809 was motivated neither by German nationalism nor by revolutionary ideas. It resembled the resistance of the Spaniards against the French in the defense of their ancient traditions and their inherited religion. It was fought by "reactionary," not by "progressive" forces. When the peasants of Tyrol rose at the beginning of 1809, their main enemies were not the French but their Bavarian fellow Germans. Their loyalty was not to a German nation which did not exist for them—nor did it exist anywhere at that time except in the hearts and dreams of a few German intellectuals—nor to an Austrian monarchy with the peoples of which they had hardly any contact, but to God, Emperor, and their land Tyrol. Their fundamentalist religion had been deeply offended by the "enlightened" reforms of the King of Bavaria whose subjects they had become; they felt only repugnance for this modern secular regime. Their Emperor was the Habsburg prince to whose ancestors their forefathers had owed loyalty, their fatherland was Tyrol. As one man they rose in defense of tradition. Within a month the whole of Tyrol was liberated from Bavarian rule. Tyrolian sharpshooters under the leadership of Andreas Hofer (1767-1810) were victorious on the Iselberg near Innsbruck. A few weeks later, however, Austria's defeat sealed Tyrol's fate. Yet Hofer did not give up the struggle, even against a numerous French army. Its superiority, however, proved too great; a second battle on the Iselberg decided against the Tyrolese. Hofer, who escaped, was betrayed while in hiding, arrested, and executed by the French in Mantua on February 20, 1810.[9] His memory was often celebrated in the years to come by Austrian patriots and German nationalists. He and his fellow fighters, however, had been neither. They were faithful to their native mountains, which circumscribed their political horizon, and to their ancient privileges and customs, which dominated their thoughts and feelings. Nevertheless their example, almost as much as that of the Spaniards, served as an inspiration to rising German nationalism.

Less enthusiastic and determined than the people of Tyrol in their defense of the House of Habsburg were the other nationalities of the Empire. None of them was yet touched by a spirit of nationalism. The patriotism of the Viennese in 1809 was of a hybrid character—half German nationalism and half Austrian patriotism—and quickly passed away. The proclamation which Napoleon sent from Schönbrunn in 1809 to the Hungarians—"I offer you the integrity of your territory, of your liberty and of your constitutions, whether as they have existed or as they may be modified by yourselves . . . You have national customs and a national language! Resume therefore your existence as a nation!"—remained without effect.[10] The Hungarian peoples remained loyal to the House of Habsburg—or rather this traditional loyalty hardly presented a problem to them—and the nobility was interested in maintaining the historical state rights and privileges of the kingdom separated from the other lands of the monarchy. While in these other lands the central power succeeded in overcoming the resistance of the medieval Estates, in Hungary the Estates remained powerful and retained control over monetary contributions and the raising of recruits. The meetings of the Hungarian Reichstag (diet) in 1805, 1807, and 1811 were filled with the struggle of the Estates against the centralizing and modernizing tendencies of the monarchy. In assuming the title of Emperor of Austria, Francis wished to emphasize the unity of all the lands under his rule. Many Hungarian nobles, on the other hand, regarded him only as King of Hungary and wished him to transfer his residence from Vienna to their midst. The resistance of the Hungarian Estates hindered the over-due modernization of the country. For a long time it did not share in the progress of the western parts of the Habsburg monarchy. It remained backward, and its medieval constitution represented an idol which the nobility in the name of patriotism sought to protect by all means—the more, because all its privileges rested on it.[11] Sporadic demands to re-place Latin by Magyar as the official language of the kingdom were rejected.[12] From 1811 to 1825 the Austrian government did not recall the Reichstag. But of all the parts of the monarchy, Hungary was the only one in which, thanks to the strength of the aristocracy, something like a public opinion was represented by the lower nobility.

The last attempt which was made in the Napoleonic era to rouse the population of the monarchy to action was the unfortunate conspiracy of Archduke Johann and Baron Hormayr to call the peoples of Tyrol and the Alps in 1813 to a people's war against Napoleon, while Francis and Metternich still hesitated to join the "War of Liberation." This

"Alpenbund" conspiracy planned an uprising on Easter Day, April 19, 1813, but the leaders were arrested on March 7, the Archduke was forbidden to enter Tyrol for twenty years, and Hormayr and others were imprisoned. The Austrian war of 1813-14 against Napoleon was conducted without the popular patriotic participation which the government had briefly sought in 1809. Austria's resistance to Napoleon in 1809 did not kindle the flame of German nationalism. Metternich quickly came to the conclusion that German nationalism was no real force with which policy would have to reckon or on which policy could rely. Austria's defeat in 1809 vindicated those who regarded Napoleon's domination as final. The marriage of the Habsburg princess to Napoleon, the alliance of Austria and Prussia with France against Russia, seemed to mark the climax for the union of all German lands under Napoleon. Yet German nationalism began its growth at that very time of apparent triumph of Napoleon. The inspiration of this nationalism had geographically and spiritually nothing to do with Austria as it developed under Francis I and Metternich.

XXIV

Romanticism and the Rise
of German Nationalism

THE growth of German nationalism was prepared by two movements of very different origin and nature. The older one, romanticism, was in its beginning little concerned with politics and the state. It was an aesthetic revolution, a resort to the imagination, almost feminine in its sensibility; it was poetry more deeply indebted to the spirit of music than the poetry of the eighteenth century had been, rich in emotional depth, more potent in magic evocation. German romanticism, however, wished to be more than poetry. It was a philosophy, an interpretation of life, nature, and history—and this philosophic character distinguished it from romanticism in other lands. Its philosophy of history was sharply opposed to the rationalism of the eighteenth century and of the French Revolution; romanticism mobilized the fascination of an often legendary past to fight against the "abstract" principles of 1789. In that indirect way romanticism came to concern itself with political and social life and with the state.

The other movement was political in its very origin and substance; it sought to reform Prussia and to apply some of the experiences of 1789 to the reconstruction of that state. It was a rational and conscious effort of administrators and soldiers, without the fascinating and bewildering contradictions of romanticism. In its spirit it was rather a continuation of the eighteenth-century Enlightenment, but with a new understanding for popular forces and national integration learned from the French Revolution.

Neither of these two movements had any clear-cut program for a modern German nation-state. While the romanticists emphasized the peculiarity of the German mind and thus furthered the growth of a common German cultural consciousness, the Prussian reformers stressed the organization and power of the Prussian state; the memory of their intentions and achievements made Prussia, half a century later, the center of crystallization for German political consciousness.

Romanticism started as a movement of intellectuals, many of them unsettled bohemians, types that are often found in the vanguard of movements of cultural renovation which coincide with a period of beginning social change. They were the spiritual children of the Storm and Stress which had preceded them by thirty years, and they were in ardent opposition to the mature Goethe, who had long outgrown his own brief Storm and Stress period. They admired Goethe as a creative man of letters, as the embodiment of the princely artist, but they rejected his concept of the individual. Goethe's goal of education was the well-rounded harmonious man, the "Persönlichkeit," the personality, which willingly subordinates itself to binding forms and to the obligation of universal law, which rejoices in measure, symmetry, and proportion, which acknowledges the limits of the human and the humane. The romantic individual, on the other hand, regarded himself as unique— not as a representative of a universal order, but as a law unto himself, rejecting all limits imposed by measure or by society and proclaiming the right to full freedom for his creative genius.[1] Like the Stormers and Stressers, the romanticist felt himself hemmed in by the society which he found around or rather beneath himself. But he did not accept the titanic loneliness of the Storm and Stress. He was drawn longingly towards a community of like-minded free individuals who would live an unhampered and full life according to their innermost emotions. The extreme complexity and the anguished groping of this search for a community was heightened by the underlying all-demanding subjectivism; the unique individual longed for a total self-assertion of all his conflicting desires and yet felt the tragic need for fulfillment in the miracle of a true harmonious union in which all the conflicting opposites of life would be reconciled, of a new Golden Age which seemed accessible only to the magic power of the artist. Art became to the romanticists the new religion.

In their quest for the miraculous the romanticists found the rationalism and common sense of the eighteenth century shallow and superficial. The decisive force of the individual was not to be found in intellect and reason, according to the romanticists; it resided in his sentiments and emotions, which distinguished him from all others and rendered him unique among men. There was no need for rational agreement; the strength of the individual's desires in which his true ego expressed itself validated them; the passion of longing established the right to its object. The more passionate a man was, the more fully he lived. Passion was the prerogative of the artist, poet, seer, who obeyed deep dark impulses in his innermost self. This discovery of the irrational and subconscious enriched poetry and the understanding of man. There was, as Goethe recognized, a threat to the rational order of law and society in this newly discovered depth. It was a depth to lose oneself in rather than to measure and control. The desired and desirable could easily appear to poetic imagination as the impossible and the indispensable which had to be achieved at any cost. The world itself could be turned into a mere instrument of full self-realization or self-enjoyment.

The ideal community of the utopian dream refused to accept the hard limitations of reality imposed by law and necessity in the interests of equal fellowmen. It promised to unite all in an organic way: everybody would be fully himself without any limitations, and yet at the same time fully part of the whole, in a loving embrace without conflict or friction. In such a perfect community, individual and society were no longer in need of legal and constitutional guarantees in their relationship. Individual and community became two sides of the one perfect life, which would be all in all, beyond and above legal distinctions and the need for them. Anarchic individualism found its complement in the total community. Both these extremes existed outside the real society, with its necessary adjustments and compromises; they led a "pure life" in the imagination of the romantic artists. To mistake imagination for reality or even for a desirable reality was bound to spell danger to the free individual and to a society based on law.

The various and often contradictory currents of the romantic movement began as an artistic revolt against eighteenth-century culture and literature; these did not warm the lonely and searching heart. Even worse seemed the fact that this apparently uninspired and uninspiring civilization was inflated with philistine pride in the recent progress of man, with the utilitarian satisfaction of the middle class, with the presumptuous emptiness of common men. The romanticists found in the eighteenth century neither chivalry nor poetry, neither miracle nor mystery. French rationalism and the French Revolution had looked down upon the past and especially upon the Middle Ages. The romanticists found in this very period the wondrous fairyland which they sadly missed in the present. Repelled by the contemporary world, they discovered inspiration and beauty, meaning and guidance, in the past. Therein they seemed to follow Justus Möser and Herder, the earlier forerunners of German nationalism.[2] But Möser was a practical statesman and jurist, and his love of the sturdy rural freeholders of the Middle Ages was deeply rooted in his personal experience. Herder's vision was infinitely broader. Like the romanticists, he saw great creative forces at work in every phenomenon of nature and history, a dynamic pantheism of organic growth; yet for him all these forces were held within a context of enlightened humanitarianism and rational morality, which were rejected by the romanticists. Though Möser and Herder understood and valued the past, they lived in the present and wished to go forward; the romanticists succumbed to the lure of history and wished to enrich the present by reviving the past. They felt it to be so overflowing with poetry, so venerable with legend and prophecy, that they could not study it with rational detachment. It seemed to them impenetrable to the analytical approach and the cautious work of scholarly reason. It could be embraced only as a whole by the intuition of a great love which plunged the longing individual into the past and merged him with its flow through the present, carrying him forward into the future.

Thus the individual found himself deeply rooted in the past, indissolubly united with it, inescapably determined by it. His thought and activity appeared conditioned by history, by the peculiar traditions of the national community, which differed from those of all others. Though the romanticists had no factual foundation for the belief, they were convinced that national characteristics were never so pronounced as in the Middle Ages. The poetry and the art of knights and guilds seemed to them to express the true national soul, its original creative force not yet corrupted by a rationalism which makes everything alike and which deprives it all of life. The nation and its past set the model—not a universal model, but one valid only for a single national community and its members. Thus the national community gained a new central importance for all cultural life. The concept of individuality, unique and all-containing, was transferred from the individual to the national community, which appeared as a higher individual, of infinite relevance and endowed with creative force. The nation was no longer a legal society of individuals entering into union according to general rational principles and for mutual benefits; it was an incomparable and unique organic growth, an original phenomenon of nature and history, leading its own life according to the laws of its growth. Civilization and law were no longer regarded as the results of conscious individual efforts, but were deemed to be the results of an unconscious growth of the community, of the immanent forces of the people. This national individuality, alive, growing, and striving, often stirred by desires for power and expansion, appeared as a manifestation of the divine with a special mission to fulfill. It overcame the stillness characteristic of the Germany of the late eighteenth century, and followed voices calling it to unfold its dynamic forces and to live and explore all its potentialities.

The national community or the state—the romanticists did not establish any clear distinction—became the source of all aesthetic and soon also of political and ethical creativity. It was a personality overflowing with life and pulsating with movement, not a mechanical and "dead" concept—for so the state of the Enlightenment appeared to the romanticists. The relationship of man to the state became intimate and highly personal; the state was an object of deep love and admiring devotion. Such a state resembled easily the feudal patriarchal realm, a great family estate held together by ties of love and mutual responsibility, deeply hostile to the spirit of rational capitalism and to the mobility of trade, but agreeable to "socialist" measures of control and protection of the individual within the community. This ideal represented a flight from reality into mythology, from action into dream. It was not a return to any real past; it was an idyllic myth and a poetic dream which transfigured the past into a Golden Age. The first and in many ways the greatest of the German romanticists, Friedrich Freiherr von Hardenberg (1772-1801), who wrote under the name of Novalis, lived in a strange borderland of poetic genius, mystic thought, and consuming malady; he hated the Prussia of Frederick the Great as a soulless rational machine, and he glorified the mediocre Frederick William III and his touchingly beautiful Queen Louise (1776-1810) as the fulfillment of true monarchy.[3]

Novalis' close friend and contemporary Karl Wilhelm Friedrich Schlegel (1772-1829) defined in 1798 their poetic ideal. Poetry "can be fathomed by no theory, and only divinatory criticism could presume to characterize its ideal. It alone is infinite, because it alone is free, and recognizes as its first law that the arbitrary caprice of the poet tolerates no law."[4] The following year Schlegel's older brother August Wilhelm (1767-1845) complained bitterly about the unpoetic character of the age:

> The times when a poet by the presentation of great events of antiquity could become the preserver of folk sagas, the beloved teacher of the nation, are perhaps gone forever. It seems almost impossible to write a national heroic poem. The word Fatherland has lost its magic power; the place of patriotism has been taken by a more general but therefore also colder interest for mankind. With the destruction of the folk religions the old saga perished too. We have been alienated from our ancestors, while the later Greeks encountered the memory of their Homeric heroes in thousands of objects. But our peaceful education, which is entirely directed toward domestic activities, seems to have made us generally less susceptible to the impression of great deeds in which warrior courage prevails.[5]

In spite of the lament over the loss of heroic patriotism, the early romanticists hardly evinced any national feeling. Though Novalis endowed the state as the true community with an unprecedented importance, he did not see it as a German national state. His famous "Fragments," some of which were published in *Athenäum* and many more left among his papers, were sometimes contradictory and often disjointed, rather the result of a deep religious intuition than part of a politico-philosophical system; nevertheless, their main tendency was unmistakable. They all wished to make the state more of an intimate reality in man's life, to fill it with higher significance.

> It is a great mistake of our states, that one sees the state too little. The state should be visible everywhere and every man should be characterized as a citizen. Could one not introduce everywhere marks of distinction and uniforms? Whoever regards this as insignificant disregards an essential part of our nation. . . . The state is too little known among us. There ought to be heralds of the state, preachers of patriotism. At present most citizens are on a rather indifferent, almost hostile footing with the state. . . . The state is a person like the individual. What man is to himself, the state is to man. The states will remain different, as long as men are different. Essentially the state, like man, remains always the same. . . . The perfect citizen lives entirely in the state; he has no property outside the state.

This all-embracing state was, however, not a political concept; it was a poetic creation, a great beautiful individual, the embodiment of that perfection to which man aspires.

> A state with intense spiritual and intellectual life will by itself be poetical. The more spiritual the state is, the more it approaches the poetical, the more joyfully will every citizen out of love for the beautiful great individual limit his own demands and be ready to make the necessary sacrifices, the less will the state need it and the more similar will the spirit of the state become to the spirit of a single exemplary man who has expressed forever the one law only: be as good and as poetical as possible.[6]

Such a new emphasis on the state could be easily explained as the result of various influences—the reawakened memory of the ancient city-state, Rousseau's glorification of it, the enthusiasm of French patriots; yet with Novalis it carried a new and different note, it sounded warmer and more intimate. It was a manifestation of the same love that he found in marriage and in religious mysticism, a perfect union and interpenetration. The ideal state was for him a divine work of art, a theocratic monarchy with a perfect prince at the head. "A true prince is the artist of artists. Every man should become an artist. Everything can become beautiful art."[7] As every man should become an artist and a king, this true monarchy was compatible with a true republic; in fact they were complementary, for the republic demanded the identification of every citizen with the state and his activization in its service. Novalis complained that in the German cities, only petty local events were discussed, that great and general questions aroused no interest and were found boring:

> This is better in republics, where the state is the main concern of every person and everybody feels his existence tied up in an immense living whole, thus broadens his imagination and his understanding with great causes, and almost involuntarily forgets his narrow self in the great totality.

True republicanism meant general participation in the whole state, intimate contact and harmony of all members of the state. Novalis was convinced that a king without a republic and a republic without a king were nothing but empty words.[8] Neither of them existed for the utilitarian purpose of making men happier; the true state made men better and stronger. It did not save them from hardship; rather, it increased the burdens imposed upon them—not, however, without at the same time increasing their strength.

> The best among the former French monarchs wished to make his subjects so rich that every peasant would have every Sunday chicken and rice on the table. But would not a government be preferable under which a peasant would rather have a slice of molded bread at home than eat a roast in another country, and yet thank God for the good luck of having been born in his land?[9]

Novalis nowhere stressed a German state as a desirable goal.

> The European stands as high over the German as the German does over the Saxon, the Saxon over the resident of Leipzig. Above the Europeans is the cosmopolitan. . . . Our old nationality was truly Roman. The instinctive universal policy and tendency of the Romans is shared by the German people. The best thing that the French gained in the Revolution is a share of Germanity.

There are Germans everywhere. Germanity is as little confined to a peculiar state as are Romanity, Hellenity, or Britannity. They all are general human characteristics which only have become here and there more general. Germanity is true popularity, and therefore an idea.[10] Though Novalis expected much from the true state, and sometimes hinted in his mysterious way at some future cultural greatness of the Germans, his vision did not encompass the Age of Nationalism; it looked backward to an idealized Christianity which had brought spiritual unity to medieval Europe; it looked forward to a new Jerusalem as the capital of the earth, where Christianity would again establish its spiritual dominion.

> Blood will not cease to flow over Europe until the nations become aware of their frightful madness, which will drive them around in a circle until, struck and soothed by divine music, they step before the altar intermingling to undertake works of peace and until a loving feast of peace is celebrated under burning tears on smoking battlefields. Only religion can revive Europe, can make the nations secure, and can reinstall Christianity in a new glory, visibly on earth in its old peacemaking office.[11]

This was the message of Novalis' strange and significant essay "Die Christenheit oder Europa" which he wrote in 1799 and submitted to the editors of *Athenäum*. These editors, the Schlegels and Tieck, rejected it because they found its historical conception too little documented and the conclusion too arbitrary. Though Novalis, a descendant of Protestant Pietists, never embraced Catholicism, his praise for the medieval Christian hierarchy was at that time too strong for his fellow romanticists, so many of whom were later to enter the haven of the Catholic Church. But though the essay had no historical foundation and mingled poetry with religious outpourings, it was a historical document of great importance. It introduced a new interpretation of history which ran counter to that of the eighteenth century and of the French Revolution. Like Bonald and De Maistre, Novalis rejected the claims of reason and progress.[12] Reformation, rationalism, and revolution seemed to him one misfortune, a deviation from the true path of Europe, a rapid descent from that summit which the spiritual universal monarchy of Christendom had reached in the thirteenth century. "These were beautiful brilliant times," the essay began,

> when Europe was a Christian land inhabited by one Christianity; one great common interest united the most distant provinces of this vast spiritual realm. Without great earthly possessions, one supreme head directed and united the great political forces. A numerous caste to which everybody had access was immediately under his orders, executed his bidding, and tried zealously to strengthen his benefits and power.

Here was a new picture of the Middle Ages—no longer the Dark Ages of barbarism, of crude savagery and ridiculous superstition, but a haven of peace and harmony, of spirituality and contentment. Novalis and the romanticists after him rediscovered the Middle Ages and presented them in the transfigured glory of magic poetry.

For Novalis the Middle Ages was still a universal period. Soon, however, the romanticists were to reinterpret it as the fountainhead of national cultures and national life, and even as the time of their exemplary development. Through romanticism history added its weight to nationalism. Even Novalis contributed to this historicism:

> We carry the burden of our fathers as we have received their good, and thus men actually live in the whole past and in the future and nowhere less than in the present. . . . The historian must often become an orator. For he recites gospels—the whole history is a gospel.[13]

From here, it was only a step to regarding the past of the nation as a gospel to which the living generations were beholden and to which they would have to repair to discover artistic and spiritual treasures that were their own. Within one decade the romanticists accomplished a great pioneer work: the literature of the Middle Ages was collected, edited, and published—the poetry of the courts and knights as well as the traditional tales of the common people.

In the beginning the romanticists found a model in Johannes Müller, whose *Geschichte schweizerischer Eidgenossenschaft* began to appear in 1786. He combined love and sympathy for medieval history with great skill in writing and the ability to evoke local color. His rhetorical brilliance, hardly supported by exact knowledge, secured to him a vast audience among the generation which came under the spell of Rousseau's sentimentalism. The emphasis which Müller put on folksongs, old chronicles, and legends endeared him as much to the romanticists as his theory that a historian needs a "soul." He wrote with patriotic fervor about the strong Swiss men of the past and thus confirmed the romantic conviction that the Middle Ages was a period of true patriotism and heroic manhood.[14] Müller was also one of the first to draw attention to the importance of the medieval epic Nibelungenlied, which was published by Christoph Heinrich Müller in 1782 after having been practically unknown for three centuries. A few years later, Johannes Müller declared in his *History of the Swiss Confederation* that the Nibelungenlied could become the German Iliad, an opinion in which August Wilhelm Schlegel later concurred. In an article in Friedrich Schlegel's *Deutsches Museum* in 1812, August Wilhelm Schlegel demanded that the Nibelungenlied be used as the chief classic in German education, to impress it upon the mind and memory of the youth, and thus to endow the history of the German people with a great poetic background.[15] His wish was soon fulfilled. Friedrich Heinrich von der Hagen (1780-1856), one of the early Germanistic scholars who popularized medieval poetry, translated the Nibelungenlied. So did August Zeune (1778-1853), the founder in 1814 of the Gesellschaft für deutsche Sprache, whose special edition of this translation, a *Feld- und Zeltausgabe*, German youth carried as an inspiration to the battlefields and into their tents in the war against France.

The first decade of the new century brought a rich crop of editions of medieval literature. This joy of discovery, this quest for national cultural roots in the untilled and promising soil of the past, set an example to the cultural national awakening of other central and eastern European peoples. Ludwig Tieck (1773-1853), who with the Schlegels and Novalis belonged to the older generation of romanticists, opened the cycle with his *Minnelieder aus dem schwäbischen Zeitalter* (1803). "If we look back," he wrote in the introduction, "upon a period hardly past which was characterized by indifference to and disregard of the letters and arts, then we shall be astonished to notice the quick change which in so short a time has come about, so that there is now not only interest in the monuments of the past but appreciation of them."

At a time when German political fortunes seemed at as low an ebb as in the Thirty Years War, when the future of the Reich was uncertain, when there was hardly anywhere an active national sentiment, the romanticists called up the past to kindle the spirit of the present. They went back to the treasures which they believed buried and yet alive in the popular tradition and in the mind of the people, in the *Volksgemüt* which had not yet been influenced by the universal rational civilization of the eighteenth century. Two years after Tieck's minnesongs, there appeared the first volume of the famous collection of folk songs *Des Knaben Wunderhorn,* which two representatives of the younger romantic generation edited, the Prussian Junker Ludwig Joachim (called Achim) von Arnim (1781-1831) and the Rhinelander Clemens Brentano (1778-1842).[16] In 1807 their friend Joseph Görres (1776-1848) explored and discussed popular almanacs and other old story books,[17] and the next decade brought the famous editions by the brothers Grimm—Jacob Ludwig (1785-1863) and Wilhelm Karl (1786-1859)—the *Kinder- und Hausmärchen* (1812-1815) and the *Deutsche Sagen* (1816-1818), an analysis of the oldest epic traditions of the Germans.

In 1808 Arnim edited the *Zeitung für Einsiedler* [Journal for Hermits], a rallying point for friends who found solace and comfort in the solitude of nature and the recollections of the past. His introduction announced the birth of a new patriotism: "Germany, my poor, poor fatherland," he wrote, "and tears began to flow out of our eyes, my eyes and the eyes of the readers." [18] Jacob Grimm wrote there:

> In our time a great love of folk songs has developed and it will also draw attention to the sagas and folk tales which still circulate among the same people and are preserved in a few forgotten places. The ever-growing realization of the true nature of history and poetry has aroused the wish to save from oblivion

what previously appeared contemptible, at the very last moment when it still could be collected.

This literature of the common people seemed to the romantic enthusiasts to be of great value—truly national and superior to modern art-literature. "Only folk poetry is perfect," Wilhelm Grimm wrote, "because God himself wrote it, like the laws of Sinai. It is not put together from pieces, like human work."

In the opinion of the romanticists the nationality of a people was based not upon its modern constitution or legislation, but upon its traditional customs and mores which grow and develop organically according to their own nature and which cannot be interfered with from without. They represented the true folk spirit, the *Volksgeist*. In their strange and quaint ways there was more wisdom and more health than in all the lofty constructions on the basis of rational principles. The folk traditions were securely founded in history and had grown up in harmony with the conditions of the land. They had stood the test of time, because they were true; the principles of 1789, the romanticists believed, had failed because they were conceived without regard for history and the peculiar conditions of a people and had falsely claimed universal validity. Had the edifice so proudly built on these abstract foundations survived a few days of enthusiasm? Had it not crumbled in chaos and disorder, in terror and war? Surely, the romanticists argued, men could not find guidance and salvation in vague and anemic rational generalizations, but only in the concrete historical tradition. Even if the regime established by the French Revolution were fitting for France, it could not be imitated in other countries, where it must fail because alien to the national character. History alone was a safeguard for national destiny; romanticism made the study of national history important to statesmen, who found therein an arsenal for fighting the spread of revolution and for establishing or maintaining national independence.

The Volksgeist determined, according to the romanticists, not only the right constitution but also the right laws of a nation. In 1794 Prussia introduced a new legal code, the Allgemeine Preussische Landrecht. It was conceived in the rational spirit of the Enlightenment, though it made all due concessions to the aristocratic and militaristic social structure of Frederick's kingdom.[19] It superseded the customary laws of the various provinces and replaced their historical growth and complex diversity by the logical uniformity of eighteenth-century legal concepts. The romanticists regarded it as a violation of the Volksgeist and of the laws of history. In May 1805 Jacob Grimm wrote to his brother Wilhelm: "I received very sad news yesterday, that a code of laws is to be introduced in Hesse. Must everything be imitated that sprouts out of the

flat Prussian sand? The news has affected me grievously." In another
letter of the same period Jacob expressed his conviction that the new
code would destroy all true juridical scholarship.[20] For true law could
be only customary law, the roots of which historical scholarship can
trace to the remote past and the almost unconscious growth of which
it can follow throughout succeeding generations. Law codified according
to abstract or modern utilitarian principle was rejected by the romanticist "school of historical law" as much as was natural law founded
on reason. Both these concepts of law seemed too universal, too rational,
and therefore unhistorical and unscholarly. When, after the defeat of
Napoleon, Anton Friedrich Justus Thibaut (1772-1840), a leading German jurist of that period, pleaded in his *Über die Notwendigkeit eines
allgemeinen bürgerlichen Rechtes für Deutschland* (1814) for the unification of Germany through the introduction of a civil law code common to all German lands, a code which would end the confusion and
diversity of the many antiquated laws, he was sharply answered by
Friedrich Karl von Savigny (1779-1861), then professor of law at the
newly founded University of Berlin. In his *Vom Beruf unserer Zeit für
Gesetzgebung und Rechtswissenschaft,* Savigny denied the vocation of
the age for introducing new legislation and codifications.[21] Law in the
true sense of the word had to be not only national but traditional, an
emanation of the Volksgeist, and courts of law acted as its representatives,
not as the exponents of a common reason. Karl Friedrich Eichhorn (1781-
1854) inaugurated with his *Deutsche Staats- und Rechtsgeschichte,* of
which the first volume appeared in 1808, research into the history of
German law with the purpose of promoting the continuity of legal
development in accord with the national character and the folk traditions. Romantic historic scholarship had its great day. It could explain,
and if need be, excuse, everything by appealing to the newly discovered
mystically creative forces of the folk, of the various Volksgeister which
formed and determined character and events, art and religion, constitutions and law.

XXV

Friedrich Schlegel

EARLIER than other German writers, Friedrich Schlegel found the way from rational universalism to a mystic nationalism.[1] Under the influence of Kant's *Essay on Perpetual Peace* he wrote in 1796 an *Essay on the Concept of Republicanism* in which he regarded political liberty and equality as indispensable conditions of the good state, and republicanism as of necessity democratic. In the enthusiasm of youth he wrote to his brother on May 27, 1796: "I cannot deny before you that the divine republicanism is still a little nearer to my heart than the divine criticism of the most divine poetry." Like many Frenchmen of that period, the young German men of letters looked to classical antiquity as the model for the ideal political form which could be no other than republican.[2] But at the same time, Schlegel discovered the greatness of the German national character, which was to him more a promise for the future than a reality of the present. "Not much attention is yet paid to the German character," he wrote to his brother on November 8, 1791. "Recently I think I have discovered that our people has a very great character." He found it so far only in a few great men—Frederick, Goethe, Klopstock, Winckelmann, and Kant:

> There is not much to be found anywhere which equals men of this kind, and they have several qualities of which we can find no trace in any known people. I see in all the achievements of the Germans, especially in the field of scholarship, only the germ of an approaching great time, and I believe that things will happen among our people that never before happened among men. Ceaseless activity, profound penetration into the interior of things, very great fitness for morality and liberty, these I find in our people. Everywhere I see traces of becoming and growth.

This early and rather isolated passage was resumed in a poem "An die Deutschen" which Schlegel wrote toward the beginning of the year

1800. He called upon the Germans to remember their spiritual mission and to recreate in religion, philosophy, and poetry the once flowering civilizations of Hellas and India. While Europe decayed, he found in Germany the source of new life which would awaken the other peoples:

> Europas Geist erlosch; in Deutschland fliesst
> Der Quell der neuen Zeit: die aus ihm tranken,
> Sind wahrhaft deutsch: die Heldenschar ergiesst
> Sich überall: erhebt den raschen Franken,
> Den Italiener zur Natur und Rom
> Wird wach.[3]

Schlegel had been converted to nationalism, but it was a purely cultural nationalism, unconcerned with the desirability of a nation-state. Had not the Greeks, without desiring or achieving national statehood, assumed the leadership of mankind in poetry, the arts, and sciences? And had not their great works clearly borne the stamp of their national character? Could not the Germans follow and become the Greeks of the new age? At about the same time Schiller expressed similar hopes in his fragmentary poem "Deutsche Grösse." [4] He felt that the greatness of Germany expressed itself in spiritual leadership. The Germans were the universal people, whose mission it was "to fulfill in themselves universal mankind and to unite in a wreath the most beautiful flowers of all peoples."

This attitude changed with Schlegel's journey to Paris in 1802. In crossing the Thuringian mountains and the Rhine River he discovered Germany, her nature and her past. His presence in France made him conscious of separation from his fatherland and of the alien character of the new environment. He was deeply impressed by the ruins of the Wartburg Castle near Eisenach, where the famous contest of the Minnesingers had been held and where Luther struggled and worked:

> If one sees objects like these, one cannot help remembering what the Germans once were, when the individual still had a fatherland. Looking at high castles like the Wartburg, one truly feels and thinks one understands why our ancestors always lived in their castles on the tops of mountains, and what joy of life was connected with it. Since men have gathered in the valleys and around the great roads, greedy for alien ways and alien money, the heights and castles stand deserted.

Thus the Middle Ages and their ruins began to recall a time of allegedly joyous living and high morality, while in the modern age, people, gathering into cities, succumbed to the lure of foreign gold and immorality.

> The poetry of former times has disappeared and with it the virtue, its sister. Instead of the *furore tedesco,* mentioned so

frequently by Italian poets, patience has become our first national virtue, and beside it humility, in contrast with the
formerly reigning mentality which caused a Spaniard who
traveled with Emperor Charles V through Germany to call the
Germans *los fieros Alemanos*. But as far as we are concerned, we
wish to retain firmly the image or rather the truth of these great
times and not become confused by the present misery. Perhaps
the slumbering lion will wake up once more, and even if we
should not live to see it, future world history will be full of the
deeds of the Germans.

Schlegel no longer turned to the Greek republic of antiquity as the
model, but to the German monarchy and knighthood of the Middle Ages.
Unlike Novalis, he no longer emphasized Christian or medieval spirituality and unity, but German virtue.

Among the world-conquering nations of the past the Germans
occupy one of the first ranks, and whether we compare them
with the Romans or the Arabs the comparison will be in their
favor. What distinguishes them above all from the Romans is
their greater love of liberty; it was with them not a mere word
but an innate sentiment. Though they were much too high-
minded to wish to impose their character upon other nations, it
nevertheless struck root where the soil was not too unfavorable,
and then honor and love, courage and loyalty grew there
mightily. Because of this original liberty of German life, which
is an everlasting character of the nation, [that life] appears in
its good times more originally and lastingly romantic than the
Oriental fairy world. Its enthusiasm was full of joy, childlike
simplicity, without coveting, not as one-sided and destructive
as the enthusiasm of those admirable fanatics who set the globe
on fire faster and wider than even the Romans—Eine gefühlte
Rechtlichkeit, die mehr ist als die Gerechtigkeit des Gesetzes
und der Ehre, eine kindlich aufrichtige und unerschütterliche
Treue und Herzlichkeit der Gesinnung ist der tiefste und hof-
fentlich nie ganz zu vertilgende Zug des deutschen Charakters.[5]

The Rhine impressed Schlegel as much as the Wartburg. It, too, seemed
to him to be a symbol of the beauty of German nature and of the
splendor of German history. His poem "Am Rheine" (1802) marked the
beginning of the romantic glorification of the river, which he called
"the all-too-faithful image of our fatherland, our history and our character." "Der alte vaterländische Strom erscheint uns wie ein mächtiger
Strom naturverkündender Dichtkunst."[6] These poetical sentiments first
found their theoretical expression in his *Philosophische Vorlesungen aus
den Jahren 1804 bis 1806*, in which he expressed his new political philosophy.[7] Eight years before, a republic had appeared to him the most

perfect form of government and the only safe guarantee of peace. Now, however, republicanism has become "a transient meteor which shines a few moments in a splendor of light but quickly goes out in a storm of civil discord and leaves behind destruction and confusion." Only the monarchy could be a true guardian of peace—not a constitutional monarchy, but the medieval monarchy of the Estates, the *Ständestaat* basing its life upon the moral guidance of the church. Like Novalis in his essay on Europe, Schlegel looked back to the medieval union of empire and church as the strongest bulwark of peace. The international tie among nations was guaranteed by the hierarchy of priests and scholars which was one and the same among all nations and above all national differences. But Schlegel went far beyond Novalis in his emphasis on nationality within this Christian universality. He demanded that the nation which as bearer of the imperial dignity exercised sovereignty over the neighboring nations must be very strong if not the strongest nation. More important was his insistence upon the nation as a new and in many ways higher reality of nature and history, a reality of supreme importance. "The concept of nation involves that all its members should form, as it were, only one individual." This fictitious corporate personality became a jealous guardian of the lives of the individuals which it comprised and which it claimed to mold. It imposed conditions which went far beyond the concept of a political nationality; it was intimately and intricately tied up with the natural and spiritual life of all its members.

To form a true nation—and that meant to Schlegel to resemble a closely knit and all inclusive family—he demanded that all its members must be held together by ties of blood, by descent from the same ancestors. The antiquity and purity of this common descent would guarantee the persistence of and the loyalty to traditional customs and habits: the greater the community of blood and the stronger therefore the perseverance of the past, the more solidly the people would form a nation. Second to a common past and affinity of blood, Schlegel rated unity of language, in which—for reasons difficult to understand because they contradict all historical evidence—he saw "the indisputable testimony of common descent." This new theory of nationalism culminated in two sentences which summed it up; the apodictic form of their statement was characteristic of the Age of Nationalism:

> It is much more appropriate to nature that the human races be strictly separated (*strenge abgesondert*) into nations than that several nations should be fused as has happened in recent times. . . . Each state is an independent individual existing for itself; it is unconditionally its own master, has its peculiar

character, and governs itself by its peculiar laws, habits, and customs.[8]

From that point of view, Schlegel protested against the assimilation of a defeated and backward nation to the higher civilization of the victor. "That would be highly immoral. The original moral character of a people, its customs and peculiarities, must be regarded as sacred." A subject nationality must be maintained as a separate entity, but it might be educated by the victor, even forcibly, as far as that was compatible with its character. In that way, Schlegel maintained, the Germans educated many nations—the Magyars and others. The French, however, Schlegel thought, were abusing their superiority to destroy the nationality of other peoples. Such an attitude justified in his opinion the union of all peoples threatened by the French for a war which would lead to the "total annihilation" of this "corrupt nation." [9] Schlegel was the first German writer of renown to issue such a strong call for German nationality and for a sacred war.

Schlegel was also the first to write patriotic poetry, exhorting the Germans to a confident struggle against Napoleon's tyranny. This poetic activity filled only a few years of his life, from 1805 to 1809; thereupon others like Arndt, Schenkendorff, and Rückert took up the mantle of national bard and soon far surpassed him in popularity. During those years Schlegel joined the Catholic Church and, a north German by birth, turned to Austria as the center and hope for German regeneration. There he became an official propagandist for the Austrian cause. In 1809 he called in strong and stirring proclamations upon the Germans outside Austria to stand by her and to brave all dangers in unity and courage. The same spirit breathed through the fervent appeal of his "Gelübde" [The Vow]:[10]

> Es sei mein Herz und Blut geweiht,
> Dich Vaterland zu retten.
> Wohlan, es gilt, du seist befreit,
> Wir sprengen deine Ketten!
> Nicht fürder soll die arge That,
> Des Fremdlings Übermuth, Verrath
> In deinen Schoss sich betten.
> Der deutsche Stamm ist alt und stark,
> Voll Hochgefühl und Glauben;
> Die Treue ist der Ehre Mark,
> Wankt nicht, wenn Stürme schnauben.
> Es schafft ein ernster, tiefer Sinn,
> Den Herzen solchen Hochgewinn,
> Den uns kein Feind mag rauben.
> So spotte jeder der Gefahr,

Die Freiheit ruft uns allen;
So will's das Recht und es bleibt wahr,
Wie auch die Loose fallen.
Ja, sinken wir der Übermacht,
So woll'n wir doch zur Todes Nacht
Glorreich hinüber wallen.

Though "The Vow" marked the end of Schlegel's patriotic poetry, he continued to elaborate his theory of nationalism. The lectures which he delivered in Vienna in 1810 *On Modern History* and the lecture series on *History of Ancient and Modern Literature* in 1812 were devoted to that task. Those of 1810 glorified the heroes of German history, especially the Habsburg princes Rudolf I, Ferdinand II, and Charles V.

> If one does not look on details but on the whole, there is no better counterweight against the onrush of the age than the memory of a great past. For that reason I thought of adding to the interpretation of the three great world-shaking periods— the migration of the Germanic tribes, the Crusades, and the Reformation—a picture of the former German nation painted in colors as strong as I could make them; of its oldest conditions when it lived in its original liberty and character, as well as of its development and culture in the Middle Ages. This demanded a special interpretative concern for the great medieval forces and forms of the state, for the relation and unifying tie of the church and of the old imperial position in Germany, Italy, and Europe, and for the spirit of knighthood.[11]

Schlegel's nationalism had all the fervor which the Age of Nationalism later developed in central and eastern Europe, but it was turned longingly backward to the period when the imperial idea—of which Schlegel thought the Germans alone worthy—and the universalism of the church still maintained some ethical unity among nations. His Catholic religion prevented him from glorifying the secularized popular state with its moral self-sufficiency.[12]

The lectures of 1812—and the periodical *Deutsches Museum*, which Schlegel then edited—were devoted to the thesis that "every literature must and should be national; this is its vocation, and this alone can give it its true and full value." The national spirit should determine language and music, painting and philosophy. But the first place belonged to poetry. It must preserve a people's memories and legends, embellish them, and perpetuate the glories of a great past, "as it happens in the heroic epics, where the miracle freely occurs and where the poet attaches himself to mythology." The spiritual growth of a nation depended on its possession of great national memories, which often lose themselves in the darkness of its origins and the preservation and glorification of which constitutes the most excellent task of poetry. Such national memories, the most wonderful heritage that a people can have, are an advantage which nothing else can replace. If a people finds itself in its own feelings elated and, as it were, ennobled by the possession of a great past, of memories from prehistoric times, in brief by the possession of poetry, it will be raised by this very fact to a higher plane. Memorable deeds, great events and destinies alone are not sufficient to keep our admiration and to determine the judgment of posterity; a people must also gain a clear consciousness of its own deeds and destinies. This self-consciousness of a nation which expresses itself in reflective and descriptive works, is its history.

The romanticists pointed to Shakespeare's historic plays as the model for the attempt to revive the national past and to make it part of the national consciousness. The theater seemed to them the most "national" of all the arts. Unfortunately the German romanticists, much stronger in reflection than in creation, were unable to create a national theater. Even the strongest dramatic talent of the time, Heinrich von Kleist, never reached the popularity of a Schiller.[13]

XXVI

The Romantic Concepts of History, State, and Liberty

For the romanticists the state became an object of poetry and adoration; they regarded it as something so lofty and wondrous, so full of miracle and mystery, that it could no longer be the work of free men founded for mutual benefit in the way that eighteenth-century thinkers had imagined. The work of Hugo Grotius defining the Western concept of the state—"Est autem civitas coetus perfectus liberorum hominum juris fruendi et communis utilitatis causa societas"—did not apply to the state of the German romanticists. The latter was, like the human being, a creation of the unfathomable will of God and of the elemental forces of nature, an ethical individual like man himself, only infinitely greater and more powerful. Joseph Freiherr von Eichendorff (1788-1857), a leader of the younger Catholic generation of romanticism, called the state "a spiritual community to make life as perfect as possible by developing the strength of mind and soul in a people, which alone could truly be called life." [1] Zacharias Werner who started as a disciple of the Enlightenment and later joined the Catholic Church and the romantic movement, defined the state as "a union which should make it possible for a group of human beings to fulfill their highest vocation. It isolates this group to give it back to mankind in an ennobled form." [2]

Yet the romanticists were individuals too strongly artistic to allow the state to impose a deadening uniformity. According to their ideal, the individual should serve and love the state with all his soul and mind, yet he should not be a robot but a free man living his own life, uniting with the others without losing his individuality. [3] They praised liberty, but it was a liberty not rooted in reason and equality but in history and peculiarity. In Eichendorff's novel *Ahnung und Gegenwart* Leontin shouted: "Es lebe die Freiheit," but he did not mean the universal liberty of 1789, which was the same for everybody and in which everybody felt himself proudly free everywhere. He found this cosmopolitan and individualistic liberty of the eighteenth century as loathsome as he found the natural religion of that period which regarded all religions as equal manifestations of the Divine, without gradations or preferences. To him liberty was the ancient and vital freedom—"jene uralte, lebendige Freiheit"—which he found among proud and simply living mountain peoples who could not live otherwise but as honor dictates.[4] The romantic concept of the ethical state, and its patriarchal union of love, was compatible with the existence of strong and independent individuals conscious of their position and their privileges. But it rejected the new Western age of individualism, of economic rationalism, of equal rights; it was a defensive attitude which looked longingly to the good old times and to more primitive communities which preserved their ancient traditions and their social order.[5]

Novalis and Eichendorff were poets, the brothers Schlegel were literary historians and critics,[6] and Adam Müller (1779-1829) was the political philosopher of romanticism.[7] With the vagueness characteristic of the movement, the limits between poetry and scholarship were neither clearly drawn nor observed. Yet amid all its contradictions—the romanticists were not systematic thinkers nor did they often achieve the perfection of finished labor; their work mostly remained fragments or lectures—romantic political philosophy held fast to the thesis that the state was not man's work nor established for the benefit of the individual, who was indissolubly part of the state and inevitably determined by its past.

> Men cannot be imagined outside the state. . . . The state is the intimate union of all physical and spiritual needs, of the whole physical and intellectual wealth, of the whole inward and outward life of a nation into a great energetic whole infinitely full of movement and life. . . . It is the totality of all human concerns (Der Staat ist die Totalität der menschlichen Angelegenheiten).[8]

In these words Müller expressed the sharp opposition of romanticism to the liberal theories of the state.

Müller and his friends were equally firm in their uncompromising rejection of the economic doctrines of liberalism. They saw in Western capitalism "the most general manifestation of that antisocial spirit, of that arrogant egotism, of that immoral enthusiasm for false reason and false enlightenment" which were the roots of the French Revolution.[9] Müller regarded the highly praised liberty and equality of the eighteenth century as a change from rural serfdom to wage slavery and found the latter infinitely worse. He had no doubt that the whole capitalistic system was incompatible with the divine order of things. To the optimism of the eighteenth century, which looked so confidently toward the future, Müller opposed just as resolute an optimism concerning the past. While the two forms of optimism may have been equally unfounded, the past was known to the memory of men and accessible to historical research; the future was known to God alone. This may explain why in the long run utopias which placed the Golden Age in the future—especially in the not too distant future—exercise a greater attraction than those placing it in the past—especially a not too distant past.

Müller's revolt against the Enlightenment's faith in progress was a revolt against his own youth. He was born in the Berlin of Frederick II, the son of a Prussian official; while a student in Göttingen he came under the influence of Adam Smith; only later, under the influence of Burke and of his friend Gentz, did he turn to an organic theory of the state:

> If one regards the state as a great individual encompassing all the small individuals, then one understands that human society cannot be conceived but as an august and complete personality—and one will never wish to subject the inward and outward peculiarities of the state, the form of its constitution, to arbitrary speculation.

In 1805 Müller joined the Catholic Church; he remained for a few years in Dresden and Berlin in close touch with Prussian conservative circles before he found in Austria his political and spiritual home. After 1817 he became ever more traditionalist and removed from the main stream of German intellectual and political life, given over entirely to praise of the past and the vain hope for its return. But in his middle period, in the years between 1806 and 1810, which were of such decisive importance in the development of German thought, he helped to arouse the spirit of national resistance to Western ideas and to strengthen the Germans' confidence in their character and mission. After the defeat of Austria at Austerlitz and of Prussia at Jena, when the German cause seemed lost and when it found hardly a friend in Germany, Müller in Dresden delivered lectures on German scholarship and literature in which he told his audiences:

> The development of the scholarly mind in Germany is the most important event in modern intellectual history. It is certain that foreign intellectual life in all its variety will have to attach itself in the course of time to that of Germany, and that, as German tribes have founded the political order of Europe, the German mind [*Geist*] will sooner or later dominate it.[10]

Müller recalled the greatness of the German mind at a time when the consciousness of the nation seemed almost extinguished. But he spoke not only of past greatness. Politically prostrate, Germany yet seemed destined for spiritual leadership. The German mind, more than any other, Müller claimed, was a universal mind, in which the cultures of other nations found their consummation and their harmonious mediation, a mind tolerant towards all others and infinite in its longing.

> The German mind is forced to ascribe to itself its obedient and pious understanding of everything alien as an advantage over all other nations, even if this penetration and understanding may sometimes degenerate into the idolatry of foreign habits and persons. We find our own happiness not in the suppression of the civilization of our neighbors, but in its highest flowering, and thus Germany, the fortunate heartland, will not need to deny its respect for others while its spirit will dominate the world.[11]

When Müller delivered his addresses, the millenary Holy Roman Empire of the German nation had crumbled. The whole political and social life of Germany seemed in a process of complete transformation under the impact of Western ideas. Even some German governments appeared eager to introduce reforms, to discard the past, to abolish ancient privileges and customs, and to promote a greater mobility of social classes and economic life. Against these rational innovations, which Müller condemned as mechanical and unorganic, he called up the power of the dead and the necessity of continuity:

> Only the traditions and the history of the past—die Geschichte der Vorwelt—can transform the meaningless letter of present times, also of the state, into a word of light. The ancestors evoked by history are not merely witnesses called to testify; they respond, they continue to act full of the warmth of life, because the spell of the heart has roused them: in their presence one performs in a loftier way and with greater freedom. Man should not act for himself and out of himself alone, as an absolutely new beginning. His deeds should continue the deeds of the ancestors. He should attach himself to a community which has already been in existence—all communities are one but the nearest would be the best to him; he should derive the blood of his instinctive advice, the spirit of his decision, from older and ever older ancestors. Such is the immortality of all greatness and goodness on earth: wherever worthy new life stirs, the old life always lives on, and only cold and vile souls speak of it as if it had gone forever and crumbled into dust. The great and immortal soul for the welfare of which the hero exposed his mortal body, must be called his true body.

The individual could find his own immortality only in the immortality of the national community; only in it could his life and actions acquire meaning.[12]

In his subordination of the present generation to the past, Müller followed Edmund Burke. In his identification of the individual's longing for immortality with the continuity of ancestors and fatherland, he anticipated Fichte. Burke was a teacher to whom Müller referred again and again with admiration and gratitude. He called him "the greatest, profoundest, most powerful and most human statesman of all periods and all nations" and claimed that he belonged more to the Germans than to the British, who never understood him fully.[13] But of the practical wisdom of Burke, of his deeply ingrained respect for individual liberty and constitutional rights, of his understanding for the living forces of history, Müller knew little. His political sense was hardly developed. Like Fichte, he wished to call the Germans to a fatherland of the mind, a celestial city which would first be built in some awakened hearts and which through some miraculous transformation would finally triumph over the enemy.[14] The victorious emerging state was hardly defined as a state of the German nation—Müller was little concerned with the problem of German unification. It was a state opposed at every point to the individualistic ideas of 1789 and to economic liberalism. It was a theocratic state, much less inspired by Burke than by the Vicomte de Bonald and his *Théorie du pouvoir politique et religieux dans la société civile*, which had appeared in Constance in 1796, twelve years before Müller delivered—in the winter of 1808-1809—his lecture on *Die Elemente der Staatskunst*.

In this lecture Müller developed at length his theory that "the state is the union of many families not only living together at one time but also following each other through time, a union not only infinitely great in space but also immortal in time." He denied that the people formed a society the purpose of which was to assure the well-being and development of individuals. He opposed emphasis on the present and on the pursuit of happiness. Against them he stressed eternity and duty:

> A people is the august community of a long line of past, living, and future generations. They all form a great intimate union for life and death. Each single generation, and in each generation each individual, guarantees the common union and is guaranteed by it. This beautiful immortal community presents itself in a common language, common customs and laws, in thousands of beneficent institutions, in many ancient families who link the various periods of history more closely together, finally in the one immortal family which forms the center of the

state, the royal family, and its own true center, the present king.[15]

Thus the hereditary nobility, with the royal house at its head, was to be the foundation of state and nation.

Müller believed that the tragic errors of the Revolution originated in the belief that the individual could separate himself from the eternal community of the state, and that the state was designed merely to assure the security and prosperity of its members. If that were true, every generation would be free to begin anew. But in the immutable nature of things, the individual had none of these freedoms, and the state was so inextricably linked up with everything human that man could not hear or see, think or feel, live or love without the state.[16] For the state, too, was a divine creation. Science and scholarship would lose all vigor and life when they ever tried to develop in their own right without serving the state.

Müller extolled the sovereignty of the state. The highest good of a nation was its peculiarity, the way in which it was different from all others. A world in which there would be only one government, one law, one system of weights and measures, would lack that creative force which springs from the conflict of the peculiarities of men. Müller, therefore, rejected the idea of perpetual peace, whether it be assured by universal monarchy or by a league of republican nations (permanenten Völker-Kongress). He regarded perpetual peace not only as an impossibility but as a misfortune which would bring human development to a standstill. Only "the true war" can provide a firm cement for nations. "Common peril, sorrow and tears bind better than prosperity. A true war would saturate the existence of every individual with the life of the state." [17] Yet Müller accepted at times a supranational Christian order, as did the Holy Alliance. "The concept of the fatherland, deeply as it might be felt, is not sufficient; there is only one world-idea, the center of all order because it is the idea of world order itself: the Christian religion." [18]

From Dresden, Müller returned for a short while to Berlin. There, in the company of Prussian noblemen and romantic poets, he noted with satisfaction that "the better ones among us have been fortunately cured of cosmopolitanism. It was a chapter in our history through which we had to pass." In the lectures *On the King and the Nature of the Prussian Monarchy* which he delivered in 1810, Müller stressed that it must be for everyone a point of honor to have a definite fatherland. To declare that one belongs to a cosmopolitan society of independent minds must be as insulting as to declare that one was without sex or honor. The basis of our honor is "our enduring readiness to stake our life for something higher. What is this higher? Is it something unknown and indefinite? No, the next higher is the national existence. Its defense is the highest touchstone of honor known to us." [19] Recalling the hopes of his youth, he declared :

> I, too, dreamt much of a union of that great nation of which we are only a branch. I, too, expected revolution and heroes and changes in the mentalities of people which would favor the realization of my dream. The great confederation of European nations, which will certainly come some day, will also wear German colors. Everything great, thorough, and lasting in all European institutions is German—that is the only certainty which has remained from all those hopes.

But that hope remained for the future.

> Our concern is the nearest and the complete, an enthusiasm for our own fatherland, for our own royal lord and for his century-old crown, which he regards with truly royal devotion as something higher than himself.[20]

In Berlin, Müller paid his respects to the Prussian monarchy, but soon he followed the Schlegels to Austria. Whether in Berlin or in Vienna, whether praising the Hohenzollern or serving the Habsburgs, Müller no longer changed his fundamental conviction. He rejected the theories of "that frightful and yet so ridiculous fraud of the French Revolution," because they did not take account of the sacred problem of continuity. However, in Müller's time, and partly through his efforts, the tide was turning and the waters of human society began to flow through healthier channels.

> It had to come to such a mad frenzy, to such a bankruptcy of the human heart, to such an intoxication of humanity that it regarded a ground covered with corpses as a park of pleasure, it had to come to all that in order that there should grow up in better nations a tremendous longing for the discredited barbarians of the Middle Ages. Burke and some Germans divined that there the lost jewel might be found. Thus the idea of nobility reappeared.

XXVII

Adam Müller and
Heinrich von Kleist

MÜLLER'S ideal of medieval society and nobility inspired the Christian-German Roundtable (the Christlich-Germanische Tischgesellschaft) in Berlin which he and his friend Heinrich von Kleist joined. The two men had collaborated in Dresden, where they founded in January 1808 the review *Phöbus*. Both were Prussian; Kleist, however, never followed his fellow north-Germans, the Schlegels, Müller, and Werner, into the Catholic Church. Among them he stood out as a man of indisputable genius, a master of German prose, and the most passionate dramatist of German literature. He expressed with a prophetic insight the dark and turbulent side of the rising German nationalism, which the optimistic nineteenth century was to veil. He was not inspired like Novalis by the Christian medieval ideals of chivalry and knighthood; neither did the pagan and carefree laughter of Siegfried and the naive joy beyond good and evil ring through his plays; the gloomy mood of doom announcing the twilight of the gods and the determined grimness of Hagen seemed to throw their tragic spell over his heroes, who by their blind desire of vengeance were driven to a frenzy of destruction and self-destruction.

Kleist was born in 1777 in a Prussian garrison town, where his father, a Pomeranian Junker, served as an officer; as a matter of course the son entered the army at an early age. But like so many of his contemporaries, he underwent the influence of Rousseau and the humanitarian cosmopolitanism of the period. He felt indifferent to the traditional values of his class and country. Prussia appeared to him a cold and utilitarian master, repugnant to the true nature and destiny of man. He left the service and even thought of renouncing his title of nobility and of living in France as a teacher.[1] But the contact with reality disappointed him; the tumultuous life of Paris offended the small-town Puritan in him.

In his middle twenties he discovered his true vocation, to create the German heroic drama, to become the equal of Aeschylus. But even then he showed little interest in the fate of the nation and in the political events of the period; he expressed his first concern with them at the end of 1805, during the war between Austria and France. In a letter from Königsberg to his friend Otto August Rühle von Lilienstern he denounced Prussia's neutrality in the war. He wished the King to call the Estates and to rouse the national spirit by setting an example, selling his gold and silver plate and giving up many of his servants and horses. Then the nation might respond with an awakened patriotism and join Austria in a common war against the French.[2] Yet in 1806, in spite of Prussia's disastrous defeat, he remained aloof from patriotic efforts and devoted himself to his career as a writer. In 1807 he settled in Dresden, the capital of a leading member of the Rhenish Confederation, where friendship for Napoleon was strong and an undisturbed literary life was maintained. His meeting there with Müller, Tieck, and Gentz introduced him more intimately to romanticism and patriotism; yet the review *Phöbus* was devoted to poetry and art. Only at the end of 1808 did the financial failure of his literary venture, within less than one year, turn his mind to nationalism.[3]

At that time Austria was preparing for war with Napoleon and its government was trying to arouse a patriotic response among its peoples. Archduke Karl, the commander of the Austrian army, was greeted as the hero-liberator of Germany. When the beginning of the war seemed to be delayed by Karl's justified doubts about Austria's sufficient preparedness, Kleist wrote a poem addressed to the Archduke, warning him against hesitation and rational calculation. Kleist emphasized that what was needed was not a successful war, but struggle for its own sake, even should it lead to the heroic honor of self-destruction:[4]

> Schauerlich ins Rad des Weltgeschickes
> Greifst du am Entscheidungstage ein,
> Und dein Volk lauscht, angsterfüllten Blickes,
> Welch ein Los ihm wird gefallen sein. . . .
> Nicht der Sieg ist's, den der Deutsche fordert,
> Hilflos wie er schon im Abgrund steht;
> Wenn der Kampf nur fackelgleich entlodert,
> Wert der Leiche, die zu Grabe geht.
> Mag es dann in finstre Nacht auch sinken
> Von dem Gipfel, halb bereits erklimmt;
> Herr! die Träne wird noch Dank dir blinken,
> Wenn dein Schwert dafür nur Rache nimmt.

The popular resistance in Spain inspired Kleist, as it did other German intellectuals. In a poem, Kleist compared Don José Palafox, the defender of Saragossa, to Leonidas, Arminius, and William Tell.[5] Arminius, the "liberator" of the Germans from the Roman conquerors, was generally popular among German nationalist writers.[6] None of their poems and plays, however, could compare with Kleist's drama *Die Hermannschlacht* in passion and fury. The events of eighteen hundred years before were interpreted in the light of Kleist's time. Two German princes—Marbod, representing Prussia, and Hermann, representing Austria—united to overthrow the Roman yoke, but only after Hermann (Arminius) had seen through the malicious Roman plan of using Marbod against him. However, Hermann did not defeat the Romans in open battle. No cunning was too dishonorable, no deception too mean not to be used by him to secure victory, and to fulfill his lust for vengeance. Hermann stood almost alone; in Napoleon's time, many Germans were only too willing to welcome the Roman "yoke"; others were pusillanimous or hesitant or concerned only with their private interests. To them Hermann opposed his message that hatred was his call and vengeance his virtue;

> Ich *will* die höhnische Dämonenbrut nicht lieben!
> So lang sie in Germanien trotzt,
> Ist Hass mein Amt und meine Tugend Rache!

Hermann's will to destroy the enemy was so strong that he was ready to sacrifice his wife and children to it. They were for him mere pawns in his war. Thusnelda, his wife, complained that his hatred of the Romans had so blinded him that he could no longer see the individual; his fanaticism made everything permissible. The dams of the human and of the humane were broken by the flood of his dark passion:

> Dich macht, ich seh, dein Römerhass ganz blind,
> Weil als dämonenartig dir
> das Ganz' erscheint, so kannst du dir
> Als sittlich nicht den einzelnen gedenken.

The drama ended with a wishful vision of Germany's complete triumph. Marbod, the Prussian, offered to Hermann, the Habsburg, the leadership of a united Germany and the imperial crown, and Hermann called upon the Germans not only to drive all Romans from the sacred soil of the fatherland but to march against Rome and to destroy the city so that nothing would remain but a black flag flying over a deserted heap of ruins. These hopes were not fulfilled. Austria was defeated, the rift with Prussia was not healed, Kleist's drama could not be staged in Vienna nor printed before 1821, when Tieck published it.[7] In vain, in his poem "Germania an ihre Kinder," did Kleist call upon the Germans to be worthy heirs of those who had conquered the Romans, and to rush with elemental force into a war of pitiless annihilation of the enemy:[8]

Schlagt ihn tot! Das Weltgericht
Fragt euch nach den Gründen nicht.

When the victory at Aspern on May 21, 1809, opened for a brief moment the prospect of Napoleon's defeat by the Austrians, Kleist and his young friend Friedrich Dahlmann (1785-1860), the future historian and politician, hurried to Prague to found there a weekly periodical, *Germania*.[9] "You can easily imagine," Kleist wrote to Friedrich Schlegel, "what this journal will contain; there is only one theme about which a German can write at present." The introduction which Kleist planned for the new journal started with the sentence: "This periodical will be the first breath of German liberty." Among the contributions which he wrote for *Germania* the "catechism for Germans, composed after the Spanish catechism for the use of children and old people" introduced two Saxons, father and son, discoursing about patriotism. To his father's question, "Tell me child, who you are," the boy answered: "I am a German."

> "A German? You are joking. You were born in Meissen, and the country to which Meissen belongs is called Saxony!"—"I was born in Meissen and the country to which Meissen belongs, is called Saxony; but my fatherland, the country to which Saxony belongs, is Germany, and your son, my father, is a German."—"You dream. I do not know any country to which Saxony belongs, unless perhaps the Rhenish Confederation. Where can I find this Germany of which you talk, where is it situated?"

But the hesitation of the father did not move the son. Even if Austria should fail and all Germany perish in the war, nevertheless, the boy declared, it was a good and desirable fight. "For God loves it when men die for their liberty and he abhors those who live as slaves."

In a second article "What is at stake in this war?" (Was gilt es in diesem Kriege?) Kleist saw German existence and destiny at stake in the war. Were the Germans not "a community entirely alien to the spirit of dominion and conquest and therefore as worthy of existence and toleration as any other?" Germans, Kleist wrote, could not think of their glory without thinking at the same time of the glory and salvation of all people on earth; their mind, soaring on the wings of imagination of poets and sages, longed for subordination under a world government constituted in free elections by the totality of all fraternal nations. The German community was equally truthful and openhearted toward friend and foe, loved by everybody for its innocence and loyalty, ever ready to receive whatever is good from without, though "the gods have preserved in it the idea of mankind (das Urbild der Menschheit) in greater purity than in any other nation."

Thus the existence of a community was at stake in the war [Kleist concluded] which belongs to the whole of the human race; to defend which even the savages of the South Sea would hurry if they knew it; a community the fall of which no German heart should survive, and which should be buried only with the blood before which the sun darkens.

Austria's war became in the poet's eyes an apocalyptic struggle. Should the war be lost, it would end in a glorious pyre and in a flood of blood which would eclipse the light of the sun in a dark red twilight. Reality turned out otherwise. The defeat of Austria at Wagram on July 6 put an end to all hopes. Germany had not risen to Austria's defense; the weekly *Germania* was never published; Kleist's call went unheeded. Napoleon's domination seemed more secure and was more willingly accepted than ever. The eyes of the few German patriots turned now to Prussia; in February 1810 Kleist reached Berlin. There, in a new drama, *Prinz Friedrich von Homburg*, he glorified no longer the Habsburgs and the unity of the Empire, but the rise of Prussia to her future greatness in the victory which the Great Elector Frederick William won over the Swedes at Fehrbellin in June 1675. The eulogy of the Prussian state and its spirit ended with the unanimous shout of the Prussian officers on the stage: "In Staub mit allen Feinden Brandenburgs!" [Into dust with all of Brandenburg's enemies!]

The Christian-Germanic Roundtable which Kleist joined was founded on January 18, 1811, the hundred and tenth anniversary of the coronation of Frederick I as King of Prussia. Its model was the Liedertafel organized by Karl Friedrich Zelter (1758-1832) in 1809, a social club which combined the cult of the fatherland with a high musical level of choral singing. Zelter, a gifted musician and a friend of Goethe, was the director of the Singakademie in Berlin, which his teacher Karl Friedrich Christian Fach (1736-1800) had founded. The Liedertafel later became the model for many similar singing associations throughout Germany and soon even in other lands among men of German descent. Its later imitations abandoned the high artistic standards of the original Liedertafel. They became purely social and patriotic groups which together with gymnastic associations formed a characteristic element of the German national movement.[10] This popular character, as well as the original high artistic standard, was alien to the Christian-Germanic Roundtable. Its members drank and sang too, but their main purpose was political: devotion to Christianity and loyalty to the monarchy, protection of historical rights and liberation from foreign domination. They represented the two classes which felt themselves threatened by the new capitalistic and industrial civilization—Prussian Junkers and romantic poets. Western influences began to undermine the privileges of the nobility and its claim to social and political leadership in Prussia. The educated middle classes saw in Prussia's defeat of 1806 definite proof of the obsoleteness of the aristocratic order and of the urgent need for Western reforms. Romantic poets and writers feared the penetration of the commercial spirit, which they regarded as hostile to the creative arts. Thus members of the nobility and some intellectuals joined for a defense against English commercialism, against French revolutionary ideas, and against the emancipation of the Jews, whom they found represented in all the hated movements.[11]

The Roundtable's founder was Achim von Arnim, its leading members Müller, Kleist, the Baron de La Motte-Fouqué,[12] and Friedrich August Ludwig von der Marwitz[13]—a wide range of personalities which reached from brilliant bohemians to staid Junkers. The hated Western spirit had invaded Prussia: some noblemen and intellectuals recognized the necessity of reform and prepared a shift from the feudal agrarian state to a modern industrial society. The heritage of the Enlightenment still dominated the majority of the educated classes. Jewish women of *esprit* and wide culture had opened literary salons where even members of the high aristocracy could be seen. Against these "evils" the Roundtable declared its irreconcilable opposition. It created its own organ in the *Berliner Abendblätter*, the first Berlin daily. Kleist became its editor; it was intended as a popular paper with a wide circulation, the first venture of this kind at a time when most German newspapers were written for a numerically small and highly educated public.[14] The strict Prussian censorship tolerated no political editorials. Instead, Kleist tried in short essays to propagate the spirit of passionate action which had characterized his *Hermannschlacht:*

> People praise the usefulness of thought and reflection before one acts. If I were a Spaniard, an Italian, or a Frenchman, I would leave it at that. But because I am a German, I shall tell my son, especially if he wishes to become a soldier, that thought and reflection should come after the action and not before. If thought enters our mind before or during the action, then it will confuse, hinder, or suppress the strength necessary for action, a strength which derives from magnificent feelings. After the action, reflection might help us to become conscious of mistakes made and to suggest improvements for the future.

In his interpretation of history, Kleist considered life a perpetual struggle with destiny, an unrelenting combat in which quickness and vigor of action decided. He no longer shared the faith of his youth in reason, progress, and peace. He believed that a nation passed at the beginning of its history through its heroic period, "which is without doubt the highest that can be achieved." When the heroes departed, the nation began to sing of them; finally when poetry dried up, the nations succumbed to intellect and reason, their vitality began to ebb, they decayed, and life became impoverished.[15] To overcome this decay, Kleist called up the old noble spirit of heroism against the new vile spirit of commercialism, *Heldentum* against *Händlertum*. But the Prussian government, then under the leadership of Hardenberg and under the influence of the reformers, could not indulge this kind of romanticism. It had to find money and intelligence to carry through the inevitable reforms. It therefore fought the aristocratic-romantic opposition and its program. On March 30, 1811, after an existence of only six months, the *Abendblätter* ceased to appear, and during the summer the Roundtable dissolved. Kleist's hopes were shattered; he had failed to arouse Germany, he had won scant recognition, his future was insecure; in November 1811 he committed suicide. But the ideas which the Roundtable represented were not dead. In the long run they proved stronger than the spirit of liberal reform which triumphed for a short while.

The patriotism of the Roundtable was more Prussian than German. Many of its members, especially the rural nobility, were opposed to nationalism; the romantic writers, on the other hand, though they placed Prussia above Germany, hoped that Germany would attach itself to Prussia. When Arnim announced his intention of publishing *Der Preusse, ein Volksblatt,* he wrote:

> We shall call this journal "The German" as soon as Germany has recovered from its long sickness, which isolates each force and leads to their mutual annihilation; now we call it "The Prussian" after the greatest among the last free German tribes. We wish to state our faith that since the Bavarian War of Succession [1778-1779] Germany has lived only in Prussia and only as far as it was connected with Prussia. Let the children who have fallen into the mud provoke and irritate the Prussian eagle. They cannot tarnish it, but with its brilliant plumage it can perhaps cleanse them; beating the enemy with its strong wings, it unfurls the flag above them.

The Schlegels and Müller looked to Catholic Austria as the bulwark of resistance against the disintegrating influence of the West; Arnim and La Motte-Fouqué saw Prussia as such a bulwark. Prussia seemed of stronger texture than Austria, more solidly built and better held together by the spirit of loyalty and industry, devotion and frugality, duty and discipline, which characterized the nobility in the lands east of the Elbe. The Prussian nobles had not succumbed to the lure of the cosmopolitan cities nor to the soft graces of the arts. Brandenburg had been a frontier land settled and guarded by valiant soldiers. From its history Arnim and

La Motte-Fouqué drew the legendary motives for some of their novels and plays. They not only sought inspiration in the past but provided Prussia with a national myth which culminated in the glorification of the monarchy and of the nobility, the "natural" link and mediator between the king and the people. Knightly chivalry and romantic poetry joined in the adoration of Queen Louise (1776-1810), who appeared as a symbol of true womanhood and royalty, of patriotic virtue and gracious beauty. The song which Arnim wrote for the opening of the Roundtable praised her as sent by God to embody hope, faith, and love and started with the assertion that the Prussian crown was confided to the king not by social contract but was won for him through Christian knightly blood.[16]

The alliance in the Roundtable of a rather primitive rural nobility and highly refined artists whose irrationalism was of intellectual origin showed the diversity of the opposition to the spirit of reform. The Junkers came from the countryside; they were simple and pious men, sober and practical, and full of distrust of writers and literature. They were convinced that too much learning and too acute an intelligence corrupted the character. They sensed in the reformers a natural ally of the rational commercial spirit, the *Krämergeist*, as Marwitz called it, which wished to replace courage by smartness and honor by profit. The reformers seemed to Marwitz to transform "the venerable old Prussia into a new-fangled Jewstate," to favor usury, to replace painstaking diligence by speculation, and to give too great an importance to international finance and bankers. He accused the liberals of undermining morality and creating unrest, of mobilizing crass materialism against the divine order, the fleeting moment of the present against the past and the future, the individual against the family, speculators and counting houses against the land and honest workshops, knowledge and conceited talents against domestic virtue and respectable character.[17]

This insistence on immobility, this disrespect for thought and the book (if it was not the Bible) could not be shared by the romantic intellectuals; but in their uprootedness and moral uncertainty, they looked longingly to the apparent solidity and unquestioning convictions of the rural nobility. From without they romantically idealized the virtues of the old order. They supplied to the vested interests an arsenal of arguments. True, when they spoke of the divine character of monarchy and nobility, of state and people, they did not mean their real representatives, but poetic symbols. Their glorification, however, served to justify the preservation of privilege and the accretion of power. The romanticists believed that their theories were nearer to the reality of life and nature than the rationalism of Enlightenment. They denied that they were theories at all, while in fact they were a poetic transfiguration of a past reality and of a vanishing life which no artifice could much longer preserve; they were the product of fertile imaginative minds who wished to subordinate intellectual complexity to the assumed simplicity and nobility of the unintellectual man, the man of action, the warrior and the tiller of the soil and, a century later, the industrial worker.[18]

Marwitz and his friends, on the other hand, did not need lofty intellectual constructions to be convinced of the moral superiority and the divine right of the Prussian state and of their class. The nobility and the army had made Prussia great: it could only continue as long as their power and spirit remained intact. Marwitz vigorously denounced the peace policy of the two kings who succeeded Frederick II. He saw in it the fruit of middle-class sentiment which preferred peace, comfort, and profit to justice and honor. He never understood that the emancipation of the peasants might reinvigorate the nation. In the reforms he saw only an imitation of Napoleon, whom he regarded as the prince of darkness, and of foreign models which could not but undermine the foundations of Prussia.

Yet he fought for a lost cause. Against the opposition of many Junkers, a few brilliant officers and statesmen carried through a modernization of Prussian society and the army and tried to arouse the spirit of nationalism among the people or at least among the educated classes. In many ways they imitated the reforms of the French Revolution—without, however, endangering the foundation on which the Prussian state had been built. They set the example of a successful adaptation of foreign and more progressive models without abandoning one's own peculiar character and traditions. On the contrary, the reform served the purpose of strengthening the latter, of increasing their power of resistance, and of facilitating the fulfillment of their mission. It was a revolution directed from above, and it was undertaken—like that in Japan in 1868 and that in Russia after 1917—at the very moment when the existing state had broken down and was faced with catastrophe. Within a few years, out of the defeat of 1806, a new Prussia rose which left behind the bureaucratic absolutism of Frederick II and tried to activize and mobilize popular forces and to find support in arts and scholarship. The state of Frederick II had been indifferent to German cultural achievements. The new Prussia attempted to fuse the military power-state and the German life of arts and letters. Through this regeneration, the work of a few energetic and farsighted men, Prussia attracted to itself a growing number of German patriots.

XXVIII

The Reform Movement in
Prussia: I. Wilhelm von Humboldt

PRUSSIA'S recovery after 1806 was due not to romanticism, not to an evocation of the German Volksgeist, but to men who understood the necessity of compromising with and making use of the Zeitgeist. As a result of their efforts, Prussia became the first German state in which state and dynasty were no longer identical and in which steps were taken to organize the various classes of the people for active cooperation in public life. The reform was not the work of the dynasty. The mediocre and rather passive King showed no enthusiasm for it and tried to keep it within narrow bounds after he had reluctantly accepted it. He showed no trace of German national feeling. He could not be called even a Prussian nationalist; he was a Prussian royalist, but without the militant and expansive inclinations of the more famous members of his house. He saw in the dynasty the real tie connecting the various provinces out of which, by royal action and historical accident, the Prussian state had grown up.[1] Nor did the class which, together with the King, had formed the Prussian state favor the reforms. The nobility, led by men like Marwitz, succeeded after 1815 not only in stopping all further reforms but in altering the existing ones in a reactionary sense. They saw in them the undoing of the genuine traditions of Brandenburg and Prussia.

Even members of the educated classes suspected the nationalism which, partly as motive and partly as a potential development, was involved in the reorganization of administration and army. Their attitude was castigated by Niebuhr, whose *Roman History* (the first volume appeared in 1811) became the first important scholarly publication by a professor of the new University of Berlin. Speaking of the hostility of Phocion to Demosthenes, Niebuhr compared it with the "aversion [to Stein] at the time of the Confederation of the Rhine."

I have known people whom I am very far from believing to have been dishonest, but who were incapable of any enthusiasm, sacrifice, and confidence. They believed that misery did not consist in being enslaved by a foreign ruler, but in the evils which follow in the train of war and in personal sufferings, and that nothing was more foolish than sacrifice of any kind, especially if there was little prospect of success. When they were told that with such principles all nationality was sacrificed and with it everything that raised human life above mere animal comfort, or when they were asked what great misfortune it could be under such circumstances to die, or whether death was a misfortune compared with servitude—they would answer, You are an enthusiast! adding with indignation, You are the cause of all our misfortunes! Those who dissented from them were even in danger of being denounced by them as fanatics and as the authors of all mischief.[2]

In 1809 Stein himself, then in Austria, complained about the "languor, selfishness, and contentment under a degrading yoke" which he found prevailing in Prussia. The French victory of 1806 brought not only peace but also personal gains to many Prussians. On January 4, 1808, Niebuhr wrote to Stein of the widespread lack of patriotism among the Berliners:

It seems as if these people possessed no feeling for the general welfare and the private happiness that flows from it; if they can only in some way continue to vegetate, they do not even show any desire for greater personal comfort and enjoyment such as in other nations rouses many to action and exertion. They feel comfortable enough if they can drag down everything superior, disturb all confidence, dissolve all allegiance. According to them not only will our yoke never be broken, but it does not even matter whether it is or not: the condition of the people would only become more painful, for it is clear that the army would continue at the highest point reached by overstraining the remaining resources of the monarchy and by defrauding the public creditor, that the War Department will waste money and the civil service starve. This set gauges our political incapacity by the fact that the King has not yet joined the Confederation of the Rhine.

Neither the Prussian nobility nor the middle classes were eager for reforms and a national regeneration. The masses were even more lethargic. Yet Prussia had been so shattered by the defeat of 1806 that only energetic and unusual measures promised a future rise from the deep fall. The army had ignominiously collapsed, the officers and officials had surrendered without resistance. Regenerative forces, whether men or ideas, could not be found in Prussia; they had to come from without.

The majority of the reformers were not born as subjects of the king of Prussia, but came there only as mature men. Stein came from the Rhineland, Hardenberg and Scharnhorst from Hanover, Niebuhr from Danish Holstein, Gneisenau and Fichte from Saxony; only Humboldt, Schleiermacher, and Clausewitz grew up in Prussian lands. Many of them—especially Stein, Gneisenau, and Fichte—never felt a lasting devotion to Prussia.

What they represented was not the Prussian tradition, but a new mental climate in which various intellectual currents of the period mingled. From abroad they received the liberalizing influence of 1789 and of the English constitution, with which some of them became acquainted while students at the University of Göttingen. Kant's younger colleague Christian Jacob Kraus (1753-1807), who taught practical philosophy and political economy at the University of Königsberg, was an enthusiastic admirer of Adam Smith, and Kraus's lectures exercised as deep an influence on the Prussian reformers as Kant's teaching of the *Rechtsstaat* did.[3] The new concept of the state as an organism of great ethical significance had already been made familiar by the romanticists. The strongest single influence which most of the reformers experienced was the intellectual climate created by German classical humanism and its emphasis on the dignity of personality. Through the reforms the Prussian power-state and German intellectual life, *Macht und Bildung,* reality and ideal entered a union which the state of Frederick II had not known.[4]

If the Prussian state was thus to receive a new start in life through its permeation with intellectual and moral forces, one of the immediate tasks before the reformers was the creation of a new system of national education. The task was accomplished by a man who had little in common with the administrative and military program of the reformers, a man of letters who had lived his life aloof from affairs of state, Wilhelm von Humboldt (1767-1835). In youth Humboldt had been deeply impressed by the classical humanism of Goethe and Schiller. Like them he regarded the classical world as an unsurpassable model:

> Nothing modern can be compared with something ancient;
> no human being should measure himself with the gods. . . .
> By transforming everything which approaches his circle, the
> Greek becomes himself a symbol of mankind, and that in its
> tenderest, purest, and most perfect form.[5]

This attachment of Humboldt's to the classics was not a passing mood of his younger years. While he participated in the abortive peace conference at Prague in July 1813, where he played a decisive role, he found time to study a description of the almost perfectly preserved frieze of the cella in the Greek city of Phigalia, which had been discovered in the preceding year by the British archeologist Charles Robert Cockerell (1788-1863), a notable representative of the classical revival in architecture. "God," Humboldt exclaimed,

> God, how one feels attracted to the stillness of the ruins and the noble figures of antiquity! I cannot deny, and it must lie deeper than the preoccupations of early youth: antiquity is the only period that wholly and vitally grips me, and I am in the purest and strictest meaning a genuine pagan, a complete antithesis to everything modern, including the Middle Ages, and everything which is founded on it.

During the difficult negotiations of Châtillon-sur-Seine he read Plutarch, and he wrote from there in a letter of March 2, 1814: "Antiquity remains eternally young to me. I find life and death, mankind and myself, heaven and earth in it. What more does man desire?" [6]

In the last years of his life Humboldt's quietist attitude found inspiration in Indian literature, especially the Bhagavadgita. But one of his last sonnets reaffirmed his lifelong faith in Rome and Hellas. "However far," he wrote, "frontiers of knowledge may expand to the Ganges and beyond, nothing can stir and delight the deepest in our heart as Hellas does":

> Wie man nicht sollte jenen Kreis verlassen,
> Den, von erhabener Trümmer Glanz umschwebet,
> Die sieben Hügel zaubrisch in mich fassen,
> So sollte man, da voll in Hellas Werken
> Das Höchste ist das Irdische erstreben,
> Nicht mehr auf fremder Töne Lockung merken. [7]

Faithful to the worldwide conception of Goethe's Weltliteratur, Humboldt explored many peoples and civilizations. At no time in his life, however, did German literature or the German past stir Humboldt as deeply as the great monuments of other cultures.

While Hellas remained Humboldt's spiritual ideal and guide, personal liberty was his political credo. He knew well that the desire for liberty and the respect for it are not innate in natural man or widely present in historical nations, but are the rare fruit of civilization, and that they have been found in few periods of history and few lands. For that reason he exalted their importance. He was deeply conscious of the strength of the fascination exercised by command and dominion. After all, he was born in Potsdam and reared on one of the country estates of the Mark Brandenburg. With his highly developed sense of individuality, he knew and appreciated, as the men of the eighteenth century had not done, the historical individualities of the various nationalities. But he never acknowledged them as a factor determining and fettering the spontaneous life of the individual. "Just as nationality interested him more than the state, so the individual interested him more than the nation." [8]

Goethe's main interest centered on nature, in which his discriminating eye joyfully and gratefully observed the splendor of the multiplicity and the mystery of the growth of form. Humboldt was attracted by the diversity and wealth of individuality in human society. He understood that the growing perfection of language and of the means of artistic and philosophical expression would increase individuality and the differences of the various nationalities, and that "the study of man would gain most by the study and comparison of all nations, of all countries and periods." [9] In 1797, working on a study of the character of the eighteenth century, he wrote: "We, however, get accustomed to study as much as possible and to make this knowledge the center of our judgment." [10] The comparative anthropology which he planned could have become the first comparative analysis of nationality and of national characters, and with a more historical approach at a later stage, an introduction to the study of the history of nationalism in its various forms. This interest in the diversity and the living aspects of nationality caused Humboldt later to devote himself to the exploration of language and its share in molding and expressing national character.

For Humboldt, nationalism did not represent a value in itself; the nationalities received their value from the fullness with which they mirrored and represented the truly human and from the scope of the widest possible freedom which they opened to the spontaneity of the individual and to his striving for individual perfection. It was on man that nationality and mankind reposed. "What binds me to Germany," he wrote to Goethe from Paris, "what else is it than what I gained from my life with you and with the circle from whom I have now been separated for almost two years?"

The German debacle of 1806, the dissolution of the Empire and the collapse of Prussia aroused in Humboldt the desire for active participation in political life and in the transformation of the Prussian state. Rereading in 1818 his correspondence with Schiller, he wrote to his wife how he was impressed by the fact that these many letters contained not one word about public affairs. At the time of his correspondence with Schiller, he remarked, everything of public interest was regarded only as a damaging intrusion into the true life, the life of the mind. "Now, on the contrary, one believes that man cannot find his true fulfillment and realize his intrinsic value without taking a lively interest in everything that concerns the state." Nostalgically Humboldt thought back to the old times and was convinced that under the previous conditions scholarship and letters, and the whole moral and intellectual life of the nation, had fared better. Perhaps without much conviction he comforted himself with the hope that this decline of the intellectual and moral life might cease and that the character of the nation might ultimately gain by the awakened interest in national affairs. The succeeding century of German history hardly bore out his hope. Even Humboldt believed during the passing enthusiasm of 1813—to which he succumbed while Goethe did not—that "Germany must be free and strong, not only to be able to defend itself against this or that neighbor but also because only an outwardly strong nation preserves the spirit from which all blessings flow."

Humboldt never admired efficiency as such, but the free interplay of movements and personalities. "Without them man becomes a machine. One admires what he does; one despises what he is." As Prussian minister of education, Humboldt demanded an education which would form man into a harmonious personality and develop his potentiality into spontaneous activity, an education of the individual for the sake of the individual and not of the state. He was convinced that such educated and freely developed individuals would as citizens transform the absolutist state of the past into a national state in which all would be able to participate. Education was not primarily to transmit knowledge or technical training, but to provide the general cultural background and to form the human being before training the professional man:

> All schools which are instituted not for a single profession or class but for the whole nation or the state must aim at a general human education (*eine allgemeine Menschenbildung*). What the necessities of life, of a trade or profession demand must be acquired separately and after completion of the general education. If the two get mixed up, we will produce neither complete men nor complete experts in the various professions and trades.

This educational system culminated in the creation of a new university. As a result of the peace treaty of 1807 Prussia lost most of her universities, among them the famous University of Halle. It was the King himself who coined the sentence: "The state must replace by intellectual forces what it has lost in material strength." The University of Berlin was opened in the fall of 1810 with a small student body, but with a number of prominent professors—Fichte and Schleiermacher, Savigny and Friedrich August Wolff. It established as its policy that scholars of the various fields, in close cooperation and intercourse, should not only teach but above all promote new knowledge.[11] Humboldt demanded that they regard "knowledge as something that has not yet been fully discovered and can never be fully discovered but must be constantly sought." The University's finances and administration depended on the state, but the students were free to select their courses and professors, and the latter were free to teach and to write without censorship or supervision. This "academic freedom" and the dedication to scholarship and research did a great deal to raise academic standards. German universities soon modeled themselves upon the example of Berlin. They put a new emphasis upon research and assured to their faculties an undisputed social position. But at the same time the system, so productive in the field of pure scholarship, tended to separate scholarship from life and to arouse a feeling of conceit among the scholars, who regarded themselves as a superior caste.

Though Humboldt had become a minister of the state and devoted much of his time to building a better and stronger state, he never abandoned his youthful attitude of critical reserve against the power of the state. In his famous *Ideen zu einem Versuch, die Grenzen des Staates zu bestimmen* he distinguished clearly the state, with its apparatus of outward restraint, from the nationality, the free society of individual lives:

> The constitution of the state and the national community, closely as they may be interwoven, should never be confused. If the state constitution imposes upon the citizens, either by superior power and force or by custom and law, a certain relationship, there exists in addition another relationship, freely chosen by them, infinitely multifarious and often changing. The latter, the free working of the nationality in its members, really preserves all the values, the yearning for which leads men to form a society.[12]

The influence of the state seemed to him dangerous because it tended to destroy the diversity of individuality which a free society protects.

> The very manifoldness which originates in the association of various individualities is the highest good that society can confer, and this manifoldness certainly always gets lost to the degree to which the state interferes. Then it is no longer the members of a nation who live in association, but single subjects who enter into relationship with the state, with the spirit which dominates its government. In such a relation the superior might of the state hinders the free interplay of forces. . . .

While states demand uniformity, man must aim at manifoldness and variety.

> This alone produces well-rounded and forceful characters, and certainly nobody yet has fallen deep enough to prefer for himself prosperity and happiness to greatness.

Whoever, on the other hand, would prefer prosperity and happiness for others to their human greatness in liberty, might be rightly suspected of misjudging mankind and of wishing to transform men into machines. Even the best paternal administration, bringing prosperity and economic security at the expense of liberty, could have no truly salutary effect. For if men are guided instead of deciding for themselves, they work not as fully human beings but only with mechanical efficiency.[13]

Wilhelm von Humboldt was statesman enough to wish to realize his ideal of the free individual in a liberal and tolerant society. But what formed the very essence of English political life and of English nationalism could not succeed in Prussia, with its different traditions and governmental power, its underdeveloped middle class, and its glorification of service and subordination to the state. Nor was Humboldt the man to carry through such a reform program. Though he rejected the example of Sparta, the source of much of Prussian inspiration, he did not clearly see the fundamental difference which existed even between the Athenian democracy of Pericles and modern individual liberty.[14] But he was opposed to any glorification of the moral autonomy and self-righteousness of the state. He wished to limit it severely by the rights of the individual and of a supranational European community. In that sense he remained, even during the Napoleonic wars, a son of the eighteenth century, of its individualism and of its cosmopolitanism.[15]

In the *Denkschrift für die Deutsche Verfassung* which Humboldt submitted in December 1813, he regarded the restoration of the Empire as it existed before 1806 and of its old constitution as desirable, but he understood that it was impossible. Under these circumstances he welcomed the proposed German Confederation. He emphasized that Germany should become neither a united national state like France nor a centralized federation, a "Bundesstaat," as it became in 1871. In the interests of domestic liberty and of European peace, Germany should form a loose confederation, a "Staatenbund." He regarded the division of Germany as a condition for the preservation of liberty and diversity within and as a safeguard against aggression and expansion without. He rejected, and for the very same reasons as did Johann Stephan Pütter and other authoritative German political scientists at the end of the eighteenth century, the formation of a strong center in the heart of Europe. Pütter had warned "the peace-loving world against the pernicious hour of German unity." He had praised the Holy Roman Empire as constituted by the Treaty of Westphalia (1648) and concluded: "Woe to the liberty of the continent if the hundreds of thousands of German bayonets should ever obey one ruler!"[16] In the last years of this empire, Humboldt's friend Schiller in his Prologue to *Wallensteins Lager* lamented the passing of the peace which the Treaty of Westphalia had made possible for Europe:

> Zerfallen sehen wir in diesen Tagen
> Die alte feste Form, die einst vor hundert
> Und fünfzig Jahren ein willkomm'ner Friede
> Europas Reichen gab, die teure Frucht
> Von dreissig jammervollen Kriegsjahren.

Humboldt wished to preserve German weakness in the interests of European peace. For, as he wrote in his *Denkschrift* of September 30, 1816, no one could prevent Germany

> from becoming a conquering nation, which no true German could desire. One knew very well what great preeminence in intellectual and scientific education the German nation had achieved as long as she did not attempt a foreign policy, while it was still unresolved how such a policy would affect the cultural development.

Out of this concern for German civilization he did not desire a united German power. As a European he knew, like Goethe, that Germany's true interests coincided with those of Europe. "In no way should one forget the true and essential purpose of the German Confederation, as far as it ties in with European policy," he wrote. "This purpose is to make peace secure." Therefore he did not hesitate to propose to put Germany under "foreign" custodians. He wanted Britain and Russia, as great European powers, to guarantee the German Confederation. He envisioned Germany secure in its independence and organized to defend it, but unable to disturb the peace of Europe.[17] Thus the great reformer of Prussia's educational system was neither a German nationalist nor a Prussian in the sense in which the words were understood later in the nineteenth century. He remained rooted in the individualist and cosmopolitan idealism which characterized the German mind before the rise of nationalism and of romanticism. For that reason he could enliven Prussia's culturally arid past with the beauty and the human values of German classicism. Much of Prussia's universal appeal and intrinsic strength rested later on her power to absorb this spirit which was originally alien to her.

XXIX

The Reform Movement in Prussia: II. Baron vom Stein

HUMBOLDT felt happier in the world of ideas than in the contact with practical affairs of state. Heinrich Friedrich Karl Freiherr vom und zum Stein (1757-1831) was a man of action with an intuitive gift for the problems of administration. Neither of the men felt "Prussian." Though Humboldt was born in Prussia, his mind belonged to Greece and to Europe. Stein was born in western Germany, a member of the semi-sovereign imperial nobility, a grand seigneur whose ancestors had for centuries ruled independently a tiny domain which he inherited. Though he served for many years as an official of the king of Prussia, he never took on the outlook of a bureaucrat or a courtier, and he had no affection for the Prussians or for the Prussian state. He longingly thought back to the period when the German Empire had not yet been undermined by the rise of the territorial princes. Like so many of the imperial nobility, he felt a deep loyalty to the imperial crown. On December 1, 1812, he wrote to Count Münster:

> I am sorry that you think me a Prussian. . . . I have only one fatherland and its name is Germany. . . . I am devoted with all my heart only to it and not to any one of its parts. At this moment of great historical development I am entirely indifferent to the fate of the dynasties; they are mere instruments. I wish Germany to become great and strong, to regain independence and nationality.

Stein was willing to abandon Prussia, to see her divided and Austria enlarged at her expense; he looked to Austria to resume the imperial dignity. If it were possible, he wished to restore a united Germany ruled by the Emperor as in the twelfth and thirteenth centuries. What he admired in the old Reich were the traditional but vanishing corporate liberties which protected small cities and the lesser nobility from total dependence on princely power and gave to their representatives self-confidence and a sense of responsibility. Though he was deeply rooted in the German past, he found much of his ideal of self-reliance and independence developed in England; her institutions of local self-government and her public spirit, with its spontaneity, remained for him a source of inspiration. Through his reforms he hoped to transplant it to Prussia.[1]

Long years of service in the Prussian state, in its western provinces and in Berlin, made him familiar with the imperfections of its administration. He saw their cause in the fact that Prussia was not a properly constituted state, was not a nation. In his *Representation of the Faulty Organization of the Cabinet* on April 27, 1806, he stated that "the Prussian state has no constitution; the supreme power is not divided between the monarch and the representatives of the nation. It is a very new aggregate of many single provinces brought together by inheritance, purchase, and conquest." Prussia as a nation did not exist for two reasons: the people had no share in its administration, and the administration itself could not work efficiently because there was no unity and no plan. In his *Representation* he suggested some fundamental remedies for the latter, because he clearly foresaw the danger which threatened Prussia of losing its independence and its "ancient renown." His "most dismal anticipations" were justified a few months later.[2]

The total collapse and the unprecedented humiliation made it evident that the general apathy and public indifference of the people had to be changed into an active interest in the state. But before citizens could participate in the government, the obsolete fetters which hindered the spirit of activity and progress had to be removed. Even among the merchants and artisans in the cities illiteracy was widespread. Among nine hundred master cloth manufacturers, about one third could not sign their name at all, and another third could do it only with great difficulty.[3] Their geographic horizon was limited by Potsdam and Frankfurt-an-der-Oder; in their provincialism they did not even suspect the possibility or necessity of better education. Stein wished to spread knowledge and to arouse a spirit of initiative in the backward eastern parts of Germany. To that end freedom of person, property, and contract had to be introduced by legal reforms.

Stein's conviction of their need was shared by Karl August Fürst Hardenberg (1750-1822), a Hanoverian who like Stein had entered Prussian service. The two men differed in character and spirit. Hardenberg had little of Stein's moral strength and deep attachment to traditional values. He was more influenced by the urban Enlightenment of the eighteenth century and by the liberalism of Adam Smith. The two men agreed, however, on the need for reforms. In a memorandum *On the Government of the Prussian State,* Hardenberg and his collaborator Karl Freiherr vom Stein zum Altenstein (1770-1840) stressed the need for the transformation of Prussia into a nation animated by a common idea. "Only the participation in such an idea will form a nation, an association of men animated by the same spirit." Such an idea, Altenstein wrote, could take hold even of small states and in the midst of disaster. It would organize them for a supreme effort and would mobilize the forces of the individuals, not as mere tools of the state but in order to achieve for themselves the freest use of all their potentialities. Prussia would then no longer be a state where everybody left concern for the commonweal to the government and entrusted all its affairs to paid officials. In unreformed Prussia "each one thought only of his own existence and its isolated improvement. The result was total indifference to the administration of the state. Nobody thought of having any duty for the commonweal without being especially appointed to and paid for it." The memorandum suggested parliamentary institutions for Prussia, "eine Nationalrepresentation," so that "a nation may be formed in the Prussian state." Then the superficial and uninformed talk among even the educated classes would give way to the growth of a constructive public opinion.[4]

The Stein-Hardenberg reforms, as they became known in history, did not fulfill these high hopes. Prussia received neither parliamentary institutions nor a constitution. The political and social indifference of the middle classes continued, and political liberty remained unknown to them. Yet before 1807 Prussia had hardly been a state in the modern sense of the word; it was an agglomeration of Brandenburgers, Silesians, Pomeranians, and others, held together only by the common dynasty. The official name under which these inherited, conquered, or purchased territories were known was "all the provinces and lands of his royal majesty" (alle Seiner Königlichen Majestät Provincien und Länder). The reforms unified Prussia and lowered the formerly unsurmountable barriers which separated nobility, burghers, and peasants. The first edict of October 9, 1807, established the right of all inhabitants to possess land of every kind and to exercise any occupation. Beginning with Martinmas (November 11) 1810, serfdom was abolished. Thus the first steps were taken to modernize Prussia's economic life and to increase prosperity and the value of landed property. In November 1808 the cities received the right to elect municipal administrations, but no similar provisions were made for rural districts, where administration and justice remained in the hands of the landed aristocracy.

These were Prussia's first cautious steps on the road to liberty, but it was not a liberty conquered or even strongly demanded by the people; it was a liberty granted by the government for purposes of state. The

English historian Seeley, who viewed Prussia and Stein with admiration and sympathy though with the understanding of a Westerner, pointed out that the legislation introducing the first civil liberties showed the same spirit as that animating the laws of military reorganization which were soon to follow.

> There is no opposition of any kind to the Government, and when liberty is introduced the whole process, from the first suggestion to the execution, is conducted exclusively by Government officials. The motive throughout is that which alone disposes Stein himself to favor liberty—not any fear of the oppressiveness of government, not any pity for the condition of a population subjected to despotic rule, but on the contrary a pity for the Government, a feeling that it is not fair of the people to wash their hands altogether of public matters and to discharge the whole burden upon their rulers. And the character of the law corresponds to the motive of it. It carries an air of stern command. The people are not allowed, but commanded, to govern themselves. Much stress is laid upon the burdensomeness of the new regulations, but it is firmly asserted that the burden is one which the people have no right to evade.[5]

Even these moderate reforms aroused the ire of the traditionalists. Count Yorck von Wartenburg, the famous Prussian corps commander in the War of Liberation, declared that to Prussia's misfortune Stein had been in England and had brought his wisdom from there. He predicted the direst consequences for the reforms, the annihilation of the Prussian nobility, the devastation of the Prussian fields and forests, and the end of all loyalty.[6] In reality the reforms strengthened loyalty and economy in Prussia without changing its character as a state founded upon king and nobility.

Stein was more a patriot than he was a liberal. He was at one with the romanticists in idealizing the past. The equality proclaimed by the French Revolution was hateful to him, and individual liberty as a natural right incomprehensible.[7] Though he favored participation of the citizens in government for the sake of the state, he stressed the necessity of slow progress in that direction. "The transition from the old order of things," he wrote to Hardenberg on December 8, 1807, "to a new order must not be too hasty. One must accustom the people slowly to act independently if one calls them to great assemblies and entrusts to them the discussion of great interests." [8] What he wished to do was not to arouse a demand for individual liberty but for national independence:

> One must keep alive in the nation the feeling of indignation over the pressure by and the dependence upon an alien insolent people—one must accustom them to the idea of self-help, the

sacrifice of life and property which in any case will soon belong to the ruling nation; one must spread ideas on the art of inciting and directing an insurrection.

So he wrote in a memorandum on policy on August 11, 1808; and similarly he demanded in a letter to Hardenberg on August 24, 1811, the rousing of the public spirit of the nation for the struggle against the enemy.

> [Such a public spirit] can only be vitalized by institutions which kindle religious sentiments, and by such political institutions as absorb all the forces of the nation. How to arouse such a religious sense and how to direct it towards the love and defense of the fatherland, what liturgic measures to take—about that you will hear proposals by the spirited (*geistvoll*) Professor Schleiermacher.[9]

Stein was undoubtedly a religious man and had deep respect for traditional liberties. He integrated religion and his understanding of liberty into a Christian-German nationalism. For the new liberty of the French Revolution he had no use; he hated it and the French.

In a letter to Emperor Alexander I of Russia, written on February 10, 1814, Stein spoke of the French as "un peuple frivole, bavard, mobile, conduit par des chefs ou phraseurs ou criminels." One year later, at the Congress of Vienna, he noted in his diary:

> Das französische Volk ist meuterisch, aufrüherisch, wie es seine Geschichte lehrt. Dieser Zug ist eine Folge seines Leichtsinns, seiner Beweglichkeit, seines Dünkels, seiner Habsucht; Laster, die durch Religiosität und Sittlichkeit nicht mehr gebändigt sind.[10]

This hatred of the French was by no means the result of the long struggle against the French; it was also expressed in Stein's earliest writings. He welcomed the war against the French Revolution because it would "increase the repugnance of the horrible (*scheussliche*) French nation." One year later, on May 21, 1794, he wrote to his friend Friedrich Wilhelm von Reden:

> All Frenchmen of all color and denomination are unbearable to me, mainly because they lack truth of character, common sense, and kindness. I doubt whether one will be able to conquer and subdue the whole of France, but I do not doubt that one will be able to take a good part of it and to destroy Paris, the seat of all abominations, and I confess that I would like to see this spectacle.

Stein found nowhere in history such immorality (*moralischen Schmutz*) as in French history, and he saw its climax in the Revolution, which from the beginning took "a vicious and criminal direction," because after the fall of monarchy and nobility the nation could show its true character without fear of punishment. Thus the war against France, from its beginning in 1792 to its end in 1815, appeared to Stein to be a struggle against immorality, and he was convinced that the struggle would enhance German ethical energies. Stein was one of the very few representative Germans who held such a violently anti-French attitude throughout the period of the French Revolution and the Napoleonic wars.[11]

When Stein was dismissed from office, under pressure of Napoleon, he left *A Political Testament,* dated November 24, 1808, in which he pleaded for a continuation of the reforms. He suggested the abolition of patrimonial jurisdiction and of the still existing corvée, a reform of the nobility, the introduction of national representation to inform the king's unrestricted power of the wishes of the nation, and an improvement of education and religious instruction. Some of these reforms were carried out by Hardenberg after he became Chancellor in 1810. He abolished the medieval guilds, introduced freedom of contract and equality of taxation, and emancipated the Jews. But a constitution and political rights remained unknown in Prussia for many years. Instead of them, the country received reforms in the military system, which proved of more lasting importance than any other reform. They were the work of Stein's close collaborator Gerhard Johann David von Scharnhorst (1755-1813). He found support in three other brilliant military men, who together became the fathers of the nineteenth-century Prussian army: August Graf Neidhart von Gneisenau (1760-1831), Leopold Hermann Ludwig von Boyen (1771-1848), and Carl von Clausewitz (1780-1831). Their reforms militarized the nation without endowing it at the same time with political rights.[12] They aroused the admiration of all later Prussian patriots and historians. Even Seeley was full of lyrical praise in speaking of them.

> The series of measures commenced by Scharnhorst has determined the result of the greatest struggles of the nineteenth century and has given to Prussia a new period of military ascendancy, grander and not less interesting than the brilliant period of Frederick the Great. The three principal wars of Prussia since her great disaster, those of 1813, 1866, and 1870, have a character of greatness such as no other modern wars have; the objects of them, and the spirit in which they were waged, were as high as the intelligence with which they were guided. They have in a manner reconciled the modern world to war, for they have exhibited it as a civilizing agent and a kind of teacher of morality.[13]

Constitutional and financial reforms seemed the work of cold and calculating reason; in the duty of military service and in the united dedication to war there appeared poetry and enthusiasm, the mystic force of creative action which Fichte demanded, the intimate identification with the state of which the romanticists wrote. When Gneisenau submitted to the King plans for a popular insurrection and suggested in his memorandum of August 8, 1811, that the clergymen in the countryside, recalling the religious struggles of the Maccabees, should preach a crusade against France, the King noted in the margin of the memorandum, "good as poetry." This sobering remark called forth Gneisenau's indignation:

> Religion, prayer, love of the monarch and of the fatherland
> are nothing but poetry! Whoever acts only from cold calculation
> will become an inflexible egotist. The security of the thrones
> is based upon poetry. This is poetry and of the noblest kind.
> I shall find comfort in it during all my life.

The influence of romanticism made itself felt in the spirit in which Scharnhorst and Gneisenau instituted their military reforms; yet the immediate practical models were found in the West, in the experiences of the American and French armies in their revolutionary wars.

Scharnhorst was neither a Prussian nor of noble descent. The son of a Hanoverian soldier, he entered the Prussian army in 1801. A man of scholarly nature, he became director of the newly founded war college, where he was joined by Clausewitz. From the beginning he stressed, against the old-fashioned drill, the importance of moral forces in the war and demanded the creation of a national army in which every citizen without exception would serve, an army founded upon the sentiment of honor, patriotic devotion, and compensation according to merit. His "revolutionary" or "Jacobin" suggestions to abolish the privileges of the nobility and to treat the soldiers humanely were submitted before the catastrophe of Jena, but his warnings remained unheeded. Only after the breakdown of the old Prussian army, Scharnhorst and Gneisenau were called to work out a new system which, in Scharnhorst's words, was founded upon two principles: the elevation of the spirit of the army and of the dignity of the common soldier; and the fusion of army and nation into an intimate union. The old army of illiterate peasant soldiers had been held together by the strictest brutal discipline. Now the problem arose how to introduce the new principles of individual dignity and equal opportunity and at the same time to preserve discipline. Scharnhorst solved the problem by trying to instill in the whole youth the spirit of a soldierly tradition in which modern patriotism, popular education, and the Prussian sense of duty would fuse. Through his efforts, corporal punishment in the army was abolished many years before it disappeared from civilian penal law.

In his proposals Scharnhorst was motivated by two practical considerations: he had to organize the forces and the resources of a relatively small state for defense against a powerful enemy, and he found himself faced with the need to apply against France the very lessons learned from the successes of the French revolutionary armies. Had not the French and American armies defeated adversaries superior in number and professional training? Scharnhorst studied closely the French revolutionary wars. In an essay "Development of the General Causes for the French Successes in the Revolutionary War and Especially in the Campaign of 1794," he came to the conclusion that "the formation of the national militia had aroused the military spirit of the nation and produced an enthusiasm for the independence of the fatherland which had hardly an equal in other countries." [14] Thus he started his reform plan of August 31, 1807, with the words: "All inhabitants of the state are its born defenders," words unknown a century before, when military operations were regarded as the exclusive task of professional soldiers.

Like Scharnhorst, Gneisenau appreciated the positive aspects of the French Revolution for the development of national strength. "The Revolution has awakened all forces and given to each force an appropriate field of action," he wrote.

> The Revolution has activized the whole national power of the French people, has transformed the living force of men and the dead force of goods into a rapidly profit-bearing capital, and has thereby destroyed the former stable relations among the states. If the other states wish to restore the equilibrium, then they have to open up and use the same resources.[15]

Gneisenau's conviction of the need for reforms which the study of recent French history conveyed to him was deepened by the memories which he carried with him from Canada, where he spent a year as a member of the British army in 1782-1783. Though he was not involved in actual combat, he had an opportunity to learn about the fighting methods of the colonists.

After his return from America, Gneisenau entered the Prussian army and began to introduce the technique of individual warfare in the training of his troops. In the disaster of 1806 he was one of the few who showed courage and determination. He organized the defense of the Baltic fortress of Kolberg, the most creditable exploit of the war. It proved "in the most striking manner the change that was coming over the age, the new forces that were mustering," the strength and need of public opinion and civilian cooperation. There for the first time on a local scale, Gneisenau used the patriotic forces which the Stein-Scharnhorst reforms of the following years tried to arouse. He was supported by the city's mayor, Joachim Nettelbeck, a widely traveled and enterprising man, and by a daring Prussian cavalry officer, Schill, who raised and led a "free corps" of volunteers, the first example of an incipient popular resistance movement against Napoleon.[16]

Gneisenau, the military man, showed among the reformers the greatest understanding for Western liberal ideas. He was no German nationalist and hardly a Prussian patriot. In a letter to Count Ernst Friedrich Herbert Münster, a Hanoverian in British service, Gneisenau suggested on November 2, 1812, that northwestern Germany should not only be occupied by an English expeditionary force but should be united permanently with Britain and thus share in the benefits of British government. Gneisenau felt that from the point of view of human liberty it was not important whether Germans were ruled by Germans or by Englishmen; what counted was the question which government safeguarded better individual freedom and had the greater experience in constitutional liberty. "These German peoples," Gneisenau wrote, "thus united with Britain will feel most happy under a free constitution." In a letter from London to Hardenberg on January 6, 1813, Gneisenau again proposed that northwestern Germany should form a great state under the Guelph dynasty in personal union with Britain. Such a British controlled and protected state in northwestern Germany would constitute, Gneisenau wrote, a bulwark protecting Prussia from France. Perhaps he hoped that the blessings of a free constitution might spread from a British Germany to other German lands. Gneisenau's hatred of Napoleon was hatred of tyranny, not of an alien race. He believed that the overthrow of Napoleon demanded a strong military spirit in the whole people and presupposed a prosperous and enlightened nation, civil liberty, and public morality. Political freedom and military strength were in his opinion interdependent. He wished to strengthen Prussia by granting her a free constitution which would become the envy of all nations. Liberty was to him not only a means, it was an end in itself.

While Gneisenau's liberalism was firmly rooted in the eighteenth century, Clausewitz, a generation younger than the two military reformers, anticipated later developments. "No book in the world," he wrote in 1807, "is more necessary for the statesman than Machiavelli; those who affect a distaste for his principles are a kind of humanistic fops." In his hatred of the French Clausewitz even denied that the Revolution and its enthusiasm had inspired the French to military prowess. Was it proof of newly awakened energy, he asked, that the French people were willing to join the army when they faced a worse terror at home, when they met in their towns only the ghosts of brothers and fathers, mothers and children who had fallen victim to the guillotine? They simply acted "heroically" out of fear; they escaped from murder at home to the lesser murder at the front. Or was it praiseworthy that a million men avid for booty and plunder would have fought with varying success against armies hardly a fourth their strength and led by old men? A nation as corrupt as the French, Clausewitz was convinced, was incapable of real heroism or of true liberty. One had only to hear the French speak, Clausewitz maintained, to find their inferiority fully revealed. The wonderful wealth of the German language allowed even to the mediocre man to be original, whereas nobody could find in the French language anything but ready-made thoughts. But it was not this hostility to France which singled Clausewitz out among the German nationalists of his time; it was the subordination of ethical and political life to the requirements of war.[17]

XXX

Prussia and France

THE Germans at the beginning of the nineteenth century showed little inclination for warlike adventures. Stein and the military reformers struggled in vain to arouse a spirit of resistance in Prussia. They had to contend with the irresolution of the King and the widespread pro-French attitude of the ruling elite and of the people.[1] The uprising in Spain and Austria's preparations for war against France in 1808 made little difference. Stein, Scharnhorst, and Gneisenau hoped in vain for a popular insurrection in Prussia in cooperation with Austria. Gneisenau stressed the need for democratic and popular actions in the plans which he worked out for a general uprising of northern Germany against France. In the summer of 1808 he wrote:

> Our enemies fear nothing more than popular uprisings, and nothing else develops the strength of the nation in a more terrifying way. . . . Where the enemy has great superiority of numbers, there one retreats, devastates and scorches the land in front of him, attacks him on his flanks and in his back and cuts off his supplies. . . . Each man over seventeen years of age receives arms and is designated a soldier by a national cockade. The battalions thus formed elect their noncommissioned and commissioned officers.

Such a national militia, a nation in arms, would do away with standing armies and with the heavy financial burdens which they impose upon the people. Gneisenau believed that such popular armies could be used only for defense and would eliminate the danger of aggressive wars. He demanded that Prussia, in preparation for the popular insurrection, should promulgate a free constitution, that she should renounce solemnly any desire for conquest or annexation of any German territory; that nobility should be confined to those who would fight valiantly in the war, and that Prussia would thus win not only independence but a new national life in liberty and popular unity.[2]

In 1809 Gneisenau went to London to demand British support for the plans of the Prussian patriots. In a memorandum to the Foreign Office he again stressed the hopelessness of using against France old-fashioned military forces. Only the united force of the nation could oppose the enemy with success; to that end a free constitution had to win the heart of the people for active support of the government and ennoble the nation. Like many continental liberals in the nineteenth century, Gneisenau appealed to Britain for help to arouse the slumbering forces of Germany.

> This potent empire can indeed dispense with the continent; but it is worthy of a generous nation, which has long enjoyed a happy liberty and stable independence, to secure these highest of earthly blessings also to the offspring of the same forefathers, and thus to renovate the ties that have long united both nations, by commerce of reciprocal advantage and by war of mutual interest.[3]

But the efforts of the Prussian patriots failed in Berlin. The King decided not to help Austria against France. He could be certain of popular support for any policy which avoided war with France. The argument of the patriots that after a French victory over Austria, Prussia might be annexed to France, was rejected. The majority of the King's advisors refused to stake Prussia's existence upon the outcome of a war at a time when the near future might bring unexpected events which would change the whole situation. But nobody actually foresaw any such changes.

When the French intended to invade Russia with an army of unsurpassed size and preparedness, everybody counted upon their victory. Under these circumstances the Prussian government concluded in March 1812 an official alliance with France. As part of Napoleon's Grande Armée, contingents of all German princes, including those of Austria and Prussia, marched against Russia. In the spring of 1812 the whole of official Germany found itself in the French camp; nor was there any resistance among the common people. Only a few patriots took an anti-French stand and turned to Russia in open defiance of the German governments. Stein, who had found a refuge in Austria after his dismissal in Prussia, moved to St. Petersburg and tried to organize a German-Russian legion consisting of German residents in Russia and German prisoners of war. He called Arndt to his side to take charge of a campaign of propaganda to arouse the Germans by appeals launched from Russia. A number of Prussian officers, among them Gneisenau and Clausewitz, resigned in protest against the French alliance.

In a memorandum written in February 1812 before the conclusion of the alliance, Clausewitz justified his and his friends' attitude. He knew that in his opposition to the French alliance he spoke only for a handful among his fellow citizens. The overwhelming majority of Prussians regarded them as "cracked fools or dangerous revolutionaries or light-hearted babblers or self-seeking intriguers."

> The opinion that one could resist France, has almost completely disappeared among us. One believes in the necessity of an alliance with France without any conditions attached, in unconditional surrender, even in a renunciation of the privilege of one's own ruling house. That is the general conviction. Some go even farther in the insolence with which they insist upon the security and tranquil enjoyment of their private property and upon the necessity of sacrificing everything to it, even the honor of the king. The higher classes are the worst; not only do they desire tranquillity and security like the others, but they persecute with undying hatred everybody who does not despair like them. Thus the true patriots have been ostracized by public opinion and have been declared enemies of state and king.

Opposing the majority of his fellow citizens, Clausewitz concluded with a solemn credo:

> I believe and profess, that a people has nothing to esteem more highly than the dignity and liberty of its existence; that it must defend it with the last drop of its blood; that it has to fulfill no more sacred duty, that it has to obey no higher law; that the infamous taint of cowardly submission can never be wiped off; that this drop of poison in the blood of a people will be transferred to posterity and will lame and destroy the strength of future generations; that even the loss of liberty after a bloody and honorable struggle assures the rebirth of a people and is a seed of life in which a new tree can strike secure roots; that I would feel myself only too happy if I could find a glorious death in the struggle for the fatherland's liberty and dignity.[4]

The handful of Prussian patriots were not entirely alone in Germany. Here and there men began to doubt whether "Napoleon's genius was intended by Providence for the happiness of the world" as Dalberg had maintained in 1806, and to develop, if not a German national program, at least a German national consciousness. Hans Ernst Christoph von Gagern (1766-1852), a Rhinelander and an imperial knight like Stein, whose father had been an officer in one of the German regiments which before 1789 formed part of the French army, was until 1811 a devoted admirer of Napoleon, to whom he dedicated in 1808 the first part of his *Die Resultate der Sittengeschichte* [Results of the History of Morals].

But then he began to despair of German salvation through Napoleon. He went to Vienna, where he started to write his *Die Nationalgeschichte der Deutschen* [National History of the Germans] and participated in 1813 in the ill-fated Alpenbund conspiracy with Baron Hormayr.

In southern Germany Schelling came to the conclusion that

> German scholarship and culture (Wissenschaft) are not mere outward appendages to the nation or mere means. They are the true inner essence and heart of the nation, bound up with its existence, and it may be rightly said that it has its true existence only in them.

In 1812 Schelling planned to found a journal as the mouthpiece of the few patriotic intellectuals, who were living isolated in the various German lands, without contact with each other. This journal, Schelling hoped, would grow into a tribune of an invisible academy which had no visible abode in Germany. The periodical appeared at the beginning of 1813 in Munich under the title *Allgemeine Zeitschrift von Deutschen für Deutsche*, dedicated to the "whole German educated public." [5]

In Hamburg, under French occupation, Friedrich Perthes (1772-1843) started in 1810 a similar enterprise in his journal *Das Vaterländische Museum*. He was one of the few German businessmen who became active in public affairs, an early representative of the awakening middle classes. His journal was founded to cultivate "the religious spirit (Sinn), scholarly soundness (Tüchtigkeit) and historical truth" and to preserve "deutsche Bildung und deutsch-eigentümliche Art und Wissenschaft und Kunst." He hoped that it would become a means of communication among the few like-minded persons in Germany who would form around it first a scholarly association and later an active union, a "Tatenbund." In his new patriotism Perthes wished to preserve the cosmopolitanism of his youth. In 1807 he wrote to Johannes von Müller:

> We Germans are a chosen people which represents mankind and makes everything a universal concern. We never were a mere nation (Wir waren nie bloss national). . . . As far as we Germans had any life at all [he wrote in another letter to Jacobi on October 19, 1807] we have never lived it for ourselves but also for Europe. We have every right to regard our character as rich and deep, but we have never understood how to use our treasures.

Perthes wished to make the Germans more conscious of their nationality, but he was afraid lest a growing nationalism might make them incapable of fulfilling their universal mission.

> You would misunderstand me if you thought that I wish our people to confine themselves to themselves like other nations

and to think only of themselves and work for themselves. Certainly, many at present have such a wish. Yet what would it mean but that the Germans should no longer be Germans and should have a nationality like every other nation?[6]

In 1814 Perthes found himself on this score in disagreement with Niebuhr, who believed that people could live happily only in great and powerful states and wished to expand Prussia at the expense of Germany. Perthes, however, recognized in Prussia "a tendency which because it thought only of Prussia must endanger Germany." He was convinced "that a great spiritual struggle was imminent between those who wished to shape Germany's future through the German people and those who wished to determine it through the Prussian state." Thus Perthes foresaw the following half century of the struggle between the Prussian state and the German people which ended with the Prussian state incorporating, politically and spiritually, the German people.

Different was the nationalism of Heinrich Luden (1778-1847), who in 1806 became professor of history at the University of Jena. Two years later in his lectures *Über das Studium der vaterländischen Geschichte,* he no longer stressed the community of Europe or of mankind, but the diversity and peculiarity of each nation, regarding the division into nations as a beneficial and eternal work of nature. All manifestations of culture and life, he taught, are invested in each people with a unique character which belongs only to this people.

> Therefore it is and must be the first aspiration of each people to preserve its independence, to remain free and independent of the domination of any other people, to assure the free development of its peculiar character, and to prevent an alien people from imposing the alien meaning of an alien life. For all life loves itself and wishes to preserve itself and to expand; it wishes to subject everything in order to be entirely free. That is the reason why each people is animated by an ambition to tower above all other peoples, to be highly regarded by them, to command them, as is the ambition of individuals against other individuals.

Luden praised this competitive struggle among nations, the fierce and ambitious battle for survival and dominion, as an iron law of nature; he was convinced that the individual could satisfy the longings of his heart and fulfill the meaning of his life only through full identification with his nation.

> For that reason the wise man or the man with a human soul will love his people as he loves himself because the people is in him as he is in the people; for that reason the man who

abandons his fatherland abandons himself: the most condemnable act that can be done (*das Verdammungswürdigste, welches geschehen mag!*).

Luden's nationalism was skeptical about the rights of man and lukewarm over parliamentary liberties.[7] His teachings aroused the students in Jena; one of their student corps, the Vandalia, which consisted of students from Mecklenburg—all German student associations, called corps, were organized according to their territorial origin, the German province or state from which they came—decided to change the territorial form of organization into a national one, a great patriotic association, called Burschenschaft, which would include students from all parts of Germany and thus help to overcome the particularist spirit. Their plan matured later under the influence of Jahn, when the students returned from the War of Liberation. Many among them had volunteered following Luden's appeal. He himself stayed on to publish a patriotic journal which he characteristically called *Nemesis*.[8] In its first issue he contributed an article "Das Vaterland, oder Staat und Volk" which maintained that only a state built upon the ethnic principle can be a true fatherland, that state and nation must coincide. Where that does not happen, people will always strive to form a nation-state. Only such a state could guarantee peace, culture, and prosperity. Luden's teaching inspired not only Germans. Many Slav students from the Habsburg monarchy were enrolled at that time in Jena: from there they carried the seeds of nationalism to their native lands.

Herder taught them the excellence and fundamental importance of the Slav vernaculars and that no true civilization could be built except on the basis of the mother tongue. Luden went further; his political nationalism taught them to strive for a nation-state and justified it. Luden accepted from Jahn and Fichte the emphasis on folk, on purity of language and descent, and the faith that the Germans were purer in race and more original in their language than other people, especially the French, and therefore superior to them. But more important was his insistence not yet shared by Fichte that political and ethnic frontiers must coincide and that only a fatherland which united the whole nationality could provide a truly human life, culture, and happiness. Where folk and state were not identical, where a state included various nationalities or language groups, there, Luden was convinced, only misery, half-heartedness, and split personalities—"Halbheit, Zerrissenheit, Unlust und Jammer"—could exist.

Not only poetry and history were put into the service of the new nationalism. Music, too, played its part. Carl Maria von Weber (1786-1826), a true romanticist, composed Theodor Körner's "Leier und Schwert" for male choir, and Ludwig Spohr (1784-1859), a follower of

Jahn, conducted in 1810 and 1811 the first German music festivals. They were held in a highly patriotic mood in the tiny town of Frankenhausen in the equally tiny principality of Schwarzburg-Rudolfstadt. The locality was chosen because it was situated at the foot of the Kyffhäuser, a mountain in central Germany which became a symbol of German nationalism. According to a widespread legend Frederick II, the last great medieval emperor of the Hohenstaufen dynasty, was sleeping in the mountain and would waken when called to deliver his people and to restore the splendor of the Reich. Later on, Frederick II was confused with Frederick Barbarossa, his grandfather; at the beginning of the nineteenth century, when the romanticists made the Kyffhäuser legend popular, Barbarossa and not his grandson became its hero. During the music festival, Albert Methfessel, then a popular singer and lieder composer, standing in the ruins of the ancient Kyffhäuser castle, appealed to Barbarossa to rise from his sleep and to drive out the enemy. These music festivals with their large orchestras and choirs marked the transition from the chamber music of the small courts and towns of eighteenth-century Germany to a new music which no longer intended to delight individuals but to reflect the emotions of crowds and to stir them into action. The patriotic poetry of the War of Liberation could never have gained the widespread popularity which it enjoyed in Germany for more than a century without the help of music.[9]

Among the men who contributed to the awakening of German nationalism in the Napoleonic era, four stand out—Fichte, Schleiermacher, Arndt, and Jahn. They came from northern and eastern Germany, and though only two of them were born in Prussia, they all came to regard Prussia as their spiritual home. All four were Protestants and all began their careers as students of theology. They came from humble or middle-class origins. Schleiermacher and Jahn were the sons of ministers. Their views differed in many ways; together they presented the varied pattern of the influences which linked 1813 with 1871 and determined more and more the outlook of the rising German middle classes, especially in the Protestant parts of Germany.

XXXI

Johann Gottlieb Fichte

OF ALL the German intellectual spokesmen for nationalism in the Napoleonic age, none was as eager to mold his people and the world according to his will as Johann Gottlieb Fichte (1762-1814). The son of a poor Saxon artisan, he became Kant's foremost disciple, though a wayward one, and the first professor of philosophy at the newly founded University of Berlin. Fichte was not primarily a scholar like Kant. Though his philosophy may strike Western readers as strangely abstract and void of any relation to reality, Fichte regarded it as the true foundation of action. He scorned contemplation which would dispassionately witness and analyze the course of events. "I do not wish only to think, I wish to act," he wrote as a young man. Life had meaning for him only as action, as personal creation, as an imposition of his will upon others. To an unusual degree Fichte was a domineering personality; the acquaintance with Kant's philosophy and his own reinterpretation of its central position in the aggressive spirit of the Storm and Stress opened to him the way to combine thought and action. To him, the objective world which claimed to determine and limit the ego on all sides, revealed itself as a creation, as an idea of this very ego, dependent upon it. The ego, as far as it is a rational ego, or to use Fichte's words, a pure ego, is not dominated by nature but dominates it in freedom. This pure ego in its autonomous and spontaneous activity, or the metaphysically free individual who follows his own moral law, becomes the absolute in whose creative act theory and activity coincide. To such a view human history is an ever progressing activity to greater autonomy and freedom, and the life of political societies is an advance through ever more perfect rational constitutions. It is easily understandable that from such a philosophical standpoint Fichte approved of the French Revolution, its rational voluntarism, its abstract universal legislation.[1]

In 1793 Fichte published his first political essay, an appeal for freedom of thought. It was characteristic of Fichte that he wrote it in the form of a lecture. It appeared dated "Heliopolis, in the last year of the old darkness," so convinced was Fichte that an entirely new period was at hand. But more important than this brief "Reclamation of the Liberty of Thought from the Princes of Europe Who Have Heretofore Suppressed It" was his "Contributions to the Rectification of Public Opinion on the French Revolution" which appeared in the same year. Here Fichte developed for the first time his philosophy of the state. It was a radically rationalist and moralist philosophy, proposed by an individualist and cosmopolitan. Turning to the princes who fought the French Revolution to preserve the European equilibrium and the independence of their countries, Fichte exclaimed:

> You fear for us subjection to a foreign power, and to secure us against this misfortune, you yourselves prefer to subject us. Do not be so confident that we regard the situation in the same way as you do. It is easy to believe that you yourselves prefer to subject us rather than to leave it to somebody else. But what we cannot understand is why we should prefer it so much. . . . Do you think that the German artist and peasant are very much interested whether a Lorrainese or Alsatian artist and peasant from now on finds his town or village in the geographic handbooks in the chapter on the German Reich and no longer in the chapter on France, and that he will throw away his chisel and his plow to see this brought about? [2]

In these years Fichte showed himself indifferent to patriotism. The fatherland of every man was the land of individual liberty. This ideal seemed to Fichte at that time realized in France. In May 1794 he wrote to his wife about the French who were then occupying parts of the Rhineland:

> The general attitude (Stimmung) of the inhabitants whose countryside has been devastated by the French is nevertheless much in their favor. The common man loves them and they feed the indigent; only the privileged classes are furious against them. In Mainz and in Frankfurt there is a general desire for their return. Everybody without exception hates the Prussians and the Austrians, laughs at them, and derides them for their defeats. [3]

A few years later Fichte spoke of himself as "a young man who had abandoned his fatherland and did not feel bound to any state." [4] He expressed himself even more strongly in a letter which he wrote in May 1799, when the attacks of fundamentalist theologians had forced him to abandon his chair at the University of Jena:

> Nothing is more certain to me than the fact that unless the French do achieve the most tremendous superiority and bring

about a change in Germany, at least in a considerable part of it, no German who is known for ever having expressed a free thought will in a few years find a secure place.[5]

More important than this indifference to the German nation, which later changed, was Fichte's controlling idea, which in spite of variations and aberrations—sometimes of even diametrically opposed positions— remained with him until his death: the conviction that the end of history is a free and fraternal association of independent individuals everywhere, a worldwide anarchy based upon the full realization of the moral law, the Kingdom of God on earth. In his "Contributions to the Rectification of Public Opinion on the French Revolution" the disciple of Kant rejected eudemonism. A pursuit of happiness appeared an unworthy end of life, the true end of which could be nothing other than the growth and spread of *Kultur*. Fichte defined *Kultur* as "the exercise of all our forces for the purpose of total liberty, of total independence from everything which is not our self, which is not our pure ego." [6] Under the influence of Rousseau, Fichte believed man to be by nature good, and freedom to be natural to him; therefore society had to allow and to assure free course to man's rational nature. The state, like all organizations of restraint from without, was against nature, an unnatural institution and thus unethical. At the end of the rational education of man—and this education Fichte then understood as creative self-education[7]—stands the total accord of the will of the ego with the law of reason. Only for the transitional period could the state be justified; ultimately, in the world as it should be, it would wither away.

Fichte's conception of society and therefore of nationality was throughout nonhistorical and nonpolitical. In his *Einige Vorlesungen über die Bestimmung des Gelehrten* (1794) he wrote: "The state like all human institutions which are only means, aims at its own destruction. It is the purpose of government to make government superfluous." But he followed this statement with the caveat: "Now this moment has not yet arrived, and I do not know how many billions of years will have to pass [before it arrives], and it is not meant at all to be applied in life." Fichte was not dealing with historical reality or political responsibility. In spite of his desire to transform reality, he developed a philosophy which he knew was unapplicable to life and its conditions. His concern was with the ultimate, with the ever valid, beyond the vicissitudes of necessity and contingency, true to Schiller's words:

> Was sich nie und nirgends hat begeben,
> Das allein veraltet nie!

In his *Staatslehre*, which he wrote in 1813 and which was published only after his death,[8] Fichte predicted the same supranational and metaphysical goal of history and politics, this time to be attained through Christianity, which will replace the juridical state-order.

> so that the whole human race on earth will be encompassed in a single closely united Christian state which according to a common plan will vanquish nature and enter the higher sphere of another life. . . . Christianity is not only a theory; it must become the principle of a constitution. We must arrive on this earth at a point where God alone and all-inclusively may rule as an ethical substance through free will and understanding, so that all men may become true Christians and citizens of the heavenly kingdom, and that all other rule over man may simply and clearly disappear. . . . In such a realm of Christianity the traditional government by constraint will gradually wither away, because it will no longer find anything to do. . . . The former state-by-restraint will quietly, without any force being used against it, die off due to its own uselessness (Nichtigkeit) brought about by the course of time, and the last heir of sovereignty, should such a one exist, will be obliged to enter the general state of equality.[9]

In his early years Fichte expected that the French people, rising above themselves in the fire of the Revolution, would lead mankind on the road to absolute freedom and rational morality. Twenty years later this role, the leadership of mankind, was transferred to the Germans. He had found the French wanting; in the *Staatslehre* he trusted that the Germans instead would establish the final kingdom. The contents of this Reich had not changed—it was and remained liberty and equality.

> Through the Germans, the Reich must start from perfected individual liberty, not the other way about; it must start from the personality formed prior to any state and then formed in the various states in which the Germans are at present organized and which later must disappear as mere means to a higher end. Thus they will be able to represent a true realm of law as it has never yet appeared on earth, with all the enthusiasm for the liberty of the citizen which we see in the ancient world, but without the sacrifice of the majority of men as slaves without which the ancient states could not exist, with liberty founded upon the equality of all human beings—"alles dessen, was Menschengesicht trägt." [10]

It was not the nation or the state which determined the course and goal of human history. Fichte was at no time a nationalist in the sense that he would have ascribed to nationalities or to nationalism any value in themselves. His guiding principle was a universal, rational philosophy. This philosophy had an active task, the "transformation, rebirth, and renovation of the spirit in its deepest root: the creation of a new organ and out of it a new world, in the temporal order." [11] The philosophy was Fichte's. He pointed out the way in which in his opinion only one nation in Europe was deep and spiritual enough to lead mankind, the Germans.

Though mankind was one in spirit and should become one in reality, in the various stages of history one nation, a different nation at each stage, seemed to be destined to take the lead. Fichte concluded the fourteenth of his lectures *Die Grundzüge des gegenwärtigen Zeitalters,* which he delivered in the winter of 1804-1805, with the words: "What is the fatherland of the truly educated Christian European? In general it is Europe; in particular it is in each age that European state which has assumed the cultural leadership." If this state committed political errors, it might perish, but others would take its place.

> Let then earth-born men who recognize their fatherland as the soil, the river and the mountain, remain citizens of the decayed state. They retain what they wish and what makes them happy: the sun-loving spirit will be attracted irresistibly to where light and right dwell and will turn to them. In this cosmopolitan understanding we can be completely indifferent to the actions and fates of the various states, for ourselves and for our descendants, to the end of days.[12]

Thus at the beginning of 1805 the earthly destiny of a nation—including the German nation—was a matter of indifference to Fichte. Only that nation counted which led in the realization and spreading of Kultur, and that meant of Fichte's philosophy. It was in 1806, in the patriotic dialogues *Der Patriotismus und sein Gegenteil* that Fichte discovered that the Germans were the most probable people to assume the task. His patriotism, now proclaimed for the first time, was still a cosmopolitan patriotism. The fatherland had no autonomous existence; it was only a place for the realization of the cosmopolitan idea. "Cosmopolitanism," Fichte wrote,

> Cosmopolitanism is the dominant will, that the purpose of existence, of humanity be really achieved by humanity. Patriotism is the will, that this purpose be first fulfilled in that nation of which we ourselves are members, and that the result shall spread from it to the whole of mankind.

Thus by definition cosmopolitanism must become patriotism.[13] The German patriot would therefore wish that the purpose of humanity should first be achieved among the Germans and that the result would then spread to the whole of mankind.

Fortunately the German was in a uniquely favored position. For the purpose of humanity could be achieved only through the acceptance and realization of Fichte's philosophy; and what people were better prepared for it than the Germans, among whom this philosophy originated and in whose language it was written?

> The greatest capacity for understanding this knowledge lies with that nation which had the force to create it. The German alone, by possessing the knowledge and understanding the age through it, can perceive that this is the next objective of humanity.

From there it was a short step to the conclusion that only the Germans were capable of understanding the task of the age, and that only their understanding could be truly called patriotic.

> The German alone can therefore be a patriot. He alone can for the sake of his nation encompass the whole of mankind. Contrasted with him, from now on, the patriotism of every other nation must be egoistic, narrow, and hostile to the rest of mankind.[14]

This conclusion was solemnly drawn in the introduction to the famous eighth address of Fichte's *Reden an die deutsche Nation* where he proclaimed:

> The German alone—the original, not the institutionalized, withered man—der ursprüngliche und nicht in einer willkürlichen Satzung erstorbene Mensch—has truly a nation, and . . . he alone is entitled to count on one and is capable of loving his nation in the true way, according to reason.

In reality the Germans owed this privileged position only to the fact that they could understand Fichte's philosophy. Fichte was convinced that Europe must perish if she did not accept the true philosophy. If the Germans would not save human culture, no other European nation would be able to do it.

> Should the German not assume the government of the world through philosophy, the Turks, the Negroes, the North American tribes, will finally take it over and put an end to the present civilization.[15]

Though Fichte's nationalism never abandoned its philosophical and universal—it might almost be said its nonpolitical and nonmilitary—aspect, the events of 1806 brought with them a new and Germanic interpretation. When the war between Prussia and France broke out in 1806, Fichte, who had left his native Saxony and had found a home in Prussia, had no doubt about the issues at stake. In the one camp was Napoleon, who represented to him "arbitrariness, which has no knowledge whatsoever of what it wills except that it wills to be unlimited and steely." He did not see Napoleon as Goethe or Hegel did, as the embodiment of world reason, but as an appearance without the true life of reason behind it, as a purely "negative greatness." In the other camp was Prussia, which appeared to Fichte as the last refuge of ethical liberty and of reason, the European state which in the present age had assumed the cultural leadership. Thus mere appearance and true existence faced each other. Prussia's defeat would mean the destruction of true Kultur, of the spiritual mission of mankind. Fichte wished to accompany the Prussian army into battle. He felt, he wrote about himself,

> that he would not fall behind anyone in courage if he had learned how to handle arms; he lamented that the present age did not allow him—as Aeschylus and Cervantes had been allowed to do—to prove his word by forceful deed, and he maintained that in the situation which gave a new task to his life he would prefer deeds to words. Now however, as he could only talk, he wished to talk swords and thunderbolts. Nor did he wish to do that without danger and in security. He would express in the course of his addresses truths which before the court of the enemy were punishable by death.[16]

When the French armies approached Berlin, Fichte did not stay and face Napoleon as Johannes von Müller did. He went to Königsberg, and there he wrote in 1807 his essay on Machiavelli, an article much more in agreement with the traditions of Frederick's and Bismarck's Prussia than with the cosmopolitan rationalism which Fichte professed in 1793 as well as in 1813. He turned with the same vehemence as Arndt or Jahn did against the "fashionable" philosophy of pacifism, which he castigated as superficial, anemic, and puny, above all as infatuated with perpetual peace—"gar flach und kränklich und armselig, ganz besonders aber verliebt in den ewigen Frieden." [17] He expected peace, not perpetual but long-lasting, only from the permanent and highly armed military preparedness of all great nations, and was convinced that conflicts must last, because

> every nation wishes to spread its own ideas and ways of life—"das ihr eigentümliche Gute"—as far as it can, and that it wishes as far as it is in its power to incorporate the whole of mankind, and this due to a compulsion (Trieb) which God has implanted into men and on which the society of nations, their mutual friction and their development rest.[18]

According to Fichte—at least the Fichte of 1807—the prince in his private life was bound by the rules of general morality, in the relation to his people he was bound by law, but in relation to other states there is neither law nor right, except the right of the mightier, and this relationship lays the divine and majestic rights of destiny and of world government upon the responsibility of the prince and into his hands, and raises him above the command-ments of individual morality into a higher ethical order, the material concept of which is contained in the words: Salus et decus populi suprema lex esto.[19]

The rational despotism of Machiavelli appealed personally to the despot in Fichte, who wished to force man to become free and moral and to live up to Fichte's ideal.[20] Like most utopians who believed that the perfect world could soon emerge if only men would will the right thing, he combined an absolute pessimism about the corruption of the present age and society—which justified and made necessary the ap-plication of ruthless means—with an absolute optimism about the goal and its attainability. The higher his esteem for ultimate man—the true rational man—the more impatient he was with actual man—a passing phenomenon without true substance. Thus the prophet of a utopian abstract morality became an advocate of extreme concrete im-morality, and yet would regard himself as justified in the name of a higher ethics.

Who has a right to be the supreme leader?—Wer hat ein Recht, Oberherr zu sein? . . . The highest human intelligence of its time and its people. . . . The expression of unreason within the world in which one person exists who understands better goes against the right of this person and he has a per-fect right not to tolerate it, if he can prevent it, and to force the others if he is strong enough.[21]

The Fichte of the crucial years after 1806 seems a different man from the proponent of a league of nations ten years before. In the *Zweiten Anhang des Naturrechts* (1796), he had stated that war could be re-garded as the legal and just means to secure legality in the relationship of states: the only drawback was that there was no means to make certain that the defender of the just cause emerged from the war vic-torious. "Because among states not everyone has as much might as he has right, war might promote injustice as much as, or perhaps even more than, the just cause." But as war remains the only means by which force can be applied to a state, ways should be found to make certain that the better cause will be victorious. This can be achieved only in the way that several states unite in defense of the just cause. Fichte was one of the first to suggest a league of nations, for which he used the word "Völkerbund." All its members would solemnly agree to act jointly for the defense of their independence and of the league covenant. The league would act as a court and at the same time have executive powers. Naturally—Fichte added realistically—there could be no guarantee that the judgment of the league of nations would always be just. But such an objection against international justice seemed to him as little valid as against domestic justice.

> As long as pure reason does not appear in person on earth and assume the judicial office, there must always be a supreme judge who, because he is human, can err or have evil intentions. The task is to find the one of whom this would be feared the least. This one is the nation, in the relation among citizens; and the league of nations, in the relation among states.

A league growing in strength and extent could become an instrument to secure peace.[22]

But this concern with peace was absent in Fichte's nationalism after 1806, which culminated in the famous *Reden an die deutsche Nation*. The nationalism of the *Reden* presupposed the universal intercourse of nations; the nationalism of the *Geschlossene Handelsstaat* which Fichte wrote in 1800, one year after he had made Berlin his permanent home, was of an entirely different character. In either case, nationalism was an educational enterprise, in the first case spreading from a center of regeneration to the whole of mankind and undertaken in its interest, in the latter case confined to one nation alone, which would create an ideal society in complete isolation from the rest of the world. Such a nation would develop its national character to an unprecedented degree. "It is clear," Fichte wrote,

> that in such a secluded nation, the members of which live with each other and very rarely with foreigners and which receives its peculiar way of life, institutions, and habits from these meas- ures of isolation, which loves devotedly its fatherland and every- thing patriotic, a very high degree of national honor and a very sharply defined national character will quickly develop. It will become another and entirely new nation.[23]

The *Geschlossene Handelsstaat* presents an extreme utopia of a closed society for the task of realizing state-directed socialism and to secure work for every citizen. To that end the state must attain complete self- sufficiency and close its frontiers to all commercial exchange with foreign lands. Fichte rejected free trade and the commercial civilization of inter- course and exchange.

Thus Fichte, in his isolationist period, rejected the thought of German leadership or of the education of mankind by the Germans. In a frag- ment which he wrote in 1807, "Die Republik der Deutschen, zu Anfang des zweiundzwanzigsten Jahrhunderts, unter ihrem fünften Reichsvogte," he declared that it was not by accident that the Germans had been placed in the midst of nations which, as soon as they had achieved some degree of education, wished immediately to exercise influence, whereas the Germans wished to keep their ways of life for themselves and not to impose them upon others. Therefore the German nation seemed to him destined to stand as a bulwark to guarantee to all European nations the freedom to pursue their own ways of life toward the common goal.[24] Here Fichte revealed a respect for the diversity of nations which was close to Herder's nationalism, and which was equally distant from an imperial world mission and from isolationism. But in the *Reden* Fichte asked the Germans to assume a missionary leadership, to be inspired by that desire for saving European civilization, which in the fragment, of the same year, he had deprecated, imputing it to the other peoples in the midst of which the Germans were living.

As early as his *Die Grundzüge des gegenwärtigen Zeitalters* Fichte approved of the tendencies of the age to subordinate the citizen to the state. He regarded it as characteristic of the period that "more than ever before every citizen becomes subject to the state, permeated by it, and its tool, and that the state strives to make this subjection general and perfect." [25] But he was still far removed from regarding this modern efficient and active state as necessarily a nation-state. He was then convinced that

> all Christian Europeans were essentially one nation, recognized Europe as one true fatherland, sought from one end of Europe to the other more or less the same goals, and were attracted by them. They seek personal liberty, justice, and laws which protect everybody without exception and preference; they seek opportunities to earn a good living by industry and work; they seek religious freedom in their religions, they seek the liberty to think according to their religious and scientific principles and to express them openly and to judge accordingly. Wherever they lack one of these liberties, they long to leave; where these liberties are granted to them, there they go.[26]

This rational liberalism was abandoned a few years later, when Fichte delivered in Berlin, during the time of the occupation of the city by French troops, his passionate *Reden*—"Addresses to the German Nation." [27] Under the stress of the times and of his own emotions, the rational philosopher, the disciple of Kant, rejected the power of reasoned argument. The intensity of individual emotions seemed to him a sufficient foundation for truth.

> Whoever feels it within himself, will be convinced. Who does not feel it, cannot be convinced, for my argument is based upon

that condition. All my words are lost upon him; but who would
not wish to hazard something as insignificant as words are? [28]

Those upon whom Fichte's words were lost, who did not feel as Fichte
believed they should feel, he regarded as aliens, as un-German. While
thus abandoning reason as the foundation of understanding, he nevertheless tried to find historical and philosophical "reasons" for his emotional
urge to summon the Germans to greatness and world leadership, "reasons"
singling the Germans out among all other European nations as something different and by nature superior.

Looking upon modern European civilization as a product of the
Latin and Germanic peoples, all of them formed by the migration of
Germanic tribes after the downfall of the Roman Emipre, Fichte found
that among all of them the Germans alone had preserved their original
language, while the others had adopted an alien tongue and slowly
transformed it according to their needs. Only the Germans had a language
rooted in nature and therefore fully alive, while French or Italian,
English or Spanish tongues were dead in their roots and therefore could
sustain only a superficial life. This fundamental difference of language,
Fichte believed, caused fundamental differences of intellectual and
spiritual life. Only the Germans possessed a true culture, only they could
bring the great historical movements to fruition. They had done it with
Christianity through the Reformation. "The Christian religion originated
in Asia and had become even more Asiatic by its corruption. It preached
only dumb resignation and blind faith, and was already alien to the
Romans." When the Renaissance opened up the sources of a freer and
more spontaneous thought, the Italians used these new discoveries
merely for the intellectual delight of a small educated class. But a
German, Luther, used the new approach to the original sources for the
transformation of life and faith. Only the German people answered his
call, not in a passing enthusiasm, but by laying the solid foundation for
a new life. They alone brought to full fruition what with the others remained a quickly abandoned attempt.

Another example which Fichte adduced to prove the unique vitality
of the Germans among the modern nations was the comparison of the
free cities in Italy with those in Germany.

> Let us compare . . . on the one side we see permanent un-
> rest, internal feuds, even wars, the unending change of consti-
> tutions and rulers; on the other, peaceful tranquillity and con-
> cord. How could it be manifest more clearly that there must
> have been an inner difference in the mentalities of the two
> nations? The German nation is the only one among the modern
> European nations in which the middle class has proved by its

deeds for centuries that it can sustain a republican constitution.

To such a degree did the leading German philosopher of the period misinterpret history: the subservient acquiescence of the middle classes in the sleepy German towns seemed to him a safer guarantee for liberty than the tumultuous activities of less orderly and less servile communities.[29]

These lessons of the past, Fichte pointed out, could also be applied to the present age. The French Revolution was an attempt to create the perfect state. Fichte explained its failure by the fact that the French nation was unfitted and unprepared for it. Only a nation which could solve the task of the education to human perfection could create the perfect state. Through their language, mind, and history the Germans alone were destined for it. Throughout the centuries the Germans had been stimulated by attempts other nations had made, but with them they remained incomplete and superficial. Out of their creative and spontaneous depth the Germans alone had carried them to realization. Through a system of true national education, the Germans had to be recalled to an understanding of themselves and of their mission. They had to be turned away from the depravity into which they had fallen by being unfaithful to themselves and by following alien ways. Spiritually purified through a new education, the Germans could show mankind the way to the perfect state.

Fichte never doubted that he and his philosophy could lead the Germans by creating through education a new and truly virtuous man. But given man's natural inertia, it was not sufficient to point the way. The teacher had to force the pupil into virtue. "If you really wish to have any influence over your pupil, then you must do more than merely admonish him: you must remake him and make him in such a fashion, that it will be quite impossible for him to will anything but what you wish him to will." Fichte and the new educators of whom he dreamt were to remake German youth—the older generation he considered lost —into perfect men, which to Fichte was synonymous with perfect Germans. Then the Germans would be able to live up to their mission and mankind would witness the advent of the ideal state.

In his *Reden* Fichte was carried away by the same utopian dream as had excited him in 1793: only this time he had lost his faith in the French people and in the nature of man. Man had to be totally remade, and this task could not begin with the French; only the Germans had proved capable of becoming the embodiment of reason on earth. Fichte did not think of the concrete and historical German of his time or any time. He spoke of an ideal German, of his idea of the Germans, of something which has never yet been realized on earth. Yet again and again he seemed to confuse the ideal and the real and to attribute to the actual Germans those qualities which in other passages were clearly reserved to the "true" German completely remade by the new education. This confusion of historical reality and metaphysical ideal was a dangerous legacy which Fichte's *Reden* bequeathed to German nationalism, and not only to German nationalism. It helped to strengthen the fateful myth of the spiritual superiority of the actual members of a historical nation, and to increase scorn and suspicion of alien influences.

Fichte's patriotism was a call to spiritual regeneration; its effects were different. "If one reads his 'Reden' attentively, one discovers everywhere how far his patriotism is removed from the patriotism which he has powerfully kindled by the 'Reden'." [30] For Fichte did not divide mankind into Germans and non-Germans but into those who believed in the spontaneous originality of man and the infinite perfectibility of the race, and those who did not. The former, wherever they were born and whatever language they spoke, belonged to the Germans, to the *Urvolk*, to the *Volk schlechtweg*, the true nation, the nation per se—which was not a historical and even less a biological reality, but a metaphysical idea. All those who did not believe in progress and liberty, even if they were Germans by race and language, were alien. Fichte's education wished to produce devoted citizens, as the Greeks had done—not, however, in the narrow and exclusive spirit of the ancient polis, but in a broad and cosmopolitan content—"mit allgemeinem und weltbürgerlichem Geiste." [31] But on many occasions in the *Reden* Fichte bestowed high praise upon the actual Germans and claimed for them virtues which history might not always concede.

> There are nations which, while they wish to preserve their peculiar quality and wish to see it honored, concede to other nations their peculiar qualities, and do not begrudge them; without doubt the Germans belong to these nations, and this trait is so deeply rooted in their whole past and present life that they have become easily unjust against themselves in order to be just to foreigners and to antiquity.[32]

The Germans were extolled as the people of justice and were regarded, thanks to their language, as the only true representatives of creative poetry and profound thought. Fichte was convinced that "a dead language [like French or English] does not know poetry in the higher sense," nor is it given to it to open up new horizons in philosophy or to delve deeply into the mystery of the human soul.[33] Thus Fichte praised the actual German nation and established its claim to European and world leadership. It was this, and not the demand for the reeducation of the Germans into rational and perfect human beings, which German nationalism read in his *Reden*. The rising German nationalism of the

Napoleonic age received the assurance that the Germans as the happy possessors of an original language were superior to the French, who, though partly of Frankish descent, had to stultify their intellectual life by the use of a derived language.[34]

In the eighth address, "On the Higher Meaning of Nation and Patriotism," Fichte started with an affirmation, typical of him, that "only the German, the original man, truly has a nation, and that he alone is capable of a true and rational love for his nation." Yet in his description of this love of nation or fatherland, Fichte transcended his own narrowness. He gave a moving picture of the deep emotions which underlay often unconsciously the nationalism of all peoples:

> The natural instinct of man is to find heaven on this earth and to fuse the Eternal with his daily terrestrial work; to plant and to raise up the Everlasting within the temporal, so that the temporal may be connected with the eternal not merely in an incomprehensible way, impenetrable to mortal eyes, but in a manner visible to the mortal eye itself. What noble man would not wish to live on in his children, and again in their children, to repeat his own life anew in an improved way, and in their lives, ennobled and perfected, to live on this earth even long after he was dead?

Thus in a secularized age nationalism fulfilled the individual's longing for immortality and seemed to guarantee his survival in the biological way of flesh and blood, for Fichte's idealism a strangely materialistic approach.

"What noble man," Fichte continued to ask—

> What noble man will not wish by his actions and thought to sow a seed for the never-ending perpetual perfection of his race, to inject something new and unprecedented into the age which should remain and become the inexhaustible source of new creations?

Though there seems to be no reason why the effects of one's thoughts and actions should be preserved within or be confined to one's nation, Fichte was convinced that only the people from whom the individual descended could provide the framework which can guarantee perpetual survival, because each nation is a distinctive manifestation of the Divine. For this is, in the higher sense of the word, a nation:

> the totality of men living in community with each other and reproducing themselves naturally and spiritually forever, a totality which lives and represents a definite and peculiar law of the development of the Divine. The faith of the noble-minded man in the eternal survival of his activity here on earth is there-

fore founded on the hope of the eternal survival of his nation
out of which he had developed himself, and of its distinctive
characteristics. These characteristics are the Eternal to which
he entrusts the eternity of himself, the eternal order of things,
to which he makes his own contribution for eternity. He must
desire its continuation, for through it alone can the short span
of his life on earth be expanded to eternal life. . . . His conception of his own life as an eternal life is the bond which unites
first his nation and through it the whole of humanity most
intimately with himself and introduces all their wants, to the
end of the days, into his expanding heart. This is his love for
his people, first of all respecting and trusting them, enjoying
them, honoring himself through his origin. The Divine has appeared in them, and the original spirit has honored them by
making them its immediate channel into the world. Thus the
Divine will continue to break through in them. Therefore man
will be active for them and sacrifice himself for them. Life,
merely as life, as continuance of changing existence, has never
had value for the noble-minded man apart from this; he wished
it only as a source of the Eternal. Only the independent survival
of his nation assures him this eternity. He must be willing to
die that his nation may live, and that he may live in it the only
life which he has ever desired.[35]

Thus patriotism, according to Fichte, desires the flowering of the
Eternal and the Divine in the world, in ever purer and more perfect
form in an unending progression. It cannot be found in the tranquil
civic love of the constitution and laws of a country, but only in the consuming flame of a higher enthusiasm to which the nation is merely the
cloak of the Eternal, for which the noble man sacrifices himself joyfully,
while the ignoble, who exists only for the sake of the noble, must be
made to sacrifice himself.[36] Such a patriotism seems characteristic for
all nations, each one being a mirror of the Eternal in a peculiar form.
Yet Fichte emphasized the degree of originality which determined the
value of a nation, and none but the German possesses full originality.
Above all the French are not a nation by nature, but purely by history.
Through historical events, through racial intermingling and the reception
of alien influences, they seem to Fichte to have drifted so far away from
the nourishing soil of their origins, that they are no longer a "real"
nation.[37] Thus the whole conception of the *Reden* with its lofty idealism
and concern for mankind's progress, served practically one purpose: to
prepare the Germans for the struggle against Napoleon and the French.
Fichte claimed that through him the ancestors were talking to the Germans of his day, the ancestors who had resisted Roman world domination and world civilization with their bodies and their minds. Should the

new Germans succumb to the new Romans, the French, then it would have been better if the ancient Germans had not resisted the old Romans. But the Germans must resist the French not only out of obligation to their ancestors, they must do it in the interest of mankind. Fichte had proved that among all modern nations the Germans alone were capable of highest human perfection; thus their end would mean the end of all the best hopes of mankind and of all civilization.[38]

In his *Reden* Fichte had no clear vision of a political future for Germany. He saw the country defeated and disunited; he wished to arouse a spirit of resistance, which would overcome the greatest obstacles and ultimately win its goal. He believed that enthusiasm and determination always win if they fight a lesser enthusiasm—"Nicht die Gewalt der Arme, noch die Tüchtigkeit der Waffen, sondern die Kraft des Gemüthes ist es, welche Siege erkämpft." [39] No better foundation, Fichte was convinced, existed for the strength of a nation than the system of national education which he proposed. There would be no longer any need for standing armies: in the new youths, dedicated to the state and prepared for it in body and mind, the nation would possess such an army as no previous period had ever known. These youths would be equally trained as soldiers and as workers; thus the nation could rely upon them for economic production as much as for military defense.[40]

But that was the hope for the future. For the time immediately ahead Fichte had only one piece of advice, the unity of the Germans and their independence from all alien influences. National independence appeared a supreme value, higher than all considerations of humanity or of individual liberty. He approved of Arminius, who rejected a higher, universal, and more human civilization for the sake of independence.

> Freedom meant to them just this: remaining Germans and continuing to settle their own affairs, independent and in accordance with the original spirit of their race, going on with their development in accordance with the same spirit, and propagating this independence in their posterity.

Thus Fichte came back to the Germans of the primeval forests of two thousand years before, far away from the "entirely new self" which his philosophy was to fashion. Seven years later, in his last year, he warned against constructing the concept of what is German, *Deutschheit*, from history. Then he knew that the spirit of Arminius and of his warriors was long dead and that their racial descendants were irretrievably lost in the impenetrable darkness of the past.

The lack of any clear political conception continued in Fichte's last writings, his *Staatslehre* and his *Entwurf zu einer politischen Schrift im Frühling 1813*. As little as his contemporaries could he foresee a political union of the various German states. In many ways he returned to the liberal concepts of his youth. He put a greater emphasis on the people than on the princes. He demanded a free and strong public opinion and constitutional liberties. He even seriously questioned whether national unity and independence without individual liberty were worthwhile. He wrote in the *Entwurf:*

> If we did not keep before our eyes what Germans should become, it would make little difference whether a French marshal like Bernadotte, who has at least in the past seen inspiring visions of liberty, or a conceited German aristocrat, unmannered, crude and insulting, ruled over a part of Germany.[41]

His eighteenth-century Heavenly City legacy determined Fichte's last words to the Germans. In the midst of the war of 1813, he turned from the vexing reality of the struggle to the comforting Utopia. In the face of the growing strength of the Prussian state, the political immaturity of German thinkers, and the weakness of the German middle classes, Fichte proclaimed a spiritual existence, without a state and beyond it, as the significant trait of the German national character. He concluded his *Entwurf* by quoting his own words from the *Staatslehre*, in which he expected the Germans to realize "the citizen of liberty in the perfect realm of law," a goal for which, he believed, thousands of years had prepared the Germans and toward which he saw them slowly maturing.[42]

Among the German nationalists of his time Fichte occupied a unique position. His concept of Germanism separated him from the romanticists who saw in nationality a historical growth, not a manifestation of the timeless absolute, the result of irrational forces rather than the embodiment of reason. Fichte was rooted in the intellectual and moral climate of the eighteenth century and the French Revolution, which the romanticists rejected and abhorred. To the rational rights of the French he opposed the "Vernunftreich" of the Germans, to the arbitrary dictatorship of Napoleon the idealistic autocracy of the leader-philosopher. Like the romanticists, he never responsibly faced the concrete problems of political and social reality. High above them, he soared to the Heavenly City of ideal Germans, who were nothing but ideal Fichtes, and who would build the Kingdom of God on earth, a realm of liberty and equality—for which Robespierre had striven in vain—according to the doctrine and in the spirit of Fichte.[43] He was driven by a strong and dominant urge to act and to impose his will, a philosopher king who wished to lead mankind by the scientific infallibility of his reason and the iron determination of his will. His intolerant and arrogant lust to create and dictate led him into many strange and dangerous bypaths.

But beyond their maze and threatening darkness there shone for him the light of his conviction that a universal order of morality was the only true principle of a constitution, a conviction to which he remained faithful from the revolutionary and rational mysticism of his youth to the Christian mysticism of his last year:

> We must arrive on earth at a stage that God alone rules over all, as ethical essence, through free will and insight; that all men without exception may become true Christians and citizens of the heavenly kingdom, and that all other dominion over men may wholly and fully disappear.[44]

XXXII

Friedrich Schleiermacher

FICHTE was Germany's first national philosopher; Friedrich Daniel
Ernst Schleiermacher (1768-1834) was its first theologian in whom nationalism and religious sentiment entered a close union. But Schleiermacher was more clearly imbued with national feeling than Fichte.
His individualism and enthusiasm had their roots less in the contemporary
movement of romanticism than in the inherited pietist tradition of his
family.[1] Pietism stressed the individual and his emotional life, but the
pietist individual was not a hermit secluded from the world; he felt
himself a member of a community inspired by a common enthusiasm.
In the emotional attachment to that community the individual found his
true life. The feeling of community had thus its source in the most
intense emotions of the individual. Schleiermacher's first important work,
his *Speeches on Religion, Addressed to Its Cultured Despisers* of 1799
and his *Soliloquies* (Monologe) of 1800 mobilized these emotions for
the service of religion. Yet in the *Soliloquies* he went further. In a way
alien to pietism, he treated the state as a force destined to enhance the
individual's life to the highest degree.

> Wo sind vom Staat die alten Märchen der Weisen?—Where
> is the strength which the highest development of existence
> should give to man, the consciousness which everybody should
> have of being a part of the fatherland's reason and imagination
> and force? Where is the love for this higher existence that man
> has conceived, a love which would rather sacrifice the narrow
> personal consciousness than lose the state, which would rather
> risk life than see the fatherland perish? Where is foresight
> closely watching lest the country be seduced and its spirit cor-
> rupted? Where is the individual character of each state, and
> where are the works through which it will be revealed? The
> present generation is so far from even suspecting what this
> side of humanity signifies, that it dreams of reorganizing society

as it does of human ideas in general. Every man, whether he lives in one of the new states or one of the old states, would like to pour all states into the mold of his own, like some sage who lays down a model for the future in his works and hopes that one day all mankind will venerate it as a symbol of its salvation. They all believe that the best state is the one which is felt least and which imposes least upon man the feeling of its necessity. Those who regard the most wonderful work of art ever created by man, a work which elevates him infinitely, as no more than a necessary evil, as an indispensable mechanism to hide their infirmities and to make them more innocuous, will feel only as a limitation what in reality should increase their life to the highest degree.

Thus Schleiermacher not only connected the state intimately with the individual but regarded it as the supreme fulfillment of the individual's life. Pietist influences were here transformed by romanticism into a political creed alien to original pietism. Common to both of them was the insistence upon the emotional life as the deepest root of religion and upon the perception of the eternal and the infinite in the midst of the finiteness of temporary life. In such a way, man as a citizen partook through the depth of his emotional loyalty in the higher life of state and national community.[2]

In 1804 Schleiermacher, the son of a Protestant army chaplain, became professor at the Prussian University of Halle. When it was closed as a result of Prussia's defeat in 1806, he moved to Berlin, where he was later appointed to the university. From 1806 to 1814 he was the most prominent nationalist preacher. His sermons gained a well-deserved reputation for clarity of thought and deeply felt emotional warmth. The ideas which he expressed were not original with him: they could be found in Herder and the romanticists, in Fichte and in the Prussian reformers. But with him they gained a rare persuasive power: among the German nationalists of the period he was certainly the greatest orator. Through him Prussian patriotism and Protestant religion entered into a close union, not an alliance for the defense of common interests, but a newly discovered affinity and interdependence. Schleiermacher breathed a new life into the dry bones of the Prussian state and of the rationalist or dogmatic theology of the eighteenth century. In the late summer of 1806 he wrote a significant postscript to the second printing of his *Addresses on Religion* in which he accused Napoleon of wishing to force a neo-Catholicism upon the German Protestants. In powerful words he challenged "the mightiest on earth" and predicted that he would not succeed in imposing his new universal order. "Germany is still here, its invisible strength is undiminished, and it will resume its calling with unexpected strength, worthy of its old heroes and of its much praised prowess."

Even before Prussia's downfall, Schleiermacher had not the slightest doubt of what was at stake in the war. On June 20, 1806, he wrote from Halle to Charlotte von Kathen:

> Remember that no individual can stand or save himself if that in which each and all of us are rooted—German freedom and German feeling—is lost; and it is these that are at stake. Believe me, sooner or later a general struggle will come, the objects of which will be our mind (Gesinnung), our religion, our intellectual life (Geistesbildung) no less than our external independence and worldly goods, a struggle which must be carried on, not by kings with their hired armies, but by the peoples with their kings together, a struggle which will unite monarchy and people by a more beautiful bond than has existed for centuries, and in which everyone without exception must join as the common weal demands.

After Prussia's defeat, Schleiermacher did not abandon his patriotism. The misfortune which had befallen the fatherland only strengthened his devotion. While the fate of Prussia was still undecided and the possibility existed that it might disappear entirely in the catastrophe, Schleiermacher wrote:

> I have only one resolution: to follow my immediate father-land Prussia as long as it exists and is worthy. Should it entirely succumb, then I will search as long as I can for the German fatherland where a Protestant can live and where Germans rule.

Though diminished and humiliated, Prussia survived the catastrophe. It showed its strength in its reforms. On November 24, 1809, Schleiermacher wrote:

> I can never despair of my fatherland. I believe too firmly in it, I know too definitely that it is an instrument and a people chosen by God. It is possible that all our efforts will be in vain and that hard and oppressive years will come for the time being —but the fatherland will certainly emerge from them after a short while in glory.[3]

Schleiermacher attacked those who believed that men have to serve mankind instead of serving first their own people. He attributed this cosmopolitanism either to shortsightedness or to arrogance. Those whom God has called to great achievements in religion or scholarship have always been men, Schleiermacher maintained, who were devoted with their whole heart to their fatherland and people and wished to heal and strengthen them. For it was not want or necessity which attached them to their land, but "an inner lust and love, an innate common existence, an indestructible accord." [4] He knew that the life of society and of the nation were changing, that a new age was dawning. "All political order as it has existed so far, has been on the whole an untenable thing, an empty appearance," he wrote to Georg Reimer at the end of November 1806.

> The separation of the individual from the state and of the educated classes from the masses has been much too great, so that state and masses could not really exist and develop. This situation must disappear, and only from its ruins can truth emerge. A general regeneration is necessary and will come as the result of these events. Nobody can yet see how, but we wish to be present and to participate as soon as the course of events calls upon us or carries us away. No one—least of all those who participate in any way in intellectual life—should think of leaving Germany.

Little more than two years later, the course of events seemed to take the desired direction. From Berlin, Schleiermacher wrote to Brinckmann on February 11, 1809: "All private concerns, even the most intricate ones, disappear before one's participation in public affairs." He approved of the Prussian reforms which prepared for a closer union of government and people, but he emphasized that even the most excellent internal regime would not be of real help without outward independence. The sermons which Schleiermacher preached during all those years served the purpose of preparing the people for the struggle to regain their full independence.

When finally in March 1813 the long desired event happened and Prussia entered the war against Napoleon, Schleiermacher concluded his sermon of March 28 with a prayer which summed up his nationalism and his religion and set the tone for many sermons throughout the coming century:

> Merciful God and Lord! Thou hast done great things for us by calling our fatherland to fight for a free and worthy existence in which we can promote Thy work. Continue to be gracious unto us. Victory comes from Thee, and we all well know that we do not always know what we are doing when we ask from Thee what seems good to us. But with greater confidence than ever, with a strong faith, we entreat Thee to bless the arms of our king and his allies, because it seems to us that Thy kingdom and the noblest goods which past centuries have acquired for us would be in peril if our present efforts should fail. In whatever way Thou wilt decide the fortunes of war, may its blessings not evade us, may everybody be purified and strengthened in his

inward life. Let everybody do what he can, be it much or little. Let all of us be fortified in our trust in Thee, in our obedience to Thy will, an obedience unto death, as was the obedience of Thy Son.

When the news of an impending peace congress in Prague in July 1813 reached Schleiermacher, he protested, very much to the King's indignation, against a premature peace.

> Germany in general and our state especially still need to make an immense effort to achieve worthy conditions of salutary development, efforts which can only be made during a war and which one could find only with greatest difficulty in peace time.[5]

Schleiermacher reconciled his nationalism and his religion in the faith that God assigned to each people its separate calling on earth and imbued it with its peculiar spirit so that He might glorify Himself by each people in its peculiar way. For that reason he could preach that "only that people relies on the Lord which wishes at all costs to preserve the peculiar purpose and spirit with which He has endowed it. It alone strives to uphold a deed willed by God." In spite of his pietist upbringing, Schleiermacher belonged to a different age and rejected the quietism, the indifference to political affairs of original pietism, which regarded national misfortunes as visitations by God for lack of religious devotion. According to the pietists, national disaster did not call for political efforts, but for increased devotion on the part of the individual to his struggle with sin and the rebirth in men of their inner life. Schleiermacher's sermons were not guides to the still and pure flame of the inner light; they were calls to action, fervent in the desire to change the outward world, to participate, with the mighty forces on earth, in the course of history. In that respect Schleiermacher was nearer to Fichte than to his fathers. Fichte called upon the Germans in an imperative way like a new lawgiver: "Thou shalt." Schleiermacher added the deeply felt and reassuring: "God wills it." [6] Yet the world of action to which he belonged was more consistent and earthly than that of Fichte; it was the actual world of rising nationality and practical statesmanship, in which Schleiermacher's brother-in-law Ernst Moritz Arndt (1769-1860)[7] was the most indefatigable propagandist in the struggle against Napoleon.

XXXIII

Ernst Moritz Arndt

ARNDT was born in Swedish Pomerania and, like most Germans of his time, felt in his youth no attachment to Germany, but only loyalty for the territorial prince—in his case the King of Sweden.[1] His reactions to the events in France were not different from those of the majority of German intellectuals of that period. He even first welcomed Napoleon in an ode, "Der Mächtige." [2] But he discovered his German patriotism sooner than other German writers; from 1801 on he regarded Napoleon as the archenemy. His opposition was not motivated by the defense of individual liberty against tyranny; it was, rather, a conscious rejection of the very cosmopolitanism which made so many Germans hail Napoleon's plans for world order. In the years 1798 and 1799 Arndt traveled widely in parts of Germany, Italy, and France. There he discovered the reality of nationality and the deep differences which, as he believed, language and geographic conditions created. He welcomed this diversity and turned against those who saw in the union of the European nations a progressive step toward a higher order. The fruit of this newly found nationalism was *Germanien und Europa,* which he wrote in 1802 and which appeared the following year.

"For the benefit of the whole world as well as for the benefit of each individual nationality there must not be any universal union," he postulated. Each nationality should develop through the cultivation of its own national character, and its constitution must be adapted to this character. Arndt rejected the then widely held view that it was enough for the Germans to excel by the universality and intensity of their intellectual life and that they did not need the bond of a common state and political strength:

> That Germany has gone as far as it has in the cultural field, it certainly does not owe to its political disunity. I believe that it would have progressed farther if it were politically united. . . . Only if we had a fatherland, if we had the highly human

and highly political ideas of an independent, united, and strong nationality, then we would gain steadfast habits, a firm character, and a perfect form. Then alone the highest and most wonderful humanity could grow from such earthy roots to gleaming sunny heights.[3]

Arndt had no clear concept of German political unity, but he emphasized the need of new and stronger ties for the still existing German Reich and promised to devote all his strength to awaken the demand for it and to keep the thought of it alive. He had found his way from the local loyalty of the Swedish subject to German nationalism. From Stockholm he wrote to his friend Charlotte von Kathen on June 4, 1807:

I shall not abandon my German fatherland and its sacred cause as long as there is a drop of warm blood in me. I feel now more intimately than ever that I belong to the Germans and that I could not and would not belong to any other people.

Arndt was one of the first to insist on German political unity. Like Stein and other German patriots who could not imagine a Germany cut off from its historical traditions, Arndt envisioned the restoration of the imperial dignity of the Habsburgs. The events of 1814 disillusioned him. The Habsburgs themselves abandoned the thought of the restoration of the Empire and relinquished the old Habsburg lands on the Rhine and in Swabia in which Austria had stood guard on the western border of Germany. On the other hand Prussia, by the acquisition of new provinces in the West, took up the watch on the Rhine and became more representative of the German nation, uniting Catholics and Protestants and stretching from the old eastern march on the Baltic to the Moselle and the Meuse. From then on Arndt looked upon Prussia as the leader toward Germany's political unity. He regarded the Prussian monarchy as the embodiment of the popular will, and he wished to endow it with added strength by the mobilization of popular forces in support of the state. He strove for a synthesis of the people's nationalism of the French Revolution with the traditional hierarchical structure of German society. He never despaired of realizing his ideal of harmony between princely will and popular will in Prussia. He made it his task to create an educated public opinion which would favor such a solution. He almost attained it when in his eightieth year, as a member of the Frankfurt parliament, he implored the King of Prussia to accept the imperial crown offered to him by the National Assembly. He died ten years before Bismarck realized his dream, one of the last survivors of the period when German intellectuals abandoned the universalism and humanism of the eighteenth century for a newly discovered militant nationalism.

French nationalism was born in the enthusiasm of a revolution, in an attempt to reform the state and to build a better society. German nationalism was born in the war against France, not primarily in an attempt to secure better government, individual liberty, and due process of law, but in an effort to drive out a foreign ruler and to secure national independence. The word liberty did not mean primarily, as it did for the Western peoples, the assertion of the rights of the individual against his government, but of the independence of the nation against foreign rule even if this rule happened to be mild and more progressive than that of domestic rulers. When the Western peoples strove for regeneration, they were primarily concerned with individual liberty; in central and eastern Europe the demand for regeneration often centered on the unity and power of the group. Arndt, Schleiermacher, and Jahn believed that only a long war of liberation could regenerate the Germans and therefore wished to prolong the war against France. On December 1, 1812, Arndt complained in a letter from St. Petersburg to Adam Georg Friedrich von Horn, an officer in the Russian German legion, that most people looked frightened or dumbstruck when he told them that if the Germans wished to become really free they must continue the war against the French for at least five years and longer. French nationalism found a political entity which it could transform; German nationalism had to create a political entity out of elements which it found in language and common descent, in past history and geography.

In the second part of his *Geist der Zeit,* which he published in 1809, Arndt asked: "I wish to speak to my people, but how shall I address you, oh German people? What and where are you? I seek but cannot find you." French nationalist thinkers were bound to the reality of their nation and the responsibility which reality imposed; the Germans could roam freely far into the past and into the future. Though it did not lack elements of moral regeneration within, German nationalism was primarily a call to arms against the aliens. Arndt recognized this clearly:

> May a general love grow among us, and a lasting hatred against the crafty foreigners, for only then shall we be saved and the liberty of our children assured. It is the highest religion to strive and die for those objects which are sacred to mankind and which deteriorate under any tyranny [for Arndt and his generation the truly hated tyranny was foreign tyranny]; it is the highest religion to love the fatherland more dearly than laws and princes, fathers and mothers, wives and children.[4]

Arndt's love for the fatherland was inextricably linked with hatred of the foreign enemy, hatred of all those at home who supported the "enemy" or accommodated themselves to his rule.

Yes, I hate; it is my joy and my life that I still can hate; I hate deeply and hotly; but I hate nothing more hotly and deeply than you, lazy and good-for-nothing fellows who are not ashamed to voice German shame in the German language. How should a man who wishes to do something in the world not hate, for who can love without hating? And I love my fatherland and its honor and liberty above all; I love my liberty; I love the sanctuaries which past centuries have bequeathed to us to preserve them. I love science and the light which despotism would like to annihilate from the earth. Therefore I cry out my ire before God and man; therefore I call for hatred in life and death, hatred, the only powerful saviour and helper.

Arndt never ceased to stress his rejection of universality and his insistence upon separated nationality. Rationalism and enlightenment might favor the unification of mankind, which would put an end to the hatreds and divisions inherited from the past and to the wars between nations. The progress of the human race, the cosmopolitans proclaimed, could be seen in the fact that through the forces of reason mankind was becoming one and that ancient prejudices and superstitions waned. Thus the age was one of philanthropy and enlightened love. In his "Address of Hope for the Year 1810" Arndt did not deny that there might be some truth in this interpretation, but only for the contemplative man.

Active man will be guided by something else and will be guided so through all eternity, by a dark force which is also of the age, and by a darker love which he would not like to explain to himself even if he could, by that deep love of his people, its way of life, its language which from childhood has become an inseparable part of the innermost recesses of his being.

Arndt regarded it as nature's wonderful secret that these dark forces did not change but remained the same throughout history. Against the hopes of enlightened rationalism, the old dark forces of the past prevailed and determined man. Man might think of mankind, but he could act and live only out of his national past, out of his national character.[5]

The German national character seemed to Arndt determined by common language and common descent. They formed the uniting bond among all Germans and constituted them a German nation. In both respects the Germans excelled all other nations. They represented the purest race, they spoke the purest language. This twofold purity guaranteed their creative superiority.

The Germans are not bastardized by alien peoples, they have not become mongrels. They have preserved their original purity more than many other peoples and have been able to develop slowly and quietly from this purity according to the lasting laws of time; the fortunate Germans are an original people. In this respect we have important evidence as regards our ancestors from one of the greatest men who ever lived, from the Roman Tacitus. This extraordinary man, who with his prophetic eyes penetrated the depth of the human heart and the depth of nature, the present time and the future, clearly saw the worth of our fathers, and prophesied their splendid future; and so far history has not contradicted him. Above all, he saw most clearly how important it was for the future greatness and majesty of the German people that they were pure and resembled only themselves, that they were no mongrels. For he saw his Italy, which had once been the mistress of the world, a bastardized canaille, cursed and outcast, defile the memories of the Fabricians and Cornelians, and his proud Roman soul bled and writhed because there were no longer any true Romans.[6]

More than purity of race, however, in Arndt's eyes language constituted a nation. It seemed to him the best guarantee of the differentiation among nations. That various nations used the same language and yet maintained their separate nationalities did not trouble Arndt. He was deeply influenced by Herder and Fichte. Like Herder, he regarded it as the greatest tragedy when a people abandoned its language and accepted an alien one, for he regarded language as the outward image of the innermost recesses of the mind of a people, the instrument which from childhood molds man's thoughts and feelings. Arndt believed that language helped to produce and to keep alive those antipathies and dislikes which protect the independence of a people better than fortified cities and unsheathed swords. Otherwise peoples might lose their peculiarities and would be in danger of becoming "solche Allerweltmenschen, die man Sklaven und Juden nennt." But Arndt went far beyond Herder, in whose eyes a small, peaceful, and pastoral people could have a wonderful language, with an expressive beauty and worth that did not depend on statehood or political power. Arndt was convinced that "only a whole people, only a whole great people, always certain that it is a glorious and mighty people, only a whole people in real possession and in the effective exercise of a vital and free political life, can have a whole language." [7]

Like Fichte, Arndt believed that among the European peoples, whom he identified with the Germanic-Latin peoples, the Germans alone had an original language, the *Ursprache*, not a mixed mongrel language like the others. The creative superiority of the Germans over the French and the Italians, over Englishmen and Spaniards, was based on this originality of language, as it was on the purity of the race. All creative power originated with the nation. "All great things which a man does, forms, thinks, and invents as a hero, an artist, a lawgiver or an inventor

—all that comes to him only from the nation." [8] Arndt was certain that God decreed the diversity of languages so that mankind would not become a lazy and good-for-nothing gang of slaves. Here the interpretation of God's will by Arndt differed from that of the Bible, according to which God instituted the diversity of languages not to improve men but to punish them for building the Tower of Babel. What was presented in the Bible as a curse appeared to Arndt a blessing.[9]

Fichte and Arndt were not alone in stressing the importance of language.[10] Friedrich Schlegel shared their conviction:

The use of a foreign language for legislation and for transactions in civil law is always most depressing, yes, one could say entirely unjust. The use of a foreign language for the affairs of the state, and connected with it, also for the life of higher society, cannot remain without damaging effects on the native language. . . . A nation that allows itself to be deprived of its language, loses the last support of its spiritual and intellectual independence and in reality ceases to exist.

Schlegel, too, went far beyond Herder in his linguistic nationalism. He wished to accord the right to their own tongue only to independent and powerful nations. He used the argument of language to strengthen the Germans in their struggle with the French. He rejected its application to the Slavic and other "backward" tongues in their struggle against the Germans.[11] The German language appeared so superior that other languages struck the ear of the German hearer almost as subhuman. A German army volunteer reported his impressions of Paris in 1815:

What mirrors the soul of a people, molds and embodies its ideas, is the language, which therefore has a peculiar character corresponding to the quality of the people. The French language is not an orderly organic language but resembles animal noises (*Gequäck, Geklatsch, Geschnatter*).[12]

The only language equal to German in creative beauty was, for the Germans of that generation, the Greek language.

But the German language had more than creative values: it was the only visible and uniting bond which remained to the Germans after the dissolution of the Reich. It linked the Germans to their glorious past, it united them as brothers for a common effort and a common understanding. Leonhard Graf von Rotkirch und Panthen addressed in his poem "An die deutsche Sprache" (1810) the language which was "born in an oakgrove" as:

Unser Stolz und uns're letzte Zierde,
Schlingst der Eintracht letztes heil'ges Band
Ums besiegt zerrissene Vaterland.

He pictured the German language as roaming centuries ago in unadorned poverty through primeval forests, calling the Cherusci to battle and jubilating when Roman power lay broken. He hoped that language would again call up Teutonia to battle:

> Ja du wirst, Teutonia, erwachen,
> Der Begeistrung heilig hehre Wut
> Wird zur hohen Himmelsflamme fachen
> Deinen tief in Staub gebeugten Mut.

Then in the poet's vision a victorious people will spread the German tongue throughout the world. It will become the voice of the sagas, and with delight Apollo will hear on its strings the sound of Hellas. A few years later, the miracle which Count Rotkirch expected from the German language happened. In his "Germania" in 1814 he happily affirmed:

> Wo kraftvoll frei erklingen deutsche Töne
> Sind Brüder, sind Thuiskon's edle Söhne,
> Germania ist aller Vaterland.

Theodor Körner's "Jägerlied" (1813) restated in Arndt's spirit the union of language and fatherland, of brotherhood and blood, of vengeance and sword:

> Aus West, Norden, Süd und Ost
> Treibt uns der Rache Strahl,
> Vom Oderflusse, Weser, Main,
> Vom Elbstrom und vom Vater Rhein
> Und aus dem Donautal.
>
> Doch Brüder sind wir allzusamm;
> Und das schwellt unsern Mut.
> Uns knüpft der Sprache heilig Band,
> Uns knüpft ein Gott, ein Vaterland,
> Ein treues, deutsches Blut.

The most important of these songs in honor of the German language was Arndt's own "Des Deutschen Vaterland," in which he answered the question "What is the German's fatherland?" with the famous assertion that it was neither Prussia nor Austria, Bavaria nor Thuringia; it was not a state which existed, not a political community anywhere on the map—it was the German tongue which gave to all Germans a common fatherland. The song which was the most popular German patriotic song until it was replaced two generations later by the "Wacht am Rhein" called upon the Germans to create one fatherland out of all lands where German was spoken. This land was the home of truth and loyalty, where every Frenchman would be called enemy and every German friend:

Was ist des Deutschen Vaterland?
So nenne mir das grosse Land!
So weit die deutsche Zunge klingt
Und Gott im Himmel Lieder singt,
Das soll es sein!
Das, wackrer Deutscher, nenne dein!

Das ist des Deutschen Vaterland,
Wo Eide schwört der Druck der Hand,
Wo Treue hell vom Auge blitzt
Und Liebe warm im Herzen sitzt—
Das soll es sein!
Das, wackrer Deutscher, nenne dein!

Das ist des Deutschen Vaterland,
Wo Zorn vertilgt den welschen Tand,
Wo jeder Franzmann heisset Feind,
Wo jeder Deutsche heisset Freund—
Das soll es sein!
Das ganze Deutschland soll es sein!

Arndt's nationalism was born in the struggle against France. It is understandable that the French appeared to him superficial and vainglorious, satisfied with an easy and graceful surface. "The Frenchmen are a talking, the Germans a thinking people." [13] French civilization seemed tied up with the court and the capital, not with the people, and the events of the French Revolution confirmed him in the opinion that Paris directed France at the expense of the rural countryside, which Arndt saw as the depository of national virtues. He denied to the French individuality of character, and from this defect he deduced their gregariousness and their eagerness to conform to the standards of society and to obey the whims of despots. How could a people like that become a model for other nations?

> Can men educate who themselves are no men, who give you artificiality for nature, elegance for beauty, illusion for virtue, fashion for morality, and chatter for thought? Who understand, appreciate, and esteem nothing foreign? . . . Incapable of eternal ideas, of deep enthusiasm, of blissful ecstasy and human longing, for which they even lack words; making fun of the holiest and highest of mankind for the sake of wittiness—

truly a people like that could have only one good effect upon the Germans, to arouse them to an appreciation of their own superiority of character.[14] The hatred of the French found its strongest expression in 1813 when Arndt became the trumpet calling to battle:

> I hate all Frenchmen without distinction in the name of God and of my people. . . . I teach this hatred to my son, I teach it

to the sons of my people. . . . I shall work all my life that the contempt and hatred for this people may strike deepest roots in German hearts and that German men may learn to understand who they are and whom they confront.[15]

Arndt rejected the absolute monarchy, which he regarded as a product of French and rationalist influences. Himself of peasant stock, he found more life and truth, poetry and religion in the people. He did not look backward to the Middle Ages or to the feudal order; he looked forward to the rise of a nation in which all classes would actively participate, in which a vigorous public opinion would stand guard against excesses of the government and would assure necessary adjustments for orderly progress. If he looked abroad for political guidance he did not look to France, which he found oscillating between revolutionary chaos and absolute monarchy, a people servile and licentious, but to England and Sweden, where in his opinion Germanic ways were better preserved. Both offered him the spectacle of a united nation, a goal which he set before the German nation.

> Sweden is a unified kingdom and has long been under one rule; her great kings, heroes, prophets, soothsayers, and poets belong entirely to her, belong to every man, and every man is proud of them. We Germans have had for many centuries only division of territory and of hearts, and in many places we are so divided from one another that some great German names are known only in one locality and some even curse what others bless.[16]

Patriotism and liberty were needed to form the Germans into a nation. Arndt found many beautiful words about patriotism, but he interpreted liberty more as national independence and the right to follow, without any foreign interference, traditional and ancestral ways than as the safeguard of individual rights. In the *Kurze Katechismus für deutsche Soldaten* which he wrote in 1812 in St. Petersburg for the members of the German legion formed in Russia, he fought those "miserable, cold and calculating men" who say:

> Fatherland, Liberty, beautiful and high sounding names without meaning! Wherever man is happy, there is his fatherland, and where he is least plagued, there is liberty; everything else is empty dreams and illusions.[17]

Arndt did not believe that man could find a new fatherland by migration and that he could migrate for the sake of political or religious freedoms which were denied to him in his old land. He maintained:

> The fatherland is not there where men can lead the most abundant carefree life, but there where he spent the innocent

years of childhood and the joyous years of youth, where he heard the first sweet sounds of friendship and love, where he first saw stars shining and springs flowing. . . . There is his fatherland. All the pulses of his heart beat for it, . . . and though it may be barren rocks or desert islands, and though poverty and hard work may be his lot, there he must love it, for he is human. His liberty is there where he can live according to the mores, customs, and laws of his people, where what formed the happiness of his ancestors makes him happy too, where no foreign people and no foreign law hold sway over him. Such a fatherland, such a liberty are the most sacred values that the good man has on earth and desires to have. But in some ways the calculating idle talkers—"die Klügler und Schwätzer" —are right too: Fatherland and liberty are a lofty dream, an exalted idea which soars high above the earth, a sacred and incomprehensible illusion (Wahn) which the human heart can never penetrate because it is beyond earthly man. When the names "fatherland" and "liberty" sound in our souls with all their sweetest love and loyalty, then the eternal, the immortal, the immeasurable through which we resemble God takes hold of us and transforms us into seers, heroes, and martyrs.

For Arndt nationalism was not as for Fichte an intellectual discovery, nor was it primarily a political program, a guide for statesmanship; it was the outpouring of sentiment, the overflowing of a heart, a religious experience, the immersion of the individual into the élan, the security, the ecstasy of mass comradeship. "I have seen misfortune," Arndt wrote in 1813,

I have suffered, but suffering scarcely moved me to tears. But when I thought of the Volk and saw it, and when the great feeling of it gripped me, I have always had to weep in the depth of my soul. When a great crowd moves before me, when a band of warriors passes before me with flowing banners and sounding trumpets and drums, then I feel as if my feeling and acting were not an empty illusion. I feel the indestructible life, the eternal spirit, and the eternal God. . . . I am egoistic and sinful like other men, but in this exalted human feeling I am immediately freed from all sins, I am no longer a single suffering man, I am one with the Volk and God. In such moments doubts about my life and work disappear. The compulsion of my feelings tells me that I do right. I shall use this justification by my love and my hate because I must.[18]

In the same book, in the third part of his *Geist der Zeit*, Arndt suggested to the Germans the remedy in which he found justification and salvation—the fraternal union of all individuals in the self-identification with the nation.

German man, feel God again, hear and fear the eternal, and you hear and fear also your Volk. You feel again in God the honor and dignity of your fathers, their glorious history rejuvenates itself in you, their firm and gallant virtue reblossoms in you, the whole German fatherland stands again before you in the august halo of past centuries! Then, when you feel and fear and honor all this, then you cry, then you lament, then you wrathfully reproach yourself that you have become so miserable and evil: then your new life and your new history will start. . . . From the North Sea to the Carpathians, from the Baltic to the Alps, from the Vistula to the Schelde, one faith, one love, one courage, and one enthusiasm must gather again the whole German folk in a brotherly community. It must learn to feel how great, mighty, and happy its fathers were in obedience to one German Emperor and one Reich, at a time when a host of discords had not yet inveighed one against the other, when a swarm of cowards and knaves had not yet betrayed them. . . . Above the ruins and ashes of their destroyed fatherland the Germans must tearfully join hands and pray and swear all to stand like one man and fight until the sacred land will be free. . . . Feel the infinite and sublime which slumbers hidden in the lap of the days, those bright and mighty spirits which now glimmer in isolated meteors but which soon will shine in all suns and stars; feel the new birth of time, the higher cleaner breath of spiritual life, and be no longer misled and confused by the insignificant and small! No longer Catholics and Protestants, no longer Prussians and Austrians, Saxons and Bavarians, Silesians and Hanoverians, no longer of different faith, different mentality, and different will—be Germans, be one, will to be one by love and loyalty, and no devil will defeat you! [19]

That such a nation might be formed, Arndt insisted in 1813, the Germans must show greater loyalty to their fatherland and to their folk than to the princes. The princes existed for the sake of the fatherland and the folk, not folk and fatherland for the princes. All the blessings came to man from the fatherland and the folk, not from the princes. Princes changed, folk and fatherland were eternal. They, and not the princes, were truly by the grace of God the representatives of the divine on earth. All men, from the prince to the lowest beggar, must be imbued with the feeling that the fatherland belonged equally to all and that all belonged equally to the fatherland. In that sense, Arndt insisted in 1814, all states were growing more democratic. By democracy, he warned, he did not mean Jacobinism, but rather a limited monarchy.

Each people which by its constitution has representative bodies and estates composed of all classes of inhabitants has a democratic constitution. Where the peasants and the burghers, those largest and most venerable sections of each people, have received public representation, there one can speak of a democratic constitution. The spirit and the power of the masses represented in these two classes will of necessity seize hold of the other estates and will give them a folkish mentality.

Of all the constitutional liberties, Arndt regarded freedom of the press as the foundation and bulwark of all other liberties. He saw in the estates the natural and organic stratification of a healthy nation, but he insisted on the participation of all estates in the common national life. Thus he worked for a synthesis of the German princely and hierarchical state with the people's state of the French Revolution.[20] He always emphasized the need for a strong and healthy peasantry, and in his later years he appreciated the importance of a growing German middle class.

Arndt objected to large standing armies, which he regarded as the possible instrument of princely absolutism. Instead he asked, like Jahn, for a nation in arms, an education of the whole youth for military service, with professional soldiers employed only to guard the frontiers and the fortresses. But this democratic army organization did not involve pacifism. In an Old Testament style which he used in his *Phantasy of a Future Germany* (1812), he interpreted the will of God in the chapter "Of God, the Unity of Nations and Church, and of Perpetual Peace," saying:

> Tell this lazy people: I am not the God of their perpetual peace; I am the God, the avenger, the terrifying, the destroyer who lusts for struggle and war. Otherwise all history which is My history would be a lie; for its beginning is war and its end will be war. Their peace is death and rotting, My war is life and movement. To shed blood is always a horror, but not the blood which flows for liberty, for freedom and virtue. War and struggle, the live movement of live forces, that is My lust, thus My name is called, that is Myself, I, God the Lord.[21]

Arndt's political plans for the new Germany rejected the bureaucratic police state of eighteenth-century Prussia as strongly as they rejected autocracy, which may guarantee economic security but stultifies intellectual liberty.

> The worst state of all is the unlimited and lawless rule of a single man, the despotism where arbitrariness can, and generally does, tie down all free minds and where the greatest virtue is enclosed in . . . servile patience which affords the only security. In such a state, it is a misfortune to have a mind and to be agitated by daring and virtuous impulses. Because in such a despotism man cannot be much more than a servile animal, he

feels happiest the more he resembles a voracious and patient beast.[22]

Arndt's constitutional monarchy was to be an institution of very great strength and power, not only equal to the parliament with which it shared legislation but superior to it, especially in everything concerning foreign policy, military organization, and domestic administration.[23] In spite of all differences, Bismarck's constitution for Germany, more than half a century later, realized the salient traits of Arndt's vision of a constitution "appropriate" to the German tradition. But more than Bismarck, Arndt stressed the responsible and free activity of the citizen as the bulwark of national strength. He wished to educate the German to be a citizen, though not a free individual according to the ideas of classical humanism.

> Only a people in which the impulses of society and of individualism are in harmony can be called a happy and just people and will know how to create and to preserve liberty. Whoever wishes always to be only Volk will be ultimately as much reduced to nothing as one who wishes always to be only a human being. But the man who knows how to unite with dignity the human being and the Volk, he will be a citizen.[24]

This true balance between individualism and nationalism Arndt thought best realized among the English.

> The Frenchman wishes to be a courtier, the Englishman a citizen, the German a human being. The middle of the three walks in greatest security; for French and German history have proved sufficiently how bad it is if through longing to be a courtier or a human being one neglects being a citizen.[25]

Arndt was one of the creators of the modern German consciousness. Like most nationalists he was neither an original nor a systematic thinker nor a great poet. But he had power and sincerity. In spite of the biblical language and imagery of much of his writings—the Pietist influence of his youth surviving in his style—he was much closer to reality than Fichte or the romanticists, and he never descended to the coarseness and vulgarity of Jahn. He preserved enough of rational clarity and intellectual responsibility not to succumb to the blind adoration of "the people."

> Nur durch die Einzelnen wird ein Volk, und nur durch die unterrichteten und gebildeten Einzelnen, wenn diese eine volle Weltkraft in ihrer Brust und in ihrem Leibe tragen, wird ein Volk brav und glücklich.[26]

But Arndt did not put his hopes in the ideal of humanism and universality which had inspired Kant, Goethe, and Beethoven.

In the midst of terrifying revolutions which unhinge the world they hoped that the education of the mind, the enlightened spirit of the time, as they call it, would produce a moderation and unification of the noblest forces of the Europeans. This would put an end to the old pernicious struggles and would revive all the good and beautiful of the ancient world in even more glorious forms. Viewed from the lofty height, political events—the overthrow of old thrones and constitutions, destructive wars, annihilation of nations—seemed to them to be of minor importance, nay, even perhaps helpful for the sublime purpose of the age as they understood it.

Arndt rejected this view. He was convinced that their imitation Hellenism could not arouse the enthusiasm of the people and that their philosophical cobwebs would not be able to lift the heavy sorrow from a plagued world. In the same second volume of his *Geist der Zeit* in which he published these lines, he printed his first four German war poems, among them the famous "Lob des Eisens," the praise of the hard black iron which he contrasted with the gold which a cowardly world demanded:

> Gold schreit die feige Welt,
> Und Gold macht feige Knechte, . . .
> Drum preis' ich das Metall,
> Das schlechte, schwarze Eisen.

Germany seemed to him "the sacred heart of old Europe" and without its strength no salvation for Europe was possible. Geographically, Germany was the meeting ground and the synthesis of northern and of southern Europe; historically, most European peoples had been formed by tribes who had migrated from the German heartland. Therefore the Germans could feel almost like parents of all the Europeans and understand them. Intellectually the Germans have learned from the cultures of all other nations and have inherited them, and thus developed a more universal humanity.

In that sense, the nationalist Arndt could join with the classical humanists in proclaiming a universalism, but it was a German universalism with the German as the representative pan-human being.

> I wish to say *Germanus universum petit* and in this noble sense I wish to call him a Greek. On the higher level, he is a citizen of the world, the whole world is his, he seeks the whole world. He will go out, as far as the sun's rays dart and the winds blow. He wishes to see everything, to learn, to grasp, to understand everything, to explore and to assimilate the habits, plays and arts of all peoples. . . . The German is a universal man (*Allerweltmensch*), to whom God has given the whole

earth as a home, and who, the more he has discovered and explored that home, will the more intimately love his own smaller fatherland and the better he will build it.[27]

Arndt remained convinced even after 1848 when his hope of a Germany united by Prussia's leadership seemed foiled, and the German Confederation under Austria's chairmanship was restored, of the realization of his hopes of 1815. On January 9, 1853, the old man, then in his eighty-fourth year, wrote:

> But the idea of the unity and might of the greatest world-nation of the present earth will and must finally break through with the help of God and in the course of nature. All those who know and all those who think must not cease to uphold this prophecy.[28]

XXXIV

Friedrich Ludwig Jahn

LIKE Fichte and Arndt, Friedrich Ludwig Jahn (1778-1852) underwent in his youth the influence of the French Revolution and came to
understand the new forms of democratic enthusiasm and the mobilization
of a whole people for national ideas.[1] He was born in the Mark Brandenburg. In the spirit of a new Prussian nationalism, he wrote in 1799 a book
on the promotion of patriotism in the Prussian realm, which he opened
with the characteristic quotation:

> Der grösste Staat ist schwach, der ungezählte Heere,
> Doch keine Patrioten hat.

And from the same then widely read German poet, Uz, Jahn quoted his
other motto:[2]

> Von allen Helden, die der Welt
> Als ewige Gestirne glänzen,
> Durch alle Gegenden, bis zu der Erde Grenzen,
> Bist Du, oh Patriot, mein Held.

> Der Du, von Menschen oft verkannt,
> Dich ganz dem Vaterlande schenkst,
> Nur seine Leiden fühlst, nur seine Grösse denkest,
> Und lebst und stirbst fürs Vaterland.

The influence of the French Revolution revealed itself in Jahn's proposals
to strengthen patriotism: the introduction of national festivals to commemorate the great days of Prussian history, the building of monuments,
especially on the fields of victorious battles, and the stress on instruction
in national history. Many years later, Jahn wrote: "History was my
oldest playmate in youth, she has remained my friend and companion
throughout life." The history that inspired him was the great deeds of
the Hohenzollern monarchs. The first book which he published showed
no trace of German nationalism; it was devoted to a glorification of

Prussia. It tied in with his later and more mature nationalism through its naive and often coarse boastfulness, which Jahn and many of his followers thought essentially patriotic and German:

> The uneducated peasant in the German states of the Prussian Reich always shows his pride in his fatherland. A fight starts quickly at the county fairs in the frontier towns whenever the superiority of the Prussians is not recognized. Almost always the Prussians win, and even if they are in a minority they never tolerate the taunts of their adversaries. I often heard it said at such occasions: One Prussian defeats three Saxons, Hanoverians, Mecklenburgians or Swedes.

Jahn was convinced that a traveler in Germany would immediately notice a great difference when he set his foot on Prussian soil. There the people appeared different. "Männlicher kriegerischer Gang, fester mutvoller Blick, fröhliches Grüssen zeichnet den Preussen aus." No wonder that with their manly, soldierly walk, their firm, courageous glance, their cheerful greeting, the Prussians felt superior not only to mankind in general, but even to all other Germans. Since the Prussians could not help but feel their superiority and their merits, and since strangers stared at them admiringly, as if they were beings of a higher kind—"da sie von Fremden als Menschen höherer Art angestaunt werden"—patriotism and pride in their fatherland was more deeply rooted in their hearts, and the call of their beloved king sufficed to kindle the hidden spark to a burning flame. "Even little boys at play are already animated by this patriotic spirit. They play more warlike games than anywhere else, and of a playmate who flees or does not behave with proper courage, they say: That's no true Prussian." [3]

Thus young Jahn glorified his native state and prince without any awareness of a German national community. Within the next decade he changed, but he carried over into his German nationalism much of the Prussian attitude and the lasting conviction that "the history of the Prussian states under the rulers of the House of Zollern is a magnificent column in the temple of the history of mankind." [4] In 1800 he met Arndt in Greifswald, and his experiences in the following years shifted his attention and his enthusiasm from the Prussian state to the German folk. In 1806 he wrote the first draft of his *Deutsches Volkstum*, which appeared in 1810. This work is essential for an understanding of the new nationalism. In it the influence of romanticism combined with that of the French Revolution and of the Prussian tradition. The emphasis was no longer on the activization of the citizen in a society founded on law and no longer on the loyalty of the subject to his hereditary monarch, but on the originality of a deep-rooted creative force, the German Volk. The Volk became for Jahn one of the elemental forces of nature, a supreme part of God's own creative effort and in itself a millenary creative force.[5] Jahn did not confine himself to theory. During the crucial years of the formation of German nationalism he became its indefatigable propagator and organizer. Little is known of the Deutsche Bund which he and some friends founded in 1810, after the dissolution of the Tugendbund, to which Jahn did not belong. More important was his influence upon three movements which remained characteristic of German nationalism and spread to other peoples in central and eastern Europe: military free corps of patriotic volunteers; gymnastic associations for the training of patriotic fighters; and student fraternities imbued with nationalistic enthusiasm. All three groups were animated by a revolutionary activism, responding to emotional appeals, and all stressed disciplined dedication to national service; this they identified with a strangely conceived "freedom" which had little in common with Western concepts of individual liberty.

Under the influence of the French Revolution, Jahn demanded the reform of the Prussian army. There he found himself in agreement with Scharnhorst; both wished to imbue the army with the spirit of a conscious nationalism. In 1806, in his first project of a national militia, Scharnhorst wished to exclude from it not only foreigners but even Prussian subjects of Polish nationality.[6] "In France as well as in England," he wrote, "it was the formation of the national militia which aroused the military spirit of the nation and created an enthusiasm for the independence of the fatherland without parallel in other countries." Scharnhorst succeeded only partly. He made the Prussian army more efficient; he did not render it more democratic. The old spirit remained, though now equipped with new weapons. "The peculiar sharp and cutting nature of Frederick's army was preserved, as well as the proud sentiment of aristocratic caste honor among the officers," Treitschke noted with approval.[7]

Jahn wished to go farther than Scharnhorst. Both demanded universal military service for rich and poor alike, access for everybody to all commissioned ranks, the introduction of examinations for officers, and the abolition of corporal punishment. But Jahn wished to base the whole military strength of the fatherland upon the national militia, in which the soldiers would elect the noncommissioned officers, and these in turn would choose subaltern officers, while colonels and generals would be appointed by the king. He believed in an army of volunteers, held together and driven to great deeds by a burning patriotic spirit. The wars of liberation seemed to realize, though only to a small extent, his hopes. In February 1813 Scharnhorst authorized the formation of a free corps, a band of non-Prussian volunteers, mostly students, under the command of a Prussian officer, Adolf Freiherr von Lützow (1782-1834). It was intended as a German corps, not as part of the Prussian army. Therein it differed from the free corps of Major Ferdinand von Schill (1776-1809), who had acquired fame as a Prussian army officer in the defense of Kolberg in 1807 and in 1809 led his regiment of Prussian hussars, without the authorization of his king, to independent action against Napoleon to help Austria against the French. He was defeated and fell in the defense of Stralsund, a Baltic seaport in Prussian Pomerania, in May 1809. Though his expedition, like the fight of the Tyrolian peasants in the same year, served as an inspiration to the rising German nationalism, he and his soldiers fought as Prussians, not yet as Germans. Lützow's free corps, though it originated in Prussia, served the German cause: among the armed forces of 1813 it alone could claim to represent Germany. In its black uniforms—which accounted for its being known as *die Schwarze Schar* or as Lützow's *Wilde Jagd*—the free corps, consisting of infantry, chasseurs, and cavalry, impressed German imagination in later years more than it actually harmed the French army. Its spirit lived on in the free corps which mushroomed in Germany after 1918, debased in the intervening century through a growing cult of violence which the more ferocious utterances of Jahn anticipated.

Lützow's free corps was designed for guerrilla warfare in the rear of the enemy. It was practically annihilated when it was ambushed near the Prussian village of Kitzen on June 17, 1813, by German forces of the Rhenish Confederation under the command of a Württemberg general. In that battle, the gifted poet of the War of Liberation, Karl Theodor Körner (1791-1813), the son of Schiller's close friend Christian Gottfried Körner, was wounded; two months later he died in another battle. Jahn and his friend Friedrich Friesen (1785-1814)[8] formed the link between the free corps and the German gymnastic organization which they founded in 1810 in Berlin when both taught there at an educational institution founded in Pestalozzi's spirit by a Dr. Plamann. Jahn was at that time also an instructor in the classical high school (Gymnasium) in Berlin-Kölln, the famous Graue Kloster, founded in 1574, where he had been a student himself. He gathered the students around him, led them to the open spaces of the Hasenheide in the southern part of the city, and started to instruct them in gymnastic drill and athletics. At the beginning of June 1811 he opened there the first gymnastic ground (Turnplatz). From then on the movement grew rapidly, and a new discipline, the Turnkunst, was worked out. Its purpose was the training of youth to be able, ready, and willing to fight for the fatherland and to form the nucleus of a future patriotic army devoted to service whenever the call would come. The Turnerschaft was consciously German. Its loyalty did not belong to the existing states, but to the nation which it hoped to create by its disciplined unity and vigilant preparedness. Physical education itself was not the goal; it was a means to a national end. Even less had it anything to do with sport in the English sense of the word. The ideals of fair play, of the good loser, of the gentleman, did not fascinate Jahn's mind. The Turnerschaft, though civilian in its appearance, was military in purpose and spirit, a potential army trained for the ardently longed-for day of the battle against the enemy.

Jahn rejected the conspiratorial character and the secrecy of many of the organizations of the period which followed similar goals. In a letter to a gymnastic teacher several years later he denied the widespread assumption that his gymnastic organization had originated in the secret Tugendbund:

> It has been a public association, as it still is and as it will and must remain. The time has come now when everything must become manifest that was formerly hidden in darkness. The soul of the gymnastic association (Turnwesen) is the life of the people itself (das Volksleben), and this thrives only in the open, in light and air. One destroys this life of the people by any kind of hiding, by secret vices and airs, secret associations and secret police.[9]

The gymnasts had their own special dress, in their conversation they used only the brotherly "thou" and their language was deliberately coarse. They believed that polished language was used only to hide truth —for that purpose the French language, the language of diplomacy and civilized society, seemed to them especially destined—while a true German was always forthright, outspoken, and sincere. Jahn was a master of coarseness in language; he hated words of foreign origin and was a fanatic for the purification of the mother tongue.[10] The gymnasts were to be German in everything. They were to be the people's vanguard, an enthusiastic and resolute elite upon which Jahn believed the salvation of the people depended.

At the end of 1809, Jahn wrote in a letter:

> Noch leben die alten Gefühle, noch immer suchen wir das alte Ziel, nur nicht mehr in der Menschheit, sondern in der Deutschheit. Diese scheinbare Beschränkung ist eine wahre Steigerung. Alles Volksheil und jede Erlösung und Wiedergeburt ist von wenigen Begeisterten noch allezeit ausgegangen. Und immer mussten durchaus erwählte Wütriche erst der Knechtschaft Ketten erklirren, ehe die Freiheit mit Riesengewalt ihr siegreiches Racheschwert zückte.[11]

Fanaticism and fury were the instruments of liberty, as Jahn understood it. To them everything was to be forgiven: "Den Weltschöpfer und Einheitsschaffer verehrt jedes Volk als Heiland," Jahn wrote in 1814, "und hat Vergebung für alle seine Sünden." The hero who by fanaticism and fury created national unity will be venerated by the people as a saviour and all his sins will be forgiven. For nothing could be allowed to stand in the way of the one ultimate goal: that the folk might establish its state, a true Volksstaat, a nation in the "democratic" sense of the word, where all members were united in equality and all division of classes was abolished. This spirit, proclaimed with a fresh and happy aggressiveness, animated the songs of the Turnerschaft:

> So hegen wir ein freies Reich,
> An Rang und Stand sind alle gleich!
> Freies Reich! Alles gleich! heissa juchhe!

And just as the gymnasts bounced over their bars with the firm strength of their bodies, so they expected to bounce into the future Volksstaat with the firm strength of their conviction:

> Über jede Schicksalsbeugung
> Schwingt uns unsre Überzeugung.
> Diese macht uns alle gleich,
> Stiftet unser neues Reich.

At the outbreak of the War of Liberation most of the young gymnasts joined the free corps as volunteers.[12] Many of them, after the war, became founders of the Burschenschaft movement, which carried Jahn's ideas into the academic world.

In 1812 Jahn and Friesen drafted a project for the reorganization of student life at the universities and submitted it to Fichte, then the rector of the University of Berlin, who, however, rejected it as "un-German." Jahn turned to the University of Jena. There, in one of the small German principalities, a common German nationalism could hope more easily to triumph over the traditional patriotism of the German states. Luden in his course on history had prepared the field. When the first Burschenschaft was founded in Jena on June 12, 1815, it was planned as the organization of all Christian German students in all German-speaking universities. It was to unite them, irrespective of class or caste or of the state or province from which they came. The members emphasized in dress and speech their Teutonism and replaced the easy-going ways of the German students, especially their overindulgence in dueling and beer, with patriotic and "Christian" seriousness. This "Christian" character found, however, its foremost practical expression in a violent anti-Semitism. Upon the suggestion of Jahn the Burschenschaft accepted black-red-gold as the colors of German unity. The origin of the new "tricolor" is unknown; probably the colors of the student corps Vandalia contributed, and those of Lützow's corps, which had its black uniforms adorned with red and gold. Symbolically the colors represented the struggle out of the black night of slavery through red blood to the golden day of liberty.

Jahn turned with his hopes to youth. The older generation seemed to him corrupted; its corruption explained the decline of German power and the victory of France. Germany had to be reborn and the old true German character restored in the hearts of the new generation. But how could the Germans achieve regeneration and nationhood? In England and France the nation was founded upon a political association, the state; its regeneration was accomplished by a political and social revolution which transformed the state and invigorated the nation. No similar political association existed in Germany. If the Germans wished to find a uniting bond, they had to find it, Jahn believed, in some reality more ancient and more "essential" than the state. This reality he found in the mystical force of Volkstum, in the inner creative life of the Volk which was itself a necessary part of God's eternal creation. The Volk existed before the state; it was its foundation. All true history was a history of Völker, of nationalities. This discovery led Jahn to the conclusion that scholarship must develop a new discipline, the study of Volk and all folkish life. His *Deutsches Volkstum* was the cornerstone of the new science.

Jahn's old Prussian patriotism was not dead in 1810. Austria appeared to him to be "too great a mixture of races, where the happiness of the ruler is prayed for in seven languages." In Prussia the overwhelming majority of the people were German.

> Thus I expect in and from Prussia a timely rejuvenation of the old venerable German Reich and in the Reich a leading people which will walk the august road to immortality in world history. . . . If Germany will develop its immense forces, which never have been used united, it can establish eternal peace in Europe and become the guardian angel of mankind.[13]

To assume this leadership Prussia would have to transform herself. Frederick the Great created a state, but the state could not endure because it was not based upon Volkstum.

> However great he has been by himself, he did not understand the sublime loftiness of folkdom—Er ahnte nicht die Hehrheit eines Volkstums. Well he understood how to build a state, but he did not found any folk in it. . . . A state without folk is nothing, a soulless artifice; a folk without a state is nothing, a bodiless, airy phantom, like the Gypsies and the Jews. Only state and folk together form a Reich, and this cannot be preserved but by the Volkstum.

To Jahn only the Volksstaat, the people's state, seemed a real state, a true political and spiritual community destined to endure. It was high time for the Germans, Jahn thought, to rehabilitate the word Volk in all its glory. From it Volkstum received its meaning as well as Volkstümlichkeit, people as well as popularity. For the Germans their Volkstum was Deutschtum, their Volkstümlichkeit was their original inner life uncorrupted by alien influences. Jahn believed that the decline of Germany originated in the treason Germans committed when they abdicated their inner original life, their Volkstum, their Deutschtum, and looked to foreign peoples for guidance. Germany could find salvation only in herself: "We are not yet lost! We can still be saved! But only through ourselves." [14]

Jahn appealed to readers for whom the lofty thoughts of "Volk, Deutschheit und Vaterland"—the precedence of Volk and Germandom over Fatherland is characteristic—were still a reality. He reminded them that for two thousand years honesty and straightforwardness, loyalty and seriousness, truthfulness and industry had been part of the German folk character, but that lately the name "German" was no longer held in highest regard. The Germans, the most popular people of Europe, must begin to understand what their true character was. While Rome was a never satiated people's hell—"eine nimmersatte Völkerhölle"— Germany was a people truly representing humanity, a pan-human people. (Dostoevsky and the Slavophils spoke in the same way about the Russians.) Jahn called the Germans "ein menschheitliches Volkstum, das alte ehrwürdige Mittelvolk und Mittlervolk Europas." But this German people had been ruined by the "unfortunate and shameful" Peace of Westphalia.

> It was unfortunate because it separated the Netherlands and Switzerland from us. The Rhine ceased thereby to be the old German protective stream, for at its source and at its mouth lived henceforth only German half-brothers. It was even more shameful because foreign nations dictated the conditions of peace to the Germans.[15]

Herder was the first man to develop the concept of the folk, but for him all the Völker were true manifestations, unique and individual, of the universal divine force, all equally near and dear to God; he rejected the superiority of any one people, of any special God-given mission.[16] Jahn—and later Dostoevsky—singled one people out as the one which in its universality represents, and understands, the whole of humanity, and was mankind's holy people. To such a people a sublime fate was reserved: to bring salvation and happiness to mankind, to be a blessing to the earth, and to civilize its inhabitants.

> The holy office of the people which has to make the world happy, is difficult to learn, and even more difficult to fulfill [Jahn wrote] but it is a virtue that lusts to bless the earth as

its saviour and to implant in the peoples the seeds of true humanity. . . . There is still room and sustenance for greatness on this earth. There are still holy wars of mankind to fight. The whole earth is a promised land, still unconquered for justice, happiness, and virtue.

An immense civilizing task awaited the people which was the highest representative of mankind.[17] It had to combat all the backwardness, the superstitions, the depravations under which mankind had suffered for thousands of years.

For that high purpose, the peoples must preserve themselves pure and unmixed. Jahn was convinced that the eternal laws of nature have doomed every intermingling of races and peoples. Rome perished for that very reason. "The purer a people, the better. The day when a universal monarchy will be founded will be the last day of mankind." Peoples were different, and this difference had to be preserved. There could not exist, and there should not exist, a universal model for mankind. The ideal of a world government, of a world language, of a world religion was wrong, for it contradicted the supreme ethical and creative value, the originality of each people.[18] It was true that Jahn glorified the longing for unity: "Das Streben nach Einheit ist das schöne Weihgeschenk der Menschheit, ein Gott, ein Vaterland, ein Haus, eine Liebe." [19] But this desire for unity at least as far as the earth was concerned—for Jahn recognized theoretically one God—stopped at the border of the fatherland, or rather, of the Volk. To Jahn the supreme and indisputable value in history and nature, the source of all creativeness, was the folkish life. He solved the conflict between his German nationalism and Christian universality in a characteristic way, not much different from the way which, in a similar dilemma, Dostoevsky chose. "Which of all the still existing folkdoms corresponds best to pure Christianity?" Jahn asked. His answer carried for him the force of conviction: "The final judgment cannot possibly point to any other but to the genuine, true, pan-human German folkdom." [20]

Jahn believed that Germany had arrived at the pitiable state and plight in which he found it by abandoning its folkdom, imitating foreign peoples and speaking foreign languages. Jahn never tired of calling upon the Germans to protect mind and character against all alien influences. His usual coarseness grew in vehemence when he spoke of the French language

> It has fooled your men [he told the Germans], enticed your youth, dishonored your wives. Germans, feel again with a manly and high mind the value of your noble, living language; draw from its never drying sources, dig up the old springs and leave Lutetia's stagnant pool alone! [21]

In the teachers of foreign languages Jahn saw dangerous spies, in the foreign languages a hidden poison. The Germans would be happier, according to him, if they could rid themselves of their greatest vice, their low esteem for themselves, and acquire the "fault" of their neighbors— pride—to which Germans were more entitled than all the others. He hoped for a true German rebirth, the glorious morning of the rediscovery of their folkdom

> In the whole history of a people, its most sacred moment arrives when it awakens from its torpor, rises from its deathlike existence, becomes for the first time conscious of itself, thinks of its sacred rights and of the eternal duty of preserving them, and finally recognizes that by the suicide of its folkdom it can only lose itself among other peoples. It is the beginning of a new and long-hoped-for period of creation when a people after many terrible years can reveal to itself, to its contemporaries, and to posterity, loudly and freely and without reservations, how it fell into humiliating serfdom by imitating foreign models. A people which grasps with joy and love the eternity of its folkdom can celebrate at all times the festival of its rebirth and the day of its resurrection.[22]

For that purpose the nation needed a new education.

Jahn developed a detailed program of national education. He demanded the writing and studying of patriotic history and the creation of popular literature. Every young German, the sons of princes and the children of laborers, should be trained in manual work, in gymnastics, and in military sports. A German fashion had to be introduced; and popular festivals, not dedicated to universal ideals like liberty or reason, but to German historical events, should regularly unite the people. Monuments and elaborate funerals of men who had merited well of the nation should arouse the public spirit.[23] In all these suggestions the influence of the French Revolution could easily be recognized, but the emphasis had shifted. The universal message which animated the French Revolution, at least in its beginning years, was lacking. Nationalism had become narrower and more self-centered. In this form it spread in the nineteenth century. People's armies, nationalist gymnastic organizations, patriotic and highly political student activity, the emphasis on the sacredness of nationality, on the originality and uniqueness of the folk language and indigenous civilization—all this influenced the awakening of the nationalities in central and eastern Europe, and later in Asia, much more than the English tradition of liberty or the ideas of 1789.

An all-embracing national education, Jahn was convinced, would create a people's state endowed with strength and vitality.

The effects of such a German national education will be

infinite; like everything good they will spread beyond the frontiers of the state and will survive beyond its duration. The citizen will feel, think, and act with the state, through it, for it, and in it; he will be one with it and his people in life, woe and love. Through all the changing times, the folkdom and its sacredly treasured originality—"heilig bewahrte Ursprünglichkeit"—will mirror itself from generation to generation with ever increasing beauty.

This folk-state would be a national democracy in which the people would collaborate through its representatives in the work of legislation and through its military preparedness be ever ready to defend the fatherland. Jahn demanded a parliament which would not be "an institution for the deaf and dumb" consisting of mute approvers and applauders. For Jahn had learned sufficiently from the West to understand that no government was more secure than one founded on the free participation of its citizens. Nor did he approve of standing armies. He demanded the strength of a "Friedensvolk," of a peaceful nation, which would efficiently prepare the youth for a defensive war and thus in case of need have ready a nation of warriors against which any conqueror would be powerless.[24]

During the war of liberation, Jahn pleaded for the creation of a greater Germany, including Switzerland (which he called Oberland), the Low Countries, Denmark, Prussia (which he called Nordreich), and Austria. Then only would Germany be able to fulfill its high humanitarian mission of universal mediator. This new Germany should build a new capital, for which Jahn suggested the name Teutona, situated on the Elbe River, approximately in the center of the roads which would connect the frontier cities of the Reich—Geneva and Memel, Fiume and Copenhagen, Dunkirk and Sandomir.[25] Jahn desired a powerful Germany. Weak nations which lacked the will to power appeared to him afflicted with the gravest malady, and he recommended for them what Hippocrates advised against cancer: "What medicine does not heal, steel heals; what steel does not heal, fire heals."[26] This ferocious medicine of fire and blood has since inspired many a struggle for the supreme good of national independence and glory. Max von Schenkendorf (1783-1817), one of the most popular poets of the War of Liberation, professed a similar faith in his poem "Das Eiserne Kreuz":

> Denn nur Eisen kann uns retten,
> Nur erlösen kann uns Blut.

Bismarck made the road to salvation through fire and sword even better known when he wrote on May 12, 1859, to Alexander Graf von Schleinitz, the Prussian minister of foreign affairs, who hesitated to break with

Austria over the reforms of the German Confederation: "I see in our federal relations an affliction of Prussia which we shall have sooner or later to cure, *ferro et igne.*" And he repeated Schenkendorf's advice of "iron and blood" in his famous speech of September 30, 1862, before the budget commission of the Prussian Chamber of Deputies.

The War of Liberation did not fulfill Jahn's hopes. It was a European war, not a German war. The peace settlements were characterized by a sense of moderation. They did not realize the dreams of the German nationalists. Jahn was convinced that Germany needed her own war to consummate the national awakening and to create a true German nation, and he remained faithful to this conviction for the rest of his life. In a letter of October 2, 1831, he wrote:

> May God soon grant to Germany what I wrote in 1815, after the return from Paris, in the guest-book of the Wartburg: Germany needs a war of her own and through her own means to feel her strength. She needs a war against Frankdom (Franzosentum) to form herself in the fullness of her own folkdom. . . .[27] [It must be a truly German war.] Germans can be helped only by Germans; Latin and Slav allies—"welsche und wendische Helfer"—drag us ever deeper into perdition. Recently the whole world has been called up, from the Ural and Caucasian mountains to the columns of Hercules, to defeat the French. God has given the victory to the Germans, but all the allies— "Mitgeher und Mitesser"—want to act as guardians for Germany. Germany needs her own war. . . . Its time will come; for no people can be born without passing through the pangs of birth.[28]

As time went on Jahn became ever more nationalist and aggressive. The French revolutions of 1830 and 1848 aroused in him only reactions of extreme hostility; against Belgium, Poland, and Denmark he voiced his nationalist aggressiveness. He saw now in liberalism the greatest misfortune for Germany.[29] The angry old man summed up his life work in the inscription which he wished put upon his tombstone:

> German, you who go by, and have not yet forgotten your mother tongue for French and Polish, hear my word: Shame, misery, curses, destruction, and death on you if you expect the saviour from abroad.[30]

XXXV

The "War of Liberation"

IN 1812 the disillusioning outcome of the "War of Liberation" was
still unknown. Schleiermacher's, Arndt's, and Jahn's fervent expectations
were fulfilled: Napoleon's army suffered a decisive defeat; its remnants
were streaming back from Russia towards the German frontier; the myth
of its invincibility was broken; there seemed hope that the German
people would take courage and rise against Napoleon. But only a
minority of Germans were eager to "break the yoke of foreign tyranny"
and willing to fight to that end. The King of Prussia hesitated for many
weeks before he finally, under the pressure of the patriots, decided to
declare war upon Napoleon. The famous proclamation which he issued
on March 17, 1813, from Breslau, the capital of Silesia, marked the
beginning of the "War of Liberation," the first official acknowledgment
of the rising German nationalism. In spite of its high reputation in German history, the royal call "To My People" (An mein Volk) could
hardly be called a nationalist document. It bore no trace of the passionate
language of Schleiermacher or Arndt. It was the work of a Prussian
official, Theodor Gottlieb von Hippel.[1]

"To My People" explained in simple language how the King had
hoped to avert war by the punctilious fulfillment of the engagements
entered into with the French Emperor, and how his purest and best intentions were of no avail against the insolence and faithlessness of
Napoleon. The Prussian people had borne a heavy burden from 1806
on. Now the hour had come to put an end to it. The King did not appeal
to the Germans nor even to his former subjects with a promise to
"liberate" them. Modestly he confined himself to the inhabitants of the
four provinces left to him after 1806. He did not call these subjects by
their later national name, "Prussians"; he still addressed them as
"Brandenburgers, Prussians, Silesians, Pomeranians, Lithuanians!" He
recalled to them "the times gone by, of the Great Elector and the great
Frederick! Remember the blessings for which your forefathers fought

under their leadership and which they paid for with their blood!" He set before them no new objectives, no picture of a German nation or of German unity: it was a traditional call for king and fatherland.

Theodor Körner,[2] who was then in Breslau, read his own national enthusiasm into the royal proclamation. "Must not all German princes blush," he asked the next day with poetic exaggeration,

> who read such a gospel and do not believe in it? No king and no prince has ever used such a language addressing his people as long as German has been spoken. This thunder will not die away in the air; let us take care that the lightning strikes. How we must thank God that He has granted us to live through such a great and wonderful time! Everybody faces the great struggle for the fatherland with free and proud courage, and everybody hastens to be the first to bleed for the sacred cause. There is only one will, only one wish in the whole nation, and the much abused "victory or death" gains a new sacred significance. King and people, state and fatherland are united in a most intimate community. The nation does its utmost to prove its devotion and loyalty, and the King does his utmost to recognize it.

In a popular poem of the day, Körner proclaimed the rising of the nation, the breaking of the storm, the people's crusade:

> Das Volk steht auf, der Sturm bricht los. . . .
> Es ist kein Krieg, von dem die Kronen wissen,
> Es ist ein Kreuzzug, 's ist ein heil'ger Krieg.

He was only partly right. The crowns knew little of the war: the King of Prussia and the Emperor of Austria entered it only reluctantly; the other German princes opposed it. It was a crusade, a sacred war, for only a part of German youth; the majority of Germans either continued to fight faithfully for Napoleon or waited for the outcome of the struggle. The last words of Körner's letter of March 18 characterized the war more truthfully: the Prussian nation or at least a part of it did much to prove its devotion and loyalty to the throne and the King did more or less gracefully his very best to recognize it. A national patriotism was shown by those non-Prussian students who joined the Prussian army. Among them were Körner and other members of the Lützow corps. Only when the Allied armies, the majority of whom were Russians and non-German Austrians, were unexpectedly and convincingly successful, did more Germans begin to join in the war effort.

In the early months of 1813 Scharnhorst's plans for universal military service were for the first time put into force in Prussia. Some official efforts were finally made to turn the war into a national people's war. All citizens received the right to wear the Prussian colors as a national cockade and thus to manifest their patriotism by an external symbol. A new decoration was created by the King—the Iron Cross, granted to officers and men alike for heroism in battle. (It was revived for the wars of 1870, 1914, and 1939.) This decoration was interpreted as a symbol of the fatherland's iron time and of the crusaders' struggle. "Iron was the time through which we lived, iron alone is the reward which our hero-king promises to the victor," Hippel said in an address on June 24, 1813, at the dedication of a Freemason Lodge in the army.

> Let simplicity and force, as in this most useful of all metals, be the symbol of our lodge; let the sacred cross be its sign, so that people may recognize the sacredness of the cause for which we stand and for which we mean to live and die. The warriors among us should regard themselves as God's warriors, to free the frontier of the German fatherland from the fetters of the alien despot, like those warriors of God who took the cross and went forth to return to the faithful the place where the Saviour was born and suffered.

Another royal decree accorded honors to the memory of those who died in the war by inscribing their names on tablets in every church of the kingdom. It was further ordered that at the end of the war, church services should be held everywhere in which the minister would recite to the congregation the names and deeds of those who out of its midst had died for king and fatherland, and report on what was done for their widows and orphans.

In spite of much real zeal for king and fatherland, the mobilization was not everywhere received with enthusiasm. Severe punishments were threatened for all those who did not join the armed forces and for those officials who would continue to support the enemy or facilitate his actions. Only at the universities was patriotic enthusiasm widespread. What Luden did at Jena, Hendrik Steffens (1773-1845) did in Breslau. Steffens was a Norwegian who had taught at the Danish University in Kiel and later at Jena, where he came under the influence of Schelling. In 1811 he became professor of physics and natural philosophy at Breslau. On February 3, six weeks before the King decided to break with France, Steffens called on the students taking his course to volunteer for the army. His lecture became famous. In his memoirs, written more than two decades later, Steffens gave an account of his patriotic mood at the time:

> I had spent two hours alone in a strange state of excitement. What I wished to say stirred all my innermost being. What had weighed heavily upon my mind for five years, I could now de-clare publicly. Under such circumstances I became the first to

state loudly that the day for the salvation of Germany, nay of the whole of Europe, had arrived. My inner commotion seemed without limits. In vain I tried to order my thoughts; spirits seemed to whisper to me and to promise their aid. I longed for the end of this torturing loneliness. One thought only predominated: how often have you complained, I told myself, that you have been thrown into this forlorn corner of Germany: and now it has become the all-comprising and exciting center. Here a new epoch in history begins, and you are privileged to express what moves this crowd. Tears ran out of my eyes, I fell on my knees, a prayer quieted me. Thus I went among the crowd and mounted the platform. I do not know what I said. Even if I had asked myself at the end of my address, I could not have given any account of it. It was the oppressive feeling of unhappy years which now found expression; it was the warm feeling of the crowded multitude which was on my tongue. I did not say anything unexpected. What I said was in the mind of all, and my talk made therefore a deep impression like an echo out of the soul of each member of the audience. It is obvious that while calling the youth to join, I declared my own resolution to share the struggle with them.

Steffens had no clear idea how to fulfill his promise to join the army. He decided to go and see Scharnhorst. As soon as he entered, Scharnhorst, who had heard of Steffens' talk, embraced him and said, deeply moved: "Steffens, I congratulate you. You don't know what you have done!" In his memoirs Steffens concluded the report of this experience with the words: "It was my most beautiful glory." He joined the army and saw active service from the beginning until the occupation of Paris. With all his enthusiasm for Germany, Steffens was critical of the narrow-minded nationalism of Jahn and the gymnastic movement. "Do not cite the Ancients," he warned the gymnasts:

> Sparta, which sacrificed with the most obstinate consistency the citizens to the state, appeared through this very consistency strong and firmly united but also arrested on a low level and in a harsh form—"in einer herben Form." In Christian states, in which understanding of the individuality of life appears inherent—"in welchem der Sinn für eigentümliches Leben als innewohnende Liebe erscheint"—that form would be a real atrocity.[3]

Patriotic legends glorified the spring of 1813 as a patriotic uprising in which all hearts were united in one great national effort. The year 1813 has become a landmark in the history of German nationalism, like 1789 in France. But 1789 symbolizes a fight for individual rights and constitutional liberties; 1813, a struggle for national independence without a message for Europe or for mankind. Nor was the enthusiasm for the war in 1813 general. The princes regarded it as a war of princes, who counted on the loyalty of their subjects. The Prussian King remained deeply distrustful of Stein and Gneisenau and their "revolutionary" plans. The events of February and March 1813 which started the "War of Liberation" originated with a small number of determined patriots—"enragés," they appeared to many conservative minds. They forced the hand of the reluctant King. His appeal to the people was followed by many; upon others it had to be enforced. There was no strong echo outside the four eastern provinces of Prussia. "It was the first great disillusionment which the Prussian patriots experienced."

Only in Prussia did the war assume a national character. Gneisenau's militia was realized under the names of Landwehr and Landsturm, which corresponded to the *levée en masse*, the nation in arms. In January 1813 Arndt in *Was bedeutet Landsturm und Landwehr?* proposed that all men over thirty-five should help the defense of the fatherland without receiving uniforms and armed with whatever weapon they found.

> The difference between warrior and citizen was abolished, and universal military service was carried to its most extreme conclusion. It was the return to total war. Modern civilization, to diminish the horrors of war, had developed the usage that only the soldier in uniform should be treated as an enemy while the civilians should be spared. When now civilians were caught in arms, they could not be considered legitimate soldiers, nor could they claim treatment as soldiers who surrendered; war reappeared in its whole primitive savagery.[4]

Arndt referred to the old German community in arms as the model which the French Revolution restored. He praised the example of the Vendée, of Spain and Russia, where national and religious passions had influenced the war. The Prussian army never consistently carried out Arndt's proposals. The character of the population did not lend itself easily to it; the North German was too docile and too civilized for a war of chaotic and uncontrolled passions. With Prussian territory quickly liberated from the enemy, no opportunity for the use of the Landsturm arose. The cautious nature of the king integrated what remained of the Landwehr into the regular army and thus deprived it of its revolutionary democratic character.

For many years the question was discussed whether the war was a "people's war" fought with the enthusiasm of a rising nation, or a war conducted and directed by the authorities. The Prussian general staff clung firmly to the latter theory. In the *Beihefte des Militär-Wochenblattes* the general staff published in 1845 and 1856 its report on the

Landwehr in Silesia, Pomerania, and Western Prussia—Prussian provinces which then formed about half of the territory of the monarchy and
which were largely inhabited by Poles. The calling up of the Landwehr
met there with very little success. The Prince of Anhalt-Köthen-Pless
was quoted as saying in a letter of May 17, 1813, that the peasants of
Upper Silesia "do not know patriotism." The definitive work of the
general staff on the Prussian army in the War of Liberation, published
immediately before World War I, insisted that the large majority of the
people did not act spontaneously but "had to be called up in the name
of its king and had often to be forced to do its patriotic duty." Undoubtedly much national enthusiasm, resentment against the foreigners,
and desire for vengeance existed among the educated classes, but the
masses were hardly touched by these sentiments. The Napoleonic period
awakened nationalism among the German intellectuals; it spread to the
people only many years later.[5]

Among the nationalist intellectuals, some went to great lengths, like
the professor of modern history at the University of Berlin, Friedrich
Rühs.[6] In a long scholarly work he presented "the whole of modern
history as a chain of unrest and wars which all originate in the fact that
a single nation, the French, was able by its superior power to satisfy as
often as it wished its rude arrogance and its insatiable lust for conquest."
Professor Rühs was convinced that "the deep hatred which he shared
with all decent Germans from boyhood for the wicked and abominable
race" in no way influenced his presentation. He demanded that Alsace,
Switzerland, and the Low Countries must become part of Germany, and
he based his claim upon many historical facts.[7] His research found many
forerunners of his anti-French attitude among less-known German
pamphleteers and writers of the second half of the seventeenth century.
His conclusions were stated with firmness and deep conviction: the
Germans must hate and despise the French forever and never forget
that they have to avenge centuries of offense and humiliation. German
youth must always be taught the diabolical wickedness of the French.
All Germans must be ashamed to have personal contacts with Frenchmen; they must not cease to regard the French Revolution as the worst
stain—"der grösste Schandfleck"—of modern history. It could not be
otherwise, because the French were entirely incapable of grasping any
lofty human or political idea. Finally the French language should not
be taught in German schools, lest the youthful mind be confused and
defiled by it.[8]

With less vehemence, other scholars throughout Germany tried to do
their part for the national cause. Even men of learning who spent their
days in the faraway fields of classical philology, like Friedrich Jacobs
(1764-1847), contributed their share. Jacobs lived not in the Prussia

which had taken the lead in the war against Napoleon, but in the small Thuringian duchy of Saxe-Gotha, whose ruler August was a devoted member of the Rhenish Confederation and an enthusiastic admirer of Napoleon. After the Battle of Leipzig Jacobs called upon the Thuringians to rise.

> Do not remain cold and indifferent spectators of the deeds of your brothers; do not leave to others alone the glory of fighting for the sacred cause. Up! Sons of the German fatherland, take the sword! Let no man wait for another; let everyone press to be first. Every town and every village must become an armed camp where everyone rises when the signal is given. As in a great army, there must live in all of you only one will, to serve the fatherland with all you have and with all your blood.[9]

Generally, the mood in the War of Liberation became less nationalist the greater the distance from northeastern Germany, from Königsberg, Breslau, and Berlin.[10]

From the east came moderating voices, too. August von Kotzebue (1761-1819), the author of more than two hundred popular German comedies, who had become a Russian subject and after 1806 ceaselessly attacked Napoleon in satirical periodicals, published in Berlin in April 1813 the *Russisch-deutsches Volksblatt.* He opened the first issue with dignified words:

> Let us unite our forces, without provocation but with solemn sternness, to defeat a people whose enemies we are without pleasure, whose enemies we are only because it allowed itself to be misused, to rob us of the one good which it itself esteemed so highly: national liberty. We demand nothing else. We are willing to leave to the French their land, their emperor, their honor. But we wish him no longer to rule our land and our princes and to encroach upon our honor.

Kotzebue drew a clear line of distinction between the fight against Napoleon, which he had helped to prepare, and the hatred with which Arndt, Jahn, and other German nationalists attacked everything French.

Not all enemies of Napoleon shared Kotzebue's restraint. Ernst Raupach (1784-1852), another popular German writer for the stage who spent part of his life in Russia, printed in January 1813 in St. Petersburg an address to the Germans entitled "Napoleon the Tyrant, the Oppressor, the Perverter of Germany." More famous, however, became his poem "An das deutsche Vaterland," which called upon the Germans in the spring of 1815 to crown their victory by doing God's work in destroying Paris forever, so that no traces might remain of this modern Babylon, the home of all vices and abominations, the source from which all mankind was poisoned:

Und ist es vollbracht
In blutiger Schlacht,
Und hat sich das deutsche Ritterschwert
Als Schrecken des Feindes wieder bewährt,
Und hat euch der Himmel
Im Schlachtengetümmel
Zu seinen Streitern wieder erklärt:

Dann seid ihm dankbar: zerstört ihm die Hölle,
Wo Bosheit und Laster nur Ehre geniesst;
Verschüttet mit Trümmern und Bränden die Quelle,
Aus welcher das Gift in die Menschheit fliesst;
Dass staunend der Wandrer in künftigen Jahren
Nicht finde den Ort am verödeten Strand,
Wo die Höhlen der Mörder und Frevler waren,
Wo die gottvergessene Babel stand.

With even less poetry but with equal vigor, Johann Friedrich Schink wrote his "Schand- und Schimpfode," in which he called Napoleon the scum of mankind—"Abschaum der Menschheit."

Blutsauger, Völkergeissel, Weltzertreter,
Pest, Räuberhauptmann, Henker und Bandit,
Du menschgewordener Satan, Missetäter,
Wie selbst der Abgrund keinen sah und sieht!

This truly "insulting ode" was written to celebrate the Battle of Leipzig on October 18, 1813, which forced Napoleon to retreat from Germany and changed the minds of many Germans about Napoleon's future. Arndt suggested that the memory of the battle be celebrated every year on October 18 by songs and speeches around campfires, preferably on mountaintops. This custom was observed in 1814 in Berlin, where Jahn lighted the flame on the Hasenheide, in Frankfurt-am-Main where Goethe with Marianne von Willemer was present, and near Essen where a poem by Johann Gottfried Christian Nonne (1785-1853) was sung:

Flamme empor!
Steige mit loderndem Scheine
Auf den Gebirgen am Rheine
Glühend empor!

Siehe, wir stehn
Treu im geweiheten Kreise
Dich zu des Vaterlands Preise
Brennen zu sehn!

Singing around the campfire has remained one of the favorite manifestations of German patriotic student and youth organizations; but the commemoration of the Battle of Leipzig soon ceased. The hope that it would parallel Bastille Day as a "Fest aller Deutschen" was not fulfilled; the government opposed it. For when the Battle of Leipzig was fought, most Germans outside Prussia and Austria still sympathized with Napoleon. The two leading literary periodicals in Germany at that time—the *Allgemeine Literaturzeitung* of Halle (1785-1849) and its namesake of Jena (1804-1848)—had been staunch supporters of Napoleon until the Battle of Leipzig. It was then still within people's memory that a highly respected historian and writer like Ernst Ludwig Posselt (1763-1804) had proposed to inscribe Napoleon's name in giant gold letters on a high mountaintop where it could shine over Germany.[11]

But even after the Battle of Leipzig some Germans were not ready for such a quick about-face as most of the princes and writers then performed. Lord Aberdeen wrote to Lord Castlereagh from Germany on December 24, 1813:

> I am sorry to inform you of the loss of one of our new friends. The King of Württemberg has written to Bonaparte to say that the alliance [with Austria against France] has been forced upon him, and that he looks forward to the time when he may be able to assist him with effect.

Pro-Napoleonic sentiments were strong in Saxony, the homeland of Fichte and Treitschke. The Saxon army, especially its rank and file, revolted as late as May 1815 when they were attached to Blücher's army in Belgium, to demonstrate their loyalty to their own royal house. Blücher suppressed the revolt with the utmost severity. In a letter to the King of Saxony from Liége on May 16, 1815, he threatened in case of need to shoot down the whole Saxon army. Many Saxons regarded not France but Prussia as their enemy. On the anniversary of the Battle of Leipzig in 1814 an anonymous author wrote a patriotic song for Saxons in which he expressed their loyalty to the Saxon King Friedrich August I (ruled 1763-1827) who since the Battle of Leipzig had been held captive by the Prussians. The anonymous writer complained bitterly of the imminent subjection of Saxony to foreign domination. Were Frenchmen committing this crime? he asked. No! It was German rapacity which threatened the existence and liberty of Saxony. The author vowed eternal hostility to Prussia and called upon the Saxons to fight for king and fatherland against the Prussian invaders:

> Nein, Teutsche sind's! Pfui, Fluch der Schande!
> Sie fesseln ihn, und List und Trug
> Ersinnt die fremde, rohe Bande,
> Sie hat des Raubes nicht genug.
> Nach uns gelüstet ihre Gier,
> Doch ew'ge Feindschaft schwören wir. . . .

Und soll der schwere Kampf beginnen
Für König und für Vaterland—
Auf! mag das Blut in Strömen rinnen—
Es waffne sich der Sachsen Hand!
Und wer noch seinen König ehrt,
Der schwöre zu dem Racheschwert.

The persistence of local loyalties and the other factors which resisted the growth of a German nationalism in 1813 were later forgotten. The propagation of the legend of 1813 was supported by the many poems and songs which patriotic enthusiasm produced.[12] Among younger writers who became widely popular, there also stood south Germans like Friedrich Rückert (1788-1866), Johann Ludwig Uhland (1787-1862), and Gustav Schwab (1792-1850).[13] An older Swabian, Philipp Joseph von Rehfues (1779-1843), who shared the admiration for the French in his younger years, later published in his *Europäisches Magazin* patriotic "Reden an das deutsche Volk" which attracted the attention of Stein, who made him commissioner for the liberated German lands on the left bank of the Rhine. The future of these lands was one of the two great problems which preoccupied the German patriots of the day; the other was the creation of a united Germany, the restoration of the Reich which had collapsed in 1806. One of the popular poets of the war, Max von Schenkendorf, expressed in August 1813 the widespread hope for future Austro-Prussian unity:

Nicht mehr nun trennt uns Süd und Norden,
Ein Lied, ein Herz, ein Gott, ein Orden,
Ein Deutschland hoch und schön!

Neither of these two problems, however, was solved in a way to accord with the desires of the German patriots. The Rhine on both its banks, from its source at the St. Gotthard to its mouth in the North Sea, did not become German, and German unity was restored in a very limited form. Both problems continued to be central concerns of German nationalism and shaped its future course. Germany felt elated by the victory in 1815. The Prussian Landwehr returned from France with the triumphant song:

Die Welt ist umgedreht;
Hoch oben Teutschland steht. . . .

which expressed the popular wonder of the sudden change in Germany's fortunes. But no national program or national will corresponded to the victory. German nationalism had not yet found its political form.

XXXVI

Josef Görres and the Meaning of the War of 1813

IN THE early morning hours of January 1, 1814, the Allied armies under the command of the Prussian Field Marshal Gebhard Leberecht Blücher (1742-1819) crossed the Rhine. The evening before, Archduke Johann noted in his diary:

> Now I live free with my fatherland and have no longer to tolerate arrogance. Germany, the wonderful land, this people leading in strength of heart, mind, and scholarship, has risen through its power and will, and has regained its due place in the sun. If a lasting peace and a firm order soon return, as I do not doubt they will, if tranquillity again renders the people happy, then I shall gladly say with Simeon: *Nunc dimitte servum tuum*, for I have seen the day of liberty for Germany. I found my faith confirmed.

These words expressed the elated feelings of many Germans at the time. Germany east of the Rhine was free of French control. But what would be the fate of the lands west of the river, which had been under French administration for almost twenty years? In the treaty of Basel (1795) Prussia, and at Campoformio (1797) Austria, agreed in principle to the cession of the left bank to France. In 1803 the Rhine became definitely by treaty rights the frontier between France and Germany. During the peace negotiations in 1813 and 1814 the allies repeatedly offered Napoleon the Rhine as France's frontier. His character and past did not allow him to accept. The hesitations of the German and Allied statesmen, who at best were lukewarm about the German character of the Rhine, increased the fears of the German patriots. In November 1813 Arndt opened their campaign with his powerful plea for the Rhine as Germany's river, not Germany's frontier. The *Preussische*

Correspondent published on February 16, 1814 a poem "The Frontier" by Friedrich Leopold Count Stolberg:[1]

> Du Grenze? Nein, nicht Grenze, du alter Rhein!
> Du Lebensblut, dem Herzen Teutoniens
> Entströmend, beiden Ufern Segen
> Spendend und hohes Gefühl und Freude!

But the most powerful voice raised for the annexation of the left bank of the Rhine to Germany was that of Josef Görres, who on January 23, 1814, began to publish in Koblenz his *Rheinischer Merkur*, which appeared every other day for two years and became the most influential German newspaper. Through it Görres became the first German political journalist.[2]

In his youth Görres, a Rhinelander by birth, enthusiastically welcomed the French Revolution and the French army as messengers of liberty. "In the first days of my youth," he wrote years later, "the ideas of republicanism and of the reform of mankind's political situation in its social conditions suffused my whole being." In 1797 he published his *Der allgemeine Friede—ein Ideal* in which he praised permanent peace as the supreme ideal and the French nation as the restorer of the rights of men. In the same year he published a journal *Das Rote Blatt* which appeared, in French revolutionary fashion, every tenth day. There he attacked monarchy, aristocracy, and clericalism and praised the French constitution, but protested also against abuses of the French administration. A visit to Paris at the end of 1799 made him feel the deep differences between the German and the French character. He became convinced that language and national traditions separated peoples more than cosmopolitan policies united them. He withdrew from political life and soon discovered (under the influence of Arnim and Brentano, with whom he formed a friendship in Heidelberg in 1806) the world of medieval legends and tales. From the universal republic of the French ideals of 1789, he turned his longing to the imperial tradition of the German Middle Ages.

In 1810 he published under the pseudonym Orion two articles, "On Germany's Fall and the Conditions of Its Rebirth" and "Reflections," in Perthes' *Vaterländisches Museum*. There he deplored the tragedy of a people which had abandoned its peculiar character and tried to imitate foreign ways:

> Darum ist es unter allen Verblendungen die unseligste, wenn ein Volk seine Eigentümlichkeit verlässt, wenn es misskennend seine innerste Natur, in fremde Kreise hinübertaumelt, und, entsagend individueller Sinnesart, zu erstreben sucht, was nicht seines Berufes ist, und gering dagegen achtet, wozu ihm die Kraft verliehen wurde.[3]

In the second article he expressed his deep pessimism about Germany's future:

> How can the German people, with its fragmentary, confused, and inconstant efforts, win the esteem of the celestial powers who demand deeds and easily see through empty words? How can the nation which has forgotten itself for so long not be finally forgotten by fate? . . . What we need above all is a firm and consistent public opinion which would express decidedly and unmistakably the peculiar character of the nation. Public opinion is, to use a dramatic picture under dramatic circumstances, the chorus in the political tragedy; as the chorus has disappeared from the stage, so public opinion, with the exception of England, has disappeared from all modern states.

When Prussia took up the struggle against Napoleon in the spring of 1813, Görres remained skeptical: it seemed to him a senseless effort doomed to failure. Only the victory at Leipzig and the advance of the Allied armies to the Rhine changed his mind. Now he saw the opportunity of giving Germany what it sadly lacked, an organ of public opinion. As such he created the *Rheinischer Merkur.*[4]

The example of England guided him in his insistence on a free press, and for a short time he succeeded in his plans. In a nation without political will or public opinion, where representative institutions were unknown and political parties did not exist, where the few newspapers were hardly more than anemic and servile sheets tolerated by an arbitrary censorship, where freedom of speech was unknown and almost unthinkable, Görres through a number of fortunate circumstances was able to publish a paper which was written with vigor and incisiveness, which was widely read and discussed, and which exercised an influence with which the governments had to reckon. In spite of growing difficulties with the Prussian censorship he managed to issue the paper for two years. As long as Görres attacked the French, he was tolerated by the German governments. When he began to remind the German princes that nations are strengthened by domestic liberty, his paper, in spite of his predilection for feudalism and the medieval order and his rejection of Western democracy, came quickly to grief. The fulfillment of his wishes for a German Rhineland brought Görres misfortune. On January 3, 1816, King Frederick William III of Prussia ordered the suppression of the *Rheinischer Merkur,* for Koblenz and the Rhineland were now part of the Prussian state. One year later Görres had to flee from Germany. As a political refugee he came to Strasbourg, in French Alsace, where the French administration showed itself more liberal than Prussia.

Görres' journal was an attempt to give political direction to the confused German longing of 1813; it failed because the paternalistic absolutism of the princes proved stronger than the dreams of fusing peoples and princes into a union. The weakness of the patriotic intellectuals was due to the lack of a strong and economically independent middle class, but even more to their emphasis on the nation as the end and on liberty only as a means, and to the vagueness of their concept of people. "People" was not the bearer of demands in opposition to government or ruling classes, it was a semimystical all-inclusive concept, a metaphysical quality which implied goodness and righteousness and was the fountainhead of all political strength and wisdom.[5] "Strong peoples alone can render princes strong," Görres wrote—as one of the few liberals among the German nationalists—

> and only those peoples have been strong at all times who participate in public affairs. Where the state lives only in few individuals, their loss leads easily to the fall of the state, and the state sinks and rises with them; where, however, the community participates in the state, the state lives an indestructible life which regenerates itself permanently.

For popular participation in government, Görres proposed a complex constitution which took good care that the old and traditional prevailed over any innovation:

> Man is founded—and let us be grateful for it—on his past existence, with roots which reach deep beneath the soil, far into the most ancient times, whence they draw their invisible strength. The people which throws away its past bares its most sensitive nerves to the storms of an unpredictable future. Woe to us and to our constitution if our new form should be so new that it would reflect only the needs of our present time.[6]

No wonder Germany's first political journalist withdrew a few years later from political life and devoted himself to a cult of the traditions of the Catholic Middle Ages.

Under these circumstances Görres' efforts to create a public opinion in Germany which would demand popular rights and challenge the absolute authority of princes and censors were doomed. While he failed as a liberal, he was more successful as a nationalist. A growing number of Germans began to regard it as the foremost national concern to reclaim all the lands west of Germany which by ties of history, language, or "blood" were deemed German. Arndt and Görres were among the first to put forward forceful arguments of "historical rights" for national expansion. They were supported by the romantic fascination with the past. Nationalism has always shown its most dangerous implications in its wish to restore situations of past centuries and to disregard or to belittle developments which in the intervening years have changed the past beyond recognition and beyond any legitimate hope for revival. Claims to territory advanced on behalf of "historical rights" have often been rendered more alluring and dangerous by pseudo-ethical considerations. When other Germans opposed Görres' and Arndt's insistence on a limitless war against France and demanded moderation, warning against wars of annihilation, Görres answered that he never thought of annihilating the French—an impossible task, as he pointed out, in the case of twenty million men. On the contrary, he wrote, France should be preserved so that the Germans would see in it

> the mirror of all detestable badness. Thus France has become for us the true antithesis in the struggle in which all our moral forces are called forth; it is a center of devouring fire and the totality of all evil, . . . and the struggle with it will with its hardness force the missing unity upon our people and thus avert from us civil war.[7]

In the same vein a volunteer in the German army wrote from France, after describing the French as a people with animal stupidity on their brow, an empty expression in their eyes, and with their crisply curled hair showing their wild sensuality:

> We who have crossed the Rhine and come to the Seine have to avenge two things upon the French people: an outward violation of our earthly goods, and a moral violation of our soul. The first was the arrogance of the wars of conquest; the second was the bitter scorn of contempt with which they identified the *bête allemande* with stupidity itself. The wrath which this attitude awakened deep down in our hearts remained a long time restrained by the yoke which fate imposed upon us, but finally it has frightfully erupted, with a volcanic explosion, into the black flame of a national war.[8]

The men who proclaimed the war as an ethical crusade to eradicate evil from the earth and who demanded vast annexations were mostly writers and intellectuals, not generals and statesmen.[9] Görres and others used to expatiate with deep emotion on the beauty of Strasbourg Cathedral, which Master Erwin at the end of the thirteenth century built into one of the great monuments of Gothic art. It had inspired Herder and the young Goethe to appreciate Gothic art—which they identified with Germanic art, overlooking the fact that Master Erwin and other German Gothic architects were influenced by the great cathedrals of medieval France. Görres called up the Alsatian and Swiss past, architecture and literature, folkways and dialects, as witnesses that the Alsatians and the Swiss belonged by history, language, and descent to Germany. What counted less was the fact that the living Alsatians and Swiss did not wish to belong to Germany. Görres himself noted how faithfully the Alsatians sided with the French and how strongly they resisted the invading German armies. But though he saw clearly how much the Alsatians wished to remain French, he could not help but proclaim that they "are ours and belong to us by God's will and by right." [10]

Turning from Alsace to Switzerland, Görres demanded that the Swiss end their neutrality:

> They should now declare once and for all whether they wish to belong to the Romance peoples—"Welschland"—or to Germany, so that the Reich will know what it can expect from them, whether they wish to be its frontiersmen or the enemy's spying eyes who watch us from their mountains.

And with superb confidence he added:

> We do not doubt their decision once they have found themselves and have renounced their habitual pettiness. The German, wherever he is, cannot lose or forfeit his true nature, and even if he has abandoned himself to alien ways, he quickly finds the way back to his old nature (Sinnesweise). Thus we greet them in our soul as our brethren; they will not hold back when we too have eliminated all our impurities and everything alien. Switzerland is geologically the center of southern Germany, as the Riesengebirge is the center of northern Germany, and in neither case can we allow the center to fall outside Germany's periphery.

With similar arguments Görres wished to include the Netherlands and Belgium within Germany. Yet all these peoples, whatever "the voice of history and of blood," wished to stay outside Germany. They preferred their personal freedom to the "elemental call of nature." [11] Through the French Revolution and especially through Napoleon's administration, the Alsatians, in spite of their German past and language, had become French in mind and intention; their free decision integrated them into the new nation and determined their loyalties.

Görres believed in the precedence of the "natural" ties of blood over all other loyalties.

> In itself every nation (Stamm) is a completely closed and rounded whole; a common tie of blood relationship unites all its members. As all speak one language, so must all be internally of one mind (Gesinnung) and must stick together like one man. That is their first rule and law. This instinctive urge which binds all members into a whole is the law of nature and takes precedence of all artificial treaties. The treaties must all be of necessity based on "nature," otherwise they are void. . . . The voice of nature in ourselves warns us and points to the chasm

between us and the alien. The irreconcilable in the nature of two nations who do not wish to fuse, the hatred which causes the mutual repulsion among nations, because they ought to remain separate according to the divine plan, the ruin and the violence of all universal monarchies warn us not to act against nature.[12]

But apparently history and blood were not always strong enough to overcome individual judgment and the inclination of the present. Even in Germany Görres had to complain that everywhere, especially in Westphalia and in the lands of the former Rhenish Confederation, very many longed for the return of the French. The twenty years of French influence did not leave only detestation in German hearts, but often preference for the French system.[13]

As the heritage of the past determined Görres' territorial claims, so it also influenced his picture of Germany's political reorganization. He hoped that the heir of the imperial tradition, the Habsburg Prince Francis, would again become emperor of all the Germans. The emperor should no longer be a powerless shadow, but should be invested with the whole dignity of the medieval emperors and with the supreme command of all military forces. At their head Görres wished to place an imperial field marshal (Reichsfeldherr), for which post he proposed Archduke Karl, and in case Karl should decline the burden, the Austrian commanding general Prince Schwarzenberg, with Gneisenau as his adviser. While the field marshal would advise the emperor in all military affairs, a prime minister should advise him in the political and civilian field. Görres had no doubt that Stein would be the right man and that upon that rock Germany could be firmly founded.

> In all German lands the estates (Ständeversammlungen) must be called together and must receive the rights which belong to them for God's sake and for the sake of princely promises; not as an act of grace nor as something which the Germans must win by strenuous fighting and efforts, but as something which cannot be denied to them in equity. The estates must have full power to stop abuses which oppress the people, to remove officials in whom they have no confidence, to change all institutions which are contrary to the spirit of the people. As the estates have come out of the people, they will be a guarantee to them that all the words spoken to them are true and all promises made to them will be fulfilled. Finally one should arm the people everywhere and should no longer be suspicious of the people in arms. One should allow freedom of meeting and association for the best among the people so that they mutually strengthen each other in their readiness for sacrifice and for courageous resistance to the grave dangers threatening us. Germany should count only upon itself; to rely upon alien help is hazardous.

All must be wide awake and active in a spirit of unity. Security
lies not in numbers but in the spirit which animates them.[14]

Such was the regenerated German nation which Görres and his friends
wished to see as the outcome of the War of Liberation. It was not a
free nation in the Western sense of the word; there was no insistence
upon individual rights and equality of opportunity; the stress was on
national union and active devotion of the citizen to the defense of the
commonweal. But even this goal was not achieved.

Görres' hope for the restoration of the imperial dignity and of the
rights of the estates in a modernized form was shared by many German
intellectuals. The princes, however, desired otherwise, and they could
carry out their will without serious resistance, because the majority of
the people were not interested. In vain Arndt complained in his pamphlet
Der Deutsche Bund wider das Deutsche Reich in the summer of 1815:
"Poor, loyal German people! You shall have no emperor. They, your
princes, wish themselves to play emperor." With disarming simplicity
he called upon the princes to "make the German people into a people—
for which it lacks nothing but your agreement," overlooking the fact
that modern nations are not made by princes. Niebuhr was better informed when he wrote at the same time: "The name of liberty has
become dear to many, but only a few understand that liberty is not a
matter of enjoyment but of labor and danger." With even greater understanding, Steffens remarked that the young warriors returning from
France asked themselves: "Where is the Germany for which we were
asked to fight? It lives in us. Show us where we can find it, or we shall
be forced to seek it for ourselves." Few scholars or statesmen believed
then in a united, strong Germany. Most of them believed that the peace
of Europe and of Germany would be better served by a loose confederation, strong enough to resist any attack on Germany, not united enough
to impose German leadership on neighboring countries. Niebuhr was one
of the few who demanded a centralized German nation-state. He regarded Prussia as the instrument for the realization of Germany's destiny.
In his *Preussens Recht gegen den sächsischen Hof* (1814) he supported
Prussia's claims to the annexation of Saxony because in his opinion
Prussia was not a land like other German states, but "the common fatherland of every German who excels in scholarship, in arms, or in the
administration." He believed that no German princely house had shown
greater loyalty to the common German cause or more sympathy for it
than the Hohenzollern, and claimed that the Dutch and the German
Swiss should unite with Germany.

At that time, however, Niebuhr represented a minority among German scholars. The famous jurist Anton Friedrich Justus Thibaut (1772-
1840), professor in Heidelberg, demanded the unification and rational

modernization of civil law in Germany to facilitate communication and economic development, but he regarded the existence of several governments as preferable to the creation of one large state. He believed that overexpanded states fall victim to internal tensions and exhaustion. The historian Arnold Hermann Ludwig Heeren (1760-1842), a professor in Göttingen, praised the German Confederation as it emerged from the Napoleonic wars as a guarantee of peace, as the "Friedensstaat von Europa." Heeren believed that Germany, as a centralized nation-state in the very heart of Europe, a compact mass disposing of great resources in manpower, natural, and industrial products, could hardly resist the temptation of using its geographic and strategic advantages and becoming the "Kriegsstaat von Europa." [15] Heeren's enlightened nationalism was moderated by his European conscience and his vision of the growing unity of the earth. Probably because of his Hanseatic origin—he was born in Bremen and studied and lived in Göttingen, where English influence was strong—he was convinced that future historians would deal with a "Welt-Staaten-System" and that the coming era of sea power and world order would usher in a happier future for mankind.[16] He was one of the first Continental writers to foresee that the European balance of power would give way to a world balance of power, that the stage of history was broadening and would soon encompass the whole earth.

The eighteenth-century legacy of a common Europe was still strong among German intellectuals even at the end of the Napoleonic wars. None of the princes and their ministers thought in nationalist concepts, least of all Francis of Austria and Metternich. Francis did not covet the imperial crown, offered him repeatedly by the minor German princes and the free cities, who viewed the restoration of the imperial crown as a protection against the rapacious desires of Prussia and the middle states. Francis was even less impressed by the many memoranda and poems, articles and pamphlets, with which Stein and Görres and the romanticists propagated the restoration of the Empire. The Habsburgs preferred the acquisition of the Lombardo-Venetian kingdom, with its non-German population, to a recovery of the Habsburg possessions in southwestern Germany. In vain Rückert called upon Francis in his poem "An Habsburgs Adler":

Nicht die fremde Pomeranze ist's, die dir gehört zunächst,
Der Reichsapfel, der im Glanze hier an deutschen Eichen wächst.[17]

The Habsburg monarchy emerged in 1815 for the first time as a geographically compact entity, uniting ten different nationalities in a system based on geography, common defense, and economic cooperation. German historians of the time showed some understanding of the value of such supranational states. In his *Grundideen der Politik der österreichi-*

schen Monarchie, which he published in Frankfurt-am-Main in 1815, Karl Ludwig Woltmann (1770-1817) insisted that Germany and Austria were not nation-states but federations (Staatenvereine). To him the federal union of various nationalities did not seem a weakness, but a source of strength and wealth; he was convinced that a multinational Austria and a loosely confederated Germany would help preserve the European equilibrium and peace.[18] Three years later, the future master of German historiography, Leopold Ranke (1795-1886), wrote in an essay published only after his death:

> Situated in the center of Europe, Austria is composed of the most varied nationalities, and yet it is so far a true unity that in 1809 the *plures* could show the highest enthusiasm for the *unum.* It represents as it were visibly the unity of Europe, for it unites all the races of the continent into one state. That makes it the leading power of Europe; all others are one-sided, either Slavs or Germans or Latins: Austria overcomes this one-sided-ness. There they all learn that they can live side by side together. Each race is related to Austria; through Austria the various races are related to each other. Therefore the power of Austria is thoroughly European. It might be said that it is the only true European power. Vienna alone was the site where the European peace conference could be held; Austria alone is the power which can maintain the peace and enhance it to a true unity. It can do it if it does not reject the new form which Europe wishes to assume, but will know how to represent it.[19]

Austria under Metternich's leadership had neither the strength nor the wisdom to follow this course. It did not become the representation of the European movement, but a symbol of conservative inertia. It avoided the pitfalls of nationalism, but it did not wake up to any of the great forces which then, and at least until 1866, counterbalanced the growing absorption with national unity and power among the Germans: the faith in the dignity of the individual which Kant and Schiller bequeathed to German idealism; the Christian conscience which moderated nationalism not only in Stein and Schleiermacher but even in Arndt;[20] and finally the surviving awareness of European unity. Many German intellectuals, later forgotten in the mounting tide of nationalism, were then good Europeans. Michael Alexander Lips (1779-1838), professor of history and political economy in Erlangen and later in Marburg, a staunch liberal hostile to all remnants of feudalism, suggested in 1814 the formation of a liberal European union. Karl Christian Friedrich Krause (1781-1832), a prolific writer and philosopher who aroused more attention in Spain than in his native land, elaborated in 1808 the plan for a federation of mankind (Menschheitsbund) and published in 1814 a draft of the constitution of a European federation which he considered a regional system within a future world government.[21]

A lonely German in Paris, a survivor from the eighteenth century, Count Gustav Schlabrendorf (1750-1824), one of the early friends of the French Revolution, affirmed in 1814 his continuing belief in the ideals of 1789, but placed them in a broader context which the experience of the intervening years of European conflict had taught him: "States as little as individuals can form themselves and prosper in isolation," he told a German visitor who came to see him after the fall of Paris:

> They succumb to dull inertia or wild fury. They lack a thousand qualities which are produced and preserved by neighborly competition. That was also the reason why the French Revolution could not immediately succeed: one people alone cannot carry through such a task. People used to say that France was too large for the new form of state. I say to the contrary, it was too small. But now when the Revolution is no longer an isolated French fact, because the whole of Europe has taken part in it, willingly or otherwise, and will in future take part even more, the Revolution can succeed as the common work of so many peoples. The peoples of Europe belong more closely together than one believes; they advance on the whole in the same direction and according to the same principles.

Count Schlabrendorf was convinced that in the nineteenth century the principles of 1789 would continue and develop and that free states would be formed throughout Europe. But he warned against any attempts in the new constitutions to force anybody to be free.

> Let even in the republic all those who so desire be servile toadies. I wish the forms of the states to be such as to allow everyone, without being a hero and ever ready to fight for it, to live always as a free man and with dignity. Such a liberty is England's great advantage; it was entirely absent in old France.

Like Mme de Staël the Count was convinced that England owed its victory over France to its free constitution. With greater clarity, however, he foresaw that England, the mother country of liberty, to whom the original inspiration for freedom in eighteenth-century France was due, was in danger of falling behind France if England did not advance and adopt the principles of 1789. To his German visitor he named the emancipation of the Catholics, the contentment of Ireland, and the "inevitable" reform of Parliament as the three decisive steps which would transform eighteenth-century England into a modern nation.[22] The character of the English constitution, the heritage of the Glorious Revolution, made in

England the transition possible without violence or upheaval. It alone, among the major European nations, solved the problem posited by the French Revolution for the Age of Nationalism: how to assure the optimum coexistence of the patriotic concern for the commonweal with the dignity of free men acting on their own initiative and responsibility, how to harmonize the moral demand of the liberty of the individual with the social necessity of the unity of the state.

Notes

NOTES FOR CHAPTER 2: *France in 1789*

1. Among recent books on the French Revolution of interest for our subject
are Jacques Godechot, *La Grande Nation: L'Expansion révolutionnaire de
la France dans le monde de 1789 à 1799*, 2 vols. (Paris: Aubier, 1956)
and *Les Révolutions 1770-1799* (Nouvelle Clio, Paris: Presses Universitaires de France, 1963). French expansion, without preconceived plans,
was based on ideology (popular sovereignty), natural frontiers, and military and economic imperialism. Similarly R. R. Palmer regards the French
Revolution as part of "The World Revolution of the West, 1763-1801"
(*Political Science Quarterly*, March 1954, pp. 1-14) and the various
revolutionary movements in Europe and America as "one big revolutionary
agitation, not simply a French Revolution due to purely French causes,
and foolishly favored by giddy people in other countries" ("Reflections on
the French Revolution," *Political Science Quarterly*, March 1952, p. 66).
See his *The Age of the Democratic Revolution*: Vol. I, *The Challenge*; Vol.
II, *The Struggle* (Princeton University Press, 1959 and 1964).—In Hans
Kohn, *The Idea of Nationalism* (New York: Macmillan, 1944) the
French Revolution is also treated as the manifestation and climax of a
crisis of the *ancien régime* throughout the Western world, including the
Russia of Alexander Radishchev. It was a search for a new basis of society
and social morality, rejecting the authoritarian oligarchic character of
traditional society. But I believe that this crisis was resolved, or not resolved, in very different ways in the various countries and that the kind of
resolution or nonresolution corresponded to the character of nationalism,
as it then developed in the various countries, each people searching for
a new identity, different in each case, and trying to follow its "own"
road to nationalism. In that sense the French Revolution was a French
national phenomenon. An understanding of the new phenomenon of
nationalism anywhere between 1760 and our own time can be gained
only by a comparative study of the various developments, not by studying
the history of any national unit alone, as has been done until recently.—
Of other new publications, stressing social aspects, see Albert Soboul,
Précis d'histoire de la Révolution Française (Paris: Editions Françaises,
1962) and A. B. Cobban, *The Social Interpretation of the French Revolution* (Cambridge University Press, 1964). Two recommended general-
background studies are those by Georges Lefebvre, *La Révolution Fran-*

çaise, 2nd ed. (Paris: Presses Universitaires de France, 1957) and *Napoléon* (Paris: Alcan, 1935); and as another general survey, M. Thompson, *Napoleon Bonaparte: His Rise and Fall* (Oxford: Basil Blackwell, 1952).

2. Philippe Sagnac, "Les Origines de la Révolution française: L'Influence americaine," *Revue des études napoléoniennes*, Vol. XXII (1924), pp. 27-45, and his *La Fin de l'ancien régime et la Révolution américaine* (Paris, 1947). See also Bernard Fay, *The Revolutionary Spirit in France and America*, tr. by Ramon Guthrie (New York: Harcourt Brace, 1927), and the important criticism of the book by Henry Commager in *The New Republic*, May 9, 1928; Louis Gottschalk, *The Place of the American Revolution in the Causal Pattern of the French Revolution* (The American Friends of Lafayette, 1948).

3. Billardon de Sauvigny, *Vashington, ou la liberté du nouveau monde*, ed. by Gilbert Chinard (Princeton University Press, 1941). This tragedy in four acts was produced in Paris at the Théâtre de la Nation on July 13 and 14, 1791. The passage quoted is from Act I, Scene v. On Washington as a model of Republican virtues, see Gilbert Chinard, *George Washington as the French Knew Him* (Princeton University Press, 1940).

4. Hans Kohn, *The Idea of Nationalism*, pp. 265-268.

5. André Chénier, *Oeuvres complètes*, ed. by Paul Dimoff (Paris: Delagrave, 1908), Vol. II, pp. 252-258:

> O sainte égalité! dissipe nos ténèbres
> Renverse les verrous, les bastilles funèbres. . . .
> Non, je ne veux plus vivre en ce séjour servile;
> J'irai, j'irai bien loin me chercher un asile. . . .
> Où, loin des ravisseurs, la main cultivatrice
> Recueillera les dons d'une terre propice:
> Où mon coeur, respirant sous un ciel étranger,
> Ne verra plus des maux qu'il ne peut soulager;
> Où mes yeux éloignés de publiques misères
> Ne verront plus partout les larmes de mes frères
> Et la pâle indigence à la mourante voix,
> Et les crimes puissants qui font trembler les lois.

6. Hans Kohn, *The Idea of Nationalism*, pp. 234 f., 391 ff.

7. "And after this, do we often lament that our state has too little to offer to self-made men (*hominibus novis*)? Never, I maintain, has a state offered so much as does ours, wherein if a man of humble birth (*ignobili loco natus*) shows in his life a character such as to support the high standing which rank confers, his advancement is dependent only on hard work and a blameless record. Indeed, a man who has nothing but humble birth to support him often goes further than he would, had he the same defects though born of high degree." Cicero, "In Defence of Cluentius," XL, 111 f., tr. by H. Grose Hodge (Loeb Classical Library, 1927), pp. 339 ff.

8. James Michael Eagan, *Maximilian Robespierre: Nationalist Dictator* (New York: Columbia University Press, 1938), p. 23. Robespierre's nationalism

does not evolve from a religious Christian matrix as nationalism did in England or the United States, but becomes itself a religion, the realization of the "general will" (*vox populi, vox Dei*). Robespierre no longer based politics on religion, but religion on politics. In a similar way Kant no longer based morality on religion but religion on morality. Aimé Patri wrote of "a striking similarity" between Robespierre's religion and Kant's postulates of practical reason.—See also, on Robespierre, Alfred Cobban in *The English Historical Review*, Vol. LXI, pp. 45-80 and Vol. LXIII, pp. 29-51; Jean Massin, *Robespierre* (Paris: Club Française du Livre, 1956); and from the point of view of social history, Walter Markov (ed.), *Maximilien Robespierre 1758-1794: Beiträge zu seinem 200. Geburtstag* (Berlin: Rütten & Loening, 1958). In his opening essay Lefebvre praises Robespierre as the proponent of social justice and popular democracy.

9. Alphonse de Lamartine, *Histoire des Girondins* (Paris: Armand le Chevalier, 1865-1866), Vol. III, Book 47, p. 159. On the influence of antiquity on the French Revolution, see, above all, Harold T. Parker, *The Cult of Antiquity and the French Revolutionaries* (University of Chicago Press, 1937); Louis Bertrand, *La Fin du classicisme et le rétour à l'antiquité dans la seconde moitié du XVIIIe siècle et les premières années du XIXe en France* (Paris: Hachette, 1897); L. Hautecoeur, *Rome et la renaissance de l'antiquité à la fin du XVIIIe siècle* (Paris: Fontemoing, 1912); Abbé Augustin Sicard (1742-1822), *L'Education morale et civique avant et pendant la Révolution* (1700-1808) (Paris: Poussielgue frères, 1884).

10. "Les futurs révolutionnaires sont presque tous les dociles élèves des Jesuites et des Oratoriens; or, ni la discipline, ni les programmes, ni les méthodes d'enseignement des collèges ne tendent à la liberation de l'individu. Si quelques esprits, comme Brissot, Condorcet, Billaud-Varenne, s'insurgent contre cette 'barbarie,' l'immense majorité accepte cette culture vouée au passé gréco-latine, étroitement classique, où Homère, Plutarque, et Virgile constituent l'apport principal; les discours les plus révolutionnaires, plus tard, en témoigneront. Rien ne laisse pressentir une culture nouvelle." Pierre Trahard, *La Sensibilité révolutionnaire, 1789-1794* (Paris: Boivin, 1936), p. 28.

11. Albert Sorel, *L'Europe et la Révolution française*, 8 vols. (Paris: Plon, 1889-1905), Vol. I, pp. 219 f.

12. Constantin François, Comte de Volney (1757-1820), who became a teacher at the newly established Ecole Normale in 1794, stressed in his course *Leçons d'histoire* the dangers of becoming fascinated by history, especially the history of ancient times, Biblical or classical. He clearly foresaw the consequences of the warlike spirit of modern nationalism: ". . . de même que nos ancêtres de moyen âge se sont trompés en adoptant une morale qui contrarie tous les penchants de nature au lieu de les diriger, de même il est à craindre que l'âge présent ne se trompe aussi en en prenant une qui ne tend qu'à exalter les passions au lieu de les modérer; de manière que, passant d'un excès à l'autre, d'une crédulité aveugle à une incrédulité farouche, d'une apathie misanthropique à une cupidité dévorante, d'une patience servile à un orgueil oppresseur et in-

sociable, nous n'aurions fait que de changer de fanatisme, et quittant celui des Goths du neuvième siècle, nous retournerions à celui des enfants d'Odin, les Francs et les Celtes, nos premiers aïeux; et tels seraient les effets de cette moderne doctrine, qui ne tend qu'à exalter les courages, qu'à les pousser audelà du but de défense et de conservation qu'indique la nature; qui ne prêche que moeurs et vertus guerrières, comme si l'idée de la vertu, dont l'essence est de conserver, pouvait s'allier à l'idée de la guerre, dont l'essence est de détruire; qui appelle patriotisme une haine farouche de toute autre nation, comme si l'amour exclusif des siens n'était pas la vertu speciale des loups et des tigres; comme si dans la société générale du genre humain il y avait une autre justice, d'autres vertus pour les peuples que pour les individus; comme si un peuple guerrier et conquérant differait d'un individu perturbateur et méchant, qui s'empare du bien de son voisin, parce qu'il est le plus fort; une doctrine enfin qui ne tend qu'à ramener l'Europe aux siècles et aux moeurs féroces des Cimbres et des Teutons; et cette doctrine est d'autant plus dangereuse que l'esprit de la jeunesse, ami du mouvement et porté à l'enthousiasme militaire, adopte avidement ses préceptes." *Oeuvres complètes de Volney* (Paris: Firmin Didot Frères, 1846), p. 578.—"On a voulu nous éblouir de la gloire des combats: *malheurs aux peuples qui remplissent les pages de l'histoire!* Tels que les héros dramatiques, ils payent leur célébrité du prix de leur bonheur. On a séduit les amis des arts par l'éclat de leurs chefs-d'oeuvre: et l'on oublie que ce furent ces édifices et ces temples d'Athènes qui furent la première cause de sa ruine, le premier symptome d'extorsions et de rapines; ils provoquèrent à la fois le ressentiment et la défection de ses alliés, la jalousie et la cupidité de ses ennemis, et parce que ces masses de pierre, quoique bien comparties, sont partout un emploi stérile du travail et un absorbement ruineux de la richesse." *Ibid.*, p. 593.

NOTES FOR CHAPTER 3: *Influences on the Rise of French Nationalism*

1. *Oeuvres de Condorcet,* ed. by A. C. O'Connor and F. Arago (Paris: Didot Frères, 1847-1849), Vol. I, p. 435. See also J. Salwyn Schapiro, *Condorcet and the Rise of Liberalism* (New York: Harcourt Brace, 1934); Léon Cahen, *Condorcet et la Révolution française* (Paris: F. Alcan, 1904).
2. Lazare Carnot, submitting in August 1788 a memorandum to the Minister of War on the desirability of destroying or abandoning the French fortresses, rejected all wars not fought defensively for the preservation of the *status quo*. Wars for which a divine sanction was invoked seemed to him especially reprehensible. "If there is a country in Europe, whose particular interest is in accord on this point with the principles of this universal morality, of this great political philosophy which considers all nations as parts of the same humanity, it is undoubtedly France." Huntley Dupre, *Lazare Carnot: Republican Patriot* (Oxford, Ohio: Mississippi Valley Press, 1940), p. 33. See also Marcel Reinhard, *Le Grand Carnot,* 2 vols. (Paris: Hachette, 1955) and S. J. Watson, *Carnot* (London: Bodley Head, 1955).

3. "Es war ein herrlicher Sonnenaufgang. . . . Eine erhabene Rührung hat in jener Zeit geherrscht, ein Enthusiasmus des Geistes hat die Welt durchschauert, als sei es zur wirklichen Versöhnung des Göttlichen mit der Welt nun erst gekommen." Hegel, *Philosophie der Geschichte*, 3rd ed., pp. 535 f. See also F. Laurent, *Etudes sur l'histoire de l'humanité: Histoire du Droit des gens et des relations internationales*, Vol. XV (Paris: Librairie Internationale, 1869), pp. 41-43 on the Abbé Fauchet, and p. 73 on Volney.
4. Georges Avenel, *Anacharsis Cloots, l'orateur du genre humain*, 2 vols. (Paris: A. Lacroix, Verboeckhoven, 1865); Albert Mathiez, *La Révolution et les étrangers; cosmopolitisme et défense nationale* (Paris: La Renaissance du livre, 1918); *Oeuvres complètes de Saint-Just*, ed. by Charles Vellay (Paris: Charpentier & Fasquelle, 1908), Vol. I, p. 434; Albert Sorel, *op. cit.*, Vol. III, pp. 165, 214.

NOTES FOR CHAPTER 4: *The Revolution as National Regeneration*

1. "Toute la force de la révolution en France provenait de son caracterè national." Sorel, *op. cit.*, Vol. I, p. 549. See also Francis Acomb, *Anglophobia in France 1763-1789* (Durham: Duke University Press, 1950).
2. "It is scarcely doubtful that events would have taken a different turn if the throne had been occupied by Henry IV or even a Louis XIV." Georges Lefebvre, *The Coming of the French Revolution*, tr. by R. R. Palmer (Princeton University Press, 1947), p. 25. This is probably the best study on the origin of the French Revolution. See also Alfred Cobban, "Historical Revision: The Beginning of the French Revolution," *History*, Vol. XXIX (1944), pp. 92 ff. There is excellent material on the beginning of the Revolution in Cornwell B. Rogers, *The Spirit of Revolution in 1789* (Princeton: University Press, 1948), and in Jean Egret, *La Pré-Révolution française, 1787-1788* (Paris: Presses Universitaires de France, 1962).
3. Eagan, *Maximilian Robespierre*, p. 22.
4. Necker pointed out in his report of December 27, 1788, that "le voeu du Tiers Etat, quand il est unanime, quand il est conforme aux principes généraux d'équité, s'appellera toujours le voeu national."
5. On Sieyès, see the excellent study by Paul Bastid, *Sieyès et sa pensée* (Paris: Hachette, 1939). The author sums up Sieyès thought in a statement which Sieyès made on 18 Thermidor, year III: "J'ai souvent entendu parler de la cause finale du monde et de tout ce qu'il renferme; il est bien vrai de dire que la cause finale de tout le monde social doit être la liberté individuelle."—*Qu'est-ce que le Tiers Etat?* was published in January 1789 and went through four printings in the same year. Only the last one carried the name of the author. The definitive edition is by Edme Champion (Paris, 1888). The passage quoted is on pp. 30 f. There is an English translation, *What Is the Third Estate?* by M. Blondel, ed. by S. E. Finer (New York: Praeger, 1964). See also Karl Löwenstein, *Volk und Parlament nach der Staatstheorie der französischen Nationalversammlung von 1789: Studien zur Dogmageschichte der unmittelbaren Volksgesetzgebung*

(Munich: Drei Masken, 1922); Glyndon G. Van Deusen, *Sieyès: His Life and His Nationalism* (New York: Columbia University Press, 1932).

NOTES FOR CHAPTER 5: *Traditional Loyalties and National Unity*

1. Quoted in Edme Champion, "L'Unité nationale et la Révolution," *La Révolution française*, Vol. XIX (1890), p. 13.
2. M. Casenave, "La Fin d'un état souverain: le Béarn," *Séances et travaux de l'Académie des Sciences morales et politiques* (Séances du 25 janvier et 1 fevrier, 1930), Compte rendu (Paris: Alcan, 1930), pp. 439-477.
3. *Ibid.*, pp. 451 f.
4. In his "Observations sur le rapport du comité de constitution concernant la nouvelle organization de France" on October 2, 1789.
5. Philippe Sagnac, "L'Idée de la nation en France, 1788-1789," *Revue d'histoire politique et constitutionnelle*, Vol. I (Paris: 1937), pp. 158-163. There are some excellent studies on the nationalism of that pre-nationalistic period: Beatrice Fry Hyslop, *French Nationalism in 1789 According to the General Cahiers* (New York: Columbia University Press, 1934); Boyd C. Shafer, "Bourgeois Nationalism in the Pamphlets on the Eve of the French Revolution," *Journal of Modern History*, Vol. X (1938), pp. 31-50; C. Berlet, *Les Tendances unitaires et provincialistes en France à la fin du XVIIIe siècle* (Nancy: Imprimeries Réunies, 1913).
6. E. Bligny-Bondurand, *Cahiers de Doléances de la Sénéchaussée de Nîmes pour les Etats Généraux de 1789* (Nîmes: A. Chastanier, 1909), Vol. II, p. 589. Article VI of Chapter I of the Cahier put the need for constitutional reform strongly: "Qu'il serait également illusoire de s'occuper de remédier aux abus, si l'on ne remontait à leur source, et si l'on ne s'attachait à prévenir que la Nation n'y fut de nouveau exposée; qu'en conséquence, la constitution et les lois seront le premier objet dont s'occupera l'Assemblée nationale, afin que, ces principes étant posés, l'extirpation successive des abus en soit la conséquence naturelle, et que Sa Majesté, qui veillera à leur exécution, jouisse de la gloire d'avoir régénéré son peuple, et du bonheur, digne de son coeur royal, d'avoir opéré la felicité de ses sujets." *Ibid.*, p. 590.—The deputation of the city of Villeneuve-les-Avignon demanded that "les notables du Tiers Etat" be admitted to all military ranks, for the existing regulation of May 22, 1781, which required proof of four generations of noble ancestors from aspirants to officer rank, excluded merit and extinguished ambition and talent. *Ibid.*, p. 560.—Among the civil rights demanded were the inviolability of the persons of the deputies to the Estates General, individual liberty, and abolition of unwarranted arrest, freedom of the press, the inviolability of correspondence, equality of taxation, and ministerial responsibility. The model for all these demands was less the natural law than the British Constitution. *Ibid.*, pp. 579-581.
7. *Archives parlementaires de 1787 à 1860*, ed. by J. Mavidal and E. Laurent, 1st Series, 1787-1799 (Paris: Paul Dupont, 1867-1875), Vol. II, pp. 491 f.
8. A good example is A. J. Raup de Baptestein de Moulières, *Mémoire sur*

un moyen facile et infaillible de faire renaître le patriotisme en France, dans toutes les classes des citoyens, comme dans les deux sexes . . . et d'assurer le remboursement des dettes de l'état sans nouveaux impôts (Amsterdam, Paris: Desenne, 1789), 104 pp.

9. Aulard, *Histoire politique,* p. 51.

NOTES FOR CHAPTER 6: *Sieyès and the Third Estate*

1. Hans Kohn, *The Idea of Nationalism,* pp. 206 f.
2. Sieyès, *Qu'est-ce que le Tiers Etat?,* p. 30. Sieyès regarded the nobility as unproductive and parasitic, a useless charge on the nation.
3. A. Aulard, "Patrie, patriotisme au début de la Révolution française," *La Révolution française,* Vol. LXVIII (1915), p. 419.
4. Paul Chauvet, *1789: L'Insurrection parisienne et la prise de la Bastille* (Paris: Domat-Monchrestien, 1946).
5. The Declaration "meant to protect the individual in his natural rights against arbitrary action from the government by making clear to everyone what his rights were and by checking and balancing the separate parts of the government each by the others." It was "the reduction of Biblical ideas and philosophical tradition to the level of good citizenship." Louis Gottschalk, in *The University of Chicago Round Table,* No. 507 (December 7, 1947). See also David G. Ritchie, *Natural Rights* (London: Allen & Unwin, 1916).
6. In his "Préliminaire de la Constitution; reconnaissance et exposition raisonnée des droits de l'homme et du citoyen."
7. Emile Boutroux, "La conception française de la nationalité," *Bibliothèque et revue suisse,* Vol. LXXX (1915), No. 238. Liberty, equality and fraternity applied not only to individuals within a nation, but to the rights of nations within a universal society, demanding national liberty, equality among the nations, and fraternity of cosmopolitan collaboration.
8. Sieyès supported a strictly centralized regime because otherwise, "au lieu d'une administration générale, qui, partant d'un centre commun, va frapper uniformément les parties les plus reculées de l'Empire, au lieu de cette Législation, dont les éléments fournis par tous les citoyens se composent en remontant jusqu'à l'Assemblée nationale, chargée seule d'interpréter le voeu général, de ce voeu qui retombe ensuite avec tout le poids d'une force irrésistible sur les volontés elles-mêmes qui ont concouru à le former, nous n'aurons plus, dans l'intérieur du royaume, hérissé de barrières de toute espèce, qu'un chaos de coutumes, de règlements, de prohibitions particulières à chaque localité. Ce beau pays deviendra odieux aux voyageurs et aux habitants." Bastid, *Sieyès,* p. 363.
9. The historical title had been "King of France and Navarre." The new compromise was also symbolized in the *tricolore,* which Lafayette, as commander of the National Guard, designed by surrounding the white center, the color of the king and of the dynasty, with the red and blue of the revolutionary city of Paris.
10. Royalists saw clearly that the events of the fall of 1789 destroyed the

traditional basis of monarchy and of the nation. At the end of November 1789, the Royalist *Journal politique national*, No. 8, declared: "Je le déclare donc à la face de l'Europe: l'Assemblée nationale ayant tué la royauté dans la personne de Louis XVI, je ne vois de Souverain en France que cette Assemblée, et je révère avec elle l'Hôtel de Ville et plus encore les Districts, et plus encore la puissance du Palais-Royal, et les Forts de la Halle encore plus redoutables. Voilà mes législateurs et mes rois: je n'en connais point d'autres. Ils peuvent me compter au rang de leur sujets: et malheur, dans une Révolution, à qui, ne pouvant dresser des échafauds, ne dresse pas des autels. Le Représentant du plus petit canton, une fois député, ne dépendra plus de ses commettants: il leur sera étranger et sacré, comme représentant de la France entière; il leur sera également inviolable et irrevocable, comme membre du Souverain."—An anonymous pamphlet, *Souhait de Bonne Année à la France*, of January 1, 1790, expressed the wish that God might protect "that monarchy which he seemed always to single out from among the other states of the universe"; that the French, united in name, might also become united in sentiments and interests; and that the nation would oppose a change in the nature of its government, the abuses of which should be corrected, but the essence of which should not be destroyed.

11. The best analysis of the social implications from a Leninist point of view is to be found in Daniel Guérin, *La Lutte de classes sous la Première République: Bourgeois et "bras nus," 1793-1797*, 2 vols. (Paris: Gallimard, 1946). See the review by R. R. Palmer, in *Journal of Modern History*, Vol. XIX (1947), pp. 324-333.

12. See the excellent study by Georges Lefebvre, "Foules révolutionnaires," *Annales historiques de la Révolution française*, Vol. IX (1934), pp. 1-26. He points out that revolutionary mobs who take justice into their own hands and commit what appears to be lawless barbarism do not feel any guilt, but are convinced that they punish justly. "A travers toute la Révolution, on surprend çà et là l'idée d'une 'justice populaire' sommairement organisée, et, à défaut, plus sommairement appliquée encore, mais qui mériterait d'être étudiée de près, car elle jetterait sûrement beaucoup de lumière sur la mentalité collective révolutionnaire et même sur la mentalité collective des masses populaires en général." *Ibid.*, p. 19. Regarding the self-idolization of the revolutionary masses, M. Lefebvre says, "La société nouvelle qui naît ou va naître s'adore elle-même, consciente de sa perfection." *Ibid.*, p. 20. See also George Rudé, *The Crowd in the French Revolution* (New York: Oxford University Press, 1959). A special case of mass psychology in the very early days of 1789 is discussed in Jean Collot, "L'Affaire Reveillon, 27 et 28 avril 1789," *Revue des questions historiques*, Vol. CXXI (November 1934), pp. 35-55, and Vol. CXXII (1935), pp. 239-254. This incident was one of the first flare-ups of what Hippolyte Taine called "anarchie spontanée." Thomas Carlyle graphically explains the psychological situation of revolutionary masses: "Another thing we will not again specify, yet again beseech the Reader to imagine: the reign of Fraternity and Perfection. Imagine, we say, O

Reader, that the Millenium were struggling on the threshold, and yet not so much as groceries could be had,—owing to traitors. With what impetus would a man strike traitors, in that case. Ah! thou canst not imagine that; thou hast thy groceries safe in the shops, and little or no hope of a Millenium ever coming." *The French Revolution,* Vol. III, Bk. iii, Ch. 8 (London: George Bell, 1902), p. 181.

NOTES FOR CHAPTER 7: *Self-Determination and Equality*

1. Louis Villat, *La Corse de 1768 à 1789,* 2 vols. (Besançon: Millots Frères, 1924-1925).
2. See Sarah Wambaugh, *A Monograph on Plebiscites, with a Collection of Official Documents* (New York: Oxford University Press, 1920), pp. 33-40 and 173-268; Jules Viguier, "La Réunion d'Avignon et du Comtat-Venaissin à la France (août 1789-septembre 1791)," *La Révolution française,* Vol. XXI (1891), pp. 424-449; Vol. XXIII (1892), pp. 149-160; and Vol. XXVI (1894), pp. 150-168.
3. Quoted in Crane Brinton, *The Jacobins* (New York: Macmillan, 1930), p. 155, from A. Philippe, "La Société populaire d'Épinal," *La Révolution dans les Vosges,* Vol. IV, p. 133.
4. A member of the Jacobin club in Strasbourg proposed that the Jews be obliged to marry Christians. *Les Sociétés politiques de Strasbourg pendant les années 1790 à 1795,* ed. by Frederic Charles Heitz (Strasbourg: F. C. Heitz, 1863), p. 311. See also Philippe Sagnac, "Les Juifs et la Révolution, 1789-1791," *Revue d'histoire moderne et contemporaine,* Vol. I (1899-1900), pp. 5-23 and 209-234; Henri Lucien-Brun, *La Condition des Juifs en France depuis 1789* (2nd ed., Lyon: A. Effantin, 1901).
5. Montesquieu, *The Spirit of Laws,* Book XV, Ch. 1, tr. by Thomas Nugent (World's Great Classics, New York: Colonial Press, 1900), Vol. I, p. 235. Montesquieu goes on to state that in despotic countries where people live in political servitude, slavery is more tolerable than in others, and the condition of the slave there is hardly more burdensome than that of a subject. Everyone in those countries might as well be satisfied with the bare necessities of life. In opposition to Aristotle (see Hans Kohn, *The Idea of Nationalism* p. 52) and following Locke (*ibid.,* p. 181), he maintained that "as all men are born equal, slavery must be accounted unnatural" (Ch. 7, p. 240), and rejected the excuse that there is work so unpleasant that only slaves will do it. "No labor is so heavy but it may be brought to a level with the workman's strength, well regulated by equity and not by avarice. . . . I know not whether this article be dictated by my understanding or my heart. Possibly there is not that climate upon earth where the most laborious services might not with proper encouragement be performed by freemen. Bad laws having made lazy men, they have been reduced to slavery because of their laziness." Ch. 8, p. 241.
6. Camille Desmoulins, *Oeuvres,* ed. by J. Claretie (Paris: Charpentier, 1874), Vol. I. p. 277.

7. Carl Ludwig Lokke, *France and the Colonial Question: A Study of French Contemporary Opinion, 1763-1801* (New York: Columbia University Press, 1932). The racial unrest in St. Domingue and the war with England and Spain furnished the occasion for the rise of Toussaint l'Ouverture. Other studies on the subject are Carl L. Lokke, "French Dreams of Colonial Empire under Directory and Consulate," *Journal of Modern History*, Vol. II (1930), pp. 237-250; Charles Oscar Hardy, *The Negro Question in the French Revolution* (Menasha, Wis., 1911); Gustav Roloff, *Die Kolonialpolitik Napoleons I* (Munich: R. Oldenbourg, 1899); Prosper Marie Boissonnade, *Sainte-Domingue à la veille de la Révolution et la question de la représentation coloniale aux Etats Généraux, janvier 1788-juillet 1789* (Paris: Guenther; New York: Stechert, 1906); Armand Brette, "Les Gens de couleur libres et leurs députés en 1789," *La Révolution française*, Vol. XXIX (1895), pp. 385-407; Gaston-Martin, *La Doctrine coloniale de la France en 1789. Les colonies pendant la Révolution*, No. 3, Cahiers de la Révolution française, Centre d'Etudes de la Révolution française (Paris: Recueil Sirey, 1935); Léon Deschamps, *La Constituante et les colonies: La réforme coloniale* (Paris: Perrin, 1898).

8. A. Aulard, "Patrie, patriotisme au début de la Révolution française," *La Revolution française*, Vol. LXVIII (1915), pp. 415-443 and 481-525; Vol. LXIX (1916), pp. 35-59. The spokesman for the National Guards of the Dauphiné replied to those of Vivarais, who had proposed the federation of the two departments: "La nouvelle division du royaume en départements fait disparaître ces limites féodales qui semblaient annoncer autant de peuples différents que de provinces; elle a pour but de procurer à tous les mêmes lois, le même ordre de choses, les mêmes moeurs, et de nous réunir à jamais par le même amour de la patrie. Nous ne sommes plus des Dauphinois, vous n'êtes plus des Languedociens: nous sommes des Français libres, citoyens et soldats." *Ibid.*, p. 440.

9. Women, too, played a considerable role in these national festivals. Some of them demanded to be allowed to take the oath which bound all Frenchmen into one great family. In Romans, "the women, dressed in national fabrics, were decorated with *tricolore* ribbons, the outward sign of the patriotism which they hold in their hearts. Several mothers with suckling babies in their arms carried them to the altar of the fatherland to dedicate them to the nation of which they are the hope." Quoted from contemporary minutes by Aulard, *ibid.*, p. 46.—In his *Histoire apologétique du Comité ecclésiastique* (1791), Durand-Maillane wrote: "On ne savait ci-devant où était la patrie. Les Français croyaient la voir tout entière dans leurs rois, et ils les adoraient; mais les uns dans un état pénible de servitude et d'oppression, et c'était le plus grand nombre; les autres pour leurs propres avantages, et ceux-ci ne s'aimaient qu'eux, en affectant plus d'amour pour leurs bienfaiteurs. Cet égoisme se trouvait aux villes: les municipalités vivaient comme etrangères, et souvent comme ennemies entre elles. Enfin la Révolution est venue, et, pour la première fois, chacun de nous a goûté les délices de cette masse de liaisons qui, comme nous l'apprend Cicéron, réunit les citoyens à leur patrie comme au centre de

toutes leurs affections." *Ibid.*, pp. 58 f.—See also "Louis XVI proclamé empereur des Français au Champ de Mars, le 14 juillet 1790" (Paris: Cordier & Meymac, 1790), reprinted in *Annales révolutionnaires,* Vol. VI (1913), pp. 90-91.

10. A different inscription, composed in a different spirit, was to be found on one of the triumphal arches on the Champ de Mars on July 14, 1790: "Les Droits de l'Homme étaient méconnus depuis des siècles: ils étaient rétablis pour l'humanité entière."

11. *Poésies nationales de la Révolution française, ou Recueil complet des chants, hymnes, couplets, odes, chansons patriotiques* (Paris: Michel Fils Ainé & Bailly, 1836), pp. 32 f.

12. *Ibid.,* p. 38.

13. Manifestations of this unity were frequent all over France. In Strasbourg the newborn sons of two members of the National Guard, a Catholic named Brodard and a Protestant named Kohler, were baptized on the altar of the fatherland, each child having a godfather of his faith and a godmother of the other. The two ministers who performed the ceremony embraced publicly afterward. In the city of Montauban the inhabitants declared in their *profession patriotique* on June 9, 1790: "In the name of the fatherland and of liberty, all of us, Frenchmen united in the same spirit, without distinction of religion, rank or profession, declare to all Frenchmen, our brothers, that we regard ourselves as all equal before the law, observing, with different cults, the same principles and the same morality expressed in the laws of society." Far behind them seemed "the religious quarrels of the centuries of ignorance." The young citizens of Brittany and Anjou, assembled in January 1790 in Pontivy "to close the ranks of brotherly friendship," decided unanimously not to recognize any divisions but to regard themselves as "an immense family of brothers which, always united under the banner of liberty, will be a formidable bulwark against which the efforts of the aristocracy will break. Et, pour mettre le dernier sceau à nos engagements sacrés, nous arrêtons qu'un serment solennel et public appellera sur nous la protection du dieu de paix, que des coeurs purs invoquent avec confiance."

14. Louis Blanc, *Histoire de la Révolution française,* 12 vols. (Paris: Langlois & Leclercq, 1847-1862), Vol. IV, p. 365.

NOTES FOR CHAPTER 8: *Divisions and Unity in the New Nation*

1. Condorcet was one of the first to demand the vote for women. In July 1790 he published an article, "Sur l'admission de la femme au droit de cité." Women participated actively in the Revolution. Some tried to found Sociétés Patriotiques des Citoyennes; many Sociétés Fraternelles des Deux Sexes admitted both men and women over eighteen and played a role in popularizing the demands of advanced democracy.

2. "Anti-aristocrates, patriotes, voilà ce que sont les ouvriers parisiens. Démocrates, ils ne pensent à l'être que lorsque les bourgeois les y font penser, et, quant au mot de république, il semble encore ignoré dans les

faubourgs." Aulard, *Histoire politique*, p. 81. "Les orateurs du parti démocratique, état-major sans armée, se sentaient alors fort en avance sur l'opinion de la masse, et toute leur ambition, tout leur espoir, c'était d'arriver à faire comprendre aux prolétaires qu'ils étaient lésés, qu'il y avait une nouvelle classe privilégiée." *Ibid.*, p. 82.

3. See the excellent study by Karl Dietrich Erdmann, *Volkssouveränität und Kirche* (Köln: Kölner Universitätsverlag, 1949).

4. *Ibid.*

5. Fernand Baldensperger, *Le Mouvement des idées dans l'émigration française* (*1789-1815*) (Paris: Plon, 1924), Vol. I, pp. 299 f. Joseph de Maistre expressed the same thought: "Tant que le Roi est à sa place, il est lui seul la patrie; au moment même où il disparait, la patrie est tout, et c'est elle qu'il faut défendre à tout prix pour la rendre au roi." "Mémoire sur la position de la Maison de Savoie en octobre 1813, quatrième supposition," *Oeuvres complètes*, 14 vols. (Lyon: Vitte & Perrussel, 1884-1886), Vol. XII, pp. 380-399.—The other great theoretician of the counter-revolution, the Vicomte de Bonald, defended the emigration and its patriotism on the same grounds. In his *De l'émigration,* he wrote: "L'émigration, forcée pour quelques-uns, fut légitime pour tous. Le sol n'est pas la patrie de l'homme civilisé; il n'est pas même celle du sauvage, qui se croit toujours dans sa patrie lorsqu'il emporte avec lui les ossements de ses pères. Le sol n'est la patrie que de l'animal . . . pour l'homme en société publique, le sol qu'il cultive n'est pas plus la patrie que pour l'homme domestiqué la maison qu'il habite n'est la famille. L'homme civilisé ne voit la patrie que dans les lois qui régissent la société, dans l'ordre qui y règne, dans les pouvoirs qui la gouvernent, dans la religion qu'on y professe, et pour lui son pays peut n'être pas toujours sa patrie." *Oeuvres* (Paris, 1852), Vol. II, p. 370. See also Sir Bernard Mallet, *Mallet du Pan and the French Revolution* (New York: Longmans, Green, 1902). On the emigration in general, see Jean Vidalene, *Les émigrés français, 1789-1825* (Publications de la Faculté des Lettres de l'Université de Caen, 1963).

6. For Condé, see Joseph Viaud, *Les Epoques critiques du patriotisme français* (Paris: Bloud, 1910), p. 80; for Villers, see Baldensperger, *Le Mouvement des idées,* p. 317.

7. Huntley Dupre, *Lazare Carnot,* p. 251.

8. Joseph de Maistre, *Considérations sur la France,* ed. by René Johannet and François Vermale (Paris: Vrin, 1936), pp. 43, 45. Maistre was convinced that the contemporary praise for the United States was unjustified. He did not trust the stability and institutions of the new nation and drew attention to the jealousy and wrangling among the various cities for the honor of being the seat of the Congress, prophesying that Washington would never be built. *Ibid.,* p. 94.

9. Bonald, *Oeuvres* (Paris; 1817) Vol. VI, p. 118. "La révolution a moins corrompu les moeurs qu'elle n'a affaibli les esprits. La connaissance des hommes et de la société parait surtout entièrement effacée; et on ignore à la fois ce qu'il y a de mauvais dans le coeur de l'homme et ce qu'il y a de

bon." *Ibid.*, Vol. VI, p. 192. It is not without interest that Bonald looked upon the restored monarchy and church in the Spain of Ferdinand VII as an ideal.

10. A. Aulard, "Le patriotisme et la Révolution française: Les émigrés," *La Révolution française*, Vol. LXX (1917), pp. 385-415, especially p. 404. See also Jacques Godechot, *La Contre-Révolution, Doctrine et Action, 1789-1804* (Paris: Presses Universitaires de France, 1961) and Duc de Castries, *Le Testament de la Monarchie:* III. *Les Émigrés 1789-1814* (Paris: Arthème Fayard, 1962).

11. B. Mirkine-Guetzevitch, "Le 150e anniversaire de la République française," *Renaissance*, Vol. I (New York, 1943), p. 112.

12. Aulard, *Histoire politique*, p. 278.

NOTES FOR CHAPTER 9: *Missionary Nationalism and the Problem of Liberation*

1. The decree of May 22, 1790, concerning the right of making peace and war reserved the right to declare war to the legislature upon the formal request of the king. If in urgent cases the executive should take war measures, it must immediately notify the legislature. "If, on receipt of this notification, the legislative body regards the hostilities already begun as a culpable aggression on the part of the ministers or any other agent of the executive, the author of this aggression shall be prosecuted for treason (*lèse-nation*); the National Assembly declaring to that effect that the French nation renounces the undertaking of any war for the purpose of conquest, and that it will never use its forces against the liberty of any people" (Art. IV). The Constitution of 1791 repeated this declaration in Title VI, dealing with relations with foreign nations.—The citizens of Strasbourg in a meeting on the Place d'Armes on March 18, 1790, voted an address to the National Assembly: "Sur cette place où nos pères ne se sont donnés qu'à regret à la France, nous venons cimenter par nos serments notre union avec elle; nous avons juré et nous jurons de verser jusqu'à la dernière goutte de notre sang pour maintenir la Constitution. Si Strasbourg n'a pas eu la gloire de donner l'exemple la première aux villes du royaume, elle aura du moins celle d'être, par l'énergie du patriotisme de ses habitants, un des boulevards les plus forts de la liberté française." Merlin de Douai maintained: "Le peuple alsacien s'est uni au peuple français parce qu'il l'a voulu; c'est donc sa volonté seule, et non le traité de Munster, qui a légitimé l'union." See also Pierre Muret, "L'Affaire des princes possessionnés d'Alsace et les origines du conflit entre la Révolution et l'Europe," *Revue d'histoire moderne et contemporaine*, Vol. I (1899-1900), pp. 433-456 and 566-592.

2. *The Political Writings of Joel Barlow* (New York: Mott & Lyon, 1796), p. 233. Hans Kohn, *The Idea of Nationalism*, pp. 298 f.

3. Savoy was incorporated into France on November 27, 1792, and Nice on January 31, 1793. The Duchy of Savoy formed part of the Kingdom of Sardinia, but the inhabitants of the seven provinces spoke French and

sympathized with the Revolution. See Sarah Wambaugh, *A Monograph on Plebiscites*, pp. 41-45 and 269-301; Jules Masse, *Histoire de l'annexion de la Savoie à la France en 1792*, 3 vols. (Grenoble: Albier, 1891-1895). The Allobroges were a Celtic tribe which settled in Savoy at the time of Hannibal. The choice of the name further attests to the current enthusiasm for the Roman world.

4. Sorel, *L'Europe et la Révolution*, Vol. I, p. 551.
5. Letter of February 1, 1792, *The Diary and Letters of Gouverneur Morris* (New York: Scribner's, 1888), Vol. I, p. 509. The demand for war against the Emperor was supported by the revival of the traditional anti-Austrian policy of the monarchy. This policy was identified with the great days of France, while the friendship with Austria, which had been inaugurated by the choice of Marie Antoinette as future queen, was judged to have brought defeats and misfortunes.
6. One of the leaders of the Feuillants, Antoine Barnave (1761-1793), later wrote that the revolutionists "imagined that all the cabinets of Europe nurtured plans in accord with their own views, and in their newspapers endowed with an aspect of consistency all the circumstances that would alarm the nation and make it wish to force its way by a violent explosion out of the situation in which it found itself." *Oeuvres*, ed. by Béranger de La Drome, 4 vols. (Paris: Challamel, 1843), Vol. I, pp. 208 f.—"Robespierre's opposition to the war was realistic, based upon a knowledge of the internal condition of France rather than upon any dread of the horrors of war or any repugnance to use it as an instrument of national policy." Eagan, *Maximilian Robespierre*, p. 49.—While Robespierre opposed the war through fear that it would strengthen his domestic enemies, he insisted on February 10, 1792, that at least all necessary preparations for war be made. He demanded that all citizens be called up without distinction for the defense of the fatherland, that the army be indoctrinated with a revolutionary spirit, that everyone be continuously on the watch for domestic enemies, and that the manufacture of arms be intensified. On March 26, 1792, he called for a last effort to avoid war by a solemn proclamation in all languages of the sacred principles of the Revolution. If this were done, he expected to see the despots beg humbly for peace and give the French entire satisfaction. But if the despots refused, then, he proclaimed, "We shall wage war; let the whole nation rise and let us wage the war of the people and not that of kings." See Georges Michon, *Robespierre et la guerre révolutionnaire, 1791-1792* (Paris: Marcel Rivière, 1937).
7. It is worthwhile to consider the growing distrust and animosity between the revolutionary terrorists speaking French and those speaking German, "the language of slaves," in the Alsace. Both came from outside Alsace— the French largely from neighboring French departments or from Paris, the Germans from beyond the Rhine. Few indigenous Alsacians participated in the terror. One of them was a shoemaker, Johannes Jung (1760-1794), who after his execution was praised for his exclusive devotion to the fatherland ("Jung kannte nichts als sein Vaterland"). Friedrich

Cotta spoke of him and others in his address "Die Fülle der Vaterlandsliebe" [The fullness of patriotism], delivered in memory of the martyrs
of liberty on October 31, 1794. Another German friend of the Revolution
was Johann-Friedrich Butenschön (1764-1842), a Holsteiner who was
saved from execution by the Thermidor and ended his life peacefully as
professor in Mainz and later as "pfälzischer Konsistorial- und Kreisschulrat"
in Speier. See Roger Jaquel, "Euloge Schneider en Alsace," *Annales
Historiques de la Révolution Française*, 1932, pp. 1-27, 103-115, 336-342;
1933, pp. 61-73; and especially 1935, pp. 218-248; his "Un Terroriste
Alsacien, le Cordonnier Jung (1760-1794)," in *La Bourgeoisie Alsacienne,
études d'histoire sociale* (Strasbourg: F.-X. Le Roux, 1954); and his "Les
Jacobins Allemands en Alsace," in *L'Alsace et la Suisse à travers les siècles*
(Strasbourg, F.-X. Le Roux, 1952).

8. Quoted in Woldemar Wenck, *Deutschland vor hundert Jahren:* Pt. II.
   Politische Meinungen und Stimmungen in der Revolutionszeit (Leipzig:
   F. W. Grunow, 1890), pp. 48 f.

9. Even Robespierre, not yet the leader in the implacable war against
   Europe, was convinced that the Revolution would spread, but at that
   time he regarded its firm establishment in France a better means to that
   end than a war of uncertain outcome. On February 10, 1792, he said: "C'est
   ici qu'il faut préparer la révolution du monde au lieu de la faire avorter
   en portant le fléau de le guerre chez des peuples qui ne nous ont point
   attaqués et en qui nous ne devons voir que des frères." And on March 26,
   1792, he declared: "Une fois établie en France, la liberté, par le cours
   naturel des choses, étendra d'elle-même ses paisibles conquêtes dans le
   reste du monde; quand les peuples sont assez éclairés et assez malheureux
   pour vouloir être libres, ils le sont. Les tyrans tombent d'eux-mêmes
   quand ils sont mûrs. L'heureuse contagion de nos principes et le spectacle
   de notre bonheur ameneront insensiblement cette époque, et alors
   l'Allemagne n'aura pas plus besoin de nos armes pour secouer le joug du
   despotisme que nous n'avons eu besoin du secours de l'Allemagne pour
   renverser la Bastille et conquérir une constitution."

10. Emile Bourgeois, *Manuel historique de politique étrangère*, 4 vols. (Paris:
    Berlin Frères, 1901), Vol. II, pp. 52 f. Similarly, Jean Jaurès, in his
    Histoire socialiste (1789-1900) (3 vols., Paris: Jules Rouff, n.d.), Vol. II:
    La Législative (1791-1792), writes: "Mais d'autre part, cette grande
    aventure de la guerre a fait tant de mal à notre pays et à la
    liberté, elle a si violemment déchainé, dans la France de la philosophie
    et des droits de l'homme, les instincts brutaux, elle a si bien préparé la
    banqueroute de la Révolution en césarisme, que nous sommes obligés de
    nous demander avec angoisse: Cette guerre de la France contre l'Europe
    était-elle vraiment nécessaire? Etait-elle vraiment commandée par les
    dispositions des puissances étrangères et par l'état de notre propre pays?
    Enfin, pour dire toute notre pensée, il nous répugnerait beaucoup de
    dégrader ou de méconnaître le patriotisme fervent, l'enthousiasme sacré
    qui se mêla à la grande aventure guerrière; mais si à l'origine même de
    cette aventure héroique nous démêlons une part d'intrigues, de roueries,

de mensonges, c'est notre devoir d'avertir les générations nouvelles. Je crois pouvoir dire, après avoir bien étudié les documents, que, pour une bonne part, la guerre a été machinée. La Gironde y a conduit la France par tant d'artifices, qu'on n'a pas le droit de dire que la guerre était vraiment inévitable" (pp. 795 ff.).—"Mais, si tout cela est vrai, il y a bonne part, la guerre a été machinée. La Gironde y a conduit la France de la Révolution, et la guerre va éclater. Nous savons, nous, que cela n'est point vrai; que Brissot, dans ces interrogations menaçantes, supprime toutes les nuances, ne tient aucun compte des difficultés sans nombre qui paralysaient les puissances, des réserves que neutralisaient leurs déclarations. Nous savon déjà, notamment, qu'à Pilnitz l'empereur d'Autriche et le roi de Prusse n'ont pris que des engagements incertains, subordonnés au concours des autres puissances qui, comme l'Angleterre, se dérobent. Mais enfin, si cela est vrai, il n'y a plus en effet à hésiter. Il faut révéler à la France toute l'étendue du péril et sonner dans tout le pays la guerre sainte pour la liberté." *Ibid.*, p. 798.—"Mais provoquer les puissances, leur tenir un langage menaçant, et s'exposer ainsi à convertir en résolutions réellement belliqueuses leurs parades grossières ou leurs velléités incertaines, c'est un crime contre la Révolution, livrée ainsi à tous les hasards. Ce crime s'aggrave quand, pour décider la France à ces démarches imprudentes, on exagère à plaisir la faiblesse et les embarras de l'étranger, dont les difficultés intérieures ne dépassaient certainement pas celles de la France elle-même. Et pourtant, après avoir égaré par ces sophismes une assemblée sans information et sans réflexion, Brissot la grise de paroles fanfaronnes" *Ibid.*, p. 799.

11. A peasant, who had been taught to read and write by monks for whom he worked, enlisted in August 1792 as a volunteer. Among his papers was found a "Prayer of the French Republican Soldier" that reads: "God of all justice, eternal Being and supreme sovereign, arbiter of the destiny of all men . . . take under your blessed protection a generous nation which is fighting only for equality." Quoted from "Journal de marche d'un volontaire de 1792: Journal du sergent Fricasse," *Mémoires patriotiques*, ed. by Loredan Larchey (Paris, 1882), in Sorel, *L'Europe et la Révolution*, Vol. I., p. 540.—Such enthusiasm was in no way general, however. Another volunteer, François Xavier Joliclerc, wrote home to his mother on December 13, 1793: "When the fatherland needs us for her defense, we must fly to it as I run to a good meal. Our life, our property and abilities do not belong to us. All that belongs to the nation, to the fatherland. I know very well that you and all the other inhabitants of our town do not share these sentiments. They are insensible to the cry of this outraged fatherland, and all they do for her, they do because they are forced into it." *Volontaire aux armées de la Révolution: Ses lettres, 1793-1796*, ed. by Etienne Joliclerc (Paris: Perrin, 1905), p. 142. The same young man wrote on May 30, 1794 ("Style esclave," as he called it, preceding the date with the new date, "Ce 11 prairial de la République française, une, indivisible et impérissable"): "You say that the volunteers from our village write letters like sermons. I ask you, who is the citizen

of Froidefontaine who dares to call himself a volunteer? . . . No, no, there are no volunteers. Some of them were bought, as one buys hogs, and the others were forced to leave by the decrees of the Convention. Thus they are in no way volunteers, and I am the only one of the town to whom this beautiful name belongs. I take glory in it and I will uphold it at the risk of my life." *Ibid.*, p. 168.

12. The international spirit was different in 1790. Then, on May 18, Volney proposed to the National Constituent Assembly the convocation of an *Assemblée des nations* to elaborate a statute of equality for all nations; all enjoying the same natural rights and accepting the same rules of justice; none having the right to invade another's territory and deprive it of liberty and natural advantages; such an invasion to be repulsed by all member nations acting together, as any act of aggression tended to endanger the liberty and safety of all. In this spirit the French nation renounced war and any desire for territorial aggrandisement. A. Aulard, "La Société des nations et la Révolution française," *La Révolution française*, Vol. LXXI (1918), pp. 104-121; B. Mirkine Guetzkevich, "La Révolution française et l'idée de rénonciation à la guerre," *ibid.*, Vol. LXXXII-LXXXIII (1929-1930), pp. 255-268; E. Fournol, "Le Caractère international de la Révolution française," *ibid.*, new series, No. 7 (1936), pp. 216-228. "Au seuil de 1793, il ne restait plus rien de l'esprit international de 1790, rien qu'un principe nu. Le champ de la guerre était libre, et devant la conquête révolutionnaire, et devant les esprits nationaux. L'esprit international et l'esprit national enfermés dans le même berceau avant de se combattre annonçaient déjà leur séparation. L'idéalisme lui-même n'était plus international pour tous les peuples, mais national pour chacun." Fournol, *ibid.*, p. 226. See also Danton's warning, on April 13, 1793, against the dangers of an ideological war and the discussion in Jules Bardevant, *La Révolution Française et le Droit de la Guerre Continentale* (Paris: Larose et Forel. 1901) pp. 164-165.

13. It is psychologically and historically unjust to accuse the French patriots of insincerity, as René Johannet does: "Pour peu que l'on se familiarise avec la littérature nationalitaire, si abondante en Europe depuis un siècle et demi, on est vite frappé de son insincérité quasi-totale. Tous ces gens-là, qu'ils soient de France, d'Allemagne, d'Italie, ou d'ailleurs, masquent des appétits (quelquefois légitimes) derrière des théories plus ou moins adroites." *Le Principe des nationalités* (new ed., Paris: Nouvelle librairie nationale, 1923), p. 109.

14. See Hans Kohn, *The Idea of Nationalism*, pp. 482-487; Henri Pirenne, *Histoire de Belgique* (Brussels: Maurice Lamartin, 1926), Vol. VI, pp. 37-40; Orient Lee, "Les Comités et les clubs des patriotes belges et liégeois, 1791, an III" (Paris: Thèse d'Université, 1931); Suzanne Tassier, *Histoire de la Belgique sous l'occupation française en 1792 et 1793* (Brussels: Falk Fils, 1934).

15. Sarah Wambaugh, in *A Monograph on Plebiscites*, emphasized that the plebiscites in Belgium and in the Rhineland were fakes. In its further annexations the French Revolution abandoned the plebiscite except in

the case of the small territory of Mulhouse, an independent state in the Upper Alsace, in close alliance with the Swiss Confederation, which united with France on January 28, 1798, and in the case of the Republic of Geneva, where the citizens voted under military coercion for union with France in April 1798. See Edouard Chapuisat, *De la Terreur à l'annexion. Genève et la République française, 1793-1798* (Geneva and Paris: 1914).

NOTES FOR CHAPTER 10: *Revolutionary Terror and National Virtue*

1. An article in *La Révolution de Paris et de Brabant*, No. 141 (March 17-24, 1792), wrote of the Phrygian bonnet: "Avec l'air du 'ça ira,' on mène le 'peuple' au bout du monde, à travers les armées combinées de toute l'Europe. Paré d'un noeud de rubans aux troix couleurs, il oublie ses plus chers intérêts pour ne s'occuper que de la chose publique et quitte gaiement ses foyers pour aller aux frontières attendre l'ennemi. La vue d'un bonnet rouge de laine le transporte, et qu'on n'en prenne pas occasion de le railler! Son enthousiasme est des plus respectables et des mieux fondés. On lui a dit que ce bonnet de laine était en Grèce et à Rome l'emblème de l'affranchissement de toutes les servitudes et le signe de ralliement de tous les ennemis du despotisme. C'en est assez pour lui. De ce moment, chaque citoyen veut avoir ce bonnet. . . ." See also the popular song, "Le Bonnet de la liberté," 1793, in *Poésies nationales de la Révolution française*, pp. 123 f.

2. At that time the Parisian masses first used the red flag in opposition to the official tricolor. It had originally been the flag of martial law. The *Décret contre les attroupements, ou loi martiale* of October 21, 1789, stated in Article II that declaration of martial law was to be made public by hanging a red flag out of the main window of the town hall and by carrying another through streets and squares, while, according to Article XII, after the reestablishment of order the red flag was to be withdrawn and replaced for eight days by a white one.

3. "Le peuple français se compose des patriotes, le reste est ilotte ou n'est rien." From a letter from Saint-Just and Le Bas to the Committee of Public Safety of 7 frimaire (November 27, 1793), quoted in Charles Vellay, "Lettres Inédites de Saint-Just (1791-1794), *Revue historique de la Révolution française*, Vol. I (1910), p. 491.

4. The text of this speech was found among Robespierre's papers after his death, by the Commission charged with their examination, and was published. The passage is on p. 16 of the original pamphlet. Reprinted in *Oeuvres de Maximilien Robespierre*, ed. by Albert Laponneraye (Paris, 1840), Vol. III, p. 702. Montesquieu wrote in *L'Esprit des lois* (Book V, Ch. 11): "Virtue in a republic is a most simple thing; it is love of the republic; it is a sensation and not the consequence of acquired knowledge; a sensation that may be felt by the meanest as well as by the highest person in the state."

5. Albert Mathiez, in his *Les Origines des cultes révolutionnaires (1789-1792)* (Paris: G. Bellais, 1904), wrongly saw a connection between the

patriotism of 1789 and the revolutionary religion of 1793. Even in 1793 the revolutionary religion included only a minority of Frenchmen among its adherents.

6. "Tout était conforme à la science; l'égalité des jours et des nuits, à l'équinoxe d'automne, ouvrait au 22 septembre l'ère de l'égalité civile. Ainsi, on refletait dans la loi les pensées constellées de l'univers. La grande République se trouve, comme une portion du firmament, inscrite dans la sphère celeste, elle s'ordonne comme l'équation de la géométrie des mondes. Quelle garantie pour l'édifice nouveau! Qui pourra le renverser puis-qu'il a pour lui l'armée des étoiles?" Edgar Quinet, *La Révolution*, 2 vols., 7th ed. (Paris: Librairie Internationale, 1869), Vol. II, p. 88.

7. "Voilà le fond de l'homme dans toute la Révolution. Il veut la liberté, du moins il croit la vouloir. Mais l'idée qu'il s'en fait a été formée sous le despotisme de l'ancien régime. Elle est pleine encore du génie intraitable du passé. Chacun devenu roi dit royalement: 'Tel est mon bon plaisir.' Malheur à qui pense et sent autrement! Celui-là est un ennemi qu'il faut extirper comme rebelle." *Ibid.*, p. 241.—"The people of Paris had thought themselves to be the kings of France because they had been told that the people were the sovereign; they now began to think of themselves as the kings of the world, because they were told that the world wished to accept their laws." Sorel, *L'Europe et la Révolution*, Vol. II, p. 110.

8. Marat was full of contempt for the people, for the common man. "He wishes the people to be led by a wise man. Perhaps he dreams of a dictatorship of persuasion for himself. Later on, he will demand a dictator-ship of any kind." Marat was one of the earliest adherents of general suffrage, but what he wished was "une démocratie césarienne." Aulard, *Histoire politique*, p. 80. See also Louis R. Gottschalk, *Jean Paul Marat: A Study in Radicalism* (New York: Greenberg, 1927).

9. *Oeuvres complètes de Saint-Just*, Vol. II, p. 76. See also the interesting discussion of the general will on April 24, 1793, *ibid.*, Vol. I, pp. 428 f. On Saint-Just see Pierre Trahard, "Le révolutionnaire idéal selon Saint-Just," *Europe*, Vol. L (1930), pp. 413-422.

10. F. A. Aulard, *La Société des Jacobins: Recueil de documents pour l'histoire du club des Jacobins de Paris*, 6 vols. (Paris: Librairies Jouaust, 1889-1897), Vol. V, p. 490.

11. In an article published on Feb. 26, 1792, in the *Journal de Paris*, "de la cause des désordres qui troublent la France et arrêtent le développement de la liberté," André Chénier wrote: "Une simple équivoque a suffi à tout: la constitution étant fondée sur cette éternelle vérité, *la souveraineté* du peuple, il n'a fallu que persuader aux tribunes du club qu'elles sont le *peuple*. Cette définition est presque généralement adoptée par les publicistes, faiseurs de journaux. Et quelques centaines d'oisifs réunis dans un jardin ou dans un spectacle, ou quelques troupes de bandits qui pillent des boutiques, sont effrontément appelés le *peuple;* et les plus insolents despotes n'ont jamais reçu des courtisans les plus avides un encens aussi vil et aussi fastidieux que l'adulation impure dont deux ou trois mille usurpateurs de la souveraineté nationale sont enivrés, chaque jour

par les écrivains et les orateurs de ces Sociétés qui agitent la France." *Oeuvres en prose de André Chénier*, ed. by Louis Moland (Paris: Garnier Frères, 1879), p. 126. "La doctrine que toute délation, vraie ou fausse, est toujours une chose louable et utile, y est nonseulement pratiquée, mais enseignée au moins comme ce que les Jésuites appelaient une *opinion probable*." *Ibid.*, p. 127.—"On y attaque aussi quelquefois des coupables, et on les y attaque avec une férocité, un acharnement, une mauvaise foi, qui les font paraître innocents. Là, se distribuent les brevets de patriotisme. Tous les membres, tous les amis de ces congregations sont de bons citoyens; tous les autres sont des perfides. La seule admission dans ce corps, comme le baptême de Constantin, lave tous les crimes, efface le sang et les meurtres. . . . Ces Sociétés, se tenant toutes par la main, forment une espèce de chaîne électrique autour de la France. Au même instant, dans tous les recoins de l'empire, elles s'agitent ensemble, poussent les mêmes cris, impriment les mêmes mouvements, qu'elles n'avaient certes pas grand'peine à prédire d'avance." *Ibid.*, p. 128.—In another article, "Sur les sociétés patriotiques," published on April 27, 1792, Chénier goes on to speak about the Jacobins: "Ils diront qu'en prêchant les lois et la paix vous ne cherchez qu'à semer le trouble, puisque vous cherchez à soulever tous les citoyens contre leur tyrannie, et que vous ne les laissez point régner en paix. Ils appelleront vos écrits des écrits *infâmes*, comme si la raison, le courage, l'amour des lois et de la liberté, l'horreur pour les tyrans, et surtout pour la pire espèce de tyrans, je veux dire ceux qui tyrannisent au nom de la liberté, pouvaient être des choses *infâmes*; mais ces messieurs se sont promis d'altérer toute la langue, comme ils ont déjà perverti le sens des mots *Patriotisme, Civisme, Liberté, Egalité, République*, etc., et, dans leur nouveau jargon, un ouvrage est *infâme* lorsqu'il dévoile des *infamies*." *Ibid.*, pp. 171-172. See also the interesting discussion between Marie-Joseph Chénier and his brother André about the Jacobins. Marie-Joseph's articles are reprinted in this volume on pp. 390-406; and André's answer on pp. 187-205.

12. *Mémoires de B. Barère*, ed. by Hippolyte Carnot and David (Paris: Jules Labitte, 1842), Vol. IV, p. 408.—"Discours sur la réorganisation de l'armée," on Feb. 12, 1793, *Oeuvres complètes de Saint-Just*, Vol. I, p. 416.

13. "Fragments sur les institutions républicaines," *ibid.*, Vol. II, pp. 506, 530. Saint-Just's prescriptions for the true republic contained much of the civilized spirit of the eighteenth century, and thus were contradictory. Many passages expressed distrust of government and a deep concern for the freedom of the individual. "The freedom of the people rests in its private life; do not disturb it. Disturb only the ungrateful and the evil ones. Let the government be not a power in its relation with the citizen, but a means of harmony; let it be a power only to protect that state of simplicity against force itself. . . . Do not oppress, that is all. Everyone will know well how to find his happiness. A people among whom the prejudice was instilled that it owed its happiness to the government

would not retain it very long." *Ibid.*, p. 507. "Il faut faire peur à ceux qui gouvernent. Il ne faut jamais faire peur au peuple." *Ibid.*, p. 530.

14. *Ibid.*, pp. 504, 517. According to Saint-Just a republican government had as its principle either virtue or terror. "What do those want who want neither virtue nor terror?" Virtue alone could establish a new form of government. "All arts have produced their marvelous works: the art of government has so far produced only monsters." It is interesting to note that since the death of Saint-Just the word "vertu" has been hardly used in France. Saint-Just also understood that "le bonheur est une idée neuve en Europe," but he abhorred those who had "a horrible idea (une idée affreuse)" of happiness and confounded it with pleasure.

15. *Ibid.*, p. 129. In another letter from the front, Saint-Just wrote appreciatively of an officer: "C'était un homme de résolution, il faisait la guerre comme il la faut faire ici, il ne laissait point respirer l'ennemi." Vellay, *Lettres Inédites*, p. 491.

16. "Rapport sur la nécessité de déclarer le gouvernement révolutionnaire jusqu'à la paix." Oct. 10, 1793, Saint-Just, *Oeuvres complètes*, Vol. II, p. 84.

17. *Ibid.*, pp. 85 f. The same contrast between French ardor and German inertia is noted in a letter from Saint-Just's friend Gateau to the adjunct minister of war Daubigny, praising Saint-Just's arrival among the armies of the East and the axe-blows he dealt "to the indolence and German stupidity of the Alsatians." The letter continues: "He has revivified, reanimated, regenerated everything . . . the holy guillotine is in the most brilliant state of activity and the beneficent terror is producing here in a miraculous way what one could not hope for from at least a century of reason and philosophy." Edouard Fleury, *Saint-Just et la Terreur* (Paris: Didier, 1852), Vol. II, pp. 45 f. See also Eugene Newton Curtis, *Saint-Just, Colleague of Robespierre* (New York: Columbia University Press, 1935); Albert Ollivier, *Saint-Juste et la Force des choses* (Paris: Gallimard, 1935); Geoffrey Bruun, *Saint-Just, Apostle of the Terror* (Boston: Houghton Mifflin, 1932).

18. "Rapport sur la loi contre les Anglais," October 16, 1793, Saint-Just, *Oeuvres complètes*, Vol. II, pp. 99 ff. Regarding the detention of the English in France, Saint-Just said: "La détention de ces étrangers ne doit les priver que des moyens de correspondre avec leur pays et de nous nuire. Cette détention doit être douce et commode: car la République exerce contre eux une mesure politique, et non pas un ressentiment." *Ibid.*, p. 101.

19. Johann Wilhelm von Archenholz (1748-1812), after spending two years in Paris, wrote in his *Minerva* (Vol. I, p. 22) that even in case of victory over all France, the Allies would have to destroy the majority of the nation to bring about a return to the *ancien régime*.

20. *Discours de Danton*, ed. by André Fribourg (Paris: Hachette, 1910), p. 52. See Scott Lythe, "Robespierre, Danton and the Levée en masse," *The Journal of Modern History*, Vol. XXX, No. 4 (Dec. 1958), pp. 325-337.

21. "In leaving the armies to be supplied by requisitions rather than maga-

322 *Prelude to nation states*

zines the Republicans effected a revolution in logistics, and in throwing their half-trained troops into battle in rushing columns or in fanned-out lines of *tirailleurs,* men who fought, fired and took cover as individuals (a practice suggested by the War of American Independence), they broke away from the Frederician system of solid battalions, and gave impetus to a revolution in tactics." R. R. Palmer, in *Makers of Modern Strategy,* ed. by Edward Mead Earle (Princeton University Press, 1944), p. 68.

22. R. R. Palmer, *Twelve Who Ruled: The Committee of Public Safety During the Terror* (Princeton University Press, 1941), p. 211. For Danton, see *Discours de Danton,* p. 230.

23. "The people hate the foreigners; they are ambitious, they intoxicate themselves easily with victory: nothing easier than to induce them to regard the aggrandizement of the Republic as the necessary condition for its independence. The whole people is imbued with some of that pride and of that contempt for kings which have naturally exalted the republican armies, in short, with the feeling that the French alone are reasonable human beings and that it is their task to command other peoples." Sorel, *L'Europe et la Révolution,* Vol. IV, p. 130.—On the nationalization of the French army, see Jules Leverrier, *La Naissance de l'armée nationale, 1789-1794* (Paris: Editions socialistes internationales, 1939); Eugène Deprez, *Les Volontaires nationaux (1791-1793)*: Etude sur la formation et l'organisation des bataillons, d'après les archives communales et départementales (Paris: R. Chapelot, 1908); Georges Michon, "L'Armée et la politique intérieure sous la Convention," *Annales historiques de la Révolution française,* Vol. IV (1927), pp. 529-546; Pierre Caron, *La Défense nationale de 1792 à 1795* (Paris: Hachette, 1912).—This "militarization" also left its mark on Babeuf's socialism. He himself compared his system of common property, administration, and distribution in *Le Tribun du peuple* of November 30, 1795, with the army. What was possible, he wrote, in the twelve French armies providing for 1,200,000 men, should be possible on a general scale for the whole nation. The question did not occur to him whether such an armed system of security and equality was compatible with liberty.

NOTES FOR CHAPTER 11: *War and The Spirit of Nationalism*

1. "Hymne à la liberté récitée à l'ouverture du Lycée, à la fin de 1792," *Poésies nationales,* p. 73. There are many other examples of the *esprit guerrier* of the new nationalism. The Marseillaise is an excellent example of the period: "Qu'un sang impur abreuve nos sillons."

2. "Strophes à l'Être suprême" (1793), by Philippe Aristide Valcour (1751-1815), *ibid.,* pp. 153 f. This new religion and its liturgy fused the rational universalism of the eighteenth century with the new patriotic fervor. Thus Theveneau, in his "Ode Révolutionnaire" (1793) addressed the hostile nations:

> Ministres impuissans de tyrans sanguinaires,
> Que peuvent contre nous vos efforts insensés?

La France brisera vos glaives mercenaires
Sur les corps palpitans de vos rois écrasés.

Sortez, sortez plutôt de votre longue ivresse;
À nos bras fraternels que vos bras soient unis:
La liberté, voilà votre unique déesse;
Vos prêtres, vos tyrans, voilà vos ennemis.

Peuples, ne formons plus qu'une seule patrie;
Marchons . . . mais quel spectacle a frappé mes regards?
Je te vois, je t'entends, divinité chérie.
Liberté, nous volons sous tes saints étendards.

Ibid., p. 157. See also the "Ode à la liberté" of the same year by Louis Vigée (1758-1820), which proclaims France unafraid because

Chez elle tout homme est soldat,
Toute famille est une armée,

and which addresses Liberty, a goddess who assures victory to those who fight under her banners, as the protectress of the French people:

C'est ce peuple dont tu fis choix
Pour assurer ton juste empire:
Que par lui tout ce qui respire
Adopte et chérisse tes lois.

Ibid., p. 168. A "Hymne patriotique pour la réunion républicaine" (1793) by Moline, to the tune of the Marseillaise, exhorts the patriots:

Nous devons tout à la patrie;
Elle veille sur nos destins.
Le Ciel, en nous donnant la vie,
Nous fit naître républicains!
Soumis aux lois de la nature,
Aux vertus formons notre coeur.
Par nos talens, notre valeur,
Etonnons la race future.

Ibid., p. 178. The new religion is well summed up in the ode "Le Français libre à l'Être suprême: Prière républicaine universelle," *ibid.*, pp. 207-210; and in the "Hymne patriotique à l'Eternel" (1794), p. 222.

3. On Sept. 30, 1792, it was decided to change the names of the streets in Paris. The Rue de Provence became the Rue Franklin; the Rue Saint George—Rue Guillaume Tell; the Rue Chantereine—Rue de la Liberté; the Rue Saint-Lazare—Rue des Belges; the Rue de Taitbout—Rue Brutus; and the Rue des Martyrs—Rue Regulus.

4. On November 8, 1793. See Lamartine, *Histoire des Girondins*, Vol. III, p. 249. Contrast the words of Mme Jeanne Roland de la Platière (1754-1794) with the exaltation of Camille Desmoulins (1760-1794) in his pamphlet "La France libre, opuscules de l'an premier de la liberté," which he published after the fall of the Bastille: "Sublime effect of philoso-

phy, of liberty and of patriotism! We have become invincible. I myself confess frankly; I who was timid feel myself now another man. Like that Lacedemonian, Otriades, who, left alone mortally wounded on the battlefield, raised himself, held up a trophy with his faltering hands, and wrote with his blood: Sparta has conquered; I feel that I could die with joy for so beautiful a cause, and riddled with shots, I also could write with my blood: France is free." Later Desmoulins himself was to change. In his periodicals, *Les Révolutions de France et de Brabant, et des royaumes qui, demandant une assemblée nationale et arborant la cocarde, mériteront une place dans ces fastes de la liberté,* which he published from November 28, 1789, to December 12, 1791, and followed for a brief while in the spring of 1792 by *La Tribune des patriotes, ou Journal de la majorité,* which he published with Louis Marie Stanislas Fréron (1765-1802), he was one of the most extreme advocates of mob enthusiasm. But with the growth of the Terror, he, a former friend of Robespierre, joined Danton in demanding a reign of clemency in his *Vieux Cordelier,* which he founded in December 1793, but of which only seven issues appeared. When Robespierre ordered the burning of the sixth issue, Desmoulins objected that "burning is not answering." Arrested together with Danton and the other Indulgents in April 1794, he answered the question about his age: "I am thirty-three, the age of the sans-culotte Jesus, a critical age for every patriot." His execution was followed a few days later by that of his wife, Lucile Duplessis, a woman of great intelligence and courage.

5. Pirenne, *Histoire de Belgique,* Vol. VI, pp. 59-75. See also Frans van Kalken, *La Belgique contemporaine, 1780-1930, histoire d'une évolution politique* (Paris: A. Colin, 1930); Jules Delhaize, *La Domination française en Belgique à la fin du XVIIIme et au commencement du XIXme siècle,* 6 vols. (Brussels: J. Lebegue, 1908-1912); Prosper Poullet, *Les Institutions françaises de 1795 à 1814: Essai sur l'origine des institutions belges contemporaines* (Paris: Plon-Nourrit, 1907). On the expansionist policy of that period in other countries, see Louis Legrand, *La Révolution française en Hollande. La République* (Paris: Hachette, 1894); Justus Hashagen, *Das Rheinland und die französische Herrschaft; Beiträge zur Charakteristik* (Bonn: P. Hanstein, 1908); Alfred Nicolas Rambaud, *La Domination française en Allemagne: Les Français sur le Rhin (1792-1804),* 3rd ed. (Paris: Didier, 1883); Philippe Sagnac, *Le Rhin français pendant la Révolution et l'empire* (Paris: F. Alcan, 1917); Paul Gaffarel, "L'Annexion du Piémont à la France en 1798," *La Révolution française,* Vol. XIX (1890), pp. 289-315 and 507-537; Raymond Guyot, *Le Directoire et la paix de l'Europe, des traités de Bâle à la deuxième coalition, 1795-1799* (Paris: F. Alcan, 1911).

6. Eagan, *Maximilian Robespierre,* p. 198.

7. Palmer, *Twelve Who Ruled,* p. 229. See also Charles Theremin, *Des intérêts des puissances continentales relativement à l'Angleterre* (Paris: 1795).

8. *Poésies nationales,* pp. 250, 254, 285 f. See also the "Ode nationale contre l'Angleterre" by Lebrun (pp. 292-296), which ends:

Tremble, nouvelle Tyr! un nouvel Alexandre
Sur l'onde où tu regnais va disperser ta cendre:
Ton nom même n'est plus.

and M. Davrigny's "L'Expédition d'Angleterre" (pp. 297-303).

9. *Ibid.*, p. 297 and p. 280.
10. *Gazette nationale, ou Le Moniteur universel,* No. 117, April 27, 1793. *Réimpression de l'Ancien Moniteur: Seule histoire authentique et in-altérée de la Révolution française* (May 1789-1799), 32 vols. (Paris: H. Plon, 1847), Vol. XVI, p. 230.
11. *Ibid.*, No. 130, Jan. 30, 1796, *Réimpression,* Vol. XXVII, p. 314. Compare the answer given in the Constituent Assembly on June 24, 1790: "The cause of the individual is the cause of the nation. If each citizen is accountable to society for his actions, society is also accountable to the citizen for the rights of whom he has made it the depositary." *Ibid.*, Vol. IV, p. 712.
12. *Ibid.*, No. 13, Oct. 4, 1794, *Réimpression,* Vol. XXII, p. 132.

NOTES FOR CHAPTER 12: *Education in the Age of Nationalism*

1. *Oeuvres de Condorcet,* Vol. I, p. 390.
2. Charles Hunter Van Duzer, *Contribution of the Ideologues to French Revolutionary Thought* (Baltimore: John Hopkins University Press, 1935), pp. 78-115.
3. *Oeuvres de Condorcet,* Vol. VII, pp. 204, 212. See also p. 415.
4. *Ibid.*, Vol. VII, p. 433.
5. *Ibid.*, Vol. I, pp. 378. In his "Observations sur le 29e livre de L'Esprit des Lois."
6. *Gazette nationale* for Nov. 7, 1793, No. 47, *Réimpression,* Vol. XVIII, p. 351.
7. "Fourth Memorandum," *Oeuvres de Condorcet,* Vol. VII, pp. 380 ff.
8. *Ibid.*, Vol. VII, p. 551.
9. Albert Mathiez, *Les Origines des cultes révolutionnaires* (Paris: G. Bellais, 1904), p. 103.
10. *Ibid.*, pp. 119, 123.
11. Albert Babeau, *L'Ecole de village pendant la Révolution* (Paris: Didier, 1881), p. 110. See also Albert Duruy, *L'Instruction publique et la Révolution* (Paris: Hachette, 1882); C. Hippeau, *La Révolution française et l'éducation nationale* (Paris: Charavay Frères, 1884); Philippe Sagnac, "L'Enseignement secondaire avant et pendant la Révolution, d'après les travaux récents," *Revue d'histoire moderne et contemporaine,* Vol. XVIII (1913), pp. 433-451.
12. Leo Gershoy, "Barère, Champion of Nationalism in the French Revolution," *Political Science Quarterly,* Vol. XLII (1927), pp. 419-430.
13. See Henri Calvet, "L'Aérostation militaire sous le Directoire," *Annales historiques de la Révolution française,* Vol. VIII (1931), pp. 213-228; Camille Richard, *Le Comité de Salut public et les fabrications de guerre*

sous la Terreur (Paris: F. Rieder, 1922); Adrien Favre, *Les Origines du système métrique* (Paris: Les Presses Universitaires de France, 1931); Louis de Launay, *Un grand Français: Monge, fondateur de l'Ecole Polytechnique* (Paris: Editions Pierre Roger, 1933), and Paul V. Aubry, *Monge, le savant ami de Napoléon Bonaparte (1746-1818)* (Paris: Gauthier-Villars, 1955).

NOTES FOR CHAPTER 13: *Arts and Letters in the Age of Nationalism*

1. Eagan, *Maximilian Robespierre,* 86. For Robespierre's attitude regarding freedom of the press, see *ibid.,* pp. 118 f.
2. Romain Rolland, "Le Théâtre du peuple," *Cahiers de la Quinzaine,* ed. by Charles Péguy, 5th series, No. 4, p. 164. The appeal was written by Barère and was signed by him, Prieur, Carnot, Billaud, and Couthon.— On David (1748-1825) see Léon Rosenthal, *Louis David* (Paris: Librairie de l'art ancien et moderne, 1905) and especially David Dowd, *Pageant-master of the Republic: Jacques-Louis David and the French Revolution* (University of Nebraska Press, 1948).
3. Julien Tiersot, *Les Fêtes et les chants de la Révolution française* (Paris: Hachette, 1908); *idem,* "Méhul, musicien des fêtes nationales et civiles," *La Révolution française,* Vol. LXXII (1919), pp. 416-445. Étienne Nicolas Méhul (1763-1817).—A characteristic review of a *Collection de tous les Airs patriotiques arrangés pour le Fortepiano* appeared in the *Allgemeine Musikalische Zeitung* (Leipzig: Breitkopf & Hartel), on December 3, 1800. The reviewer felt that such songs would hardly appeal to Germans. "The Frenchman is interested in the Revolution and grows enthusiastic in recalling the festivals where these songs were sung, all of which leaves us pretty indifferent. For the French republican they are full of life, and what appears to us to be inadequate, or perhaps even detestable, that he loves, and even the slightest evocation of revolutionary sentiments by the most unsatisfactory means awakes in him rapturous enjoyment. If you subtract their topical or local significance, most of them are so miserably composed that you cannot regard them without disgust." The reviewer found only very few of them good enough to be heard by Germans with a sense of patriotism and musical inclination. Among them, he mentioned the Marseillaise and several hymns by Gossec, Solie, and others. "It is not without interest to study the melodies and words that have filled a people like the French with enthusiasm on important occasions and have moved immense crowds to action. It would have been desirable if the melodies of the Greek national songs, especially the war songs, had been similarly preserved," he added.
4. The national festivals were celebrated in every canton of the Republic. According to Article II of Title VI of the law, the celebration was to consist of "chants patriotiques, en discours sur la morale du citoyen, en banquets fraternels, en divers jeux publiques, propre à chaque localité, et dans la distribution des recompenses." On the festivals, see the thesis by Seymour Ballard Dunn, "The National Festival in the French Revolu-

tion, 1794-1797: A Study in Revolutionary Propaganda" (Cornell University, 1939).

5. Bastid, *Sieyès et sa pensée*, p. 496.

6. Pp. 23 f. of the original pamphlet printed at the Imprimerie Nationale, 1794.

7. The historical dates that Robespierre suggested commemorating were July 14, 1789; August 10, 1792; January 21, 1793; and May 31, 1793 (Article VI). In Article VII, he recommended a festival for each of the thirty-six *decadis* that were to replace Sunday in the new republican calendar, which, in the metrical fashion, divided the year into periods of ten days. The thirty-six festivals were: To the Supreme Being and to Nature; to the Human Race; to the French People; to the Benefactors of Mankind; to the Martyrs of Liberty; to Liberty and Equality; to the Republic; to the Liberty of the World; to Love of the Fatherland; to Hatred of Tyrants and Traitors; to Truth; to Justice; to Modesty; to Glory and Immortality; to Friendship; to Frugality; to Courage; to Good Faith; to Heroism; to Disinterestedness; to Stoicism; to Love; to Conjugal Faith; to Paternal Love; to Maternal Tenderness; to Filial Piety; to Childhood; to Youth; to Manhood; to Old Age; to Misfortune; to Agriculture; to Industry; to Ancestors; to Posterity; and to Happiness. "Rapport sur les rapports des idées religieuses et morales avec les principes républicains, et sur les fêtes nationales," 18 floréal, an II (1794), pp. 25 f.—See also André Blum, "Les Fêtes républicaines et la tradition révolutionnaire," *La Révolution française*, Vol. LXXII (1919), pp. 193-200; Christophe d'Opoix, "Fête à la Pudeur, proposée comme modèle pour les autres fêtes décadaires" (an III), *ibid.*, Vol. III (1882), pp. 415-428; François Antoine, Comte de Boissy d'Anglas, "Essai sur les fêtes nationales, suivi de quelques idées sur les arts et sur la nécessité de les encourager, adressé à la Convention nationale," (Paris: Imprimerie polyglotte, an II).

8. Bernardin de Saint-Pierre, "Treizième étude da la nature: Application des lois de la nature aux maux de la société," *Oeuvres complètes*, ed. by L. Aimé-Martin (Paris: Mequigon-Marvis, 1815), Vol. V, p. 193—Rolland, *Le Théâtre du peuple*, p. 75. On Jan. 23, 1794, "in rejoicing over the anniversary of the death of the tyrant," the Parisian theaters gave free performances. The National Opera presented *Miltiade à Marathon* by Nicolas François Guillard and Antoine Marcel Lemoine, in which Aristides sang, "We have against us three parts of the world . . . cowardly tyranny against a single people"; and *L'Offrande à la Liberté* by Gossec, the climax of which was the "Hymne à la Liberté" by Chénier and "Veillons au salut de l'empire." The Théâtre de la République in the Rue de la Loi played *Le nouveau réveil d'Epiménide;* the Théâtre de la Rue Feydreau—*La Prise de Toulon;* the Théâtre National—*Manlius Torquatus;* the Théâtre des Sans Culottes (formerly the Théâtre National de Molière)—*La Reprise de Toulon;* the Théâtre Lyrique des Amis de la Patrie—*Toulon reconquis, ou la Fête du Port de la Montagne;* the Théâtre de la Cité—*La Folie de Georges, ou L'Ouverture du Parlement d'Angleterre,* and *Le Vous et le Tu;* the Théâtre de la Montagne, in the Jardin de

l'Egalité—*La Sainte Omelette*. On the theater during the Revolution in general, see E. Jauffret, *Le Théâtre révolutionnaire, 1789-1799* (Paris: Corbeil, 1869); Henri Welschinger, *Le Théâtre de la Révolution, 1789-1799* (Paris: Charavay, 1880); Paul d'Estrée, *Le Théâtre sous la Terreur, 1793-1794* (Paris: Emile-Paul Frères, 1913); Maurice Albert, *Les Théâtres des boulevards, 1789-1799* (Paris: Société Française d'Imprimerie et de Librairie, 1902); Gaston Bizos, "La Comédie littéraire sous la Révolution, *La Révolution française*, Vol. XVIII (1890), pp. 288-316; Maurice Dommanget, "Le Symbolisme et le prosélytisme révolutionnaires à Beauvais et dans l'Oise; le Théâtre patriote," *Annales historiques de la Révolution française*, Vol. VI (1929), pp. 372-391; J.-J. Barbe, "Le Théâtre à Metz pendant la réaction Thermidorienne et le Directoire (an II—an VIII)," *ibid.*, Vol. V (1928), pp. 347-365.

9. Beatrice F. Hyslop, "The Theater During a Crisis: The Parisian Theater During the Reign of Terror," *Journal of Modern History*, Vol. XVII (1945), p. 355. This article contains a valuable analysis of many characteristic plays of the period.—An interesting example of the revolutionary theater before the Terror is Marie-Joseph Chénier's *Le Triomphe de la République, ou Le Camp de Grand-Pré*, for which Gossec wrote the music and Pierre Gardel arranged the ballet. In the French camp, facing the Prussian army, soldiers and villagers dance around the Tree of Liberty; the soldiers then leave for battle, while the villagers await the outcome confidently— "Nos guerriers sont republicains"; the soldiers return triumphant, and Liberty, descending from Heaven on a cloud, congratulates them. The chorus, joined by "the different nations of the world," ends the play by singing:

> Chantons, dansons; la Patrie est contente;
> Partout ses braves défenseurs
> Ont frappé les Rois d'épouvante.
> La République est triomphante:
> Chantons, dansons; nos frères sont vainqueurs.

After the fall of Robespierre, Chénier wrote a tragedy, *Timoléon* (Paris: 1795), preceded by an ode on the situation in which the Republic found itself during the oligarchy of Robespierre and his henchmen that included the following verses:

> Liberté des Français, que d'infâmes complots
> Ont rallenti ta noble course!
> Un monstre a dévoré nos fruits à peine éclos:
> Le sang s'est mêlé dans tes flots
> Si purs, si brillans à leur source. . . .

> Mais plus de sang français; laisse frapper les lois:
> Leurs vengeances sont légitimes:
> Peuple républicain, n'imite point les rois
> Dont la fureur a tant de fois
> Puni les crimes par des crimes.

Renais chez les mortels, aimable Egalité;
Viens briser le glaive anarchique:
Revenez, douces lois, justice, humanité:
Sans les moeurs, point de Liberté;
Sans vertu, point de République.

NOTES FOR CHAPTER 14: *Nationalism and Linguistic Unity*

1. *Correspondance générale de Carnot*, ed. by Etienne Charavay (Paris: Imprimerie Nationale, 1892), Vol. I, pp. 331, 338, 345 f. The new nation-state also intended to nationalize public welfare and charities. The Constitution of 1791 proclaimed it the duty of the government "to organize a general establishment for public aid to educate children, to relieve those who are both poor and infirm, and to provide work for the poor who are capable of work but could not find it." The Assembly formed a Comité de Mendicité, under the chairmanship of François Alexandre Duc de la Rochefoucauld-Liancourt (1747-1827), who had been famous under the old regime for his philanthropies; and this committee proclaimed "the great principle, long unrecognized in social institutions: the misery of the people is a fault of the governments," and insisted that assistance for the unfortunate was a national charge. In the Constitution of 1793, Article XXI stipulated that public assistance is a sacred debt owed by society. These principles, however, remained unrealized for more than a century.

2. For Barère, see the article by Leo Gershoy, "Barère, Champion of Nationalism," *op. cit.* and his *Bertrand Barère, A Reluctant Terrorist* (Princeton University Press, 1962). The proclamation by Saint-Just, dated 25 brumaire, an II, is found in *Oeuvres complètes de Saint-Just*, Vol. II, p. 148. For the Jacobin club of Strasbourg, see Crane Brinton, *The Jacobins*, p. 149. Beatrice Fry Hyslop, *French Nationalism in 1789*, pp. 47-49, points out that there was hardly any desire expressed for uniformity of language on the eve of the Revolution.

3. See Book XI of Goethe's *Aus meinem Leben: Dichtung und Wahrheit*. See also Alois Biessle, *Die Bedeutung der französischen Revolution für die Französisierung des Elsass* (Frankfurt a.M.: Elsass-Lothringen-Institut, 1933; Schriften des Wissenschaftlichen Instituts der Elsass-Lothringer im Reich, University of Frankfurt, New Series, No. 8).

4. Ferdinand Brunot, *Histoire de la langue française des origines à 1900* (Paris: Armand Colin, 1926), Vol. VII: *La Propagation du français en France jusqu'à la fin de l'ancien régime*, p. 253.

5. Edmund Crosby Quiggin, in the *Encyclopaedia Britannica*, 11th ed., Vol. V, p. 650.

6. On the problems of the French language during that period, see Brunot, *Histoire de la langue française*, Vol. IX: *La Révolution et l'Empire* (Paris: Colin, 1927).

7. *Ibid.*, p. 408.

Notes for chapter 15: *Napoleon and Nationalism*

1. "Rapport sur les fêtes nationales," *op. cit.*, p. 6.
2. See Hans Kohn, *The Idea of Nationalism*, pp. 253 f. Napoleon later wrote that up to the age of sixteen, "I would have fought for Rousseau against all the friends of Voltaire. Today it is the opposite. Since I have seen the East, Rousseau is repugnant to me. The wild man without morals is a dog." F. M. Kircheisen, *Napoleon's Autobiography: The Personal Memoirs of Bonaparte, Compiled from His Own Letters and Diaries*, tr. by Frederick Collins (New York: Duffield, 1931), p. 253.
3. *Ibid.*, pp. 13 and 17 f.
4. Lefebvre, *Napoléon*, pp. 65 and 58. On the diplomatic methods of Napoleon's early imperialism, see Harold C. Deutsch, *The Genesis of Napoleonic Imperialism* (Cambridge, Mass.: Harvard University Press, 1938); and H. Butterfield, *The Peace Treaties of Napoleon, 1608-1808* (Cambridge University Press, 1929). On Napoleon and the nationalist movements in Europe, see Willy Andreas, *Das Zeitalter Napoleons und die Erhebung der Völker* (Heidelberg: Quelle & Meyer, 1955).
5. Napoleon treated painters in a similar way. They were attached as officers to the armies of the First Consul. "Militarized artists, subjected to the strictest discipline, they had nothing to paint but glorious battle scenes—which caused them to be called 'painters of victories'—and they could not paint them according to their inspiration; they could choose neither the day nor the hour nor the composition of the picture, and their talent was circumscribed by minute regulations worked out by officers who had little concern with art, even if one admits that it was not completely strange to them. They have left a considerable amount of work dispersed in various archives and museums and generally little known." Villat, *La Révolution et l'empire*, Vol. II, p. 114. See also V. Coffin, "Censorship and Literature under Napoleon I," *American Historical Review*, Vol. XXII (1916-17), pp. 288-308; M. Albert, "Napoléon et les théâtres populaires," *Revue de Paris*, Vol. III (1902), pp. 806-827; Robert R. Holtman, *Napoleonic Propaganda* (Baton Rouge: Louisiana University Press, 1950).
6. A. Aulard, *Etudes et leçons sur la Révolution française*, 9 vols. (Paris: F. Alcan, 1902-1924), Vol. VII, p. 146.—Sir Walter Scott, *The Life of Napoleon Buonaparte, Emperor of the French*, 3 vols. (Philadelphia: Carey, Lea & Carey, 1827), Vol. I, p. 464.

Notes for chapter 16: *The Empire of the West*

1. Matthew Josephson, *Stendhal* (Garden City N. Y.: Doubleday, 1946), p. 122. In his *Vie de Napoléon* (Paris: Calmann-Levy, 1877), pp. 2 f., Stendhal left a famous description of the patriotism of the Revolution, but, born in 1783, he knew it only by hearsay: "L'enthousiasme pour les vertus républicaines, éprouvé dans les années appartenant encore à l'enfance, le mépris excessif et allant jusqu'à la haine pour les façons d'agir

des rois, contre lesquels on se battait, et même pour les usages militaires les plus simples, qu'on voyait pratiquer par leurs troupes, avaient donné à beaucoup de nos soldats de 1794 le sentiment que les Français seuls étaient des êtres raisonnables. A nos yeux, les habitants du reste de l'Europe qui se battaient pour conserver leurs chaînes, n'étaient que des imbéciles pitoyables, ou des fripons vendus aux despotes qui nous attaquaient. . . . Alors tout était dominé par un sentiment profond dont je ne vois plus de vestiges. Que le lecteur, s'il a moins de cinquante ans, veuille bien se figurer, d'après les livres, qu'en 1794, nous n'avions aucune sorte de religion; notre sentiment intérieur et sérieux était tout rassemblé dans cette idée: *être utile à la patrie*. Tout le reste, l'habit, la nourriture, l'avancement, n'étaient à nos yeux qu'un misérable detail éphémère. Comme il n'avait pas de société, les *succès dans la société*, chose si principale dans le caractère de notre nation, n'existaient pas. Dans la rue nos yeux se remplissaient de larmes, en recontrant sur le mur une inscription en l'honneur du jeune tambour Barra (qui se fit tuer a treize ans, plutôt que de cesser de battre sa caisse, afin de prévenir une surprise). Pour nous, qui ne connaissions aucune autre grande réunion d'hommes, il y avait des fêtes, des cérémonies nombreuses et touchantes, qui venaient nourrir le sentiment dominant tout dans nos coeurs. . . . Nous avons fait plus tard des infidélités à cette religion; mais dans toutes les grandes circonstances, ainsi que la religion catholique le fait pour ses fidèles, elle a repris son empire sur nos coeurs. Il en fut autrement des hommes nés vers 1790 et qui à quinze ans, en 1805, lorsqu'ils commencèrent à ouvrir les yeux, virent pour premier spectacle les toques de velours ornées de plumes, des ducs et comtes, récemment créés par Napoléon. Mais nous, anciens serviteurs de la patrie, nous n'avions que du mépris pour l'ambition puérile et l'enthousiasme ridicule de cette nouvelle génération."

2. Kircheisen, *Napoleon's Autobiography*, p. 234.
3. *Ibid.*, p. 180.
4. See Napoleon's letters of August 2 and 22, 1798, *Correspondance de Napoléon Premier, publiée par l'ordre de Napoléon IIIe* (Paris: 1859), Vol. IV, pp. 224 f., 534 ff. See also Lt. Col. P. G. Elgood, *Bonaparte's Adventure in Egypt* (London: Oxford University Press, 1931), and Paul V. Aubry, *Monge, le savant ami de Napoléon Bonaparte* (Paris: Gauthier-Villars, 1955).
5. Pirenne, *Histoire de Belgique*, Vol. VI, p. 141.
6. *Correspondance*, Vol. XXIII (1868), p. 45 (No. 18, 300, Dec. 2, 1811).
7. Kircheisen, *op. cit.*, p. 236. On Napoleon's treatment of Italian patriotism, see *Correspondance*, Vol. II (1859), p. 63 (No. 1099, Oct. 17, 1796); *ibid.*, p. 157 (No. 1258, Dec. 10, 1796); *ibid.*, pp. 223 f. (No. 1349, Jan. 1, 1787); *ibid.*, p. 483 (No. 1724, April 12, 1797); Vol. III (1859), p. 153 (No. 1960, June 29, 1797); *ibid.*, p. 235 (No. 2013, August 16, 1797): "Les îles de Corfou, de Zante et de Céphalonie sont plus intéressantes pour nous que toute l'Italie ensemble. Je crois que si nous étions obligés d'opter, il vaudrait mieux restituer l'Italie à l'Empereur et garder les quatre îles, qui sont une source de richesse et de prospérité pour

notre commerce. L'Empire des Turcs s'écroule tous les jours; la possession de ces îles nous mettra à même de le soutenir autant que cela sera possible, ou d'en prendre notre part."; Vol. XXVII (1869), pp. 11 f. (No. 21, 063, January 4, 1814); and Vol. XXXII (1870), p. 386, reported by Dr. Antommarchi as told to him on January 26, 1821.

8. *Ibid.*, Vol. XXXII (1870), pp. 304-306. English translation in Emmanuel, Comte de Las Cases, *Memoirs of the Life, Exile and Conversations of the Emperor Napoleon*, 4 vols. (New York: Worthington, 1890), Vol. IV, pp. 104-108.

9. On April 14, 1815. Benjamin Constant, *Mémoires sur les Cent Jours*, Pt. II (Paris: 1829), pp. 19 ff.

10. Benjamin Constant, *L'Esprit de conquête* (Paris: Bernard Grasset, 1918), pp. 12 and 14 (Ch. II: "Du caractère des nations modernes relativement à la guerre."). See also *Prophecy from the Past*, ed. by Helen Byrne Lippmann (New York: Reynald & Hitchcock, 1941). On Constant, see Lothar Gall, *Benjamin Constant, seine politische Ideenwelt und der deutsche Vormärz* (Wiesbaden: Steiner, 1963).

11. Kircheisen, *Napoleon's Autobiography*, p. 238. Like Frederick II of Prussia, Napoleon permitted religious discussions, but no political opposition. "Great freedom must be allowed in writings on religious questions, so that the publication of useful truths may not be strangled under the cloak of offense to religion. However, censorship will be inflexible in the case of documents directed against the state." *Ibid.*, p. 245.

12. Las Cases, *Memoirs*, Vol. III, p. 255.

13. Barry E. O'Meara, *Napoleon in Exile, or A Voice from St. Helena* (New York: W. Gowans 1853), Vol. I, p. 249.

14. Hugh Fortescue, "Memorandum of Two Conversations Between the Emperor Napoleon and Viscount Eberington at Porta Ferrajo on the 6th and 8th of December, 1814" (London: 1823), p. 27. See also *Correspondance*, Vol. XXIX (1870), pp. 490 f.; and Las Cases, *op. cit.*, Vol. III, p. 318.

15. Kircheisen, *op. cit.*, p. 104. "Instead of sending troops, I ought to have left everything to the black men, or at most have sent a few white officials, for instance, a treasurer, and required that the white men marry Negro women."

16. Kircheisen, *op. cit.*, p. 181. See also *Correspondance*, Vol. XXXII (1870), pp. 316 f.; and O'Meara, *Napoleon in Exile*, pp. 113 f.

17. O'Meara, *op. cit.*, Vol. II, p. 225. See also Las Cases, *op. cit.*, Vol. IV, p. 145.

18. How much conscription was resented may be seen from the violent diatribe against "la loi homicide" in Chateaubriand's "De Buonaparte et des Bourbons" (March 30, 1814), *Oeuvres complètes* (Paris: Ladvocat, 1828), Vol. XXIV, pp. 20-24; and Edmond Geraud, in his journal for March 1814, quoted in H. F. Stewart and Paul Desjardins, *French Patriotism in the Nineteenth Century, 1814-1833, Traced in Contemporary Texts* (Cambridge University Press, 1923), p. 120.

NOTES FOR CHAPTER 17: *Nationalism and Liberty*

1. Auguste Barbier, "L'Idole," *Iambes et poèmes*, 6th ed. (Paris: Paul Masgana, 1849), pp. 38 f. On the evaluation of Napoleon by French historians see Pieter Geyl, *Napoleon, For and Against* (New Haven: Yale University Press, 1949).
2. Stewart and Desjardins, *French Patriotism*, pp. 130 and 131.
3. Aimée de Coigny, *Mémoires*, ed. by Etienne Lamy (Paris: Calmann-Levy, 1902), p. 229. See also Mme de Staël, *Considérations sur la Révolution française*, Pt. IV, Ch. 19.
4. Pierre Jean de Béranger, *Ma Biographie* (3rd ed., Paris: Perrotin, 1859), p. 162. See also the *Mémoires de la Comtesse de Boigne* (Adèle d'Osmond), ed. by the Marquise d'Osmond (Paris: Emile Paul, 1921), Vol. I, p. 292: "It was no longer a public matter—one had no personal connection with it, and one was not allowed to inquire about it: the Emperor had made such an effort to make it his affair and not ours, that one had finally taken him at his word. And, whatever people may have been saying about him for the last few years, in 1814 everybody, including his army and officials, was so tired that they asked for nothing but to be relieved from an effort that had ceased to be directed by a wise and reasonable will."
5. *Mémoires de Grégoire, ancien évèque de Blois*, introd. by Hippolyte Carnot (Paris: J. Yonet, 1840), Vol. I, p. 7. Grégoire's first published book was *Essai sur la régénération physique, morale et politique des Juifs* (Metz: Imprimerie Claude Lamort, 1789), a work awarded a prize by the Royal Society of Sciences and Arts of Metz on August 23, 1788. As deputy from Nancy, he presented in 1789 a "Motion en faveur des Juifs, précédée d'une notice historique sur les persécutions qu'ils viennent d'essuyer en divers lieux, notamment en Alsace, et sur l'admission de leurs députés à la barre de l'Assemblée nationale." In the same year he addressed to the National Assembly a "Mémoire en faveur des gens de couleur ou sang-mêlés de St.-Domingue et des autres îles françaises de l'Amérique." In 1808, he published a book, *De la Littérature des nègres, ou Recherches sur leur faculté intellectuelle, leur qualité morale, et leur littérature; suivie des notices sur la vie et les ouvrages des nègres qui se sont distingués dans les sciences, les lettres et les arts* (Paris: Maradan, 1808); and in an anonymous pamphlet he returned to the question in 1815: "De la traite et de l'esclavage des noirs et des blancs, par un ami des hommes de toutes les couleurs." (Paris: Egron, 1815).
6. *Mémoires de Grégoire*, pp. 305 f.
7. Dupre, *Lazare Carnot*, p. 264.
8. A. Aulard, "Les Idées politiques de Carnot," *La Révolution française*, Vol. XIV (1888), pp. 640-658; and René Girard, "Carnot et l'éducation populaire pendant les Cent Jours," *ibid.*, Vol. LII (1907), pp. 424-448.
9. Stewart and Desjardins, *French Patriotism*, pp. 160-165.
10. See the letters by Gneisenau of June 22, 24, and 27, 1815, in Hans

Delbrück and Georg Heinrich Pertz, *Das Leben des Feldmarschalls Grafen Neithardt von Gneisenau*, Vol. IV (Berlin: G. Reimer, 1880), pp. 532, 533, 539, 543. See also Karl Grievank, *Der Wiener Kongress und die Europäische Restauration 1814/15* (Leipzig: Koehler & Amelang, 1954), especially Grievank's comments on pp. 340-341.—Most French intellectuals and journalists remained anti-British until 1870. Bertrand Barère, who had published in 1798 a pamphlet *La Liberté des mers ou le gouvernement anglais dévoilé* (which was republished in France in 1942) and edited in 1803 the journal *Mémorial anti-Britannique*, pleaded in 1841, one year before his death at the age of eighty-seven, for a Franco-Russian alliance to contain English ambitions. See on the French anti-British and pro-German attitude my *Prophets and Peoples* (New York: Macmillan, 1946), Ch. II, and "France Between Britain and Germany" in my *Reflections on Modern History* (Princeton: D. Van Nostrand, 1963) pp. 112-130. Execution of Napoleon, demanded by Stein and Gneisenau, would have deprived the fallen Emperor of the opportunity of creating in his memoirs that legend which inspired so many French youths.

11. Though the official style under Napoleon remained the cold classical "Empire"—dictators of the twentieth century have shared this predilection—romanticism, with its emphasis on the Middle Ages and the French past, made its appearance. Napoleon himself, by harking back to the days of Charlemagne, gave impetus to the movement. Boileau had chided Carel de Sainte-Garde for singing in "Sarrasins chassés de France" the glories of Childebrand, the brother of Charles-Martel. In his *L'Art poétique*, chant III, Nicolas Boileau (1636-1711) wrote:

> Oh! le plaisant projet d'un poète ignorant
> Qui de tant de héros va choisir Childebrand!

and suggested Agamemnon or Achilles as a more proper subject. To the classical mind of Boileau, the national glories of France were not worthy of treatment. But in 1804 the *Mercure* asked whether the reign of Chilperic and Brunehaut was not at least as important as that of Agamemnon and Clytemnestra.—The publication of *Le Génie du Christianisme* by Chateaubriand and its reception by the French public attested to the new Gothic vogue. Edmond Géraud, whom Sainte-Beuve called "le premier des romantiques," studied the French fairy tales and turned his attention to the nation's past. In 1805 the Académie Celtique was founded for research in Celtic and Gallic antiquity; it became in 1813 the Société nationale des antiquaires de France. Also in 1805, François Just Raynouard (1761-1836) achieved his greatest success as a dramatist with *Les Templiers*, for which he took his subject not from classical antiquity, as in his previous play *Caton d'Utique*, but from the French Middle Ages; and from this period he later assembled his collection of the poetry of the troubadours. While Raynouard had been a deputy of the Legislative Assembly, Joseph François Michaud (1767-1839) was a royalist. His *Histoire des Croisades*, which he began to publish in 1811 and which was a pioneer work for his time, testified to the current admiration for medieval history.

In 1806 the medieval Jeux Floraux, which had been suppressed during the Revolution because of their traditional connotations, were revived.

12. Nationalist French historians, like Henri Houssaye, author of *1815* (15th ed., Paris: Perrin, 1894), exaggerated French grievances out of all proportion. Another nationalist historian, Edouard Driault, wrote in the *Revue des études napoléoniennes,* Vol. XXII (September 1933), p. 194, about Napoleon's son, the Duc de Reichstadt (1811-1832): "The martyred son remains a prisoner still after one hundred years in the crypt of the Capuchins in Vienna. He must join his father in the Invalides: that is the wish of all the friends of France. . . . It must become the will of all Frenchmen. We must not leave the son of Napoleon in the hands of the enemy." This wish "of all the friends of France" was fulfilled by Hitler, who during the German occupation of 1940-44 had the remains of the Duke of Reichstadt transferred to the Invalides. See on the Napoleonic legend Albert Léon Guérard, *Reflections on the Napoleonic Legend* (New York: Scribner's, 1924).

13. Slightly paraphrased from Constant, *L'Esprit de conquête,* p. 25.

14. Friedrich Nietzsche, *Will to Power,* Book IV: "On Breeding: The Masters of the World," No. 951; *The Joyful Wisdom,* Book V: "We Fearless Ones," No 362; *Genealogy of Morals,* First Essay: "Good and Evil, Good and Bad," No. 16.

15. Victor Hugo, "Buonaparte," *Odes,* Livre I, Ode 11. *Oeuvres complètes* (Paris: A. Houssiaux, 1857), Vol. I, p. 88.

16. On April 6, 1829, J. P. Eckermann, *Conversations with Goethe,* ed. by Hans Kohn (New York: F. Ungar, 1964), p. 156.

NOTES FOR CHAPTER 18: *The French Revolution and Central Europe*

1. Serano Suñer in his *Entre les Pyrénées et Gibraltar* expressed one aspect of this instinctive myth: "Without failing to admire what France could offer by way of admirable examples, we could not feel real friendship for her. A whole collective consciousness, inherited from father to son, cultivated on the school benches, spread out through the folklore, rooted in every true Spaniard, would have been opposed to it. In short, everything that formed the historical instinct of a people rose against the powerful neighbor who had grown great at our expense." A similar feeling characterized the reaction of Spanish nationalism to the Anglo-Saxons (liberal and capitalistic heretics who in the three centuries from 1588 to 1898 had destroyed noble and Catholic Spain), and determined, with varying motivations, the attitudes of traditionalist French nationalism against Britain, of Italian and German nationalism against France, of Russian or Indian nationalism against the West.

NOTES FOR CHAPTER 19: *Madame de Staël and Cultural Nationalism*

1. *De l'Allemagne,* Pt. 1, Ch. 1. Mme de Staël, *Oeuvres Complètes* (Paris: Firmin Didot, 1838), Vol. II, p. 5.

2. *Ibid.,* p. 6 (Pt. I, Ch. 2).

3. *Ibid.*, p. 1-3. In introducing her book to the French, Mme de Staël pleaded for freer intellectual exchange among nations, for less cultural self-sufficiency. Nationalist seclusion, upon which German romanticism, with its emphasis on originality, insisted, seemed to Mme de Staël stultifying for the development of the mind. "Les opinions qui diffèrent de l'esprit dominant, quel qu'il soit, scandalisent toujours le vulgaire: l'étude et l'examen peuvent seuls donner cette liberalité de jugement, sans laquelle il est impossible d'acquérir des lumières nouvelles, ou de conserver même celles qu'on a; car on se soumet à de certaines idées reçues, non comme à des vérités, mais comme au pouvoir; et c'est ainsi que la raison humaine s'habitue à la servitude, dans le champ même de la littérature et de la philosophie. . . . Car nous n'en sommes pas, j'imagine, à vouloir élever autour de la France littéraire la grande muraille de la Chine, pour empêcher les idées du dehors d'y pénétrer." The last sentence was suppressed by the Parisian censors in 1810.

4. *Ibid.*, p. 20 (Pt. I, Ch. 9). National character demands national political institutions. "Les institutions politiques peuvent seules former le caractère d'une nation; la nature du gouvernement de l'Allemagne était presque en opposition avec les lumières philosophiques des Allemands. De là vient qu'ils réunissent la plus grande audace de pensée au caractère le plus obéissant. La prééminence de l'état militaire et les distinctions de rang les ont accoutumés à la soumission la plus exacte dans les rapports de la vie sociale; ce n'est pas servilité, c'est régularité chez eux que l'obéissance; ils sont scrupuleux dans l'accomplissement des ordres qu'ils reçoivent, comme si tout ordre était un devoir." *Ibid.*, p. 9 (Pt. I, Ch. 2).

5. *Réflexions sur la Paix, ibid.*, Vol. I, p. 44.

6. In a footnote to this phrase, the author noted that in it and in the following passages she meant England. "I could not have spoken with enthusiasm of war without thinking of it as a war of a free nation fighting for its independence."

7. *Ibid.*, Vol. II, p. 254 (Pt. 4, Ch. 12).

8. *Considérations sur les Principaux Evénements de la Révolution Française,* Pt. 6, Ch. 2, *Oeuvres Posthumes, Ibid.*, Vol. II, Pt. 2, pp. 289 and 283.

9. *Ibid.*, p. 299.

10. *Dix Années d'Exil,* Pt. II, Chs. 13 and 14, *ibid.*, pp. 394, 398. "Les Anglais, avec cette admirable droiture qui distingue toutes leurs actions, rendent compte aussi véridiquement de leurs revers que de leurs succès, et l'enthousiasme se soutient, chez eux, par le vérité, quelle qu'elle soit. Les Russes ne peuvent atteindre encore à cette perfection morale, qui est le résultat d'une constitution libre."

11. *Dix Années d'Exil,* Pt. 1, Ch. 10, *ibid.*, Vol. II, Pt. 2, p. 349. Mme de Staël goes on: "Il y a sans doute des principes communs à tous les pays; ce sont ceux qui assurent les droits civils et politiques des peuples libres; mais que ce soit une monarchie limitée comme l'Angleterre, une république fédérée comme les Etats-Unis ou les treize cantons suisses, qu'importe? Et faut-il réduire l'Europe à une idée, comme le peuple romain a une seule tête, afin de pouvoir commander et changer tout en un jour!"

12. *Corinne*, Bk. 1, Ch. 4., *ibid.*, Vol. I, p. 658.

13. "Discours Préliminaire" to *De la Littérature considérée dans ses Rapports avec les Institutions Sociales, ibid.*, Vol. I, p. 205. However, Mme de Staël found the spirit of militarism especially developed among Germans. In her *Dix Années d'Exil*, Pt. 2, Ch. 9, she tells of an encounter between her son and a German captain. "Le capitaine lui avait répondu avec une brutalité qu'on ne saurait rencontrer que chez des subalternes allemands; l'on ne rencontre aussi que là ce respect obséquieux pour le pouvoir qui succède immédiatement à l'arrogance envers les faibles. Les mouvements de l'âme de ces hommes ressemblent aux évolutions d'un jour de parade; elle fait demi-tour à droite et demi-tour à gauche, selon l'ordre qu'on leur donne." *Ibid.*, Vol. II, Pt. 2, p. 387.—And in *De l'Allemagne* Mme de Staël remarks that the military spirit had always been ruder in Germany than anywhere else; "there one can still imagine those men of steel whose image one finds in the imperial arsenals."

14. *De l'Allemagne* encouraged the Germans. Goethe wrote in a letter on February 17, 1814: "The French police was intelligent enough to understand that a book like this must increase German self-confidence and has therefore had it destroyed . . . in the present moment the book has a miraculous effect. If it had appeared earlier, one would have attributed to it an influence upon recent great events." *Goethes Briefe*, ed. by Philipp Stein (Berlin: Otto Elsner, 1905), Vol. VI, p. 293. See also Comtesse Jean de Pange, *Madame de Staël et la Découverte de l'Allemagne* (Paris: Edgar Malfère, 1928). Frédéric Ancillon (1767-1837), a Prussian theologian and statesman of Huguenot descent who was as familiar with French as with German civilization, wrote to Mme de Staël in 1813: "Je suis prussien bien plus par le sentiment que par la naissance et je fais gloire de l'être car jamais on n'aura à rougir d'appartenir au peuple de Frédéric. . . . L'indépendance et la gloire de mon pays a été ma première passion et sera la dernière; l'un et l'autre sont inséparables de l'affranchissement de l'Allemagne et la noble nation qui l'habite n'est pas faite pour recevoir des lois de l'étranger. Je n'ai jamais cessé de faire des voeux pour le renaissement de la liberté germanique. . . . Dans tous les cas vous me permettrez de me réjouir de la publication de votre ouvrage, de l'attendre avec impatience et de me féliciter en ma qualité d'allemand de ce que l'Allemagne recevra l'hommage de votre génie dans le moment où elle en sera le plus digne. Le salut de votre livre est une première victoire de l'Allemagne sur ses ennemis et cette bonne fortune est l'heureux augure de ses succès."

15. These are the last words of the Preface which Mme de Staël added on October 1, 1813, to *De l'Allemagne*.

Notes for chapter 20: *The French Revolution and Eighteenth-Century Germany*

1. *Briefe von und an Friedrich von Gentz*, ed. by Friedrich Carl Wittichen (Munich: R. Oldenbourg, 1909), Vol. I, pp. 178 f. See on Gentz, Paul R. Sweet, *Friedrich von Gentz, Defender of the Old Order* (Madison: Uni-

versity of Wisconsin Press, 1941) with complete bibliography; Golo Mann, *Secretary of Europe: The Life of Friedrich Gentz, Enemy of Napoleon,* tr. by Wilhelm H. Woglom (New Haven: Yale University Press, 1946). On Klopstock and Kant see Hans Kohn, *The Idea of Nationalism,* pp. 421 and 396.

2. Adolf Wohlwill, *Weltbürgerthum und Vaterlandsliebe der Schwaben, insbesonders von 1789 bis 1815* (Hamburg: Otto Meissner, 1875) pp. 45 f. Wohlwill mentions a letter from Johann Georg Kerner (1770-1812), written probably in 1797 to Talleyrand, in which he wrote: "Je n'ai point oublié de visiter la cave, où il-y-a dix-huit mois j'ai eu le bonheur de boire avec vous à la réunion de la rive gauche." The cession of the German left bank of the Rhine to France not only did not arouse patriotic indignation—it was remembered pleasantly as an occasion for rejoicing.

3. Georg Forster, *Sämtliche Schriften,* 9 vols. (Leipzig, 1843), Vol. VI, p. 416.

4. The Hamburg poet wrote:

> Was soll uns Freiheitsschwärmerei?
> Wir haben Freiheitssinn;
> Macht mich die rote Mütze frei,
> Wenn ich es sonst nicht bin?
> Die Wahrheit warb noch nie;
> Es wirkt von selbst ihr göttlich Licht,
> Nur freien Dienst will sie.
> Und unsre Freiheit drückt uns nicht,
> Es fliesst durch sie kein Blut;
> Sie glänzt auf unserm Angesicht,
> Nicht auf dem Band und Hut.
> So nehm' an unsrer Freude Teil,
> Wes Glaubens, Volks er sei—
> Und singe Heil dir, Hamburg, Heil,
> Denn du bist wirklich frei.

See Eberhard Sauer, *Die französische Revolution von 1789 in zeitgenössischen deutschen Flugschriften und Dichtungen* (Weimar: Alexander Duncker, 1913); A. Stern, *Der Einfluss der Französischen Revolution auf das deutsche Geistesleben* (Stuttgart: Cotta, 1928); G. P. Gooch, *Germany and the French Revolution* (London: Longmans, Green, 1920); Jacques Droz, "L'Allemagne et la Révolution Française," *Revue Historique,* Vol. CXCVIII (1947), pp. 161-177, and his *L'Allemagne et la Révolution Française* (Paris: Presses Universitaires de France, 1949); Adalbert Wahl, *Über die Nachwirkungen der französischen Revolution, vornehmlich in Deutschland* (Stuttgart: Kohlhammer, 1939); Sydney Seymour Biro, *The German Policy of Revolutionary France, A Study in French Diplomacy 1792-97,* 2 vols. (Harvard University Press, 1957).

5. See Eberhard Sauer, *op. cit.,* pp. 38, 88 f. Sauer rightly characterized Germany at the turn of the century: "Nowhere is there the slightest trace of an inclination to political unrest. But what about the revolution of the mind? The masses met it with the same indifference as a political upheaval; per-

haps in no country had the revolution of the mind a less immediate effect than in Germany."

6. Karl Biedermann, *Deutschland im achtzehnten Jahrhundert,* Vol. II, Pt. 2 (Leipzig: Weber, 1858), p. 1216.

7. In 1790 some small states forbade the discussion of politics in pubs and inns, and in one place the innkeeper was made responsible for the conversation of his guests. A Berlin journal thereupon described a scene in which the guest, whom the innkeeper asked not to talk but to confine himself to eating and drinking, received to his question, "What then distinguishes man from animal?" the reply, "Paying for his food and drink." Woldemar Wenck, *Deutschland vor hundert Jahren,* Vol. II (Leipzig: F. W. Grunow, 1890), p. 165.

8. Klopstock, "Das Versprechen," *Sämmtliche Werke* (Leipzig: Göschen, 1804), Vol. III, p. 360. The *Annalen der Leidenden Menschheit,* Vol. II (1796), pp. 62 f. published an anonymous poem "Die Krieger," dated summer 1794, which was a parody of Schiller's famous ode "Die Künstler." It began:

> Wie scheusslich, Mensch, mit deinem Bajonette
> Stehst du in der geschlossenen Mörderkette
> Mit eingefuchtelter Vermessenheit,
> Mit feigem Sinn, mit wütiger Gebärde,
> Taktmässig stampfend auf der fremden Erde,
> Auf deines Treibers Wink bereit
> In gleichgeformten willenlosen Horden
> Zehntausend gegen dich Geprügelte zu morden,
> Mit mehr als tierischer Unmenschlichkeit,
> Voll Rache gegen nie gesehene Brüder. . . .

9. "Deutschland, schlummerst du noch?" Herder, *Sämmtliche Werke,* ed. by Bernard Suphan (Berlin: Weidmann, 1889), Vol. 29, p. 210. The example of Poland as a deterrent was proposed to the Germans as late as 1810 when Johann Gottfried Seume (1763-1810) told them that they were now what the Poles had been, and that in twenty-five years they would be what the Poles were now. Seume, *Sämmtliche Werke* (Berlin: Hempel, 1879), Vol. 5, p. 189. Seume was one of the few liberal German nationalists. As a young man he fought in the Russian army against Poland. After 1800 he tried to arouse German national feeling without abandoning the firm basis of eighteenth-century liberalism. He warned that "philosophically one leads men into the most miserable mysticism and politically into iron despotism or anarchical fanaticism if one transcends common sense (den gesunden Menschenverstand)." He remained to his end a republican and an enlightened rationalist.

10. See Eduard Spranger, "Hölderlin und das deutsche Nationalbewusstsein" in his *Kultur und Erziehung* (Leipzig: Quelle & Meyer, 1928), pp. 126 ff; Agnes Stansfield, *Hölderlin* (Manchester: University Press, 1944). Hölderlin wrote in 1792 to his sister: "We shall have a bad time if the Austrians

win. The abuse of power will become dreadful. Believe me and pray for the French, who fight for the rights of man."

11. These are the last three lines of Hölderlin's "Germanien," *Werke*, ed. by Marie Joachimi-Dege (Berlin: Deutsches Verlagshaus Bong & Co., n.d.), Vol. I, p. 216. See also "An die Deutschen," "Gesang der Deutschen," "Stimme des Volkes," and "Der Tod fürs Vaterland," pp. 129-135, and the note of triumphant expectation towards the end of his great poem "Der Archipelagus":

> Dann, dann, o ihr Freuden Athens! ihr Taten in Sparta!
> Köstliche Frühlingszeit im Griechenlande; wenn unser
> Herbst kommt, wenn ihr, gereift, ihr Geister alle der Vorwelt
> Wiederkehret und siehe! des Jahrs Vollendung ist nahe!

which Miss Stansfield excellently translated:

> Then, then O you joys of fair Athens, deeds done in Sparta,
> Precious and lovely springtime of Greece! then when our
> Time comes, ripe in the autumn, all you ghosts of past ages
> Come again and see. The year's completion is near.

12. Hölderlin, *Werke*, Vol. II, pp. 149-152.
13. *Ibid.*, pp. 51-55. See "Hölderlins Deutschlandbild" in Reinhold Schneider, *Dämonie und Verklärung* (Vaduz: Liechtenstein Verlag, 1947) pp. 69-97.
14. See A. Stern, *op. cit.*, p. 62. The first issue was dated December 10, 1789, and contained a long introductory poem "In Celebration of the Year 1789" which started:

> Deutschland, Erstes der Völker von allen Völkern der Erde,
> Denn umsonst wird Gallier dir und Britte sich rühmen,
> Wenn du deine Güter erkennst!—Dir, heiliges, teures
> Vaterland, und euch mit inniger Liebe vor allen,
> Söhne Brandenburgs, euch weih ich des Jahres Erinnerung,
> Meinen Feiergesang!

15. Christian Ulrich Detlev Freiherr von Eggers (1758-1813), a Danish states-man, in his *Skizzen und Fragmente einer Geschichte der Menschheit in Rücksicht auf Aufklärung* (1786; 2nd vol. 1801) wrote: "Höchstens der Bürger einer kleinen Reichsstadt frägt noch bisweilen, wie steht's in Deutschland. Jeder Deutsche zählt sich gern zu den Österreichern, den Preussen, den Sachsen, den Hannoveranern, den Mecklenburgern; nur die, welche kein besonderes Vaterland haben, nennen sich Deutsche." Karl Biedermann, *Deutschland im Achtzehnten Jahrhundert*, Vol. I, *Politische, Materielle und Sociale Zustände* (Leipzig: J. J. Weber, 1854), p. 56.
16. Arnold Berney, "Reichstradition und Nationalstaatsgedanke 1789-1815," *Historische Zeitschrift*, Vol. XCL (1929), pp. 66 f. See also Anton Ernst Berger, "Reichsheer und Reich 1794-1795" in *Gesamtdeutsche Vergangenheit*, Festgabe for the 60th birthday of Heinrich Ritter von Srbik (Munich: Bruckman, 1938).

17. Adolf Wohlwill, *op. cit.*, pp. 50 f.
18. Such a poet was Hölderlin's friend and fellow student Ludwig Neuffer (1769-1839). He expressed this dream in a poem:

> Vaterland! Dein heiliger Name glühe
> In der Bürger Herzen mit reiner Flamme,
> Von dem Thron des Fürsten bis zu des Landmanns
> Niedriger Hütte.
>
> Weggetilgt sei jegliche Spur der Selbstsucht,
> Dass am festen Bundesaltar der Eintracht
> Sich die deutschen Völker zu Einem Volke
> Mutig vereinen.

19. Seume, *Sämmtliche Werke*, Vol. V, pp. 188 ff., under the title "To the German People in the Year 1810," first printed in a Berlin periodical in 1813, when Seume's words were still regarded as true: "Hatred and division separates the German tribes; only unity could stamp out the perdition and yet we flee unity like the plague. Rather than honor publicly what is right, people jubilate when one German country devastates the other, and the public shame is celebrated like a festival."
20. Mathys Jolles, *Das deutsche Nationalbewusstsein im Zeitalter Napoleons* (Frankfurt a.M.: Vittorio Klostermann, 1936), p. 42, spoke of "a desire for peace, contrary to the character of the country."
21. See Otto Tschirch, *Geschichte der Öffentlichen Meinung in Preussen vom Baseler Frieden bis zum Zusammenbruch des Staates, 1795-1806*, 2 vols. (Weimar: Böhlau, 1933-34), which shows from a great wealth of literature —not newspapers (which hardly existed as political mouthpieces), but pamphlets, leaflets, and judicial and police records—how strongly public opinion in Prussia in all classes was opposed to war with France and favorable to Napoleon.
22. *Briefe von und an Friedrich von Gentz*, Vol. I, p. 330. See also the memorandum written by Gentz in 1800 in Paul Wittichen, "Das Preussische Cabinett und Friedrich von Gentz," *Historische Zeitschrift*, Vol. 89, pp. 239 ff.
23. Otto Hintze, "Preussische Reformbestrebungen von 1806," *Historische Zeitschrift*, Vol. 76 (1896), p. 413.

Notes for chapter 21: *The Cosmopolitanism of German Intellectuals*

1. Quoted in Woldemar Wenck, *op. cit.*, p. 69. Wieland's observation was printed in his *Neue Deutsche Merkur*, 1794, Vol. I, p. 279.
2. Campe wrote a special children's edition of *Robinson Crusoe* which was published in Braunschweig in 1801 and later translated into all languages. In his *Wörterbuch der Erklärung und Verdeutschung der unserer Sprache aufgedrungenen fremden Ausdrücke* he suggested many Germanizations of foreign words; for instance, he wished to replace *Aether* by *Luftgeist*.
3. A. Stern, *op. cit.*, pp. 19 f. Among other friends of the French Revolution the well-known musician Johann Friedrich Reichardt (1752-1814) should

be mentioned. He published two periodicals, one under the title *Deutsch-land* in Berlin, the other, called *Frankreich,* in Altona. The former journal published Friedrich Schlegel's *Versuch über den Begriff des Re-publikanismus* and the poem "Gallia und Germania," mentioned in the text. In 1804 Reichardt edited the book *Napoleon und das Französische Volk unter seinem Konsulat* by his friend, the francophile Count Gustav von Schlabrendorf (1750-1824)

4. Few Germans, on the other hand, became so hostile to the French Revolution that they would have agreed with Count Friedrich Leopold Stolberg (1750-1819), who in June 1794 wrote a poem in which he called the French the Western Huns:

> Bei meiner Mutter Asche, das duld' ich nicht!
> Ihr sollt nicht Franken nennen der Völker und
> Der Zeiten Abschaum! Nennt Westhunnen,
> Dann noch beschönigend, ihre Horden. . . .

5. Quoted from Magister F. Ch. Laukhard, *Leben und Schicksale* (Stuttgart, 1908), Vol. II, p. 177, in August Friedrich Raif, *Die Urteile der Deutschen über die französische Nationalität im Zeitalter der Revolution und der deutschen Erhebung* (Berlin: Walther Rothschild, 1911), p. 17. See also Joachim Ritter, *Hegel und die Französische Revolution* (Köln: West-deutscher Verlag, 1957).

6. Franz Rosenzweig, *Hegel und der Staat* (Munich: R. Oldenbourg, 1920) Vol. I, pp. 101-131. On the young Hegel (before 1807), see Jean Hip-polyte, *Introduction à la philosophie de l'histoire de Hegel* (Paris: Rivière, 1948). Hegel did not welcome Napoleon's defeat. "Liberation? Liberation from what?" he wrote on December 23, 1813. "They talk a great deal here about liberation. If I ever see one liberated person with my own eyes, I shall fall to the ground to prostrate myself before him." Nor did Hegel harbor any aspirations for reestablishing the German Reich. In 1816 he wrote in an essay on the constitutional struggle in Württem-berg that "the vain idea known as the German Reich . . . has found the contemptible end it always deserved, and in its stead have arisen the particular German states." In 1829, lecturing on the philosophy of history, he praised the Congress of Vienna because "the lie known as the German Reich has finally and utterly disappeared." See *Briefe von und an Hegel,* ed. by J. Hoffmeister (Hamburg, 1952), II, 14-15. See also *ibid.,* pp. 27, 23, and Hegel's Essay of 1816, in his *Schriften zur Politik und Rechtsphilosophie,* ed. by G. Lasson (Leipzig, 1913), p. 159.— Hegel's political philosophy was based not upon nationality, race, or language but on the political state: "In our days there is no need for integration and unity in the state as far as custom, tradition, culture, and language are concerned. . . . The Austrian and Russian monarchs do not even know how many languages are spoken in their states—and yet their states are models of the modern state, whose integration does not arise from the arbitrariness of language, but from the spirit and unity of a common political consciousness." Hegel's *Schriften zur Politik und Rechts-*

philosophie, pp. 24 f.—Hegel rejected all *Deutschtümelei* and Klopstock's attempt to revive the German mythology. "This imagery is not that of Germans today. The project of restoring to a nation an imagery once lost was always doomed to failure. . . . The old German imagery has nothing in our day to connect or adapt itself to; it stands as cut off from the whole circle of our ideas, opinions, and beliefs, and it is as strange to us as the imagery of Ossian or of India." Hegel, *Early Theological Writings,* transl. by T. M. Knox and R. Kroner (Chicago, 1948), p. 149. See also p. 146.—Hegel never stressed German originality, but praised the dependence of German development on "alien" culture. Nor had he any high opinion of the liberty of the ancient primitive Germans. "Ever since Tacitus, much has been said of the ancient original liberty of the Germans. But woe to us were we to confuse this state of savagery and barbarism with the state of liberty. Let us not follow the fallacy of Rousseau, who saw in the wild Indians of America the embodiment of true human liberty." Hegel, *Vorlesungen über die Philosophie der Weltgeschichte,* ed. by G. Lasson (Leipzig, 1920) pp. 758, 775.

7. Franz Rosenzweig, *op. cit.,* p. 240.
8. See Erwin Hölzle, "Das Napoleonische Staatssystem in Deutschland," *Historische Zeitschrift,* Vol. CXLVIII, pp. 277-293. Generally, German historians have devoted little attention to the Rheinbund and to pro-French sentiments in Germany. The nationalism of the later nineteenth century regarded the lack of German nationalism at the beginning of that century not as an historical phenomenon but as a moral failure. Among the existing literature there should be mentioned Jos. Hansen, *Quellen zur Geschichte des Rheinlandes im Zeitalter der französischen Revolution, 1780–1801,* 2 vols. (Bonn: Hanstein, 1931, 1933); Karl Heinrich Ludwig Pölitz, *Der Rheinbund, historisch und statistisch dargestellt* (Leipzig: J. C. Hinrichs, 1911); Michael Doeberl, *Entwicklungsgeschichte Bayerns,* 3 vols., Vol. II (1648–1825), 3rd ed. (Munich: R. Oldenbourg, 1928); Hans Karl von Zwehl, *Der Kampf um Bayern, 1805,* Vol. I (Munich: C. H. Beck, 1937); Kurt Uebe, *Der Stimmungsumschwung in der bayerischen Armee gegenüber den Franzosen 1806–1812* (Munich: C. H. Beck, 1939); Anneliese Waller, *Baden und Frankreich in der Rheinbundzeit 1805–1813* (Schramberg: Gatzer & Hahn, 1935); Georges Servières, *L'Allemagne française sous Napoléon I* (Paris: Perrin, 1904); Marcel Dunan, "La Naissance de l'Allemagne Napoléonienne" *Revue Historique,* Vol. CLXXXVIII (jan.-mars 1940), pp. 105-114.—A detailed survey of the political line of one of the smaller states of the Rhenish Confederation is in Mathias Bernath, "Die auswärtige Politik Nassaus, 1805-1812," *Nassauische Annalen,* Vol. 63 (1952), pp. 106-191. Most German patriots, and probably Napoleon himself, were for a consolidation of the Rhenish Confederation as the true and modernized successor of the old Reich, but the larger south German states insisted on their sovereignty. Many were convinced that under Napoleon's protection the Rhenish Confederation could be transformed into a Germanic Confederation. In a Bavarian memorandum of December 3, 1806, Napoleon was called "l'empereur des

Français et des Germains," and the hope was expressed that "le vaste empire des Francs se trouvera rétabli tel qu'il était du temps de Charlemagne." In the same year Dalberg wrote: "Puisse-t-il [Franz II] être empereur d'Orient pour résister aux Russes, et que l'Empire d'occident rénaisse en l'empereur Napoléon, tel qu'il était sous Charlemagne, composé de l'Italie, de la France et de l'Allemagne." Napoleon was praised by the German intellectuals because he did not follow the French kings' policy of disorganizing Germany, but tried to organize her. The Rhenish Confederation was regarded as the modernized and legitimate continuation of the old and historical Germany.

9.　　　　　Und wenn dem Helden alles zwar gelungen,
　　　　　Den das Geschick zum Günstling auserwählt,
　　　　　Und Ihm vor allen alles aufgedrungen,
　　　　　Was die Geschichte jemals aufgezählt,
　　　　　Ja, reichlicher, als Dichter je gesungen,
　　　　　Ihm hat bis jetzt das Höchste noch gefehlt;
　　　　　Nun steht das Reich gesichert wie geründet,
　　　　　Nun fühlt Er froh im Sohne Sich gegründet.

　　　　　Und dass auch diesem eigne Hoheit gnüge,
　　　　　Ist Roma selbst zur Wächterin bestellt.
　　　　　Die Göttin, hehr an ihres Königs Wiege,
　　　　　Denkt abermals das Schicksal einer Welt.
　　　　　Was sind hier die Trophäen aller Siege,
　　　　　Wo sich der Vater in dem Sohn gefällt?
　　　　　Zusammen werden sie des Glücks geniessen,
　　　　　Mit milder Hand den Janustempel schliessen.

Goethe, *Werke*, Grossherzog Wilhelm Ernst Ausgabe (Leipzig: Inselverlag, 1920), Vol. 14, p. 614. The birth of the King of Rome was also celebrated by the German poet August Count Platen (1796-1835), who was then a royal page in Munich. The beginning of the ode may be quoted less for its intrinsic value than for its characteristic expression of widespread feeling:

　　　　　Holder Sprössling des grössten aller
　　　　　Erdensöhne, so lange sich Welten
　　　　　Ew'gen Kreislaufs um Welten drehen,
　　　　　Sonnen um Sonnen.

　　　　　Sei mir freudlich gegrüsst, o Knabe,
　　　　　Romas künftiger Herrscher, dreimal
　　　　　Segn' ich feurig den Tag, an dem du
　　　　　Lächelnd das Licht sahst.

10. Hans Kohn, *The Idea of Nationalism*, pp. 413-417. An excellent article on Goethe's relations to Prussia, to military glory, and to nationalism is Hans Haussherr, "Der Minister Goethe und die äussere Politik Carl Augusts," *Historische Zeitschrift*, 169 (1949), pp. 299-336.

11. *Ibid.*, p. 427.
12. See Fritz Strich, *Goethe und die Weltlitteratur* (Bern: Francke, 1946).
13. "Dass die Griechische Mythologie als höchstgestaltet, als Verkörperung der tüchtigsten, reinsten Menschheit mehr empfohlen zu werden verdiene, als das hässliche Teufels- und Hexenwesen, das nur in düstern ängstlichen Zeitläufen aus verworrener Einbildungskraft sich entwickeln und in der Hefe menschlicher Natur seine Nahrung finden konnte." Written in 1827, as a critical annotation to an article on Goethe by French admirers. Goethe, *Werke*, Grossherzog Wilhelm Ernst Ausgabe, Vol. 13, p. 276.
14. Oskar Seidlin, "Goethe über Goethe auf Französisch," *The Germanic Review*, Vol. XXI (1946), pp. 241-246. See, in general, Wilhelm Mommsen, *Die politischen Anschauungen Goethes* (Stuttgart: Deutsche Verlags-Anstalt, 1948).
15. Max Lenz, "Deutsches Nationalempfinden im Zeitalter unserer Klassiker," *Jahrbuch der Goethe Gesellschaft*, Vol. 2 (Weimar: Verlag der Goethe-Gesellschaft, 1915), p. 296. "The mood which in those years of German subjection dominated the broadest circles of our people has little in common with the reminiscent imagination which has been bequeathed to posterity; for already the contemporaries hastened to forget what they had done and what they had believed." See also Joachim Müller, "Schillers Gedichtentwurf 'Deutsche Grösse': Zum Problem der Kulturnation in der deutschen Klassik," *Wirklichkeit und Klassik: Beiträge zur deutschen Literaturgeschichte von Lessing bis Heine* (Berlin: Verlag der Nation, 1955) pp. 163 ff.
16. Frau von Stein wrote to her son Fritz on April 24, 1814: "They say that Goethe did not wish to allow his son to go with the volunteers, and he is the only young man of the upper classes (von Stand) who has remained at home. His father does not seem to share at all our present enthusiasm; one is not allowed to speak of political matters in his house."
17. "Nur so viel will ich sagen, dass nach meiner Einsicht das eigentlich innere Wirksame bei den Franzosen jetzt am tätigsten ist und dass sie deshalb zunächst wieder einen grossen Einfluss auf die sittliche Welt haben werden. Gern sagt ich mehr, aber es führt zu weit, und man müsste sehr ausführlich sein, um sich verständlich, und um das, was man zu sagen hat, annehmlich zu machen." *Studien zur Weltlitteratur*, Goethe, *Werke*, Vol. 13, p. 491.
18. *Conversations of Goethe with Eckermann and Soret*, tr. by John Oxenford (London: G. Bell, 1883), pp. 252 f.
19. Paul Nerrlich, *Jean Paul, Sein Leben und Seine Werke* (Berlin: Weidmann, 1889), p. 514. The passage is from the *Friedenspredigt an Deutschland*, Ch. 4, "Vaterlands- oder Deutschlands-Liebe."
20. Jean Paul, *Sämmtliche Werke*, Historisch-kritische Ausgabe, Abteilung I, Vol. 14 (Weimar: Hermann Böhlaus Nachfolger, 1939), p. xix. See also Heinrich Bertram, *Jean Paul als Politiker* (Halle: Niemeyer, 1932); Fritz Klatt, "Jean Paul und der Krieg," *Preussische Jahrbücher*, February 1918, pp. 145-164.
21. Jean Paul's article was called "Nachdämmerungen für Deutschland" and

was intended as a continuation of his "Dämmerungen für Deutschland" (1809). There he welcomed the rebirth of the empire of Charlemagne (Jean Paul, *Sämmtliche Werke*, p. 128) and was convinced that Napoleon would mellow and settle down after having built a new Europe and perhaps a new Asia. *Ibid.*, p. 126.

22. Paul Nerrlich, *op. cit.*, pp. 516 f.

23. Only one year before, in his letters to Gentz, Müller had called upon the Austrians not to surrender to Napoleon: "Be heroes. Abandon the thought that you could survive the honor of the great name of Habsburg, Lorraine, Austria; the fatherland is where the army is, and your domicile where there is undefeated courage." And in 1806, after the Battle of Jena, he wrote: "If Europe should really fall, it will be impossible for me to stand it. I shall go to the Neva or Volga, wherever one wishes, only to sustain as long as I live, by words full of truth and force, the sacred fire so that it may burn high when the hour comes." *Briefwechsel zwischen Gentz und Johannes von Müller*, ed. by Gustav Schleseer (Mannheim, 1840), pp. 126, 152.

24. "La Gloire de Frédéric, discours prononcé à la séance publique de l'Académie des sciences à l'occasion de l'anniversaire de Frédéric II." The address was reviewed by Goethe in the *Jenaische Allgemeine Literaturzeitung*, February 28, 1807. He also translated the address into German and published it in the *Morgenblatt für gebildete Stände* of March 3 and 4, 1807. Goethe, *Werke*, Grossherzog Wilhelm Ernst Ausgabe, Vol. XII, pp. 366-68, 378-388.

25. Kosegarten, among many other publications, translated Richardson's *Clarissa* into German. As professor of history in Greifswald, Kosegarten succeeded Arndt, who was dismissed by the French in June 1808. Though Kosegarten later wrote German patriotic poems—*Vaterländische Gesänge* (1813)—he was violently attacked by the German nationalists. Kotzebue wrote against him, "Warum Schonung gegen einen solchen Auswurf?"

NOTES FOR CHAPTER 22: *AEIOU: Austria's Historical Consciousness*

1. Ernst Karl Winter, *Rudolph IV von Oesterreich*, 2 vols. (Vienna: Reinhold Verlag, 1934), Vol. I, p. 309.

2. Anti-Austrian observers often interpreted Habsburg policy in the age of nationalism "as if it were directed against all manifestations of the national idea in this period of an intolerant and ferocious Germanization. This opinion is completely erroneous. The truth is that the system hated German nationalism no less than the Hungarian or the Italian (which were at the period the most highly developed) but it had no objection whatever to permitting every people to speak, cultivate, even develop its own language in its local sphere." Oscar Jászi, *The Dissolution of the Habsburg Monarchy* (Chicago: University of Chicago Press, 1929), p. 81.

3. "There was undoubtedly in many parts of the monarchy a kind of moral cohesion between the Habsburgs and the peasantry of the oppressed nationalities, which was very often protected by the Habsburgs against

German and Magyar rule. . . . The writer of these lines observed very often during his trips to Transylvania that the idea of the emperor enjoyed almost a kind of religious sacredness among the backward Rumanian peasants." *Ibid.*, p. 44. Eduard Wertheimer, *Geschichte Oesterreichs und Ungarns im ersten Jahrzehnt des 19. Jahrhunderts,* 2 vols. (Leipzig: Duncker & Humblot, 1884 and 1890); Viktor Bibl, *Der Zerfall Oesterreichs: Kaiser Franz und sein Erbe* (Vienna: Rikola Verlag, 1922); Heinrich Ritter von Srbik, *Deutsche Einheit: Idee und Wirklichkeit vom Heiligen Reich bis Königgratz,* Vol. I (Munich: Bruckmann, 1935); Franz Martin Mayer and Hans Pirchegger, *Geschichte und Kulturleben Deutsch-Oesterreichs von 1792 bis nach dem Weltkrieg* (Vienna: Braumüller, 1937); Walter Consuelo Langsam, *The Napoleonic Wars and German Nationalism in Austria* (New York: Columbia University Press, 1930); H. Freiherr Langwerth von Simmern, *Oesterreich und das Reich im Kampf mit der Französischen Revolution 1790-1797,* 2 vols. (Berlin: E. Bidder, 1880).

Notes for chapter 23: *Austria's Brief National Awakening*

1. Quoted from Béla Grünwald, *The Old Hungary* (Budapest: 1910) in Jászi, *op. cit.,* pp. 70 f. "About two decades later in a very nationalistic county, it was said that the introduction of the Magyar language would endanger our constitutions and all our interests . . . and religion would be ruined, the Latin language would be eliminated."

2. Viktor Bibl, *op. cit.,* Vol. I, p. 25. The Emperor wrote in his rescript of January 28, 1790: "As we are now convinced that you prefer the old administrative forms and that you look for your happiness in them and find it there, we do not hesitate to conform to your wishes." Professor Jászi comments rightly: "The unselfish work of a whole life in the interest of the commonweal, the disinterestedness of a great man against the dark powers of the past, a long series of brilliant reforms for the people, all were suddenly forgotten, but the returning of the mystical mediaeval symbol threw them into raptures of enthusiasm." *Op. cit.,* p. 73. See also Ernest Wangermann, *From Joseph II to the Jacobin Trials: Government Policy and Public Opinion in the Habsburg Dominion in the Period of the French Revolution* (Oxford University Press, 1959).

3. Mozart's *Magic Flute* was interpreted as an allegoric glorification of the French Revolution in the *Geheime Geschichte des Verschwörungssystems der Jakobiner in den Oesterreichischen Staaten* (1795). Pamino was declared to represent liberty; Papageno, the aristocracy; the serpent, the deficit; Sarastro's priests, the National Assembly. Undoubtedly some French pamphlets and newspapers like the *Moniteur* were read in Austria. Azirmay's *Jacobinorum Hungaricorum Historia* mentions that the speeches of the French revolutionaries "sparis libellis ephemeridibus gallicis Moniteur diciis vulgabantur et in caffeariis in Hungaria legebantur." Anton Springer, *Geschichte Oesterreichs seit dem Wiener Frieden 1809* (Leipzig: S. Hirzel, 1863) Vol. I, p. 49. See also Walter Consuelo Langsam, "Emperor Francis

II and the Austrian 'Jacobins' 1792-1796," *American Historical Review,*
Vol. L (1945), pp. 471-490; Denis Silagi, *Ungarn und der geheime Mitar-
beiter-Kreis Kaiser Leopold II.* (Munich: Südost-Institut, 1960); *id.,
Jakobiner in der Habsburger-Monarchie* (Vienna: Herold Verlag, 1962);
Paul Bödy, "The Hungarian Jacobin Conspiracy," *Journal of Central
European Affairs,* Vol. XXII (1962), pp. 3-26.

4. The anthem was first sung on February 12, 1797, the Emperor's birthday,
in all Viennese theaters. The first line recalled the "God Save the King."

5. Johann Baptist von Alxinger (1755-1797) wrote:

> Triumph! sie fliehen nach langer Gegenwehr!
> So hat denn Oesterreichs geprüfte Tapferkeit
> Auch ohne Bundesverwandte Scharen
> Dich, oh Germanien, geschirmt und befreit.
>
> Doch lernt einmal, dass kein politisch Klügeln,
> Nur Eintracht retten kann, und dass sichs nirgends gut
> Als unter den weit ausgebreiteten Flügeln
> Des hohen Kaiseradlers ruht.

6. The best study of this memorable year and generally of the "Austrian
idea" is André Robert, *L'idée nationale autrichienne et les guerres de
Napoléon: L'apostolat du Baron de Hormayr et le Salon de Caroline
Pichler* (Paris: Alcan, 1933). See also Walter Consuelo Langsam, *The
Napoleonic Wars and German Nationalism* (New York: Columbia University Press, 1930); *Achtzehnhundert-neun: Die politische Lyrik des
Kriegsjahres,* ed. by Robert F. Arnold and Karl Wagner (Vienna: Litterari-
scher Verein, 1909); Helmuth Rössler, *Oesterreichs Kampf um Deutsch-
lands Befreiung 1805-1815,* 2 vols. (Hamburg: Hanseatische Verlag-
sanstalt, 1940); Eduard Wertheimer, *Zur Geschichte Wiens im Jahre
1809* (Vienna: F. Tempsky, 1889). Characteristic of the spirit of the
year is the sentence from an article "Über die Landesverteidigungs-
Anstalten in Oesterreich" in *Vaterländische Blätter,* 1808, p. 302: "Der
Geist der Nation ist umgeschaffen. . . . Die Scheidewand zwischen dem
Stande der Verteidiger und dem der Verteidigten wurde weggeräumt."
The French chargé d'affaires Dodun wrote to the French Foreign Minister
Jean Baptiste de Champagny, Duc de Cador, who formerly had been
French ambassador in Vienna, on March 1809: "En 1805 la guerre était
dans le gouvernement, mais non dans l'armée ni dans le peuple; en 1809,
elle est voulue par le gouvernement, par l'armée et par le peuple."

7. Hormayr (1782-1848), a Tyrolian, was the most interesting among them.
He wrote a large number of historical works, especially on the history of
Tyrol, and published twenty volumes of the *Oesterreichischer Plutarch,
oder Leben und Bildnisse aller Regenten des Oesterreichischen Kaiser-
hauses* (Vienna: 1807-1814). Caroline Pichler (1769-1843), whose salon
was the literary center of Vienna, was a prolific writer of novels. Her
Sämtliche Werke comprised sixty volumes (Vienna 1820-45). In addition,
she wrote *Denkwürdigkeiten aus meinem Leben,* published after her death

in four volumes by F. Wolf (Vienna, 1844). Heinrich Joseph von Colin (1772-1811) wrote many dramas and in 1809 published *Lieder Oester-reichischer Wehrmänner*, songs which were set to music by Joseph Weigl (1766-1846). His less gifted brother Matthäus (1779-1824) chose for his dramas predominantly themes from Austrian history. Ignaz Franz Castelli (1781-1824) wrote in 1809 a "Kriegslied für die Oesterreichische Armee" and in 1813 "Ein Wort zur rechten Zeit eines Oesterreichers an seine verzagten Mitbürger."

8. Before he left Schönbrunn in 1805, Napoleon assured the Viennese in a proclamation that he knew well that they had all been against the war which their ministers, bought by England, had started.

9. Andreas Hofer was born in 1767 in the inn Sankt Leonhard am Sand in Passeier and was therefore known as "Der Sandwirt." A tall man with a long black beard, he was an impressive figure. Other leaders of the uprising were the Capuchin father Peter Jochen Haspinger (1776-1858), a small man with a red beard, and Josef Speckbacher (1768-1820).

10. On May 15, 1809, *Correspondance de Napoléon Ier*, Vol. 19, p. 11. Gellio Cassi in his "Napoléon, l'Autriche, et les Nationalités" emphasizes the refusal of the Austrian nationalities to strive for independence: "Au contraire, quand on leur addressa l'appel (et Napoléon ne manqua pas de le faire), elles s'insurgèrent à un tel point qu'elles manifestèrent plus ferme leur attachement à la couronne. En effet, elles détruisirent les effets mêmes de la Révolution, que Napoléon répandait en Europe à leur bienfait." *Revue des Etudes Napoléoniennes*, Vol. 15 (1919), p. 37. On Hungary's reported "neutrality" in 1805 after the Austrian defeats, see Eduard Wertheimer, *Geschichte Oesterreichs und Ungarns*, Vol. 1, pp. 344-355.

11. Count Jozsef Dessewffy wrote to Ferencz Kazinczy in 1808: "Non barbaries, non defectus culturae apud nationem Hungaram, impedit tales propositiones fieri et executione mandare, sed commodi proprie studium." Wertheimer, *op. cit.*, Vol. 2, p. 62.

12. Only intellectuals and writers showed an interest in the Magyar language. The cities spoke German, the nobility French and German. Yet with Ferencz Kazinczy and Alexander Kisfaludy the development of Hungarian literature began (Hans Kohn, *The Idea of Nationalism*, pp. 531-533). The slogan was coined, "Magyar, be truly Magyar, and honor your language" (Magyar, légy igaz magyar; becsüld nyelvedet). The first Magyar newspaper in Pest began to appear in 1806. Its name was "Patriotic News" (*Hazai tudós tasok*). It is interesting that the Hungarian Chancellery, in its reply of November 28, 1807, to the demand for the introduction of Magyar as the official language of Hungary, declared that such a step would be undesirable in view of the fact that Hungary was inhabited by many different nationalities with various languages, and the proclamation and propagation of Magyar as the official language might provoke the resistance and national feeling of these nationalities, especially of the Greek-Orthodox Serbs, whom the Chancellery called "Griechen." In this respect the imperial officials showed greater foresight than the Magyar nationalists. It was later the resistance of these orthodox

Serbs—of whom the Chancellery warned that they would not be easily deprived of their customs and language—which destroyed the ancient Hungarian kingdom and the monarchy.

NOTES FOR CHAPTER 24: *Romanticism and the Rise of German Nationalism*

1. See, on "personality" and "individuality," Fritz Strich, *Dichtung und Zivilisation* (Munich: Meyer & Jessen, 1928), p. 35, and his *Deutsche Klassik und Romantik* (Munich: Meyer & Jessen, 1922). See on romanticism in general the articles by Arthur O. Lovejoy, Goetz A. Briefs, and Eugene N. Anderson in *Journal of the History of Ideas*, Vol. II, No. 3 (June 1941). The relevant literature on German romanticism is very large. One of the first important books, published in 1870, was Rudolf Haym, *Die romantische Schule; ein Beitrag zur Geschichte des deutschen Geistes*, 5th ed. by Oscar Walzel (Berlin: Weidemann, 1928); one of the latest was Richard Benz, *Die deutsche Romantik: Geschichte einer geistigen Bewegung* (Leipzig: Philipp Reclam Jr., c. 1937). On the political implications see Paul Kluckhohn, *Persönlichkeit und Gemeinschaft: Studien zur Staatsauffassung der deutschen Romantik* (Halle: Niemeyer, 1925); Carl Schmitt, *Politische Romantik*, 2nd ed. (Munich: Duncker & Humblot, 1925); Jakob Baxa, *Einführung in die romantische Staatswissenschaft* (Jena: Gustav Fischer, 1923); *Gesellschaft und Staat im Spiegel deutscher Romantik*, ed. by Jakob Baxa (Jena: Gustav Fischer, 1924); Kurt Borries, *Die Romantik und die Geschichte* (Berlin: Deutsche Verlags-Gesellschaft für Politik und Geschichte, 1925); Andries David Verschoor, *Die ältere deutsche Romantik und die Nationalidee* (Thesis, Groningen; Amsterdam, 1928); Gottfried Salomon, *Das Mittelalter als Ideal in der Romantik* (Munich: Drei Masken Verlag, 1922); Reinhold Aris, *History of Political Thought in Germany from 1789 to 1815* (London: Allen & Unwin, 1936), pp. 205-341; Josef Körner, *Die Botschaft der deutschen Romantik an Europa* (Augsburg: Filser, 1933). Two more general works are Julius Petersen, *Wesensbestimmung der deutschen Romantik* (Leipzig: Quelle und Meyer, 1926), and Henri Braunschweig, *La Crise de l'Etat Prussien à la fin du XVIIe siècle et la génèse de la mentalité romantique* (Paris: Presses Universitaires de France, 1947). On the differences between English and German romanticism see Hoxie N. Fairchild, "The Romantic Movement in England," part of a symposium on romanticism in *PMLA*, Vol. 55 (March 1940), pp. 1-60.

2. See Hans Kohn, *The Idea of Nationalism*, pp. 413 ff.

3. In two famous poems in the second unfinished part of his novel *Heinrich von Ofterdingen* Novalis best expressed the character of this early romanticism:

> Es bricht die neue Welt herein . . .
> Der Liebe Reich ist aufgetan,
> Die Fabel fängt zu spinnen an. . . .
> Alles muss ineinandergreifen,

Eins durch das andre gedeihn und reifen;
Jedes in allen dar sich stellt,
Indem es sich mit ihnen vermischet
Und gierig in ihre Tiefen fällt,
Sein eigentümliches Wesen erfrischet
Und tausend neue Gedanken erhält.
Die Welt wird Traum, der Traum wird Welt. . . .

And in the second poem:

Wenn nicht mehr Zahlen und Figuren
Sind Schlüssel aller Kreaturen,
Wenn die, so singen oder küssen,
Mehr als die Tiefgelehrten wissen, . . .
Und man in Märchen und Gedichten
Erkennt die ew'gen Weltgeschichten,
Dann fliegt vor einem geheimen Wort
Das ganze verkehrte Wesen fort.

4. In an essay in the periodical *Athenäum* (Berlin, 1798-1800), Vol. 1, Part 2, pp. 28 f., quoted by John C. Blankenagel, *PMLA*, Vol. 55 (March 1940), p. 3.
5. Review of *The Athenaid*, an epic in thirty books, published in 1787, two years after the death of its author, Richard Grover (1712-1785), in the *Göttingische Anzeigen von gelehrten Sachen*, 1789, p. 1988.
6. *Novalis' Werke*, ed. by Hermann Friedemann (Berlin: Deutsches Verlagshaus Bong & Co., n.d.), Vol. 3, pp. 168, 159, 163 (Fragments 947, 884, 885, 887, 919). See also Richard Samuels, *Die poetische Staats- und Geschichtsauffassung Friedrich von Hardenbergs (Novalis)* (Frankfurt a.M.: Diesterweg, 1925), and Hans Wolfgang Kuhn, *Der Apokalyptiker und die Politik: Studien zur Staatsphilosophie des Novalis* (Freiburg i.B.: Rombach, 1961).
7. *Novalis' Werke*, p. 175 (Fragment 967). See also Fragment 946, "Alle Menschen sollen thronfähig werden," and Fragment 980, which explains that there is only one king by reason of economy. "If we were not obliged to proceed economically, we would all be kings."
8. *Ibid.*, pp. 155, 174, 169 (Fragments 863, 965, 950).
9. *Ibid.*, p. 165 (Fragment 936).
10. *Ibid.*, pp. 137, 176 (Fragments 756, 972, 973).
11. *Ibid.*, Vol. 4, p. 145.
12. Though Novalis himself warned wisely: "It is strong proof how far we have really progressed, that we think so contemptuously of our progress, of the stage we have reached." *Ibid.*, Vol. 3, p. 139 (Fragment 768).
13. *Ibid.*, pp. 191, 192 (Fragments 1064, 1072).
14. Later the romanticists accused Johannes Müller of a lack of patriotism. In reality, Müller was fundamentally an eighteenth century rationalist and cosmopolitan, an enthusiast for human rights and liberty. Adam Müller in an article in *Phoebus*, a periodical which he published together with

Heinrich von Kleist in Dresden in 1808, blamed the historian for being too impartial. Such an attitude, Adam Müller conceded, could be admitted while discussing the domestic affairs of the fatherland, but it was inadmissible regarding an external enemy. The heart of the historian must include hatred besides love, which can easily be corrupted. "Every hero, therefore also the scholarly hero, needs a fatherland, a firm foundation, on which to build his army camp, his place d'armes." An historian must take a stand; a cosmopolitan mentality was contrary to true humanity, Adam Müller maintained.

15. Josef Körner, *Nibelungenforschungen in der deutschen Romantik, Untersuchungen zur neuern Sprach- und Literaturgeschichte*, ed. by O. Walzel, N.F., No. 9 (Leipzig, 1911). Zeume was also the author of *Der Rheinstrom, Deutschlands Weinstrom, nicht Deutschlands Rainstrom* ("printed on the Rhine in the second year of German liberty") which never achieved the fame of Arndt's similar book.

16. *Des Knaben Wunderhorn: Alte deutsche Lieder* appeared in Heidelberg in the fall of 1805 with the date of 1806. Two further volumes followed in 1808. The first volume contained an important introduction by Tieck. Arnim's letter "An Herrn Kapellmeister Reichardt," which appeared first in Reichardt's *Berlinische Musikalische Zeitung*, was printed as a postscript to the *Wunderhorn*. Both texts are reprinted and easily accessible in *Deutsche Vergangenheit und Deutscher Staat*, ed. by Paul Kluckhohn, *Deutsche Literatur in Entwicklungsreihen, Reihe Romantik*, Vol. 10 (Leipzig: Reclam, 1935), pp. 83-126. Under the impression of this romanticism Stendhal wrote in 1807 to his sister Pauline: "Je ne sais pourquoi le moyen âge est lié dans mon coeur avec l'idée de l'Allemagne."

17. *Die Teutschen Volksbücher, Nähere Würdigung der schönen Historien-, Wetter-, und Arzneibüchlein, welche teils innerer Wert, teils Zufall Jahrhunderte hindurch bis auf unsere Zeit erhalten hat. Von J. Görres*, Professor der Physik an der Sekondärschule zu Coblenz (Heidelberg: Mohr und Zimmer, 1807).

18. The full title of the journal read: *Zeitung für Einsiedler: Alte und neue Sagen und Wahrsagungen, Geschichten und Gedichte*. It appeared for only half a year and was then published in book form, *Trost-Einsamkeit*. It was republished as No. 3 of the *Neudrucke romantischer Seltenheiten* (Munich: Meyer & Jessen, 1924).

19. The codification was the work of Johann Heinrich Kasimir Count Carmer (1721-1801), who was appointed by Frederick II in 1779 as chef de justice to reorganize the courts and the law in Prussia, and of the jurist Karl Gottlieb Suarez (1746-1798). Treitschke characterized the introduction of the Landrecht: "Dem Jünger der Aufklärung, dem der Staat das Werk des zweckbewussten Menschenwillens war, drängte sich von selber das Verlangen auf, dass im Staate nicht ein gegebenes und überliefertes, sondern ein gewusstes und gewolltes Recht herrschen müsse; sein Leben lang trug sich Friedrich mit dem Gedanken, die erste umfassende Kodifikation des Rechts, die seit den Zeiten Justinians gewagt worden,

durchzuführen." *Deutsche Geschichte im Neunzehnten Jahrhundert,* 8th ed. (Leipzig: Hirzel, 1909) Vol. I, p. 77.

20. Hermann U. Kantorowicz, "Volksgeist und Historische Rechtsschule," *Historische Zeitschrift,* Vol. 108 (1912), p. 311. Not only law but also religion was regarded as a product of the Volksgeist.

21. A translation of Savigny's pamphlet by Abraham Hayward, *Of the Vocation of Our Age for Legislation and Jurisprudence,* was printed by Littlewood and Co., London, 1831 (?), "Not for Sale."

Notes for Chapter 25: *Friedrich Schlegel*

1. Ernst Wieneke, *Patriotismus und Religion in Friedrich Schlegels Gedichten* (Munich: F. Gais, 1913). Richard Volpers, *Friedrich Schlegel als politischer Denker und deutscher Patriot* (Berlin-Steglitz: B. Behr's Verlag, 1916). Similar was the development of Friedrich's brother August Wilhelm, who had first welcomed the Revolution and the Consulate and later changed under the influence of Mme de Staël. Otto Brandt, *August Wilhelm Schlegel, der Romantiker und die Politik* (Stuttgart: Deutsche Verlags-Anstalt, 1919).

2. The "Versuch über den Begriff des Republikanismus veranlasst durch die Kantische Schrift zum ewigen Frieden" was printed in Friedrich Schlegel, *Prosaische Jugendschriften 1794-1802,* by J. Minor (Vienna: 1882), Vol. II, pp. 57-71. There on page 68 Schlegel wrote in the Kantian way: "Nur universeller und vollkommener Republikanismus würde ein gültiger . . . Definitivartikel zum ewigen Frieden sein."

3. Friedrich Schlegel, *Sämmtliche Werke,* 2. Originalausgabe, ed. by E. von Feuchtersleben, 15 vols. (Wien: Ignaz Klang, 1846), Vol. X, p. 14.

4. See Hans Kohn, *The Idea of Nationalism,* p. 413.

5. Schlegel's "Reise nach Frankreich" appeared in *Europa,* a periodical which he edited in Frankfurt-am-Main in 1803. There he wrote also: "How immensely further would Europe be on the road to true liberty and culture, if the center of the Church in past times had not been in Italy but, as it ought to be, in Germany, where the natural greatness of the spirit and the freer heart would have better fitted the great aim." In Paris Schlegel discovered old German art; he praised Dürer for deciding to paint not like the ancients or the Italians but in a German way. He even went so far as to prefer, for national and religious reasons, old German poetry to Greek poetry and old German painting to Italian art.

6. See Fr. Schlegel, *Sämmtliche Werke,* Vol. X, p. 93, and Vol. VI, p. 212. Schlegel was also the first to sing the glory of the romantic German forest —therein being the precursor of Eichendorff. In his lectures in 1810 he called "das tiefe und wahre Naturgefühl . . . , welches die alten Deutschen auf ihren Bergen und in ihren Wäldern mit der vaterländischen Luft selbst einathmeten, den eigentlichen Grundzug des deutschen Charakters, der immer geblieben ist und die deutschen Völker durch alle Zeiten und alle Länder begleitet hat." *Ibid.,* Vol. XI, p. 26.

7. These *Philosophische Vorlesungen aus den Jahren 1804 bis 1806* were edited after Schlegel's death by his friend C. J. H. Windischmann, professor of philosophy at the University of Bonn, in two volumes (Bonn: Eduard Weber, 1836-37); a second edition appeared there in 1846.

8. *Ibid.*, Vol. II, pp. 358, 382. In his lectures, however, Schlegel was still so fascinated by the medieval Ständestaat and so hostile to all the innovations of the French Revolution that he was against universal military service and wished, in the interests of peace, to reserve military service to the aristocracy. "Es wäre im Allgemeinen schon ein gefährliches Princip, alle Bürger in Soldaten verwandeln zu wollen. Dies würde dem kriegerischen Geiste der Nation ein höchst verderbliches Übergewicht geben, über den edleren Trieb der Bildung und Entwicklung, der nur im stillen, friedlichen Wirken sich steigend vervollkommen und schöner gestalten kann. Hat bei einer Nation einmal die Lust und Neigung zum Kriege die Oberhand erhalten, so wird nichts der wilden, verheerenden Eroberungssucht Grenzen setzen können. Allen Unordnungen und Verwirrungen, die aus ihr nothwendig entspringen, ist dann Thür und Thor geöffnet, und der Geist der Zwietracht und der Zerstörung wird sich wie ein reissender Strom über die benachbarten Völker ergiessen, und alle Kunst und Bildung in seinen wilden, tobenden Strudeln gewaltsam verschlingen. Durch die Aufstellung einer eigenen Krieger-Kaste wird dieser Gefahr vorgebeugt und der Zweck den übrigen Ständen gesichert. Dies ist der Adel, der nur als Kriegerstand als nothwendig anzusehen ist; ohne diese Bestimmung aber etwas durchaus zweckloses und widersinniges seyn würde." *Ibid.*, p. 364.

9. *Ibid.*, p. 385.

10. Fr. Schlegel, *Sämmtliche Werke*, Vol. X, p. 159. The poem was also included in *Deutsche Wehrlieder*, edited by Jahn in 1813. Schlegel's stepson, Philipp Veit (1793-1877), who served in the free corps, wrote to his mother Dorothea and to Schlegel from Schönhausen near Magdeburg on July 1, 1813: "Jahn is sending you herewith the first issue of a collection of songs which are being sung in our corps or are being rehearsed. You will find there one of your own which was sung here yesterday in church to a good melody by Zelter."—His brother August Wilhelm had preceded Schlegel to Vienna. In a letter from Coppet in Switzerland, where he was with Mme de Staël, he wrote in 1807 to Countess Louise von Voss: "I often have the impression that I have been forgotten in Germany; I do not deserve it, for never did I feel more German than now." He declared that he knew only one aim for a writer in that historical age, "to present to the Germans the image of their ancient glories, their old dignity and liberty, and the mirror of the past, and thus to kindle every spark of national sentiment which might anywhere be dormant." *Briefe von und an August Wilhelm Schlegel*, ed. by Joseph Körner, 2 vols. (Vienna: Amalthea-Verlag, 1930), Vol. I, pp. 199 f.

11. Fr. Schlegel, *Sämmtliche Werke*, Vol. XI, p. 195.

12. Friedrich Meinecke, *Weltbürgertum und Nationalstaat*, 7th ed. (Munich: Oldenbourg, 1928), p. 92, objected from the point of view of the modern

German power-state as much to the Christian political ethics of the romanticists as to the rational universalism of the Enlightenment. "Beide schalten das als blinde Herrschsucht, was im Wesen des Staates selbst begründet lag, was Ausfluss seiner Selbsterhaltung und Selbstbestimmung war." Meinecke argued that besides universal morality for individuals there exists an individual morality for the state and that this individual morality justifies the apparent immorality of the power-egotism of the state. "Denn unsittlich kann nicht sein, was aus der tiefsten individuellen Natur eines Wesens stammt," a principle which would justify every strong state and every strong individual in establishing his own "nature" as a yardstick of all morality.

13. The Germans owe to the romanticists—to A. W. Schlegel and Tieck—their first famous Shakespeare translation. Shakespeare as a great national poet was praised by A. W. Schlegel, *Sämmtliche Werke*, ed. by Eduard Bocking, 12 vols. (Leipzig: Weidmann, 1846-47), Vol. VIII, p. 145; and Tieck wrote in 1793: "Shakespeare war in seinem Zeitalter, mehr als jeder andere Schriftsteller, der Dichter seiner Nation; er schrieb nicht für den Pöbel, aber für sein Volk," and in 1817: "Soll also die Bühne nur in der Eigentümlichkeit und nationalen Bildung eines Volks bestehen, so hat ohne Zweifel nach dieser Voraussetzung England das älteste Theater in Europa." *Kritische Schriften* (Leipzig: 1848), Vol. I, pp. 38, 327.

NOTES FOR CHAPTER 26: *The Romantic Concepts*
of History, State, and Liberty

1. "Eine geistige Gemeinschaft zu einem möglichst vollkommenen Leben durch Entwicklung der Geistes- und Gemütskräfte im Volk, welche ja eben allein Leben genannt werden kann." Joseph Karl Benedikt Freiherr von Eichendorff, *Sämmtliche Werke*, Historisch-kritische Ausgabe, ed. by Kosch und Sauer, 24 vols. (Regensburg: J. Habbel, 1908-13), Vol. X, p. 159.

2. Zacharias Werner (1768-1823), an East Prussian, served the Prussian government in Warsaw and in other Prussian parts of Poland, where he became one of the first German poets expressing sympathy for the Polish cause. In a fragment in 1794 he glorified Kosciuszko:

> An diesen Trümmern angefesselt liegt
> Polonia, in Ketten eingeschmieget—
> Durch fremdes Gold und durch Verrath besiegt—
> Uud starr in dumpfen Schlummer eingewieget.

> Doch seht!—der Freiheit Engel naht sich schon,
> Er fliegt—ein Gott!—vom Mississippistrande,
> Er lacht des Todes—stürzt des Miethlings Thron,
> Und bricht des Vaterlandes Sklavenbande.

See Robert F. Arnold, *Geschichte der Deutschen Polenlitteratur von den Anfängen bis 1800* (Halle: Max Niemeyer, 1900), p. 277.

3. "So wird auch der grossen Genossenschaft des Staates mit innerlich ausge-wechselten Gesellen nichts gedient, sondern der der liebste sein, der ihr, weil mit ungebrochener Eigentümlichkeit, aus ganzer Seele dient, wie er eben kann und mag." Eichendorff, *Sämmtliche Werke*, Vol. X, p. 341.

4. *Ibid.*, Vol. III, p. 325.

5. The romanticists opposed capitalism, commerce, and the "influence of money." Schlegel went as far as to oppose taxes because they might give to the moneyed classes the power to influence the state. He suggested that the state should receive its income from the ownership of land and from the monopoly of all foreign trade. To Niebuhr in his *Roman History*, the period when the Romans tilled their own fields represented the ideal, while the later period, based upon commerce and trade, represented decadence and moral corruption. Another romantic historian Karl Ott-fried Müller (1797-1840) found in Greek history his model in Sparta and its constitution, full of "deepest political wisdom." A romantic philosopher, Franz Xaver von Baader (1765-1841), charged in his *Über das dermalige Missverhältnis der Vermögenslosen oder Proletars zu den Vermögenbe-sitzenden Klassen der Sozietät in betreff ihres Auskommens, sowohl in materieller, als intellektueller Hinsicht, aus dem Standpunkte des Rechts betrachtet* (Munich: G. Franz, 1835) that plutocratic servility to gold under liberalism rendered the poor into serfs of money whose conditions were worse than those of rural serfs. See, on Baader's social philosophy, David Baumgardt, *Franz von Baader und die philosophische Romantik* (Halle: Niemeyer, 1927).

6. Like Goethe, the Schlegels deserved great credit for opening up "world literature." August Wilhelm translated not only Shakespeare but Calderón and many Spanish, Portuguese, and Italian poets and later became a student of Sanskrit and Indian literature. Friedrich Schlegel regarded his Ständestaat as related to the Indian caste system, and both as an Aryan heritage. Fr. Schlegel, *Sämmtliche Werke*, Vol. XII, p. 347.

7. Adam Müller was practically unknown in the second half of the nine-teenth century. The German neo-romanticists of the twentieth century rediscovered him. See Otto Weinberger, "Das neue Schrifttum über Adam Müller," *Archiv für Sozialwissenschaft und Sozialpolitik*, Vol. LI (1924), pp. 808 ff.; Reinhold Aris, *Die Staatslehre Adam Müllers in ihrem Verhält-nis zur Deutschen Romantik* (Tübingen: Mohr, 1929); Ferdinand Reinkemeyer, *Adam Müllers ethische und philosophische Anschauungen im Lichte der Romantik* (Osterwieck am Harz: A. W. Zickfeldt, 1926); Jakob Baxa, *Adam Müller, ein Lebensbild aus den Befreiungskriegen und aus der deutschen Restoration* (Jena: Gustav Fischer, 1930). At the same time many of his works were republished, *Von der Notwendigkeit einer theologischen Grundlage der gesamten Staatswissenschaften und der Staatswirtschaft insbesondere* (Leipzig, 1819) as Vol. XVI of the Allge-meine Bücherei der Österreichischen Leo-Gessellschaft (Vienna: 1897); his *Zwölf Reden über die Beredsamkeit und deren Verfall in Deutschland* (Vienna, 1812) and his *Vorlesungen über die deutsche Wissenschaft und Literatur* (Dresden, 1807) were edited by Arthur Salz (Munich: Drei

Masken Verlag, 1920); Othmar Spann's series Die Herdflamme published his *Die Elemente der Staatskunst,* ed. by Jakob Baxa, 2 vols., and his *Versuche einer neuen Theorie des Gelds mit besonderer Rücksicht auf Grossbritannien,* ed. by H. Lieser (Vienna: Literarische Anstalt, 1922).

8. Adam Müller, *Die Elemente der Staatskunst,* Vol. I, pp. 29, 37, 48.
9. Adam Müller, *Ausgewählte Abhandlungen,* ed. by Jakob Baxa (Jena: Gustav Fischer, 1921), p. 21.
10. "Nichts desto weniger ist die Wendung, die der wissenschaftliche Geist in Deutschland genommen, die wichtigste Begebenheit in der Geschichte der modernen Bildung. Es ist entschieden, dass die verschiedenartigsten Geisteserzeugnisse des Auslandes sich nach und nach an diesen deutschen Stamm werden anschliessen müssen, und dass, wie Germanische Völker den Staatenkörper dieses Weltteils gegründet, so Germanischer Geist über kurz oder lang ihn beherrschen werde." Adam Müller, *Vorlesungen über die deutsche Wissenschaft und Literatur,* p. 4.
11. *Ibid.,* pp. 14 f. See also pp. 48, 59 f., and passim. What Germany is to Europe, Europe is to the world. "Die gesamte Erdoberfläche unseres Planeten strebt offenbar nach einer grossen Gemeinschaft, bei deren Errichtung Europa im Ganzen dieselbe Vermittlerrolle spielen wird, nach der sich, unsrer neulichen Auseinandersetzung zufolge, die deutsche Bildung im Verhältnis zu dem Staat von Europa hinneigt. Mittelpunkt der Civilisation der Welt, nicht bloss ihr Gipfel, soll Europa werden. Alle Strahlen des unerschöpflichen Reichtums der beiden Indien sollen im Mittelpunkte zusammenströmen, aber nur um von dort aus durch die Gewalt der Vereinigung auf alle Punkte des Umkreises hin wieder gleichförmig zurückströmen zu können." *Ibid.,* p. 38. About the pan-humanism of the Germans, see also A. W. Schlegel in *Europa,* I, 269: "Es ist auf nichts geringeres angelegt als die Vorzüge der verschiedenen Nationalitäten zu vereinigen, sich in alle hineinzudenken und hineinzu-fühlen, so einen kosmopolitischen Mittelpunkt des menschlichen Geistes zu stiften."
12. *Vorlesungen über die deutsche Wissenschaft und Literatur,* pp. 163 f.
13. *Ibid.,* pp. 165 f. See also *Zwölf Reden über die Beredsamkeit,* pp. 124 ff. (describing Burke's oratorical duel with Fox on the night of February 11-12, 1791), 135 ff., 167 ff., 186 f. Müller paid his tribute also to the ora-tory of Fox and of the two Pitts, but Burke was the greatest of all in his eyes. He called Burke the "Stellvertreter des unsichtbaren Englands, Geisterseher seiner Geschichte, Prophet seiner Zukunft; . . . er hatte keine Partei in dem wirklichen Parlament und dem damaligen Volk. . . . seine Partei war bei denen, die nicht sterben in England wie anderswo, deren Geist fortsitzt im Parlament, wo ihn keine Gegenwart, und sollte sie selbst durch Foxens Mund reden, verdrängen kann. . . . Wenn die weltliche Beredsamkeit . . . in Fox ihren Gipfel erreicht hat: so hat die heilige Beredsamkeit in diesem Jahrhundert nur durch Einen Mund geredet, durch den Mund Burkes.
14. "Bilde dein angewiesenes Werk nur ruhig fort, du vielfach verwundetes und unterdrücktes, aber auch jetzt schon mit Gütern, die die spätesten

Enkel deiner Unterdrücker noch segnen werden, vielfach entschädigtes Volk. . . . Jedes Herz helfe die eine Waffe schmieden und vollenden, der wir bedürfen: Erkenntnis des einfachen, ewigen Rechts unter allen Entstellungen der Selbstsucht und des Vorwitzes um uns her. Bleibt ihr der Erkenntnis, der Wissenschaft treu, so wird sie von selbst zur Kraft und zur Handlung, die jede einseitige Macht beugen, und zu ihrer Zeit die wilde Tyrannei, die euch jetzt zu Boden wirft, bezähmen wird." *Vorlesungen über die deutsche Wissenschaft und Literatur*, pp. 167, 169.

15. "Elemente der Staatskunst," third and seventh lectures. Adam Müller, *Vom Geiste der Gemeinschaft*, ed. by Friedrich Bülow (Leipzig: Alfred Kroner, 1931), pp. 41, 81.

16. Second lecture, *ibid., pp.* 20-23, 28, 34 f.

17. Fourth lecture, *ibid.*, pp. 48-52. "In einem langen Frieden muss sich also, eben weil das Auge der Bürger fast ausschliessend auf das Innere gewendet ist, das Zarteste und Innigste des gesellschaftlichen Verbandes auflösen und nachher nur allmählich in einem längeren Kriege, durch die Notwendigkeit ein gesellschaftliches Ganzes dem Feinde gegenüberzustellen, wieder geschürzt werden." Treitschke, *op. cit.*, p. 589, praised very highly a book *Vom Kriege* by Johann Jakob Rühle von Lilienstern (1780-1847): "Nowhere did the keen political idealism of the War of Liberation find a nobler expression than in that book," which in Treitschke's opinion "proved victoriously the indestructible blissful necessity of war" and proposed "to nationalize the armies and militarize the nations." The book was largely plagiarized from Adam Müller.

18. Thirty-fourth lecture, *ibid.*, p. 236.

19. *Über König Friedrich II und die Natur, Würde, und Bestimmung der Preussischen Monarchie*, Öffentliche Vorlesungen gehalten zu Berlin im Winter 1810 von Adam Müller (Berlin: J. D. Sander, 1810), first lecture, p. 5.

20. Second lecture, *ibid.*, pp. 52 f. There is something of the spirit of Fichte's *Reden* in Müller's eighth lecture: "Um die Zukunft mit Kraft und Bestimmtheit zu empfinden, muss man erst das Nationalleben empfunden haben. Was der Privatmann "Zukunft" nennt, ist ein weites Feld des Zufalls, worüber die Wetter Gottes und seine Winde und Zeiten walten, wovon das Herz nichts ahndet: eben weil es ein isoliertes Herz, ein Privatherz ist, und weil es den unendlichen Gott von seinem einsamen Standpunkt nicht fassen kann, sein Gesetz in den Erziehungscalcül nicht aufnehmen kann. Was der nationale Bürger "Zukunft" nennt, ist dagegen etwas sehr Bestimmtes und Besonderes; das Vaterland, d.h. Gott selbst und sein Gesetz, ist ja in der Rechnung. Nicht also der Privatmann, sondern nur der nationale Bürger, kann erziehen; also ist die Nationalität selbst conditio sine qua non aller Erziehung. Wie mögt ihr denn erziehen, bevor ihr einen Altar, ein Heiligtum, ein vaterländisches höchstes Gut fest und für die Ewigkeit erkannt habt? Ohne so ein Mittelstes, Nationales, Religiöses, worauf alles bezogen werde, und welches die junge Generation und ihr ganzes Streben ordne und festhalte, erzieht Ihr nur Privatmänner, und erneuert die alte Misere."

NOTES FOR CHAPTER 27: *Adam Müller and Heinrich von Kleist*

1. Johann Georg Sprengel, *Das Staatsbewusstsein in der Deutschen Dichtung seit Heinrich von Kleist.* Zeitschrift für den deutschen Unterricht, 12. Ergänzungsheft (Leipzig: Teubner, 1918). Kleist wrote to his friend Christian Ernst Martini from Potsdam on March 19, 1799: "The greatest miracles of military discipline, the objects of wonder of all experts, became the object of my deepest contempt; I regarded the officers as so many drillmasters, the soldiers as so many slaves, and when the whole regiment performed artfully—seine Künste machte—it appeared to me to be the living monument of tyranny." Arthur Elösser, *Heinrich von Kleists Leben, Werke und Briefe.* Tempel-Klassiker, *Kleists Sämmtliche Werke,* Vol. 5 (Leipzig: Tempel-Verlag, n.d.) p. 20. Kleist's letter of November 13, 1800, to his fiancée Wilhelmine von Zenge explained why he did not wish to accept any position in the service of the state: "I shall do what the state demands from me is good. I shall become a new instrument of its unknown purposes—I can't do it . . . I would seek my pride in it to claim the rights of my reason against the will of my superiors—die Ansprüche meiner Vernunft gelten zu machen gegen den Willen meiner Obern—no, I am not fit for any governmental position—Ich passe mich für kein Amt." *Ibid.,* p. 104. See on Kleist, Walter Solz, *Early German Romanticism, Its Founders and Heinrich von Kleist* (Cambridge, Mass: Harvard University Press, 1929); Hans M. Wolff, *Heinrich von Kleist als politischer Dichter* (Berkeley: University of California Press, 1947); Helmut Sembdner, *Die Berliner Abendblätter Heinrich von Kleists, ihre Quellen und ihre Redaktion* (Berlin: Weidmann, 1939), and his *Heinrich von Kleists Lebensspuren, Dokumente und Berichte der Zeitgenossen* (Bremen: Schünemann, 1957).

2. *Ibid.,* pp. 247 f. In the same letter Kleist asked why no French émigré had been found to shoot Napoleon, "diesen bösen Geist der Welt."

3. In an interesting psychological study, Professor Eugene Newton Anderson explained Kleist's nationalism by his literary failures. "If Kleist had been successful in his writing and publishing in Dresden, he probably never would have embraced nationalism, for he felt little concern about political conditions until his own career was directly endangered. His case illustrates that of an egocentric writer forced back into the group, showing how the fate of one became identified with that of the other." French influence seemed to deprive Kleist of a stage for his dramas and even threatened to destroy the German language, vehicle of his creation and fame. Eugene Newton Anderson, *Nationalism and the Cultural Crisis in Prussia 1806-1815,* pp. 126 f. See also p. 149.

4. *Heinrich von Kleists Werke,* ed. by Erich Schmidt with Georg Minde-Pouet and Reinhold Steig (Leipzig: Bibliographisches Institut, n.d.), Vol. 4, p. 35. "We shudder as you seize the spoke of the wheel of world-destiny, on the day of decision, and your people listen full of anxiety which lot will be theirs. . . . The German doesn't demand victory, help-

less as he stands on the brink of the precipice; if only the fight will flare up torchlike, worthy of the corpse going to be buried. May he then fall into dark night from the summit which he had already half ascended. Lord! the tear will thank you if only your sword will avenge it."

5. "An Palafox," *ibid.*, Vol. 4, p. 36.

6. Hans Kohn, *The Idea of Nationalism*, pp. 144 f., 340 f., 346, 418, 648, 700. Arndt published fragments of a tragedy "Herrmann" in the second part of his *Geist der Zeit* (1809) and Jahn wrote at the beginning of 1813 a "Rede des Arminius vor der Teutoburger Schlacht." After 1813, German nationalist writing abounded in second- and third-rate glorifications of Arminius.

7. It is interesting that later German critics regarded Bismarck as the embodiment of Herrmann. "Das Erstaunliche an dieser Schöpfung Kleists bleibt indessen, dass wir Deutschen diesen gedichteten Herrmann in Fleisch und Blut besitzen dürfen; denn diese einzigartige Persönlichkeit war in voller Lebenswahrheit und Lebensgrösse unter uns vorhanden, es ist niemand anders als Otto v. Bismarck, der Gründer des Reichs, sechs Jahre vor seiner leiblichen Geburt aus dem Geiste deutschen Weltfühlens im Bilde der Kunst geschaffen." Johann Georg Sprengel, *op. cit.*, p. 16. And in the same way Elösser wrote: "Es bleibt ewig merkwürdig, mit welcher Sicherheit der dichtende märkische Junker seinen grössten Landsmann und Standesgenossen vorgeahnt und vorgezeichnet hat. . . . Herrmann outwits Varus as Bismarck outwitted the other Napoleon. . . . He has the same soldierly religion, which, after the most minute preparation, leaves the decision to the German God." Elösser, *op. cit.*, p. 288. Naturally, the "Herrmannsschlacht" pleased National Socialist scholarship. Walter Linden wrote in his *Geschichte der deutschen Literatur von den Anfängen bis zur Gegenwart* (Leipzig, 1937), p. 342: "Eine völkische Sittlichkeit wird gepredigt; entschlossener Daseinskampf um jeden Preis und unter freiwilliger Opferung aller Güter, stahlharter Schicksalswille, Vernichtung des Gegners ohne Mitleid und Rücksicht. . . . Den 'humanen' Vorurteilen seiner Zeitgenossen setzt Kleist eine Germanische Kriegerethik entgegen. . . . Es ist das Drama des Triumphes völkischer Gefühlssicherheit. In ihm lebt und wirkt eine naturhafte deutsche Menschheit, die einem tötlichen Feind ihrer Gemeinschaft ohne Sentimentalität, mit klarer und fester Unerbittlichkeit entgegenzutreten und ihn zu vernichten weiss." [A folkish morality is being preached; resolute struggle for existence at any cost and a voluntary sacrifice of all goods, a steely will of destiny, annihilation of the adversary without pity and regard. . . . Kleist opposed a German warrior ethics to the humane prejudices of his contemporaries. . . . It is the triumphant drama of the folkish sentiments certain of themselves. In it a natural German humanity lives and is at work which knows how to meet a deadly adversary of its community without sentimentality, but with clear and firm ruthlessness, and how to annihilate him.] See also Walter Linden, *Heinrich von Kleist, der Dichter der völkischen Gemeinschaft* (Leipzig, 1935); Hoppe, *Die Staatsauffassung Heinrich von Kleists* (Bonn, 1938); Fritz Mattini, *Heinrich von Kleist*

und die geschichtliche Welt (Berlin: Ebering, 1940); also Heinrich von Kleist, *Politische und journalistische Schriften,* ed. by Adam von Trott (Potsdam, Protte, 1935). A different approach can be found in Günter Blöcker, *Heinrich von Kleist oder das absolute Ich* (Berlin: Argon, 1960).

8. *Kleist, Werke,* pp. 30 f.; Germania calls upon her children:

> Alle Triften, alle Stätten
> Färbt mit ihren Knochen weiss;
> Welchen Rab' und Fuchs verschmähten,
> Gebet ihn den Fischen preis;
> Dammt den Rhein mit ihren Leichen;
> Lasst, gestäuft von ihrem Bein,
> Schäumend um die Pfalz ihn weichen,
> Und ihn dann die Grenze sein!

9. See Dahlmann's "Fragment einer Autobiographie" in Anton Springer, *Friedrich Christoph Dahlmann* (Leipzig: Hirzel, 1870), Vol. I, pp. 456-459.

10. Originally only composers, poets, and professional singers were admitted. The members of the Liedertafel called themselves Liederbrüder; the chairman, Liedervater; the conductor, Liedermeister. Later the name Männergesangverein or Männerchor was used. The original Liedertafel started each meeting with Gleim's song, composed by Zelter:

> Der König soll leben, soll leben ein Held!
> Gegeben dem Throne, gegeben der Welt!
> Gegeben dem Lande zum deutschesten Mann,
> Der König soll leben, soll leben, stosst an!

11. One of its visitors, Philipp August Boeckh (1785-1867), the famous classical scholar, wrote to the bookseller Zimmer in Heidelberg on May 1, 1811: "Brentano and Arnim gefallen sich ganz ausnehmend. Arnim ist der Stifter einer grossen Essgesellschaft, welche sich die Christlich-Deutsche nennt, und keine Franzosen und keine Philister duldet. Ich habe neulich auch darin gegessen, und es geht recht Arnimisch darin zu." Reinhold Steig, *Heinrich von Kleist's Berliner Kämpfe* (Berlin und Stuttgart: Spemann, 1901), p. 39. See also Philip Eberhard, *Die politischen Anschauungen der christlich-deutschen Tischgesellschaft* (Erlangen: Palm & Enke, 1937); Reinhold Steig and H. Grimm, *Achim von Arnim und die ihm nahe standen,* 3 vols. (Stuttgart: Cotta, 1894-1913); Hermann Becker, *Achim von Arnim in den wissenschaftlichen und politischen Strömungen seiner Zeit* (Abhandlungen zur mittleren und neueren Geschichte, Heft 37, Berlin und Leipzig, 1912); René Guignard, *Achim von Arnim* (Publications de la Faculté des Lettres d'Alger, 1953).

12. Friedrich Heinrich Karl Freiherr de La Motte-Fouqué (1777-1843), the author of many romances from the German middle ages, was also the first to write a modern dramatization of the Nibelungenlied and of the old saga in his *Der Held des Nordens* (1808). It was a trilogy consisting of

the dramatic poems "Sigurd der Schlangentöter," "Sigurds Rache," and "Aslauga."

13. On Marwitz (1777-1837) see his *Nachlass,* ed. by Friedrich Meusel, 3 vols. (Berlin: Mittler, 1908-1913); the excellent study by Sigmund Neumann, *Die Stufen des preussischen Konservatismus: Ein Beitrag zum Staats- und Gesellschaftsbild Deutschlands im 19. Jahrhundert* (Berlin: Ebering, 1930); Gerhard Ramlow, *Ludwig von der Marwitz und die Anfänge konservativer Politik und Staatsanschauung in Preussen* (Berlin: Ebering, 1930); Willy Andreas, "Marwitz und der Staat Friedrich des Grossen," *Historische Zeitschrift,* Vol. 122 (1920), pp. 44-82.

14. The other two newspapers in Berlin at that time, among them the famous *Vossische Zeitung,* appeared in the morning, three times a week, and followed a moderate liberal policy. Kleist's paper was popular in his time and cheap in price.

15. *Kleists Werke,* ed. by Wilhelm Waetzoldt (Berlin: Deutsches Verlagshaus Bong & Co., n.d.), Vol. 5, pp. 105 f. ("Von der Überlegung") and p. 96 ("Betrachtungen über den Weltlauf").

16. This song began with the verse, expressing the character of the Prussian crown and nobility:

> Unsre Krone ward erstritten
> Durch der deutschen Ritter Blut,
> Als die Heiden mussten bitten
> Um des ew'gen Friedens Gut;
> Seit die Heiden sind bekehret,
> Kam die gnadenfrohe Zeit,
> Und der Adel wahret und lehret
> Freiheit in Ergebenheit;
> Freiheit christlich deutscher Treue
> Uns mit deinem Segen weihe!
> Ew'ger Glaube lebe hoch!

Steig, *Heinrich von Kleist's Berliner Kämpfe,* pp. 27 f. Arnim and La Motte-Fouqué used among others the figure of Markgraf Woldemar of Brandenburg (1308-1319), whose successful reign was followed after his sudden death by a "time of troubles." As a result, in 1348 a pretender appeared who declared that he was Woldemar returning to save his land. For seven years most of the people believed him. The Woldemar legend played for Brandenburg a role like that of the legend of Barbarossa for Germany. In the next generation Wilhelm Häring (1798-1871) wrote, under the pen name Willibald Alexis, a great number of very popular novels from Brandenburg history, among them also *Der falsche Woldemar* (1842). Of the romanticists, Novalis and Adam Müller helped to create the Prussian myth of Queen Louise.

17. Marwitz, *Nachlass,* Vol. I, p. 495; Vol. II, 2, p. 20. Marwitz and his Junker friends were very far even from a Prussian patriotism. They insisted on the historical rights of the various provinces. The nobility of the Priegnitz declared that its province formed a separate state with a pe-

culiar constitution different from all the other provinces. Treitschke, *op. cit.*, p. 373. In reality the Prussian nobility represented a heavy drag on the strength and health of the Prussian state. Most of its members were impoverished, and though poorly educated, were determined to hold most of the official positions in the state. The reformers had no intention of abolishing the nobility, but were bent on improving its position by reforming it after the English model.

18. Amongst the leading figures of romanticism, Tieck was perhaps least interested in political questions and played no role in the turbulent years from 1806-1820. See Edwin H. Zeydel, *Ludwig Tieck, The German Romanticist* (Princeton: University Press, 1935), pp. 164 f. In his youth he had been more strongly in favor of the French Revolution than even his friends. At the end of 1792, after the start of the war, he wrote to his friend Wilhelm Wackenroder (1773-1798): "Oh, how I would love to be in France now; it must be a wonderful feeling to fight in Dumouriez' army and to put slaves to flight and even to die—for what is life without freedom? I welcome rapturously the genius of Greece which I now see soaring over Gaul. I think day and night of France." In January 1793 Wackenroder answered: "I entirely agree with you, and I can assure you that I am in full accord with your enthusiasm, and this out of the fullness of my heart." Even after the execution of Louis XVI, he wrote to Tieck on March 5, 1793: "The execution of the King of France has revolted the whole of Berlin against the French, but not me. I think of their cause as I always did. Whether they use the right means, I cannot judge, because I understand very little of history." Wackenroder, whose *Herzensergiessungen eines kunstliebenden Klosterbruders* [Outpourings of an art-loving monk] of 1797 "discovered" medieval art, influenced Tieck in that respect. He died like Novalis long before the awakening of a national consciousness in Germany; Tieck, in spite of his enthusiasm for the German past, paid less fervent tribute to the rising flood of nationalism than his fellow-romanticists who lived through the Napoleonic era. See his correspondence with Karl Wilhelm Ferdinand Solger (1780-1819) in *The Complete Correspondence Between Tieck and Solger*, ed. by Percy Matenko (New York-Berlin: B. Westermann, 1933) and passages like the interesting conversation in his short novel called "Der Geheimnisvolle," Tieck, *Schriften* (Berlin: G. Reimer, 1829), Vol. 14, pp. 337-346.

NOTES FOR CHAPTER 28: *The Reform Movement in Prussia:*
I. Wilhelm von Humboldt

1. When the King returned to Berlin in August 1814, after the defeat of Napoleon, the people prepared a great reception for him. He was rather irritated by it, declared that too much money was wasted, and continued: "I do not like the trophies of victory, the captured cannons and flags heaped together at the armory opposite my residence. One must not and dare not taunt the defeated enemy. This is miserable boastfulness, and we do not wish in our good fortune to start again that haughtiness which

brought about our misfortune. It is against all rules of propriety to cause people with whom we have just made peace to feel again humiliated by putting up cannons and flags, especially those of the Bavarians and others who ultimately fought as our allies, boldly and courageously supporting us. The festive victory arches, the elaborate trophies in the windows of the arsenal must be taken away again; tomorrow's festivities shall be a Christian feast of pious gratitude and humility before God. It is He who has done great deeds for Prussia; to Him alone belongs the honor." Eugene Newton Anderson, *Nationalism and the Cultural Crisis in Prussia*, p. 295. It is regrettable that with the triumph of nationalism in Germany this attitude of the more modest "old times" disappeared. Nor was the King eager to invade France in 1813-14. Gneisenau wrote to Boyen from general headquarters in Frankfurt-am-Main on November 11, 1813, and to Clausewitz on November 16, 1813, complaining bitterly that the King was most reluctant to cross the Rhine. He reported the King saying, "What do those on the left bank matter to us? . . . It would be a ridiculous idea to wish to march on Paris."

2. J. R. Seeley (1834-1895; after 1869 professor of modern history at Cambridge), *Life and Times of Stein* (Cambridge: University Press, 1878), Vol. I, p. 383.

3. Stein wrote of Adam Smith "that the world has never seen a more important book than that of A. S. Assuredly since the time of the New Testament no work has had more beneficial effects than this will have if it should be more widely diffused, and more deeply impressed upon the minds of all who have to do with public affairs." *Ibid.*, p. 409.

4. See, on the men and their ideas, Franz Schnabel, *Deutsche Geschichte im Neunzehnten Jahrhundert* (Freiburg-i.B.: Herder, 1929), Vol. I, pp. 283-478. Also Wilhelm Dilthey, *Gesammelte Schriften* (Leipzig: Teubner, 1936), Vol. XII, pp. 37-122; and on Prussian bureaucracy Hans Rosenberg, *Bureaucracy, Aristocracy and Autocracy: The Prussian Experience, 1660-1815* (Harvard University Press, 1958).

5. Wilhelm von Humboldt's *Gesammelte Schriften,* ed. by Albert Leitzmann and others, 15 vols. (Berlin: Prussian Academy of Sciences, 1903-1920), Vol. 3, pp. 196, 216. See on Humboldt: Rudolf Haym, *Wilhelm von Humboldt: Lebensbild und Charakteristik* (Berlin: Gaertner, 1856); Eduard Spranger, *Wilhelm von Humboldt und die Humanitätsidee* (Berlin: Reuther und Reichard, 1909); Friedrich Meinecke, *Weltbürgertum und Nationalstaat*, Chs. 3 and 8; S. A. Kaehler, *Wilhelm v. Humboldt und der Staat* (Munich: R. Oldenbourg, 1927); Ernst Schaumkell, "Wilhelm v. Humboldt und der Preussische Staatsgedanke," *Forschungen zur Brandenburgischen und Preussischen Geschichte,* Vol. 47 (1935), pp. 309-395; Paul Binswanger, *Wilhelm v. Humboldt* (Frauenfeld: Huber, 1937); Otto Vossler, *Der Nationalgedanke von Rousseau bis Ranke* (Munich: Oldenbourg, 1937), pp. 102-115; Ernst Howald, *Wilhelm v. Humboldt* (Zürich-Erlenbach: Eugen Rentsch, 1944).

6. Ernst Schaumkell, *loc. cit.,* ends as following: "Das Menschentum, das Humboldt lebte und vertrat, war das des allgemeinen deutschen Idealis-

mus, der den Einzelmenschen, das Individuum, als höchsten Wert setzte, es war kein Menschentum preussischer Prägung."

7. "As one should never leave the circle which the seven hills surrounded by the splendor of lofty ruins magically encompass, so one should no longer listen to the lure of foreign melodies, as the highest fulfillment of all earthly desires was fully reached in the works of Hellas." Sonnet 786. See on the whole problem Ernst Howald, *op. cit.*

8. Rudolf Haym, *Wilhelm von Humboldt*, p. 51. Friedrich Meinecke, *op. cit.*, pp. 42 f. wrote: "As a man who knew the human soul, he knew even then that man inclines more to domination than liberty, and as a Prussian subject, he knew that the edifice of domination not only pleases the ruler but also the parts that serve, through conscious of being parts of a whole which survives throughout the generations. But this was not his ideal; he saw a higher degree of culture not in the dominating, but in free activity."

9. See W. von Humboldt, *Gesammelte Schriften*, Vol. 1, pp. 264 ff., "Über das Studium des Altertums" (1793), and his letter to Goethe from Paris on March 18, 1799.

10. *Ibid.*, Vol. 2, p. 72. In 1795, he wrote: "Plan einer vergleichenden Anthropologie." *Ibid.*, Vol. 1, p. 379.

11. "Der Universität ist vorbehalten, was nur der Mensch durch und in sich selbst finden kann, die Einsicht in die reine Wissenschaft. Zu diesem Selbstaktus im eigentlichsten Verstand ist notwendig Freiheit und hilfreiche Einsamkeit." *Ibid.*, Vol. 13, p. 279. The university was not to be primarily a school, but an institute for research. It should treat knowledge not as something finished, but should always continue to search. The teachers were not there to communicate ready results to the students. Both were there for the sake of scholarship. *Ibid.*, Vol. 10, pp. 251 f.

12. *Ibid.*, Vol. 1, p. 236. Nationality in Humboldt's view was not based on race and descent but on the human individuality. Thus in his "Gutachten zum Preussischen Emanzipationsedikt" of July 17, 1809, concerning the emancipation of the Jews, he called it "an inhuman way of thought, full of prejudices," if one "judges a man not according to his individual qualities, but according to his descent and religion, and if one regards him, against all true concept of human dignity, not as an individual but as a member of a race and by necessity sharing certain qualities with it." *Ibid.*, Vol. 10, pp. 97-115.

13. *Ibid.*, Vol. 1, pp. 113, 118. More than thirty years later, Humboldt wrote in a letter of May 9, 1826: "In world events and the occurrences which whole states experience, the truly essential remains that which is concerned with the activity of the mind and the sentiment of individuals. Man is everywhere the center, and ultimately every man remains solitary, so that only that which has been in him and which emanates from him has an important influence on him." *Briefe von Wilhelm v. Humboldt an eine Freundin* (Leipzig: F. A. Brockhaus, 1860), p. 177.

14. *Ibid.*, Vol. 1, p. 103. Humboldt, comparing antiquity with modern times, pointed out the difference in purpose of government, stating that the

ancients were concerned only with the strength and formation of man as man, while the moderns are concerned with his well-being and prosperity. "The ancients sought virtue, the moderns seek happiness." He showed greater understanding for the fundamental difference in his *Geschichte des Verfalls und Unterganges der Griechischen Freistaaten.* There he wrote: "Only in our times has education aimed at individuality, only since Christianity has destroyed all national ties through its never entirely successful attempt to unite all nations. What we tried to achieve through individuals, the ancients tried to achieve through nationality—Wonach wir individuenweise streben, dahin suchten die Alten völkerweise zu gelangen" *Ibid.,* Vol. 3, p. 181.

15. Meinecke, *loc. cit.,* pp. 194 ff. agrees, but with an opposite evaluation. To him it seems "ein Irrtum," an imperfection, that Humboldt like Stein did not conceive "den Staat und Nationalstaat in ihrer nackten Gestalt, in jener reinen Autarkie und Autonomie, in jener unbedingten Auswirkung ihrer immanenten Machttriebe, wie es später Ranke und noch später Bismarck sahen"—as if Humboldt and his generation, still connected with the modern Western tradition, had not understood deeply enough the forces in history. They may have understood them better than Ranke and Bismarck.

16. See Hans Kohn, *The Idea of Nationalism,* p. 372.

17. See Humboldt's *Denkschrift über die Deutsche Verfassung* of December 1813, in *Ges. Schriften,* Vol. 11, pp. 95 ff. Humboldt speaks there of the Confederation as a Staatenverein. The Denkschrift of September 30, 1816, see *ibid.,* Vol. 12, p. 77.

NOTES FOR CHAPTER 29: *The Reform Movement in Prussia:*
II. Baron vom Stein

1. See, on Stein, Gerhard Ritter, *Stein,* 2 vols. (Stuttgart: Deutsche Verlags-Anstalt, 1931); Franz Schnabel, *Freiherr vom Stein* (Leipzig: Teubner, 1931); R. Flad, *Studien zur politischen Begriffsbildung in Deutschland während der preussischen Reform: Der Begriff der öffentlichen Meinung bei Stein, Arndt und Humboldt* (Berlin: W. de Gruyter, 1929); Helmut Tiedemann, *Der deutsche Kaisergedanke vor und nach dem Wiener Kongress* (Breslau: Marcus, 1932); U. Noack, "Christentum und Volksstaat in der politischen . . . Ethik des Freiherrn vom Stein," *Historische Zeitschrift,* Vol. 147 (1933), pp. 40 ff.; Walter Görlitz, *Stein, Staatsmann und Reformator* (Frankfurt a.M.: Verlag der Frankfurter Hefte, 1949); Kurt von Raumer, "Der junge Stein," *Historische Zeitschrift,* Vol. 184, No. 3, pp. 497-530; and R. C. Raack, *The Fall of Stein* (Cambridge Mass.: Harvard University Press, 1965).

2. See Freiherr vom Stein, *Staatsschriften und Politische Briefe,* ed. by Hans Thimme (Munich: Drei Masken Verlag, 1923), pp. 5-23.

3. See Max Lehmann, *Freiherr vom Stein* (Leipzig: Hirzel, 1902), Vol. I, pp. 355 f.

4. *Stimmen aus der Zeit der Erniedrigung,* ed. by Rudolf Vaupel (Munich: Drei Masken Verlag, 1923), pp. 5-23.

5. J. R. Seeley, *Life and Times of Stein,* Vol. II, p. 244. James Harvey Robinson remarked in his *Readings in European History* (Boston: Ginn, 1934) Vol. 2, p. 519, that these cautious measures "are in singular contrast to the generous and thoroughgoing, not to say reckless, provisions of the decree abolishing the feudal system in France." On the other hand, Eduard Spranger, "Philosophie und Pädagogik der preussischen Reformzeit," *Historische Zeitschrift,* Vol. 104 (1910), pp. 278-321, found them too little cautious because too much under the influence of "liberty and equality." They were also quickly regulated in a very restrictive sense. Spranger pointed out as one of their consequences that the spirit of caste amongst the Prussian nobility increased. "Es ist bemerkenswert, dass erst seitdem der Adelsgeist im Offizierkorps seine Höhe erreicht hat: denn von nun an schloss sich dieser Stand auch gegen die in Bildung und Abkunft Gleichstehenden schroff ab durch die ideellen Momente eines besonderen staatlichen Ehr- und Pflichtgefühls, das strenger als alle Geburtsschranken wirken musste." See also Walter M. Simon, *The Failure of the Prussian Reform Movement 1807-1819* (Ithaca, N. Y.: Cornell University Press, 1955).

6. "Eine eigentliche Abschaffung, man möchte sagen Verhöhnung des Adels ist dem Geiste unseres Monarchen und unseres Volkes durchaus zuwider. Wird der Gewürzkrämer oder der Schneider, der das Gut erwirbt, oder der Spekulant, der auf seinen Profit gedacht hat und schon auf Wiederveräusserung sinnt, wird er auch im Unglück seinem Monarchen zu Dienst sein mit Gut und Blut? Wird der neue Herr seine Bauern, die ihn wohl mit Ziegengemecker an der Ehrenpforte empfangen, mit sich in der Treue festhalten, wie der alte Erbbesitzer tat, der in seinem Dorfe über die Gemüter mit Liebe und Anhänglichkeit herrschte? . . . So etwas kann nur in der Kanzlei eines Bankiers oder von einem Professor, der einen schlecht verdauten Adam Smith vom Katheder doziert, ausgeheckt werden. Leider hat sich dergleichen Geschmeiss des genialen Ministers bemächtigt."

7. See Hans Thimme in Stein, *Staatsschriften,* pp. xxxiv, xl f. After 1815 Stein became more and more conservative, a follower of Metternich's Restoration, and opposed to his own spirit of reform of 1808. See Werner Gembruch, *Freiherr vom Stein im Zeitalter der Restauration* (Wiesbaden: Steiner, 1961).

8. Max Lehmann, *Stein,* Vol. II, p. 76.

9. Stein, *Staatsschriften,* pp. 45, 86.

10. H. F. K. Freiherr vom Stein, *Briefwechsel, Denkschriften und Aufzeichnungen,* ed. by Erich Botzenhart, 7 vols. (Berlin: Heymann, 1931-1937), Vol. IV (1933), p. 573; Vol. V (1933), p. 225.

11. See Stein, *Briefwechsel, Denkschriften und Aufzeichnungen,* Vol. I (1931), p. 232; Georg Heinrich Pertz, *Das Leben des Ministers Freiherr vom Stein,* 2nd ed., 6 vols. in 7 (Berlin: G. Reimer, 1850-1855), Vol. I, p. 131; Vol. II, p. 443. See also Stein's letter to his wife, of April 10, 1814 (*ibid.,* Vol.

III, p. 577), where he calls the French "diese unreine, unverschämte und unzüchtige Rasse." See, in general, Ernst von Meier, *Französische Einflüsse auf die Staats- und Rechtsentwicklung Preussens im 19. Jahrhundert,* 2 vols. (Leipzig: Duncker & Humblot, 1907-08).

12. William O. Shanahan, *Prussian Military Reforms 1786-1813* (New York: Columbia University Press, 1945); Max Lehmann, *Scharnhorst,* 2 vols. (Leipzig: Hirzel, 1886-87); Rudolf Stadelmann, "Scharnhorst und die Revolution seiner Zeit," *Das Innere Reich* Vol. V (1938), No. 1, pp. 44-65; and *Scharnhorst: Schicksal und geistige Welt* (Wiesbaden: Limes 1952); Gerhard Scholz, *Hermann von Boyen* (Berlin: Verlag für Kulturpolitik, 1936); Hans Rothfels, *Karl von Clausewitz, Politik und Krieg* (Berlin: Ferdinand Dummler, 1920); Clausewitz, *Politische Schriften und Briefe,* ed. by Hans Rothfels (Munich: Drei Masken Verlag, 1922); *Makers of Modern Strategy,* ed. by Edward Mead Earle (Princeton University Press, 1943), Ch. 5.

13. J. R. Seeley, *Life and Times of Stein,* Vol. II, p. 98. Stein strongly supported the principle of universal military service on moral grounds. See his letter to Gneisenau, March 1809 (*Staatsschriften,* p. 57) and to Gentz on September 8, 1809 (*ibid.,* p. 61) where he also suggested election of the officers by the army and an emblem for the German army, showing the symbol of freedom over broken fetters and the names of the national liberators, Hermann, Henry I, Otto I, and William of Orange.

14. "Entwicklung der allgemeinen Ursachen des Glücks der Franzosen in dem Revolutionskriege und insbesondere in dem Feldzuge von 1794," in Scharnhorst, *Militärische Schriften,* ed. by Freiherr von der Goltz (Militärische Klassiker des In- und Auslandes, Vol. XI, Dresden: Höckner, 1881). On the example of the United States, see Lehmann, *Scharnhorst,* Vol. I, p. 212. See also Reinhard Höhn, *Scharnhorsts Vermächtnis* (Bonn: Athenäum, 1952). A very good brief summary of the Prussian military reforms is in Guy Stanton Ford, "A Century of Universal Military Service" in his *On and Off the Campus* (Minneapolis: University of Minnesota Press, 1938), pp. 204-18.

15. Georg Heinrich Pertz, *Das Leben des Generalfeldmarschalls Grafen Neidhardt von Gneisenau,* 5 vols. (Berlin: G. Reimer, 1864-1880), Vol. I, pp. 30 f.

16. Nettelbeck (1738-1824) wrote a well-known autobiography *Lebensbeschreibung von ihm selbst aufgezeichnet,* 3 vols. (Leipzig, 1821-23) which was often reprinted, also in Reclam's Universalbibliothek. Ferdinand von Schill (1776-1809) was a Prussian cavalry officer who with his regiment decided in 1809 to join Austria in the war against France and so perhaps to force the hand of the King of Prussia. He and his soldiers were defeated by the French in Stralsund, where Schill himself fell.

17. See Clausewitz, *Politische Schriften und Briefe,* pp. xxv, 26, 29 ff., 39, 63 f.

NOTES FOR CHAPTER 30: *Prussia and France*

1. Stein wrote to Gneisenau on August 17, 1811: "What shall I say of the present state of the nation when, as you say, fear of war and dislike of taxation make them indifferent to the preservation of their nationality and to every sentiment of honor?" *Staatsschriften*, p. 85. A number of Prussian writers, among them well-known men like Dietrich Heinrich Freiherr von Bülow (1757-1808), Friedrich Buchholz (1768-1843), Christian Karl August Ludwig von Massenbach (1758-1827), regarded Napoleon as the embodiment of irresistible superiority. The often cited organization of patriotic Prussians which was known as the Tugendbund —its full name was "Moralische und scientifische Gesellschaft zur Übung öffentlicher Tugenden"—founded in Königsberg in the spring of 1808 and dissolved in December 1809, was without any real importance. It was influenced on the one hand by Free Masonic ideas of Lessing and Herder, and on the other hand by the nationalism of Fichte. Stein was hostile to the association, which he regarded not only as useless but as potentially harmful, a "Jacobin" club.
2. Friedrich Thimme, "Zu den Erhebungsplänen der preussischen Patrioten im Sommer 1808," *Historische Zeitschrift*, Vol. 86 (1901), pp. 78-110.
3. Alfred Stern, "Gneisenaus Reise nach London im Jahre 1809 und ihre *Vorgeschichte*," *Historische Zeitschrift*, Vol. 85 (1900), pp. 32 f., 36.
4. Clausewitz, *Politische Schriften und Briefe*, pp. 80-86. See also *ibid.*, pp. 87-119, the second memorandum by Clausewitz. On pp. 117 f. Clausewitz stressed the difference between the wars of the past, fought by professional armies with moderation and consideration, and present wars. "The war of the present age is a war of all against all. No longer does a king fight a king, an army another army, but a people another people, and king and army are contained in the people." Clausewitz believed that in the future it might not be necessary to fight by means of popular insurrections like those in revolutionary France, in Spain, and now in Germany. He hoped that after the defeat of Napoleon, Europe, reorganized "into organic states according to the laws of nature," would no longer need to recur to this desperate way of life. But even then "every war will be regarded as a national concern—eine Nationalsache—and will be conducted in this spirit, with an effort graded according to the strength of the national character and of the government."
5. Schelling, *Sämmtliche Werke* (Stuttgart: Cotta, 1861), Vol. 8, pp. 3, 138.
6. Clement Theodor Perthes, *Friedrich Perthes Leben*, 3 vols. (Hamburg: F. Perthes, 1848-1855), Vol. I, pp. 144 f. Friedrich Perthes opened a bookshop in Hamburg in 1796. In 1822 he moved to Gotha, from where he organized the German book trade and became one of the founders in 1825 of the Börsenverein der deutschen Buchhändler in Leipzig. In 1816 he published *Der deutsche Buchhandel als Bedingung des Daseins einer deutschen Literatur.*
7. It is for this very reason that Meinecke, *Weltbürgertum und Nationalstaat,*

pp. 212 ff. praised him so highly, together with Niebuhr und Ottokar Thon. The last-named was aide-de-camp of Duke Karl August of Weimar. He had served with the Lützow free corps. He was eulogized by Treitschke for his essay "Was wird uns die Zukunft bringen?" (*Treitschke, Deutsche Geschichte im Neunzehten Jahrhundert*, Vol. I, p. p. 682) because he believed that struggle and friction, not peace and tranquillity were the fate of the "true national state." He asked Germans to drive the un-German powers, Austria and England, out of Germany and to unite the whole of Germany through Prussia's sword. But these were isolated voices in German nationalism of that time. Thon's essay remained unknown to his contemporaries and was printed only after his death in 1867. On Luden, see W. E. Brown, "Heinrich Luden: A Pioneer of Nationalism," *The Contemporary Review*, Vol. CXL (1931), pp. 231-238.

8. *Nemesis, Zeitschrift für Politik und Geschichte* appeared in twelve volumes in Weimar from 1814 to 1818. In addition to many other publications, Luden wrote a *Geschichte des deutschen Volkes*, 12 vols. (Gotha, 1825-1837) which carried the history of the German people down to the thirteenth century.

9. See Hans Joachim Moser, *Geschichte der deutschen Musik*, 2nd ed. (Stuttgart: Gotta, 1928), Vol. 3, p. 136. Moser's book itself is an important contribution to the study of nationalism; in its discussion of music it breathes a highly nationalistic or chauvinistic spirit. On the Hohenstaufen and the Kyffhäuser legend, see Hans Kohn, *The Mind of Germany* (New York: Scribner's, 1960).

NOTES FOR CHAPTER 31: *Johann Gottlieb Fichte*

1. Fichte's works were edited as *Sämmtliche Werke*, 8 vols. (Berlin: Veit & Co., 1845-46) by his son Immanuel Hermann Fichte, and as *Werke*, 6 vols. (Leipzig: Felix Meiner, 1911-12) by Fritz Medicus. For political ideas the most important works, not contained in the Medicus edition, are: "Zurückforderung der Denkfreiheit von den Fürsten Europas, die sie bisher unterdrückten," ed. by Reinhold Strecker (Leipzig: Meiner, 1920); "Beitrag zur Berichtigung der Urteile des Publikums über die Französische Revolution," ed. by R. Strecker (*ibid.*, 1922); "Der Patriotismus und sein Gegenteil: Patriotische Dialoge," ed. by Hans Schulz (*ibid.*, 1918); "Machiavelli, nebst einem Briefe Karls von Clausewitz an Fichte," ed. by H. Schulz (*ibid.*, 1918); "Rechtslehre von 1812," ed. by R. Strecker (*ibid.*, 1925), which contains among other pieces, "Aus dem Entwurf zu einer politischen Schrift im Frühjahr 1813."—See on Fichte: Fritz Medicus, *Fichtes Leben* (Berlin: Reuther und Reichard, 1925); Reinhard Strecker, *Die Anfänge von Fichtes Staatsphilosophie* (Leipzig: Meiner, 1917); Ernst Bergmann, *J. G. Fichte der Erzieher* (Leipzig: Meiner, 1927); Gustav Adolf Walz, *Die Staatsidee des Rationalismus und der Romantik und die Staatsphilosophie Fichtes* (Berlin-Grunewald: Walther Rothschild, 1928); Franz Haymann, *Weltbürgertum und Vaterlandsliebe in der Staatslehre Rousseaus und Fichtes* (Berlin: Pan-Verlag Rolf Heise,

1924); Reinhold Aris, *History of Political Thought in Germany from 1789 to 1815* (London: Allen and Unwin, 1926), pp. 106-135, 345-360; Wilhelm Windelband, *Fichtes Idee des deutschen Staats*, 2nd ed. (Tübingen: Mohr, 1921); Nico Wallner, *Fichte als politischer Denker* (Halle: Niemeyer, 1926); Ernst Schenkel, *Individuum und Gemeinschaft: Der demokratische Gedanke bei J. G. Fichte* (Zurich: Rascher, 1933); Arnold Gehlen, *Deutschtum und Christentum bei Fichte* (Berlin: Junker & Dünnhaupt, 1935); Walter Becker, *Platon und Fichte: die königliche Erziehungskunst* (Jena: Fischer, 1937); H. C. Engelbrecht, *Johann Gottlieb Fichte, a Study of His Political Writings with Special Reference to His Nationalism* (New York: Columbia University Press, 1923), with a detailed bibliography. There is an excellent article by Edward L. Schaub, "J. G. Fichte and anti-Semitism," *The Philosophical Review*, Vol. XLIX (January 1940) pp. 37-52; see also M. Guéroult, "Fichte et la Révolution Française," *Revue philosophique*, Vol. CXXVIII (1939), pp. 226-320.

2. Fichte, *Sämmtliche Werke*, Vol. 6, p. 95.

3. Johann Gottlieb Fichte, *Briefwechsel, Kritische Gesamtausgabe*, ed. by Hans Schulz, 2 vols. (Leipzig: Haessel, 1925) Vol. I, p. 360.

4. Fichte, *Sämmtliche Werke*, Vol. 5, p. 288.

5. Fichte, Letter of May 22, 1799, to Reinhold. *Briefwechsel*, Vol. II, p. 104. See also Fichte's letter in the same month (dated "21. Floréal, 7") to Franz Wilhelm Jung, in which Fichte asked for employment by the French Republic, because henceforward an honest man could devote his forces only to it and humanity's hopes and existence were dependent upon its victory.

6. Fichte, *Sämmtliche Werke*, Vol. 5, p. 288.

7. "Niemand *wird* kultiviert, sondern jeder hat sich *selbst zu kultivieren*. Alles bloss leidende Verhalten ist das gerade Gegenteil der Kultur; Bildung geschieht durch Selbsttätigkeit, und zweckt auf Selbsttätigkeit ab. Kein Plan der Kultur kann also so angelegt werden, dass seine Erreichung notwendig sei; er wirkt auf Freiheit, und hängt vom Gebrauche der Freiheit ab." *Ibid.*, Vol. 6, p. 90.

8. He gave the lectures in the summer of 1813 under the title *Vorträge verschiedenen Inhalts aus der angewandten Philosophie;* they were published for the first time in 1820 as *Die Staatslehre oder über das Verhältnis des Urstaates zum Vernunftreiche.*

9. Fichte, *Sämmtliche Werke*, Vol. 4, pp. 600, 579 f., 599. The same ideal of a stateless society of free and equal individuals, but without direct reference to Christianity, was advanced in the lectures which Fichte delivered to his Free Mason Lodge in 1800: "The whole of mankind shall form a single state, based entirely on law; the relationship of the individuals in the states and the relationship of these states on earth should be ordered entirely according to the eternal law of reason—Rechtsgesetz der Vernunft. This is the purpose of all legislation in the various states and of all the alliances and agreements among the nations." *Philosophie der Maurerei (Briefe an Constant)* ed. by W. Flitner (Leipzig: Meiner, 1923) p. 33.

10. Fichte, *Sämmtliche Werke*, Vol. IV, p. 423.

11. In "Transzendentale Logik" (1812), Fichte, *Nachgelassene Werke,* Vol. I, pp. 399 f.

12. Fichte, *Sämmtliche Werke,* Vol. 7, p. 212. In 1799, after the assassination of the French delegates to the Congress of Rastatt, Fichte wrote: "It is clear that from now on the French Republic alone can be the fatherland of an upright man; . . . since from now on not only the dearest hopes of mankind but even human existence depends upon its victory. . . . I dedicate myself and all my abilities to the Republic." *Briefwechsel,* Vol. 2, p. 100. Though these lines were written under emotional stress, nevertheless they show clearly that Fichte identified the cause of mankind with one nation, at that time the French nation.

13. Fichte, *Nachgelassene Werke,* Vol. 3, p. 227 f.

14. *Ibid.,* Vol. 3, p. 234. In the *Ideen für die innere Organization der Universität Erlangen* (1805-06) Fichte contrasted the primitive ("dumpfe") patriotism of Sparta with the enlightened patriotism "welcher mit Weltbürgersinn und deutschem Nationalsinne sich sehr wohl vereinigen lässt, und in jedem kräftigen Menschen sich notwendig damit vereinigt (Atticismus könnte man ihn nennen) und es steht ein allenthalben gewandter und allenthalben sich zurechtfindender Diener des Staates da." *Nachgelassene Werke,* Vol. 3, p. 284. Fichte truly was such a forceful personality, in whom, as he said, cosmopolitanism and patriotism fused by necessity; but it is most doubtful whether he ever could have become an adroit, practical, and efficient servant of the state.

15. *Ibid.,* Vol. 3, pp. 243 f., 265 f. "The Reden substantiates the thesis that Fichte turned nationalist first of all through devotion to himself and his philosophy. Because of his burning faith in both he discovered the nation. His nationalism consisted of patriotism to himself, his philosophy, and the nation, and he hoped that the last would be guided by the first to accept the second, thereby creating a new human race." Eugene Newton Anderson, *Nationalism and the Cultural Crisis in Prussia 1806-1815* (New York: Farrar and Rinehart, 1939), p. 40.

16. Fichte, *Sämmtliche Werke,* Vol. 7, p. 510.

17. Fichte, *Nachgelassene Werke,* Vol. 3, p. 428. Luden in an article in the *Jenaische Allgemeine Literaturzeitung* in 1810 carried the discovery of Machiavelli by Hegel and Fichte to practical conclusions: "Die Moral wird den Mord eines Menschen nicht entschuldigen; dass aber für die Unabhängigkeit der Völker hunderttausend geopfert werden, hat noch keinem unmoralisch geschienen. Es gibt nur eine und ewige Tugend; und demjenigen, der ganz von einem grossen Gedanken erfüllt und in denselben aufgegangen ist, fallen die Mittel mit dem Zweck zusammen; er sieht in jenen nur diesen, während der Moralist auf der Stube abwägt und richtet. Eine verzweifelte Krankheit verlangt eine verzweifelte Kur, und der Biss des tollen Hundes kann nicht behandelt werden wie ein Nietnagel. . . . Das Bild ist trivial, aber die ganze Anschauung ist getragen von demselben Ethos, das Hegel und Fichte beseelt hat. Und auch dieselbe politische Gesinnung beherrscht ihn; aus einer ins einzelne gehenden historischen Untersuchung des Princips, die Luden fordert, würde Machia-

vellis grosser Grundsatz hervorgehen: dass das eine Notwendige, welches unter jeder Bedingung erstrebt werden müsse, die Unabhängigkeit des Vaterlandes—die Befreiung Italiens von den Barbaren—sei, dass aber die genannte Kenntnis der Zeit, des Zustandes des Landes und Volkes in jeder Beziehung nur die Art bestimmen dürfe, wie das Ziel zu erreichen sei. Das könnte eine grosse Lehre sein, auch für unsere politischen Schwätzer, die beständig allgemeine, halb begriffene Sätze aufstellen, ohne sich die Mühe zu geben, die Geschichte und den Zustand nur eines Volkes zu studieren!" Albert Elkan: "Die Entdeckung Machiavellis in Deutschland zu Beginn des 19. Jahrhunderts," *Historische Zeitschrift*, Vol. 119 (1919), pp. 427-458.

18. Friedrich Meinecke, *Weltbürgertum und Nationalstaat*, 7th ed., pp. 104 f., regards these words as "among the most significant and profound of the period." According to him they harmonized universal ethics with nationalist power egotism, though to other readers it may appear that they justified nationalist power egotism with the thin veneer of universal ethics. "Der entscheidende Schritt war hier getan, der Machttrieb des Staates als natürlicher und heilsamer [!] Lebenstrieb anerkannt und in den Zusammenhang einer sittlichen Weltanschauung gestellt." The limitless expansion of a nation—a supposition which in itself is most dubious because many nations lived without any urge for expansion, especially limitless expansion—is here judged as willed by God and justified by its own autonomous morality, without any regard for the existence of mutual obligation, of live and let live, as a foundation of civilized life. Wilhelm Windelband, *op. cit.*, p. 8, summarized Fichte's *Reden* saying: "The state of the future can be only the nation-state, especially the German nation-state. That is, as far as philosophy could formulate it, the program of the political history of the nineteenth century, in which the consolidation of the nation states forms the main interest, and the center of which, its dominating event, is without doubt the foundation of the German Reich."

19. Meinecke, *op. cit.*, approved this definition of the rights of the state, "sein Recht und seine Pflicht zur kraftvollen, rücksichtslosen Selbsterhaltung und zur Selbstbestimmung dessen, was seiner Selbsterhaltung dient." This philosophy of the absolute autonomy of the state asserting itself, without any consideration for the universal good, was unfortunately characteristic of German—and not only of German—scholarship and statesmanship in the later stages of the Age of Nationalism.

20. There is an inner relationship between Napoleon and Fichte; Fichte regarded Napoleon as a despot of evil and dreamt of the coming of a despot of good. Friedrich Schlegel spoke in a letter to Caroline in 1805 of Napoleon as "a certain Fichtean in Paris" who has applied with great originality Fichte's "I am I and create myself"—Ich bin Ich, und setze mich selber—to politics. The National Socialists felt an affinity to Fichte's strong and dictatorial voluntarism. Adolf Baeumler in "Fichte und Wir," *Nationalsozialistische Monatshefte* (June 1937) interpreted German history as a Ghibellinian revolution against the Guelphian Rome. He found the high points of German history in the struggles of the emperors against

the popes, in the Reformation against Rome, in German idealism against the West, and ultimately in National Socialism. "Fichte's position in German philosophy and our relation to him are determined by the fact that he has expressed the Ghibellinian voluntarism in the most unconditional and extreme form."

21. From the *Staatslehre* (1813), Fichte, *Gesammelte Werke*, Vol. 4, p. 444. Fichte goes on: "Auch in Absicht der Rechtsurteile steht dem höchsten Verstand das Zwangsrecht zu, nebst dem bedingenden Recht, als höchster, inappellabler Entscheider der Frage vom jedesmaligen Recht zu gelten."

22. Fichte, *Werke*, ed. by Medicus, Vol. 2, pp. 373-389.

23. Fichte, *Sämmtliche Werke*, Vol. 3, p. 509. Fichte's "Geschlossene Handelsstaat" has been aptly called a "great, common workhouse." Fichte's complete seclusion does not hold good in one important respect: he exempts scholarship from it, whatever belongs to man and not to the citizen. *Ibid.,* p. 512.

24. *Ibid.* Vol. 7, p. 533.

25. *Ibid.,* p. 152.

26. *Ibid.,* pp. 204 f. Fichte regarded the spread of these liberties of civilization all over the earth as an important task. For him it justified colonial expansion. Though it was an injustice for primitive countries and peoples to be subjected to exploitation by more progressive nations, nevertheless, he wrote, it promotes step by step the general spread of Kultur, the prime concern of world history; and this will thus continue unceasingly until the whole race which inhabits our globe will have become assimilated into a single republic of civilization including all peoples—"zu einer einzigen Völkerrepublik der Kultur." *Ibid.,* p. 163.

27. Friedrich Jansen, *Fichtes Reden an die deutsche Nation: Eine Untersuchung ihres aktuell-politischen Gehaltes* (Berlin: W. Rothschild, 1911); Josef Körner, "Die Wirkung der Reden Fichtes," *Forschungen zur brandenburgisch-preussischen Geschichte,* Vol. XL (1927), pp. 64 ff.

28. "Wer dasselbe in sich fühlt, der wird überzeugt werden; wer es nicht fühlt, kann nicht überzeugt werden, denn allein auf jene Voraussetzung stützt sich mein Beweis; an ihm habe ich meine Worte verloren, aber wer wollte nicht etwas so geringfügiges, als Worte sind, auf des Spiel setzen?" Fichte, *Sämmtliche Werke,* Vol. 7, pp. 399 f.

29. The fourth of Fichte's Reden deals with the principal difference between the Germans and the other European nations, which are regarded as descendants of Germanic tribes (*ibid.,* pp. 313, 325). The fifth Rede discusses the consequences of this difference for the intellectual life of the nations, while the sixth adduces proofs for Fichte's position from German history (*ibid.,* pp. 344, 357).

30. Fritz Medicus, *J. G. Fichte,* p. 238.

31. Fichte, *Sämmtliche Werke,* Vol. 7, pp. 374 f., 366.

32. *Ibid.,* p. 471.

33. *Ibid.,* pp. 334 and 339 f. "Nach allem wird der ausländische Genius die betretenen Heerbahnen des Alterthums mit Blumen bestreuen, und der Lebensweisheit, die leicht ihm für Philosophie gelten wird, ein zierliches

Gewand weben; dagegen wird der deutsche Geist neue Schächte eröffnen, und Licht und Tag einführen in ihre Abgründe, und Felsmassen von Gedanken schleudern, aus denen die künftigen Zeitalter sich Wohnungen erbauen. Der ausländische Genius wird seyn ein lieblicher Sylphe, der mit leichtem Fluge über den, seinem Boden von selbst entkeimten Blumen hinschwebt, und sich niederlässt auf dieselben, ohne sie zu beugen, und ihren erquickenden Thau in sich zieht; oder eine Biene, die aus denselben Blumen mit geschäftiger Kunst den Honig sammelt, und ihn in regelmässig gebauten Zellen zierlich geordnet niederlegt; der deutsche Geist ein Adler, der mit Gewalt seinen gewichtigen Leib emporreisst, und mit starkem und vielgeübtem Flügel viel Luft unter sich bringt, um sich näher zu heben der Sonne, deren Anschauung ihn entzückt."

34. Jean Paul, whom Miss E. M. Butler in *The German Mind and Outlook* (London: Chapman & Hall, 1945), p. 111, calls "a humorist, rather a rare bird in Germany, but not absolutely unknown, who had therefore a sense of proportion and also some common sense," reviewed the *Reden* in the *Heidelberger Jahrbücher* for 1809. He asked why the modern Greeks who continue to speak their primitive tongue—naturally with modification like the Germans, too—did not share the advantages of the Germans. As Fichte attributed to the fact of the still living ancestral language the religious earnestness of German Protestantism, Jean Paul asked to what then he attributed the Catholicism of southern Germany and the Calvinism of French and English speaking nations.

35. Fichte, *Sämmtliche Werke,* Vol. 7, pp. 378-383.

36. *Ibid.,* pp. 384-390.

37. *Ibid.,* pp. 566, 467, 389.

38. *Ibid.,* pp. 495-499.

39. *Ibid.,* p. 390. "Not physical strength, nor efficient armaments, but the power of the mind achieves victories."

40. *Ibid.,* p. 431.

41. *Ibid.,* p. 569. In the *Entwurf* Fichte saw clearly the lack of a German national consciousness. He rejected the idea that literature could unite the nation, for it remained unknown to the people, a private affair of the writers themselves, and hardly shared by the Catholic part of Germany. The German writers had constructed the concept of the Germans and the German nation from history. "How does that concern the people? How could a posterity so completely changed be united by the memory of Arminius' battle?" *Ibid.,* p. 569.—In another passage Fichte declared that the Germans should not continue their old history, which did not bear any fruit for them and which exists only for writers and scholars. These writers and scholars who traveled and migrated from one of the German lands to another, Fichte regarded as the only Germans. Thus, he wrote, "there have been Germans—not as citizens but beyond citizenship, and this is the great advantage." *Ibid.,* p. 572.

42. *Ibid.,* pp. 572, 573. The latter passage is found also in the *Staatslehre*. See above, Note 10 of this chapter.

43. "Um Alles zusammenzufassen:—Der Geist der alten Zeit ist irdische

Theokratie, der der modernen, himmlische; der irdische Staat muss daher durchaus auf dem himmlischen aufgebaut seyn, seinen Geist verwirklichen, und ist nur als Glied desselben zu begreifen. Hauptabsicht der neueren Zeit und eigentliches Geschäft der Vorsehung in ihr ist, dass der Glaube an das Reich der Himmel und die übersinnliche Welt nicht untergehe: —dies hält freilich heutzutage schwer. . . . Auch die Religion wird ihre Anschauungen erweitern; das Christenthum ist nicht bloss Lehre, sondern es ist historisches Princip, Staatsstiftung. Die Trägheit daher wird eben durch die Religion verschwinden; es wird Indignation entstehen über den Zustand, welcher der Bürger des ewigen Reiches unwürdig ist. Religiöse Begeisterung wird die Ketten brechen, wie zur Zeit der Reformation. Da muss sich eben erst der Himmel näher an die Erde bringen. . . . Die Welt geht aus von einer beglaubten, und endet in einer durchaus verstandenen Theokratie. Gott wird wirklich allgemein herrschen und er allein, ohne andere, die Welt in Bewegung setzende Kräfte; nicht bloss mehr als Lehrer, sondern als lebendige und lebendig machende Kraft." *Ibid.*, pp. 611, 613.

44. *Ibid.*, Vol. 4, pp. 579 f. See also the passage on pp. 523 ff.

NOTES FOR CHAPTER 32: *Friedrich Schleiermacher*

1. See Koppel S. Pinson, *Pietism as a Factor in the Rise of German Nationalism* (New York: Columbia University Press, 1934). On Schleiermacher, see Ernst Müsebeck. *Schleiermacher in der Geschichte der Staatsidee und des Nationalbewusstseins* (Berlin: R. Hobbing, 1927); Günther Holstein, *Die Staatsphilosophie Schleiermachers* (Bonn: K. Schroeder, 1922); Arthur von Ungern-Sternberg, *Schleiermachers völkische Botschaft aus der Zeit der deutschen Erneuerung* (Gotha: L. Klotz, 1933); Albert Reble, "Der Volksbegriff bei Schleiermacher," *Deutsche Vierteljahrsschrift für Literaturwissenschaft und Geitesgeschichte*, Vol. 14 (1936), pp. 361-381.

2. Schleiermacher's *Soliloquies*, tr. by Horace Leland Friess (Chicago: The Open Court, 1926), pp. 58 f.

3. Wilhelm Dilthey, *Gesammelte Schriften* (Leipzig: Teubner, 1936), Vol. 12, pp. 9-33.

4. In his sermon of August 24, 1806, "Wie sehr es die Würde des Menschen erhöht, wenn er mit ganzer Seele an der Bürgerlichen Vereinigung hängt, der er angehört."

5. Article by Schleiermacher in the *Preussische Correspondent* of July 14, 1813. This periodical was first edited by Schleiermacher, and later by Arnim and Niebuhr.

6. Salo Wittmayer Baron, *Modern Nationalism and Religion* (New York: Harper, 1947), p. 142.

7. No definitive edition of Arndt's works exists. There is an edition of his *Werke*, ed. by Hugo Rösch, of which Vols. 1-6 were published in 1892 (Leipzig: Karl Vogelsberg), Vols. 7-8 in 1902 (Leipzig: Karl Pfau) and Vols. 9-14 in 1909 (Magdeburg; Magdeburger Verlagsanstalt). In addi-

tion see the edition of selected works, *Arndts Werke*, in 12 parts, ed. by August Leffson and Wilhelm Steffens (Berlin: Deutsches Verlagshaus Bong & Co., 1912) and *Ausgewählte Werke*, ed. by Heinrich Meiser and Robert Geerds (Leipzig: Max Hesse). There is a brief selection, ed. by Ernst Müsebeck, *Staat und Vaterland* (Munich: Drei Masken Verlag, 1921). An excellent bibliography of Arndt's works is to be found in Alfred G. Pundt, *Arndt and the Nationalist Awakening in Germany* (New York: Columbia University Press, 1935). Recent works on Arndt are Hermenegild Kuhn, *Arndt und Jahn als völkisch-politische Denker* (Langensalza: Bauer, 1936); Hans Polag, *E. M. Arndts Weg zum Deutschen: Studien zur Entwicklung des frühen Arndt, 1769-1812* (Leipzig: Eichblatt, 1936); Rudolf Fahrner, *Arndt, Geistiges und Politisches Verhalten* (Stuttgart: Kohlhammer, 1937), Ibo Ibbeken, *Ernst Moritz Arndt und die christlich-germanische Bewegung seiner Zeit* (Greifswald: Bamberg, 1937). Arndt as forerunner of Communist nationalism is glorified in Herbert Seurle, *E. M. Arndt der Vorkämpfer für Einheit und Demokratie* (Berlin: Kongress Verlag, 1952). Important older literature: Ernst Müsebeck, *Ernst Moritz Arndt, ein Lebensbild:* Vol. 1. *1769-1815* (Gotha: F. A. Perthes, 1914); Paul Ruth, *Arndt und die Geschichte* (Munich: R. Oldenbourg, 1930); John R. Seeley, *The Life and Adventures of Ernst Moritz Arndt* (London: Seeley, Jackson & Halliday, 1879).

NOTES FOR CHAPTER 33: *Ernst Moritz Arndt*

1. See Richard Wolfram, *Ernst Moritz Arndt und Schweden* (Weimar: Alexander Duncker, 1933); Uno Willers, *Ernst Moritz Arndt och hans svenska förbindelser: Studier i svensk-pommersk historigrati och svensk opinionsbildring* (Stockholm, 1945).

2. Arndt did not publish this poem, written in 1799, before 1860 in his *Gedichte: Vollständige Sammlung* (Berlin: Weidmannsche Buchhandlung, 1860), p. 28. It begins:

   Wer trägt den schimmerndsten von allen Namen?

3. "Nur wenn wir ein Vaterland, wenn wir die hochmenschlichen und hochpolitischen Ideen eines eigenen, einigen, kräftigen Volks hätten, würden wir stehende Sitten, festen Charakter und Kunstgestalt gewinnen; dann nur könnte das Höchste und Herrlichste der Menschheit aus solchen irdischen Wurzeln zu schimmernden Sonnenwipfeln erwachsen." Arndt, *Germanien und Europa* (Altona, 1803), p. 429.

4. *Geist der Zeit,* Pt. 2 was published in Arndt, *Werke,* Vol. 9, ed. by E. Schirmer and R. Lorenz. The passage is on p. 120.

5. "Hoffnungsrede vom Jahre 1810" in Ernst Moritz Arndt, *Schriften für und an seine lieben Deutschen,* (Vols. 1-3 Leipzig: Weidmann, 1845; Vol. 4 Berlin: Weidmann, 1855), Vol. 4, pp. 32 ff. In 1813 Arndt published in Leipzig a pamphlet *Über Volkshass und über den Gebrauch einer fremden Sprache.* In it he expressed his wish to inculcate hatred against the French forever. "Where the nations of the world stand differ-

entiated, each one in the fullness of its peculiarity, where a proud and noble hatred separates and keeps separate the dissimilar and different characters, there each one will develop in the fullest, worthiest and peculiar way, and all will thus best fulfill the great task of mankind and the clear will of God. . . . The arts and sciences will also gain by it because nothing noble and pure can grow out of mixture and conflict but only out of the simple and harmonious and only because incredibly much time and energy are lost with vain efforts to ape the alien." The pamphlet is to be found in Arndt, *Schriften für und an seine lieben Deutschen,* Vol. 1.

6. In "Fantasien zur Berichtigung der Urteile über künftige deutsche Verfassungen" (1815), *Schriften für und an seine lieben Deutschen,* Vol. 2, and Arndt, *Ausgewählte Werke,* ed. by Meisner and Geerds, Vol. 15, p. 115. See also Arndt's "Über den deutschen Studentenstaat" (1815) in *Ausgewählte Werke,* Vol. 13, p. 304, where he wrote: "The German people is still a very youthful and poetic people." He explained this fact by their purity of race. There again he quoted Tacitus as a witness for German racial purity.

7. From *Über Volkshass und über den Gebrauch einer fremden Sprache.* Arndt called language "das geistigste und gewaltigste Band aller Bände." "Zwei Worte über Entstehung und Bestimmung der deutschen Legion" (1813) in *Ausgewählte Werke,* Vol. 13, p. 107. Here too he declared that fatherland and folk were in a certain sense identical, the fatherland being the outward, the folk the inward of a country. "Was die Menschen von einer Zunge in Sitten, Leben, Taten, Wissenschaften und Künsten Gemeinsames hatten und taten oder haben und tun—das heisst ein Volk."

8. Arndt, *Ansichten und Aussichten der teutschen Geschichte* (Leipzig: Vol. 1, p. 461).

9. The passage is from Arndt's famous *Der Rhein, Deutschlands Strom aber nicht Deutschlands Grenze* (1813), in *Schriften für und an seine lieben Deutschen,* Vol. 2; also *Ausgewählte Werke,* Vol. 13, p. 190. The book was very popular and has remained so. There were four new editions between 1920 and 1930. In 1933 Lothar Weinich published it together with the *Katechismus* in two volumes of Reclams Universal-Bibliothek. In this book generally, Arndt was very certain of God's will. "What God plans in the mighty and secret course of times, is not hidden from us, it is not to us a secret for a minute." Apparently what God wills is nationalism, what He rejects is internationalism. "Verflucht aber sei die Humanität und der Kosmopolitismus, womit ihr prahlet! Jener allweltliche Judensinn, den ihr uns preist als den höchsten Gipfel menschlicher Bildung." Achim von Arnim reviewed Arndt's *Der Rhein* in *Der Preussische Correspondent* on Jan. 28, 1814. (*Der Preussische Correspondent,* founded by Niebuhr on April 2, 1813, was edited by Arnim from October 1813 to January 31, 1814.) He compared Arndt to Hutten. See Hans Kohn, *The Idea of Nationalism,* pp. 143 f.

10. Even in his later years Arndt adhered to his high esteem for language as a separating element among nations. See his "Lasset euch nicht verführen

oder die Weltlitteratur" (1842) in *Schriften für und an seine lieben Deutschen,* Vol. 3, pp. 317 f., 330 f.

11. In the lectures *Geschichte der alten und neuen Literatur,* which Arndt delivered in Vienna in 1820. See *Sämmtliche Werke,* Vol. 2, pp. 34 f.

12. In Görres' *Rheinischer Merkur* of October 31, 1815.

13. Arndt, *Schriften für und an seine lieben Deutschen,* Vol. 1, p. 405. As against the French he praised the English. "These merchants and navigators are the truly great, free and mighty people, not the French who call themselves in their frivolous conceit la grande nation." *Ibid.,* Vol. 1, p. 519. Arndt was most violent when the French were defeated. His "Das Wort von 1814 und das Wort von 1815 über die Franzosen" (1815) begins triumphantly: "These are the incomparable, these are the invincible Frenchmen, this is the unique Napoleon." In the pamphlet itself he wrote: "Thus are the French, thus they will always be . . . as cruel as they are lighthearted, as tigerlike as they are apelike, as avaricious as they are subservient, as slovenly as they are disloyal, as glittery as they are treacherous—where has this good-for-nothing people even one certain virtue which would redeem its vices? For even its good sides are based upon empty conceit and upon screaming about an honor which must not be called honor by Germans." *Ibid.,* p. 14.

14. Arndt, *Geist der Zeit,* Vol. 2, pp. 112 f.

15. "Das Preussische Volk und Heer im Jahre 1813," *Schriften,* Vol. 1, p. 335. In a poem of that time Arndt wrote "An die Teutschen" (1813):

> Und hörst du nicht? und siehst du nicht?
> Und willst den Schimpf nicht fühlen?
> Und lassest den Franzosenwicht,
> Den Affen, mit dir spielen,
> Den Ehrendieb? den Freiheitsdieb?
> Hast du so sehr die Schande lieb?
> Der helle Klang der Schwerter
> War deinen Vätern werther.
>
> Auf deinen Wagen setzt er sich,
> Du musst zu Fusse gehen,
> Zu deinem Weibe legt er sich,
> Du musst als Schildwach stehen.
> Dein Silber und dein rothes Gold
> Er höhnend sich ins Fäustchen rollt,
> Und willst du zürnend blicken
> So bläut er dir den Rücken.
>
> So hat er sich mit Trug und Tand
> Der Herrschaft unterwunden,
> Er hält das heil'ge teutsche Land
> In Knechtschaft angebunden,
> Der Wahrheit schlägt er auf den Mund,
> Die Ehre kuschet wie ein Hund,

Mit Knochen und mit Brocken,
Fast hündisch anzulocken.

16. Arndt, *Geist der Zeit*, Vol. 1, p. 46, translated in Eugene N. Anderson, *Nationalism and the Cultural Crisis in Prussia 1806-1815*, p. 80.

17. Arndt took up the same theme in a somewhat expanded form and in the style of the Old Testament prophets in his *Katechismus für den Teutschen Kriegs- und Wehrmann, worin gelehrt wird, wie ein Christlicher Wehrmann seyn und mit Gott in den Streit gehen soll*, Ch. 12: Of Liberty and Fatherland. This *Katechismus* was very popular. It was reprinted six times between 1813 and 1815, and new editions appeared in Hamburg 1916 and Leipzig 1933. There Arndt defined "Freiheit" as a condition "wo keine fremden Henker über dich gebieten und keine fremden Treiber dich treiben," as if there would be freedom where one's own henchmen and one's own slavedrivers are in power.

18. Arndt, *Geist der Zeit*, Vol. 3, pp. 161 f., tr. in Eugene N. Anderson, *op. cit.*, pp. 100 f.

19. Arndt, *Ausgewählte Werke*, Vol. 11, pp. 180 ff.

20. "Über künftige ständische Verfassungen in Deutschland" (1814), Arndt, *Ausgewählte Werke*, Vol. 13, pp. 212 ff.; *Werke*, Bong ed., Vol. 11, pp. 85 ff.

21. Arndt, *Staat und Vaterland*, ed. by Ernst Müsebeck, pp. 5 f.

22. From an article in *Der Wächter*, published by Arndt in Cologne in 1815, quoted in *Staat und Vaterland*, p. 34.

23. In his later years Arndt insisted more and more on the preponderance of monarchy in Germany. In 1850 in an article published in the periodical *Germania* he maintained that the German people "was so monarchical by education and mentality that even the population of the two great capitals of Germany [Vienna and Berlin], who at the beginning of the German revolution had raised arms against the governments, have turned again with their sympathies to their princes. The real desires and claims of our people seem to demand only that measure of freedom in the constitution of the state and of the municipalities which is in harmony with the monarchy, and not more; what goes beyond is something alien and imported from without, which has not yet any root in the life of the German people." Quoted by Ernst Müsebeck in his introduction to Arndt's *Staat und Vaterland*, p. lxxxiv.

24. Arndt, *Schriften für und an seine lieben Deutschen*, Vol. 1, p. 404.

25. *Ibid.*, p. 468.

26. "A people realizes itself only through individuals, and a people becomes brave and happy only through educated individuals if these bear in their hearts and bodies a full world force." Arndt, *Geist der Zeit*, Pt. 1, p. 432. See also Paul H. Ruth, *Arndt und die Geschichte*, p. 89.

27. Arndt, *Versuch in vergleichender Völkergeschichte* (Leipzig: Weidmann, 1843), pp. 390 f.

28. Arndt, *Staat und Vaterland*, p. lxxxvi.

NOTES FOR CHAPTER 34: *Friedrich Ludwig Jahn*

1. *Über die Beförderung des Patriotismus im Preussischen Reich:* Allen Preussen gewidmet von O. C. C. Höpffner. (Halle: J. C. Hendel, 1800). See the text in *Friedrich Ludwig Jahn's Werke,* ed. by Carl Euler (Hof: G. A. Grau, 1884), Vol. 1, pp. 1 ff.
2. The lines are from the poem "Der Patriot" by Johann Peter Uz (1720-1796). They form the beginning and the end of the poem. See *Sämmtliche Werke von J. P. Uz,* ed. by A. Sauer, *Deutsche Litteraturdenkmale des 18. und 19. Jahrhunderts in Neudrucken,* Vol. 33 (Stuttgart: Göschen, 1890) pp. 173, 176.: "The greatest state is weak which has innumerable armies but no patriots. . . . Of all the heroes who shine upon the world as eternal stars, through all regions to the ends of the world, oh, patriot, you are my hero: you who, often misunderstood by men, give yourself entirely to the fatherland, feel only its sorrows, think only of its greatness, live and die for the fatherland."
3. Jahn, *Werke,* pp. 6 f.
4. *Ibid.,* p. 10.
5. In addition to the *Werke,* Jahn's writings were easily accessible in the popular Reclams Universal-Bibliothek, which published *Deutsches Volkstum* and *Kleine Schriften.* Of literature on Jahn, see Peter Viereck *Metapolitics: From the Romantics to Hitler* (New York: Knopf, 1941), pp. 63-89; Michael Antonowytsch, *Friedrich Ludwig Jahn: Ein Beitrag zur Geschichte der Anfänge des deutschen Nationalismus.* Historische Studien, Vol. 230 (Berlin: Ebering, 1933); Carl Euler, *Friedrich Ludwig Jahn, sein Leben und Wirken* (Stuttgart: Karl Krabbe, 1881); Fritz Karl Schade, *Untersuchungen über die ästhetischen und ethischen Anschauungen Friedrich Ludwig Jahns* (Leipzig-Borna: Noske, 1928). There is an English translation of Jahn's *Deutsche Turnkust* (1816), viz., *A Treatise on Gymnasticks, Taken Chiefly from the German of F. L. Jahn,* tr. by Charles Beck (Northampton, Mass.: S. Butler, 1828).
6. Max Lehmann, *Scharnhorst,* Vol. 1, p. 380. See also Scharnhorst's letter to Clausewitz from Memel on November 27, 1807: "One must imbue the nation with the feeling of independent action, one must afford it the opportunity to acquaint itself with itself, to take care of itself. . . . only then will it esteem itself and know how to force others to esteem it. To work in that direction, that is all that we can do. To destroy the old form, to untie the fetters of prejudice, to direct the rebirth, to cultivate it, and not to hinder it in its free growth, that is as far as our activity reaches."
7. "Das eigentümliche scharfe und schneidige Wesen der fridericianischen Standesehre unter den Offizieren." Heinrich von Treitschke, *Deutsche Geschichte im Neunzehnten Jahrhundert,* 8th ed. (Leipzig: S. Hirzel, 1909), Vol. I, p. 437.
8. On Friesen, see Erwin Rundnagel, *Friedrich Friesen, ein politisches Lebensbild* (Munich: R. Oldenbourg, 1936). Friesen was killed in the

war in 1813; thirty years later his body was buried in Berlin next to Scharnhorst's.

9. Letter of November 7, 1815. *Die Briefe Friedrich Ludwig Jahns,* ed. by Wolfgang Meyer (Leipzig: Paul Eberhardt, 1913), pp. 64 f.

10. Jahn was, with Zeume, one of the co-founders of the Berlinische Gesellschaft für deutsche Sprache. Some of Jahn's attempts at "Eindeutschung der Sprache" were the following: neutral—keinseitig; Episode—Ingeschichte; Chaussee—Schüttstrasse; praktisch—werklich; Socialist—Gesellschaftsmensch.

11. "The old sentiments are still alive, we still seek the old goal—no longer in humanity, but in Germandom. This seeming limitation is a true enhancement. All salvation of the people and every solution and renaissance has always started from a few enthusiasts. The chains of serfdom had first to be clattered by chosen fanatics before liberty with giant power brandished its victorious sword of vengeance." Jahn, *Briefe,* p. 32.

12. Among the early student gymnasts in Berlin was Franz Lieber (1800-1872), the future American political scientist, who like the other gymnasts volunteered for the war and was gravely wounded in 1815 before Namur. Among the prominent early gymnasts and collaborators of Jahn were Ernst Eiselen, who declared, "Die Turnkunst war meine Minne, sie war mir Geliebte und Braut," Eduard Dürre, Karl Euler, Wilhelm Harnisch, Franz Eberhard Marggraff, and Hans Ferdinand Massmann.

13. Jahn, *Werke,* Vol. 1, pp. 146 ff. "So ahnete ich in uns durch Preussen eine zeitgemässe Verjüngung des alten ehrwürdigen Deutschen Reichs und in dem Reiche ein Grossvolk, das zur Unsterblichkeit in der Weltgeschichte menschlich die hehre Bahn wandeln würde. . . . Deutschland, wenn es einig mit sich, als deutsches Gemeinwesen, seine ungeheuern nie gebrauchten Kräfte entwickelt, kann einst der Begründer des ewigen Friedens in Europa, der Schutzengel der Menschheit sein!"

14. Jahn, *Deutsches Volkstum* (Reclams Universal-Bibliothek, No. 2638-40), pp. 34 ff.

15. Jahn, *Werke,* Vol. 1, pp. 155 f. "Welches Volkstum steht am höchsten, hat sich am meisten der Menschheit genähert? Kein anderes, als was den heiligen Begriff der Menschheit in sich aufgenommen hat, mit einer äusserlichen Allseitigkeit sie sinnbildlich im Kleinen vorbildet, wie weiland volkstümlich die Griechen und noch bis jetzt weltbürgerlich die Deutschen, der Menschheit heilige Völker!" *Ibid.,* p. 162.

16. Hans Kohn, *The Idea of Nationalism,* pp. 445 ff.

17. "Schwer zu erlernen, schwerer noch auszuüben, ist des Weltbeglückers heiliges Amt, aber es ist eine Wollust der Tugend, eine menschliche Göttlichkeit, die Erde als Heiland zu segnen und den Völkern Menschlichwerdungskeime einzupflanzen. . . . Noch immer gibt es Raum und Stoff für jede Grösse auf der Erde.—Es gibt noch heilige Kriege der Menschheit, die ganze Erde ist das Heilige Land, noch unerobert von Recht, Glück und Tugend. Menschenfressende Horden sind noch menschlich zu machen, Blutgötzendienst ist auszutilgen und Menschenhandel und Menschenverstümmelung; es bleiben die Zwinger eingekerkerter

Jugend und Schönheit zu sprengen und alle Ketten des Wahns, worunter das Menschengeschlecht seit Jahrtausenden keucht und dumpf hinbrütet." Jahn, *Werke*, p. 163.

18. "Es versteht sich von selbst, dass jeder echte Mann seinen künftigen Kindern eine Mutter aus eigenem Volke zu geben bemüht ist. Jede andere Ehe ist tierische Paarung ohne Gatten. Wer mit einem uneingebürgerten Weibe Kinder zeugt, hat Vaterland und Vaterschaft verscherzt." Jahn, *Werke*, Vol. 2 (1887), Pt. 2, p. 700.

19. *Ibid.*, Vol. 1, p. 94.

20. "Welches von allen noch lebenden Volkstümern dem reinen Christentum am meisten zusagt? Unmöglich wird das Endurteil für ein anderes als für das echte, unverfälschte, menschheitliche deutsche Volkstum ausfallen." *Ibid.*, p. 225. Luther was especially praised as the creator of the common German language. *Ibid.*, p. 227.

21. Jahn, *Deutsches Volkstum* (Reclam edition), p. 128. See also *Werke*, Vol. 1, pp. 237, 249, 266.

22. Jahn, *Werke*, Vol. 1, p. 309. The section is entitled "Verbannung der Ausländerei."

23. Jahn demanded the collection of German folk and fairy tales arranged as an "Arabian Nights"; the reedition of old popular books like Faust and Eulenspiegel; the composition of German heroic epics, for which he found only two models in German history—Hermann, the saviour of the folk (Volksheiland) and Heinrich (Henry I, the Fowler, 919-936, the first German king of the Ottonian house), the saviour of the state (Staatsretter); and the publication of a German popular Plutarch for which he suggested the name "Deutsches Enherion," a name signifying the assembly of the Nordic heroes around Odin, in Walhalla, who every day fight, die, and are again resurrected.

24. Jahn, *Werke*, Vol. 1, pp. 281, 285, 299. Jahn called the parliament "Sprechgemeinde"; the totalitarian "parliaments" of the twentieth century, which certainly are no "Sprechgemeinden," he characterized with a sense of anticipation as a "Taubstummenanstalt von Jaherren und Beifallsnickern." He always adhered to the revolutionary ideas of the national militia, a "Landwehr": "Erst wenn alle wehrbare Mannschaft durch Leibesübungen waffenfähig geworden, streitbar durch Waffenübungen, schlagfertig durch erneuerte Kriegsspiele und Immergerüstetsein, kriegskühn durch Vaterlandsliebe—kann ein solches Volk ein wehrhaftes heissen. Wehrlos, ehrlos! So sagten unsere Ahnen, und den Sinnspruch sollten wir in alle Landwehrbanner setzen." *Ibid.*, p. 304.

25. Jahn in his "Runenblätter," written 1814. *Ibid.*, Vol. 1, pp. 416, 418. For Teutona, see *ibid.*, p. 206.

26. Jahn, *Werke*, Vol. 1, p. 419.

27. Jahn, *Briefe*, p. 335.

28. In the "Stammbuchblätter," Jahn, *Werke*, Vol. 2, Pt. 2, p. 1003.

29. In a letter written in 1831 (*Briefe*, pp. 328 f.) Jahn demanded for Prussia the Meuse frontier which Prussia had abandoned in 1815 to the King of the Netherlands and which would now become part of Belgium. "Bel-

gium, if it separates from Holland, belongs again to Germany, and its fortresses are to be occupied as German federal fortresses, so that the new monkeyshame of blue-red-white cannot establish itself there." Jahn demanded also a large German fleet and the fortification of the German coast. "The German must feel in the future that he is a German, and the German flag must be respected on all the seas; then we shall be a nation." *Werke*, Vol. 2, Pt. 2, p. 1041.

30. Jahn, *Briefe*, p. 317. Letter of December 16, 1834.

NOTES FOR CHAPTER 35: *The "War of Liberation"*

1. Theodor Bach, *Theodor Gottlieb von Hippel, der Verfasser des Aufrufs "An mein Volk"* (Breslau: Eduard Trewendt, 1863). This book, published to commemorate the fiftieth anniversary of Prussia's uprising, is in itself a highly interesting document for the Prussian-Protestant German nationalism of the sixties. See especially pp. 111 f., where the struggle against Napoleon is compared to the Reformation. In 1811 Hippel suggested that all Prussian school children should recite a catechism, of which the following questions and answers are typical: "What is your fatherland?" "Prussia, or the Prussian state." "What are we called?" "We are called Prussians as a people, Prussian subjects in relation to our king and lord, Prussian citizens in relations among ourselves and to the fatherland." "To which great people do we belong?" "To the German, which for many centuries has been the most courageous and powerful on earth." "What is the king's vocation?" "To take good care as our chief and lord, that we may be brought up in the fear of God and justice as good men and citizens, that we may be governed justly and well by the authorities and that we may be protected by his wisdom and strength as free men against alien oppression." "What do we owe the king in return?" "Loyalty and life and death." *Ibid.*, pp. 148 f.

2. Körner's war poems were published after his death in two collections, in 1814, *Zwölf Freie Deutsche Gedichte*, and *Leier und Schwert*, the latter edited by his father.

3. Steffens, in his *Turnziel* (Breslau, 1818) pp. 94 ff., 101. His memoirs appeared under the title *Was ich erlebte*, 10 vols. (Breslau, 1840-44). A one-volume edition, reduced to about one fourth, was edited by Willi A. Koch (Leipzig: Dietrich, 1938). Steffens himself proposed a synthesis of moderate conservatism and moderate liberalism. "Der ächte Bürger ist conservativ und legitim, weil er progressiv und liberal ist; gäbe er dasjenige auf, in seiner bestimmten Form, welches sich entwickeln soll, dann verlöre ja die Entwicklung selbst allen Sinn, ja liesse sich gar nicht denken; und gäbe er diese auf, so verlöre ja das, was er erhalten will, die bestimmte Lebendigkeit, er schleppte sich, einem Wahnsinnigen ähnlich, mit einer Leiche." *Ibid.*, Vol. 8, p. 226. A similar role was played by Wilhelm Traugott Krug, professor of philosophy of Leipzig, who in November 1813 organized the Saxon Banner, a contingent of Saxon volunteers who

fought in the allied ranks. His new "Gaudeamus" student song was characteristic of the time:

> Gaudeamus igitur
> Juvenes Germani!
> Ecce Galli, collaudati
> Petunt Rhenum profligati
> Fugiunt vesani!
>
> Juble, Deutschlands junge Brut,
> Lass die Freude tosen!
> Sieh die ruhmbedeckten Franzen,
> Wie sie nach dem Rheine tanzen
> Ohne Waff' und Hosen!

4. Franz Schnabel, *Deutsche Geschichte im Neunzehnten Jahrhundert*, Vol. 1, pp. 493, 503 f.

5. See *Das preussische Heer der Befreiungskriege*, ed. by the Grosse Generalstab, Kriegsgeschichtliche Abteilung, 3 vols. (Berlin: Mittler & Sohn, 1912-14). In a review of this work Max V. Szozepanski, *Historische Zeitschrift*, Vol. 123 (1921), pp. 499 ff., came to the conclusion: "Das Urteil des Generalstabswerkes übersieht, dass für eine weitergehende Betätigung des Volksgeistes, als er 1813 und 1814 hervorgetreten ist, innerhalb der damaligen Staatsverfassung und geistigen Atmosphäre der Massen überhaupt kein Platz und die höhere vaterländische Pflicht eben bei den 'Authoritäten' war."

6. Friedrich Christian Rühs (1781-1820) was born, like Arndt, in Swedish Pomerania and devoted much of his research to Swedish and Nordic history and literature. In 1810 he became professor of history at the new university of Berlin. He gave various expressions to his German nationalism. In his rejection of French or Western influences he turned to the old Germanic gods. As early as 1803 he published a poem "Der Barde, ein Preisgedicht" in his *Unterhaltungen für Freunde altdeutscher und altnordischer Geschichte und Literatur* (Berlin: Vossische Buchhandlung, 1803), pp. 6-8, where he wrote:

> O wie tief ist unsre Schande!
> Über den erzürnten Rhein
> Drang zum Hohn dem Vaterlande
> Die Armee der Franken ein!
> Auf ihr Sveven, Cauzen, Catten,
> Zu den Waffen Jedermann,
> Wer den Schimpf empfinden kann;
> Weiber, treibet eure Gatten,
> Treibt zum Kampf die Feigen an!
>
> Wodan wird uns Sieg verleihen,
> Hermann glänzt,
> Ruhmumkränzt,

Herrlich her vor unsern Reihen;
Und wer im Getümmel sinkt,
Den ergreifen die Valkyren,
Nach Walhalla ihn zu führen . . .

Professor Rühs published in 1815 the first scholarly anti-Semitic book *Über die Ansprüche der Juden an das deutsche Bürgerrecht, mit einem Anhang über die Geschichte der Juden in Spanien* (2nd printing 1816). Like most German nationalists, he regarded the emancipation of the Jews, based upon the ideas of individual liberty, equality before the law, and tolerance, as a Western idea imposed upon the Germans by French influence. He demanded that the Jews in a Christian state should not be allowed to exercise any political rights and should be excluded from trade guilds, public offices, and the army. "The army must represent national unity (die Volkseinheit) in the clearest way. Only Germans should be allowed to fight side by side with Germans." Rühs suggested that the Jews should be tolerated as an inferior class, pay for their protection, and wear a distinctive piece of garment so that "the German could always recognize his Hebrew enemy." The medieval yellow patch reintroduced by Hitler one hundred twenty years later was first suggested by the professor of history at the University of Berlin at the end of the War of Liberation. Rühs followed up his first "defense" of Germany against the Jews in 1816 with another book *Die Rechte des Christentums und des deutschen Volkes gegen die Ansprüche der Juden und ihrer Verfechter.* Rühs was in no way alone. The following year Jakob Friedrich Fries (1773-1843), a well-known philosopher and professor in Heidelberg (1805-16) and later in Jena, published his *Über die Gefährdung des Wohlstandes und des Charakters der Teutschen durch die Juden.* He saw in the admission of the Jews to civil rights a result of the misguided humanitarianism of the eighteenth century. Fries participated actively in the Burschenschaft student movement, which shared his anti-Semitism.

7. Rühs, *Historische Entwicklung des Einflusses Frankreichs und der Franzosen auf Deutschland und die Deutschen* (Berlin: Nicolaische Buchhandlung, 1815), pp. ix, xii, 4 f., 28, 101.

8. *Ibid.*, p. 206: "Aber mit Nichten; wir müssen keinen Augenblick nachlassen: der Hass und der Abscheu muss unauslöschlich und ewig werden, wir müssen nicht vergessen, dass wir Jahrhunderte voll Hohn und Beleidigungen auf Beleidigungen zu rächen haben; dass unser Erbfeind binnen Kurzem sich aufs neue wider uns erheben wird: damit er uns alsdann gegen Gewalt und List gleich gerüstet finde, muss in allen Gemüthern das Andenken an die alte Schande frisch erhalten werden: unsrer Jugend werde auf die lebendigste, ergreifendste Weise die Schande und die eingeteufelte Verworfenheit der Franzosen, das unsägliche Unheil, das sie über unser schönes Vaterland gebracht haben, immer vor Augen gestellt: an den Namen hafte sich die Verachtung so, dass von den Vogesen bis zum Belt jeder Deutsche sich schäme, wie unsre redlichen Väter in hoher Weisheit gerathen haben, mit einem Franzosen nur umzu-

gehn: weniger lässt sich hier durch Gesetze thun, als durch die allgemeine Gesinnung: dass diese entstehe, fest wurzle und sich erhalte, muss das Bestreben jedes wohlgesinnten Deutschen seyn: worin uns keine Verrätherei, die in der Maske der Philanthropie heranschleicht, irre machen soll." See also pp. 329 f. and p. 370.

9. Friedrich Jacobs (1764-1847) published in 1805 a translation of the addresses of Demosthenes against Philip as a patriotic inspiration for the Germans. (Similarly, Niebuhr translated the First Philippic). His "Für Gott und Vaterland!" was first published in the *Gothaer Allgemeine Anzeiger der Deutschen* on December 25, 1813. It was reprinted a century later in Friedrich Jacobs' *Deutsche Reden aus den Freiheitskriegen,* ed. by Rudolf Ehwald (Weimar: Gesellschaft der Bibliophilen, 1915), pp. 10 ff.

10, See Paul Czygan, *Zur Geschichte der Tagesliteratur während der Frieheitskriege,* 2 vols. (Leipzig: Duncker & Humblot, 1909-11); Hans Rosenberg, *Die nationalpolitische Publizistik Deutschlands vom Eintritt der neuen Ära in Preussen bis zum Ausbruch des deutschen Krieges: Eine kritische Bibliographie,* 2 vols. (Munich: Oldenbourg, 1935). The most important history of the period is Friedrich Christoph Förster, *Geschichte der Befreiungskriege 1813, 1814, 1815.* Dargestellt nach theilweise ungedruckten Quellen und mündlichen Aufschlüssen bedeutender Zeitgenossen, sowie vielen Beiträgen von Mitkämpfern, unter Mittheilung eigener Erlebnisse von Dr. Fr. Förster, 9th ed., 3 vols. (Berlin: F. Dummler, 1889-90). See also Carl Brinckmann, *Der Nationalismus und die deutsche Universität im Zeitalter der deutschen Erhebung* (Heidelberg: C. Winter, 1932), and Eckart Kiessmann, *Die Befreiungskriege in Augenzeugenberichten* (Düsseldorf: Karl Rauch, 1966).

11. Ernst Ludwig Posselt (1763-1804) published among other works a *Geschichte der Deutschen für alle Stände* (1789-90) and *Archiv für ältere und neuere, vorzüglich deutsche Geschichte, Staatsklugheit und Erdkunde* (1790-92), *Lexicon der französischen Revolution* (1802) and 10 vols. of *Europäische Annalen* (Tübingen, 1795-1804).

12. Franz Wilhelm Freiherr von Ditfurth, *Die historischen Volkslieder vom Ende des siebenjährigen Krieges 1763 bis zum Brande von Moskau 1812* (Berlin: Lipperheide, 1872), and *Die historischen Volkslieder der Freiheitskriege, von Napoleons Rückzug aus Russland bis zu dessen Verbannung nach St. Helena, 1815* (Berlin: Lipperheide, 1871); G. Gromaire, *La littérature patriotique en Allemagne, 1800-1815* (Paris: Colin, 1911); Sophus Stahl, *Die Entwicklung der Affekte in der Lyrik der Freiheitskriege* (Leipzig: Fock, 1908).

13. Rückert's *Deutsche Gedichte* were published in Heidelberg in 1814 under the pseudonym Freimund Raimar. Among them were the famous "Geharnischte Sonette," Armored Sonnets.—Schwab wrote in August 1814 a poem "To German Women" in which he protested against French fashions and asked German women not to bare their charms to the lewd glances of foreigners. In Prussia a Frauenverein zum Wohle des Vaterlandes was founded in March 1813, but existed only a few years.

Notes for chapter 36: *Josef Görres and the Meaning of the War of 1813*

1. On Count Stolberg, see Hans Kohn, *The Idea of Nationalism*, p. 422, and Note 4 to Chapter 21, above. Together with his brother, equally hostile to the French Revolution and Napoleon, he published *Vaterländische Gedichte* (1815). Stolberg was one of the early famous converts to Catholicism. See J. Janssen, *Friedrich Leopold Graf zu Stolberg: sein Entwicklungsgang und sein Wirken im Geist der Kirche*, 4th ed., ed. by L. Pastor (Freiburg-Breisgau: Herder, 1910).

2. The political writings, *Politische Schriften*, of Görres were edited in six volumes by his daughter Marie Görres as part of his *Gesammelte Schriften* (Munich: Kommission der literarisch-artistischen Anstalt, 1854). A new edition of *Gesammelte Schriften* was started by the Görres-Gesellschaft under the editorship of Adolf Dyroff (Cologne: Bachem, 1942). Selections were published as Görres, *Ausgewählte Werke und Briefe*, ed. by Wilhelm Schellberg, 2 vols. (Kempten: Kösel, 1911) and in two volumes, *Rheinischer Merkur* und *Deutschland und die Revolution*, ed. by Arno Duch in the collection *Der deutsche Staatsgedanke* (Munich: Drei Masken Verlag, 1921). Martin Berger, *Görres als politischer Publizist* (Bonn: Kurt Schroeder, 1921) is at least as characteristic of German nationalism in 1920 as of Görres' times; K. A. von Müller, *Görres in Strassburg 1819-20* (Stuttgart: Deutsche Verlagsanstalt, 1926); Hajo Jappe, "Die Vorstellungen von Volk und Nation, Staat und Reich im Rheinischen Merkur," *Forschungen zur Brandenburgischen und Preussischen Geschichte*, Vol. 46 (1934), pp. 112-146; Alois Dempf, *Görres spricht zu unserer Zeit: Der Denker und das Werk* (Freiburg i.B.: Herder, 1933).

3. The first article appeared in the February issue of the *Vaterländisches Museum*. For the passage, see Görres, *Politische Schriften*, ed. by Marie Görres, Vol. I, p. 125. There also on p. 127: "Gehe Jeder insbesondere und die Gesamtheit insgemein mit sich zu Rate, was ihr fromme, was befreundet ihrem Geiste sei, was feindlich; was dem gemeinen Wesen wirklich angehöre, was ihm nur angeliehen. Alles Fremdartige, das unangeeignet ins Leben eingedrungen, wird in ihm zum Krankheitsstoff, und muss ausgeworfen werden. . . . Lerne die Nation sich selbst durchschauen und ergründen, es ist ein tiefer Brunnen in ihrer Mitte zugedeckt, der zu allen Schatzkammern der Erde führt, viele Geister haben sich schon am Nibelungenhort bereichert, und er liegt immer noch unerschöpft im Verborgenen." The second article appeared in August.

4. Outwardly it appeared as a continuation of an insignificant local paper, *Mercure du Rhin*, published in Koblenz from 1811 on.

5. Arno Duch, in the introduction to *Rheinischer Merkur*, pp. xxxiii f.: "Für den Machtstaat als solchen ist in Görres' Staatslehre kein Raum, der Nationalstaat ist ihm eo ipso Machtstaat."

6. From the article "The Future German Constitution" in No. 104, August 18, 1814, *ibid.*, p. 67; and No. 116 of September 11, 1814, *ibid.*, pp. 79 ff.

Görres' semimystical concept of Volk first appeared in his *Die Teutschen Volksbücher*. See Note 17 to Chapter 24, above. There he wrote: "Welch eine wunderseltsame Zeit ist nicht dies Mittelalter, wie glüht nicht in ihm die Erde liebeswarm und lebenstrunken auf; wie waren die Völker nicht kräftige junge Stämme noch, nichts Welkes, nichts Kränkelndes, alles saftig, frisch und voll, alle Pulse rege schlagend, alle Quellen rasch aufsprudelnd, alles bis in die Extreme hin lebendig! . . . So wäre es daher verständig wohl, nicht ferner mehr so sehr zu pochen auf das, was wir geleistet, und bei unsern Vätern anzufragen, dass sie in unserm Misere uns ihren Geist nicht vorenthalten und uns erquicken in unserer Not mit dem, was Gutes und Schönes sie gebildet: sie sind immer die nächsten uns und werden es nicht entgelten lassen, was wir in den Tagen unseres Stolzes gegen sie verbrochen haben. Auch das wird uns fernerhin wenig zieren, sie herabzusetzen so ganz und gar gegen die alte klassische Zeit in Griechenland."

7. *Rheinischer Merkur*, No. 236, May 11, 1815, ed. by Arno Duch, p. 216.
8. *Rheinischer Merkur*, October 31, 1815.
9. Schnabel, *Deutsche Geschichte im neunzehnten Jahrhundert*, Vol. I, pp. 537 f.
10. *Rheinischer Merkur*, July 11 and August 6, 1815.
11. The *Frankfurter Zeitung* of January 12, 1935, published a correspondence from Saarbrücken entitled "Das Elementare," claiming that the elemental forces of history and nature were driving the Saarländers, including the Communists, back into Germany. "Die Stimme einer zweitausendjährigen Überlieferung, die den Saarländer zurück in die grosse Heimat treibt, die ihm zuruft, mit den anderen Brüdern seines Volkes gemeinsam zu kämpfen, gemeinsam zu leiden und gemeinsam zu leben, diese Stimme ist auch in dem Blute des Rotfrontlers lebendig." The Saarländers who wished to abandon the civil liberties of the League of Nations territory for the "liberty" of the Hitler Reich demonstrated with upraised arms singing:

> Drum lasst uns in den Himmel schrei'n:
> Wir wollen niemals Knechte sein!

12. *Rheinischer Merkur*, No. 25, March 11, 1814, ed. by Arno Duch, pp. 20 f.
13. *Rheinischer Merkur*, No. 92, July 25, 1814, ed. by Arno Duch, p. 227. See, on Switzerland, Hans Kohn, *Nationalism and Liberty* (London: Allen & Unwin, 1954).
14. *Rheinischer Merkur*, No. 215, March 30, 1815, ed. by Arno Duch, pp. 191 ff. See also Görres' long article "Der Kaiser und das Reich: Ein Gespräch" in *Rheinischer Merkur*, No. 175-181, January 8-20, 1815, reprinted by Arno Duch, *op. cit.*, p. 127-187, where at the end the imperial dignity is seen in its full medieval splendor, as Dante formulated it, a protector of Christianity, ruling not by force but by justice, not subjecting the nations by armed power, but winning them through harmony founded upon higher right and legality.
15. Heeren published in 1817 "Der Deutsche Bund in seinem Verhältnis zu

dem europäischen Staatensystem" (*Historische Werke,* Göttingen, 1821, Vol. 2, pp. 423 ff.).

16. Heeren's article "Über die Mittel zur Erhaltung der Nationalität besiegter Völker" was reprinted in *Historische Werke,* Vol. 2, pp. 1 ff. Besides important writings on ancient history, his main work was *Geschichte des europäischen Staatensystems und seiner Colonien* which first appeared in 1809. See also Adolf Rein, "Über die Bedeutung der überseeischen Ausdehnung für das europäische Staatensystem," *Historische Zeitschrift,* Vol. 137 (1928), pp. 28-90.

17. Rückert, *Gesammelte Gedichte* (Erlangen: Carl Heyder, 1839), Vol. 3, pp. 305 f.

18. Heinrich von Srbik, *Deutsche Einheit, Idee und Wirklichkeit vom Heiligen Reich bis Königgrätz* (Munich: Bruckmann, 1935) Vol. 1, p. 189: "I could not name any other historian or statesman of the period who produced thoughts so mature and rich on the European, German, and multinational nature of Austria."

19. See Ludwig Keibel, "Einige Jugendarbeiten aus dem Nachlass Leopold von Rankes," *Historische Zeitschrift,* Vol. 137 (1928), pp. 241 ff. On Metternich's policies, see Enno E. Kraehe, *Metternich's German Policy:* Vol. I., *The Contest with Napoleon 1799-1814* (Princeton University Press, 1963) and Arthur G. Haas, *Metternich, Reorganization and Nationality 1813-1818* (Wiesbaden: Franz Steiner, 1963).

20. See the essay "Ernst Moritz Arndts innere Wandlungen" in Friedrich Seebass, *Zehn Aufsätze zur neueren Literaturgeschichte* (Munich: Neubau-Verlag, 1947). Arndt looked upon the European problem not without understanding; he wrote in 1813 of the English: "Europe owes it to them that for two hundred fifty years no one or two rulers have dominated all others and that it has become very rare for a tyrant to suppress all intellectual life and eliminate all virtues and liberties. The French have wished to destroy the equilibrium of Europe for the last three hundred years. The English have preserved it against them; mainly thanks to them, we Germans were able to continue as an independent people until the recent unfortunate times which, thank God, are now past. England lies like an added weight next to the scales of Europe; if the one dish of the balance goes too far down, then it adds itself immediately to the other dish and thus restores the equilibrium. As a commercial state England will always be called upon to play this role; as a maritime and insular state, it can easily do it; advantage, honor, and ease coincide here in a very special way. England is a world in itself, an island powerful enough to frustrate every attempt of its enemies to land on its shores, but not powerful enough to make permanent conquests on the European continent. Europe never has to fear the danger of being attacked by the English as conquerors."

21. In 1808 Krause hoped that Napoleon would realize his world-state. He intended to write a book "Der Weltstaat durch Napoleon." He published for three months a *Tageblatt des Menschheitlebens,* probably the first journal dedicated to the cause of world government. In his *System der*

Sittenlehre (1810) he incorporated his world-state ideas. His *Der Mensch-heitsbund* was reedited by Richard Vetter (Berlin, 1900), his *Entwurf eines europäischen Staatenbundes* by H. Reichel (Leipzig, 1920). See Friedrich Ueberweg, *Grundriss der Geschichte der Philosophie*, Vol. 4, 12th ed. by T. K. Oesterreich (Berlin: E. M. Mittler, 1923), pp. 102-112.

22. E. A. Varnhagen von Ense, *Denkwürdigkeiten des eigenen Lebens* (Leip-zig: F. A. Brockhaus, 1843), Pt. III, pp. 188 ff.

Index

By the same author——

REFLECTIONS ON MODERN HISTORY

(D. Van Nostrand Company, Inc., 1963)